ADVISORY EDITOR
Ted Honderich

What Philosophy Is

An Introduction to
Contemporary Philosophy

Anthony O'Hear

Penguin Books

PENGUIN BOOKS

Published by the Penguin Group
27 Wrights Lane, London W8 5TZ, England
Viking Penguin Inc., 40 West 23rd Street, New York, New York 10010, USA
Penguin Books Australia Ltd, Ringwood, Victoria, Australia
Penguin Books Canada Ltd, 2801 John Street, Markham, Ontario, Canada L3R 1B4
Penguin Books (NZ) Ltd, 182–190 Wairau Road, Auckland 10, New Zealand

Penguin Books Ltd, Registered Offices: Harmondsworth, Middlesex, England

First published 1985
10 9 8 7 6 5 4

Printed and bound in Great Britain by
Cox & Wyman Ltd, Reading
Filmset in 9/11½ pt Monophoto Photina by
Northumberland Press Ltd, Gateshead,
Tyne and Wear

Pelican Books

What Philosophy Is

Anthony O'Hear was born in 1942 and educated in North London. He read Philosophy at the University of Warwick and went on to become a Lecturer in Philosophy at Hull University (1971–5) and subsequently at Surrey University, until 1984. He has also taught at the University of Jos, Nigeria, and Bedford College, London. He is the author of *Karl Popper* (1980), *Education, Society and Human Nature* (1981) and *Experience, Explanation and Faith* (1984). He is co-founder, with Brenda Cohen, of the Society for Applied Philosophy, and co-editor of the *Journal of Applied Philosophy*. He is currently Professor of Philosophy at the University of Bradford.

Anthony O'Hear is married, with a daughter and a son.

To Tricia, Natasha and Jacob

Contents

Preface

In this book, I attempt to introduce philosophy, as it is currently practised in the English-speaking academic world, to those with little or no background in the subject, and also to those already embarked on some course of philosophical study. The issues I deal with are, I believe, such as to be of interest and importance to any reflective person. What there is, what we can know, how language relates to the world, the nature of human beings and how they should organize their lives, individually and socially: to wonder about these things, and to attempt to do so rationally and systematically, has been part of our culture, and one of its glories, since the time of classical Greece.

In the academic study of these matters, as in any academic study, there is both gain and loss: gain through the concentration of intelligence and mutual criticism academic study permits, loss in the way the almost inevitable growth of technicality and sophistication renders the results of a study that much more difficult for the uninitiated to penetrate. My brief has been to guide the beginner into some of these complexities. I have not tried, in the first instance, to expound my own views, nor to suggest that issues are more closed than in fact they are. I believe that the work of contemporary philosophers is not known as widely or as well as it deserves to be, so my primary aim has been to survey the subject as it now stands. My survey is inevitably somewhat subjective, reflecting my own assessment of what the important themes are, but I hope that my professional colleagues will not find it wholly idiosyncratic.

In writing this book, I have drawn on the work of many people, reference to whose writings will be found in the text and in the suggestions for further reading. I am grateful to all these people for what I have learned from them. But I should also like to thank more directly those who have generously read the manuscript, or parts of it, and commented on it: David E. Cooper, Sir Alfred Ayer, Mark Sainsbury, Jonathan Glover, Richard Lindley and Brenda Cohen. Their help and support, along with that of Ted Honderich, advisory editor on philosophy to Penguin, has been invaluable. I must also thank my Workers Educational Authority students

at Spelthorne in Middlesex, on whom I tried out the chapter on metaphysics, and my tutorial students at Bedford College, London, from 1982
to 1984; many from both these groups have, unknown to themselves,
contributed improvements to the first three chapters.

A.O'H.

May 1984

Chapter One

Metaphysics

Metaphysics: Its Nature and Methods

'On What There Is' is the title of one of the most tantalizing essays of the American philosopher W. V. Quine, and it could well serve as the subtitle of this chapter, for the term 'metaphysics', originally used simply to denote the work of Aristotle placed after (*meta*) his physics, has come to be used of the inquiry into existence, into what there is.

Why should there be such an inquiry, and, given that there is, why should it be undertaken by philosophers rather than by specialists in specific subject areas? In considering this question, I shall also be saying something about philosophical inquiry generally, as the methods used by philosophers will be much the same whether they are considering metaphysics or other philosophical topics, such as knowledge, language and thought, or values, all of which we will consider in due course.

Metaphysics, and philosophical inquiry more generally, would perhaps not be necessary were it the case that we all shared a coherent and un-problematic notion of what the world consists in, and so never raised reflective questions about the nature of the world and of our knowledge of it, but a moment's reflection will show that this is far from being so. We can all agree that there are chairs and tables, dogs and people, but once we go beyond such banalities, we quickly run into problems. What about, say, nations and races? Are there things with an existence and soul over and above the wishes and actions of the individual people that compose them? Hardly a trivial question: millions of people have been killed or moved from one place to another in the belief that there are, and right-wing writers continue to recommend that we should think and act on such a belief. Then again, we might wonder whether people are composed of something more than the visible limbs and organs that make up their bodies. Doesn't the simple fact of human self-consciousness lead us inevitably to conclude that there is in each of us an immaterial self or spirit? Further, are we not aware of and motivated by a world of value, of objective right and wrong, which is absolute and irreducible to any observable facts? Don't we also have inklings of a spiritual world, in which God exists, and which we sometimes experience in moments of insight?

It might be thought that these questions, and the claims they bring in their train, could simply be swept away by a robust appeal to the findings of natural science, which appear to deliver a view of the world as entirely composed of material objects and forces and regulated by the laws governing the operations of those objects. There are, however, at least four reasons for thinking that an unreflective sweeping-away of these questions in the name of science would be premature and unreasonable. In the first place, the theories of modern science do not form a single, simple and all-encompassing view of the world. Even on their own terms, scientists are very far from being able to explain all the phenomena they deal with in their laboratories and experiments, let alone being able to predict such everyday events as the next physical movements of my dog or myself. Secondly, some of the entities postulated by modern science such as anti-matter, charms and quarks seem just as mysterious and repugnant to common sense as anything we might find in the writings of medieval theologians. We will want to have a good idea of the grounds on which scientists think they are entitled to go so far beyond the surfaces of things – the banalities of the chairs and tables we all unreflectively take for granted – before allowing their theories to be used as the touchstone of the truly real. Thirdly, science relies heavily on mathematics, and, as we shall see, many mathematicians believe that doing mathematics requires a belief in abstract entities, in fact, in infinities of them. The mathematician Hilbert said that the discovery of proofs of infinite sets of numbers of varying sizes meant that mathematicians had been granted a paradise to work in. It would indeed be an irony if the means by which people felt themselves entitled to dismiss the notion of an angelic paradise as an outworn myth turned out to involve the postulation of new paradises populated with infinitudes of abstract objects. The fourth and final reason for thinking a simple rejection of the non-material by bare appeal to scientific theory would be premature is because such a move would amount to no more than an unsupported assertion of one world view against another; the believer in non-material realities could quite properly reply that his opponent's dogmatic assertion of the scientific fails to do justice to the grounds, experiential or otherwise, on which he is claiming to perceive more in heaven and earth than can be brought within the scope of scientific observation and experiment. If, as we surely should, we wish to go beyond mere assertion and counter-assertion in these matters, we will have to examine the types of grounds on which claims to existence are advanced within various areas of discourse and to compare the grounds regarded as acceptable in one area with those of other areas, with a view ultimately to making decisions about the claims themselves. It is because one is involved in assessing the validity and implications of the grounds used within different areas of human activity that metaphysics is necessarily a general or philosophical inquiry. To take a concrete example, which also has a bearing on our original banal cases of existence, physics may tell us that what appears to us to be a solid, unchanging table is really a mass of bombinating particles separated from each other by large tracts of empty space. If (as we shall) we want to assess the comparative status of these two apparently conflicting versions of what is before us, it will be no use asking for more physics or more common sense, because what is at issue is an assessment of the claims of physics in comparison with those of common sense. This is quite different from asking from within the perspective of physics whether mesons exist or muons exist. For this one would indeed consult a physicist. But what we are asking for here is, bluntly, an assessment of the worth and status of the sort of story a physicist might tell you in answering the inquiry about muons and mesons.

Seeing metaphysical inquiries as involved in assessing the status of existence claims made within various human activities should not be taken to imply that the philosopher has some means of making such judgements which is given to him from above. The philosopher is not a god surveying and assessing human activities and checking them off against some absolute standard of existence and truth. The philosopher remains a human being. His only activities, including philosophical ones, are human activities, and the comparisons and assessments he makes are bound by this fact. Philosophy differs from other human activities not by presuming a grasp of standards higher than those implicit in non-philosophical activities, but only in the way philosophers reflect consciously on the standards implicit in other activities and effect comparisons between them.

Despite our disclaiming any privileged access to reality, there is none the less a sense in which metaphysics is a conscious attempt to do what Quine has described as 'limning the true and ultimate structure of reality'. We want to arrive at a reasoned picture of what there really is. The fact that we can only get at reality through the sorts of things we are inclined to say and think about it means that part of the work of metaphysics will involve examining whether a given area of discourse

– such as physics, religion, history or astrology – meets certain minimum standards of coherence, clarity and credibility. Coherence is the requirement that we should not contradict ourselves in what we say and think, and should be non-controversial. There are, it is true, mystical thinkers who claim that what they experience and wish to convey is so far beyond the means of human language to capture that the very attempt to speak of it at all leaves one mouthing contradictions. Whatever one attempts to say about God or Being or whatever is so inadequate as to be virtually false, and hence one is forced immediately to assert the opposite as well. Some may respect the reverence suggested in this embrace of the contradictory; my own inclination is to regard it as a form of moral and intellectual laziness. Be that as it may, it is nevertheless clear that an assertion (even if about God) which is immediately negated by the assertion of the opposite amounts to no assertion at all; if God is a person then he is not a non-person too, and to say both things successively is not somehow to increase the content of the first assertion, but is to cancel it out altogether. Contradictions say nothing at all about reality, though their utterance may say something about those who make a habit of uttering them.

Clarity is more difficult to deal with than coherence, both because there can be degrees of clarity and because people will disagree about the minimum standards of clarity required for significant discourse. Thus, we will see that Quine sets his standards high, too high in the view of many philosophers. Nevertheless, it is surely the case that if a term referring to a type of thing or property is to be used significantly, at least some users of that term must have some idea of what would count as an example of the type of thing in question and of what would count as evidence for and against a reasonable application of the term. Notice that I did not say that all users of the term must know how to pick out examples of the thing in question or what would count as evidence relevant to the use of the term. That would be too high a demand, ruling out, for example, my own recent talk of muons and mesons. Language is a social phenomenon, and there are divisions of labour here as elsewhere. But the significance of my use of terms does rely on some users of the language having an idea of what these terms refer to and also what sort of evidence would go towards showing that an application of the term was justified. Further, where a term is used referring to a class of individuals, at least some members of the linguistic community must have an idea of how to mark one such individual off from another, or, in other words, how to individuate members of that class. These demands for clarity in the use of terms should not be construed as a demand for definitions. In the case of many words with which we are all familiar, a definition that is not circular or otherwise uninformative may well be difficult or even impossible to give. The example of 'money' is often cited in this context, and we could waste a lot of time trying to define 'blue' or 'wicked'. The time would be wasted from our point of view because the clarity we are seeking is one in the use of words, of knowing what difference saying a certain term is exemplified in a given context makes to one's picture of the world. This is why I have analysed clarity in terms of abilities to *recognize* applications of those terms and what in the world would count for or against the applications of the terms, rather than in terms of replacing one word with other words, for which one could once again ask for definitions and clarifications. Looked at this way, the demand for clarity is an extension of the demand for coherence. Contradiction in our talk was ruled out because a contradictory assertion is an empty assertion. Clarity is ruled in to ensure that what we say makes some definite difference to our picture of how things are. Minimal as our demands for clarity have been, however, we shall frequently find examples of statements that fail to meet them.

To say that an area of discourse must meet minimum standards of credibility if it is to be taken seriously as an account of how the world is may strike some readers as overly subjective, given that assessing the credibility of a set of theories (whether of physics or of religion or of astrology) cannot be done in isolation from the views we already have on what is reasonable or credible. So if we discount astrological claims in general on the grounds that our understanding of physics renders such claims absurd, we are in effect simply re-expressing an existing prejudice in favour of physics and against astrology. An astrologer, starting from his position, would no doubt come to the opposite conclusion, and with as much right.

This complaint is partly justified. Assessments of credibility will initially be based on what we already accept, and it is hard to see how it could be otherwise, for the evidence used in making such assessments will consist in seeing how the set of theories up for assessment fits in with other things we believe. At the most basic level, assessing a theory about the physical world will involve seeing how it fits in with what we believe about observable phenomena. At a slightly more sophisticated level, a new theory about how things are will need to be compared with our existing theories about the nature of the world. Given that some of these existing theories have wide-ranging implications for our view of the world, an initial prejudice in their favour need not be seen as a mindless conservatism, so much as a sensible realization that we cannot undermine too many of our beliefs about the world at one time without being left with no coherent picture at all. So the fact that our assessments of credibility will depend on what seems reasonable in the light of the rest of what we believe is actually another aspect of the demand for coherence in our world picture. What at one time seemed incredible can indeed become credible at a later time, and, as I shall later suggest, it may be right that it should. But the incredible can be transformed into the credible only by a process of altering those beliefs with which the originally incredible theories were in tension. Altering those beliefs may not be an easy matter while we retain any beliefs at all about what the world is like, either because they themselves are extremely central in our view of things or because they imply other beliefs that are central to our view of the world in this way. Knowledge, in Otto Neurath's instructive metaphor, is like a ship on which we are afloat, which we can therefore change only plank by plank. The demand for credibility in an area of discourse is simply the demand that in inserting new sections into our ship they should mesh easily with the old without either straining the whole to breaking point or necessitating the wholesale removal of vital planks while leaving nothing in their place to fill the resulting gaps.

Insisting that areas of discourse meet minimal standards of coherence, clarity and credibility, then, is an indispensable task for the metaphysician and one which metaphysicians have by no means always taken seriously enough, particularly where their own pronouncements have been concerned. Nevertheless, it is only part of what metaphysics is concerned with. A very powerful motivation to metaphysical inquiry has always been the wish to propagate or deny reductive claims of various sorts, for example, that life is or is not a merely physical phenomenon, or that people are or are not just biological organisms, or that nations are or are not simply amalgams of the individuals who regard themselves as belonging to them. Arguments about such claims are by no means always enlightening, and part of the trouble is that the claims are rarely presented precisely enough to admit of rational assessment. The reductionist tends to be motivated by a craving for generality, the feeling powerfully embedded in Western scientific consciousness that the multiplicity of phenomena and types of phenomena is ultimately explicable in terms of the same basic elements operating under the same basic physical laws in different circumstances. The anti-reductionist will often reply with Bishop Butler's adage, that everything is what it is and not another thing, emphasizing the differences between phenomena where the reductionist is seeing no more than different applications of the same laws and same basic elements. Sometimes he will go on to suggest that some new type of thing or law emerges where the reductionist sees no more than difference of circumstance of application; thus living things are seen by the anti-reductionist as taking on fundamentally new properties unforeseeable if all we had were the laws and types of object admitted in physics, while, in the same way, human beings conceiving themselves as members of groups are thereby given possibilities of action and are motivated by concepts and desires of a quite different sort from what would be predictable on the basis of observations of isolated individuals.

It is worth mentioning that the divide drawn here between reductionists and anti-reductionists does not coincide at all with that between materialists (who believe all reality is matter) and non-materialists. While materialists will naturally be reductionist in some areas, attempting to explain religious experience, say, in a way that requires no appeal to anything divine, some non-materialists are, perhaps surprisingly, reductionist in claiming that everything is really spiritual, or simply an aspect of the divine, or really constructed out of mental experience. Indeed, we shall shortly see that some philosophers normally regarded as empiricist take up precisely this last position. For them empiricism is a position far removed from an uncritical materialism or a naïve acceptance of the findings of natural science. It is, rather, the belief that experience – something mental – is the stuff out of which all else in the world is constructed.

As already mentioned, arguments about attempted reductions of one subject matter to another are frequently vitiated by unclarity about just what is being claimed, and hence about what would count either in favour of or against the claim. We are often left with the feeling that the whole dispute has amounted to little more than assertions of what each protagonist finds interesting or significant in some strongly felt but none the less vague way. Thus the vitalist may feel that life is a phenomenon so wonderful and unique that no account of it in purely physicochemical terms could possibly do justice to it. The hard-headed physicist, on the other hand, may be quite unwilling to make the sacrifice of his goal of total economy and uniformity of explanation which would result from admitting even the possibility of types of law which are not ultimately reducible to physics. In order to get some sort of clarity into disputes of this sort, philosophers have suggested criteria for successful reductions of one subject matter to another. Thus, taking a reduction of biological data to physics and chemistry to illustrate the point, Carl Hempel has argued fairly typically that such a reduction will ideally show two things:

1. All the characteristics of living organisms are physicochemical characteristics – they can be fully described in terms of the concepts of physics and chemistry;
2. All aspects of the behaviour of living organisms that can be explained at all can be explained by means of physicochemical laws and theories.[1]

In such a case what would have been shown is that what is expressed through the concepts and explanatory laws of one of the disciplines can in principle be expressed through the concepts and laws of another regarded as being more general and fundamental. (The reason why physics is regarded here as more fundamental is that, in this account, it is not envisaged that all the laws and concepts of physics could be expressible in biological terms.) If Hempel's conditions were satisfied we have good reason to regard the subject matter of the one discipline – life – as reduced to something more basic – matter (although this might be contested if it was felt that there was a great deal of importance about life that had not been explained by biological theory). Strikingly, however, even in the natural sciences it is hard to think of examples where conditions such as those suggested by Hempel are actually fulfilled. Certainly biology has not been reduced to physics and chemistry in this sense, though there are those who think enough progress has been made in this direction to justify the claim that one day it will. Once we leave the natural sciences, and move to the more general reductionist claims philosophers tend to be interested in, it becomes harder to see conditions of the sort laid down by Hempel as being even in principle satisfiable. Take, for example, the empiricist reduction of the physical world to mental experience mentioned in the previous paragraph. There are no laws governing mental phenomena which could even remotely explain all that could be explained by the laws governing physical phenomena; nor, as we shall shortly see, is it possible to provide anything like a straightforward translation of physical object talk into talk of experience, if only because physical objects are taken to exist when there is no question of any actual or possible experience of them. Nevertheless, even if we weaken Hempel's conditions so as not to rule out of court reductions that do not provide fully adequate replacements of one level of laws and concepts with concepts and laws from another level, we will still expect discussion of reductive analyses to centre round the extent to which purported reductions are able to provide explanations and analyses of any sort of the phenomena to be reduced in terms of the objects and relationships admitted in the reduction. Thus, the reduction of external objects will have to show how talk about objects could possibly be constructed out of the data of experience, reduction of the notion of causality will involve claiming that talk of causal powers adds nothing intelligible to the perception of regularity among types of event, reductions of the mental to observable behaviour will attempt to show how talk of minds is really no more than a shorthand or oblique way of referring to behaviour, and so on. In considering reductions, then, we will be primarily interested in assessing the explanatory and analytical power of the reduction.

Metaphysics we have defined as the inquiry into what there is. I have suggested that, owing to the generality and comparative nature of any such inquiry, it is not something that can be undertaken from within particular sciences or areas of discourse. Often what will be involved in metaphysics is an assessment of the claims and standards of judgement taken for granted within a particular area of discourse. Are the standards of judgement insisted on sufficiently clear to allow us to see what is really at issue in the claims? Are the claims coherent? Are they credible? Are they analysable in terms of something more basic or more certain? It will be clear from what has already been said and from this list of questions that it is not possible completely to separate metaphysical discussion from discussion of the evidence which might be offered for a particular type of thing. This is true particularly in assessing reductive claims. So, although this chapter is called 'Metaphysics' and the next one 'Epistemology', the division is somewhat arbitrary, and should not be taken too seriously. There will indeed be a degree of overlap, the difference between the two chapters being partly one of emphasis (in this chapter I shall treat existence claims more directly, while in the next I shall centre more on questions of knowledge and justification) and of history (in this chapter I shall deal with things that are often dealt with under the heading of metaphysics, while the next chapter will contain more discussion of the sorts of things one might expect to find in an epistemology course). This being said, however, each of the topics that will be covered in this chapter bears fairly centrally on our conceptions of the world and of what there is. In the first section, I consider, under the title 'Things and Experiences', the relationships that might exist between the external world and our experiences of it. In particular, I consider whether it is possible to see the world and its denizens as either inferred from or constructed out of experience. I then consider an attack on the common-sense view of the world from the opposite point of view. Are its appearances of solidity and certainty undermined by the claims of science? Then we look at the status of abstract objects. Are there such things as universals, numbers and classes over and above the particular concrete individuals of everyday experience? This is followed by a section considering the way in which physical individuals might be said to stay the same, despite continual changes in the bits of matter that make them up. Does this mean that they have to have essential natures, somehow governing and regulating their behaviour? We then consider the role of causality in the world. Are there necessary causal connections of some sort which link the objects of our experience, or can all talk of causality be reduced to experience of regularities between things? Then, is the world governed by deterministic causal laws or is there a degree of randomness in the way things happen? The penultimate section considers the nature of time and of the future. Is time simply an illusion, imposed on us by our limited perspective on a fundamentally static world? Is the future fixed in such a way that there is nothing we can do to change it? The chapter concludes with a brief examination of the status of religious claims to the effect that there is a god or supernatural reality which we sometimes have experience of, or can argue for in some other way.

Despite the length of the chapter and the number of topics considered in it, I will still not be treating in it the important claims about the nature of persons and of social groups which I have used in this preamble to illustrate the nature of metaphysical positions. They will be considered in the chapters dealing directly with those topics. The reason for this is only a matter of convenience; it is not because I think numbers and time are notions of greater metaphysical interest or importance than persons or nations.

Things and Experiences

Nowhere is it more difficult to separate questions of existence from questions of knowledge than in considering the interrelationships that exist between the medium-sized enduring three-dimensional objects of our everyday experience and the experiences which we have of those objects. This is because one of the most persistent thoughts in Western philosophy since the seventeenth century has been the thought that all we are ever fully entitled to believe on matters of fact is what is given to us as the content of our immediate sensory experience. Whatever else we believe must ultimately be interpreted and assessed in terms of these experiences, and of their interrelationships. From this it is but a short step to claiming that what there truly is is experience; not objects, not people, not stars, not atoms – all these things are ultimately, from the point of view of experience, either theoretical constructs enabling us to put some order into our experiences, so as to predict the future experiences we will have economically and correctly, or the inferred causes of the experiences forever hidden to us behind the experiences. The experiences we have may be thought of quasi-physiologically in terms of the barrage of sensory stimulation we undergo at any moment, or, more subjectively (or phenomenologically), in terms of what is present to our consciousness and what we are aware of. When philosophers wish to speak of the contents of our experience which we are conscious of at any moment, they have used terms like 'simple ideas of sensation' (Locke), 'impressions' (Hume) or 'sense data' (Moore and Russell). The view we are considering would then hold that impressions or sense data are the primitive elements out of which our picture of the world and the objects it contains are constructed or inferred.

What we think of the reduction of physical objects, people and the rest implied in the suggestion that they are theoretical constructs out of experiences or inferences from our experience will depend in part on how we read and assess the claim that all we are ever fully entitled to assert is what is given to us as the content of our immediate experience, and in part on how we conceive the experiences themselves, from which all else is held to be inferred or constructed.

Why, then, are we fully entitled to assert only the contents of our immediate experience? The clue here is given by the use of the term immediate. Relative to our present sensory experience, there is much about the physical objects we ordinarily speak of which is not manifest. For example, at any one time I can see directly at most three sides of an object such as the book on my desk and actually touch only part of it. Further, for the greater part of the time in which we believe it to exist, it is not observed by us, or indeed by anyone. Its existence thus transcends the actual observations we make of it, and, relative to those observations, its continuous existence while unobserved can only be a matter of inference or construction, just as the belief that the parts of it that I am not now touching remain as they did when I was touching them is only an extrapolation from past experience. Then again, we say that the book is of such and such a colour, yet it manifests this colour only in certain lights and certain conditions. Indeed, we are familiar with many cases in which how things really are is said to be quite different from how they appear. The book we are saying is blue looks black in the dark; straight sticks look bent in water; parallel railway tracks seem to meet in the distance; mountains look blue from afar; judgements of temperature and size are notoriously dependent on the state and position of the perceiver, and so on. Even more, in the case of hallucinations and dreams, we can have experiences not qualitatively distinguishable from other experiences, but which we regard as deriving from nothing other than the mental state of the person concerned. There is, moreover, more than a suspicion that when we say how something really is we are referring simply to the way it appears to certain observers under certain so-called ideal conditions. That the book is really blue may be no more than an assertion that in 'ideal' conditions it appears this way to 'normal' observers. In appearing blue in 'ideal' conditions to a 'normal' observer, the observer's perception is surely no less dependent on causal factors, including crucially his own mental and physical state, than is the same observer's perception that the world is spinning round when it is he who is really spinning. Appearances of objects, then, even those appearances which are said to reveal how an object really is, are never due solely to the nature of the object. Naïve realism, then, the view that things are simply as they appear, is said to be untenable, both because of illusions and hallucinations, and because of the influence of causal factors of various sorts on all our perceptions.

Several points emerge from all this. What we perceive at any one time is frequently only part, spatially and temporally, of the object we take the perception to be a perception of. Moreover, our perceptual experiences are frequently said to be misleading, and this is put down to causal factors operative in the cases of illusion. But saying this only serves to remind us that the perceptions we consider to be ideal are also and equally dependent on causal factors outside the perceived object, including the states of the perceiver. Finally, in considering cases of dreaming and hallucinating, we see that experiences can exist without any object at all.

These factors taken together suggest very strongly that what we know of things in the external world is mediated through our experiences. The claims we make about the existence of things in the external world go beyond these experiences in various ways and are subject to error and correction, while the experiences themselves are the result of causal processes which seem to rule out any direct access to the objects which we ordinarily suppose are the causes of the experiences. On the other hand, if, as a result of these reflections, the objects of everyday life are fast receding from view, behind, as it were, the veil of perception from which they are inferred or constructed, the experiences themselves are correspondingly gaining in certainty. Even if the things which we are supposing to be the causes of our experiences may be very different from the way our experiences represent them as being – and of this we cannot judge for we have no access to the things themselves except through our experiences which, as we have seen, are subject to all sorts of causal factors which may be highly distorting of the true nature of the objects – the experiences themselves are sure and certain. The contents of our current experience, then, are all we can be sure of, but we can be sure of them none the less. Even if I am hallucinating or dreaming and my experiences are actually of nothing at all, I can hardly be wrong about the content of my experience; a statement about how things appear to me does not run the risk of error, providing I restrict what I say to a description of the content of my experience and make no claims about how things external to that experience might be. So we find that scepticism about the beliefs we unthinkingly have about the nature of objects in the world often goes hand in hand with a stress on the certainty and indubitability of our experiences.

Three strands of thought, then, go to establish what Quine has referred to as 'the fact that we know external things only mediately through our senses'.[2] There is the idea that, relative to sense experience, external things are inferred or constructed; then there is the thought that sense experience, even of the sort we commonly think of as standard or ideal, is due to all sorts of causal factors which, for all we can tell, may distort the nature of objects we believe the experience to be experience of; and finally there is the idea that only the content of sense experience is truly certain. I shall argue in the rest of this section that there is something correct about the first idea, but that it does not in itself establish that our perception of objects is not immediate or direct, that the second idea is deeply misleading in its implication that unperceivable objects are the causes of experience, and that the third idea is false because categorization of experience is possible only in a world manifesting objective regularities independent of us. What emerges from all this, I shall argue, in no way establishes that appearances are prior to things or that things are merely constructs out of or inferences from experience. On the contrary, it may be nearer the truth to say that appearances are but abstractions from things, and that any coherent talk of appearances presupposes the existence of enduring objects.

A. J. Ayer has argued that there are two grounds for taking sense experiences as primitive relative to the enduring physical objects of common sense. The grounds are first that the truth of a judgement about an object finally depends on the truth of some judgement of sense experience and second that our judgements about external objects assert far more than is given in the judgements of sense experience on which they depend. In Ayer's view, both these grounds would imply that there is some sort of inferential relationship between a judgement that there is a lamp in front of me and the judgement that a lamp-like pattern currently occupies my visual field: what is present to my senses, so far as the lamp is concerned, is just a visual pattern, and all the rest is inference.[3]

It is admitted by Ayer that the inference in question is not one which we would in normal conditions be conscious of making. We do not regard our consciousness as being filled with sensory patterns, whether visual, auditory, tactile or whatever, on the basis of which we then go on to conclude that there is a physical object such as a lamp or a dog in front of us. It is true that in asserting that I am perceiving a lamp-like pattern I am making a more guarded claim than if I were to assert that I am perceiving an actual lamp. The latter claim entails all sorts of consequences about the continuing existence of the lamp, about what other similarly placed observers would see, and so on: the failure of any of these consequences would suggest that I had been mistaken in my claim that I was perceiving a lamp, although it would not of course suggest that I had been wrong in saying that I had had a visual experience of something like a lamp.

If the contrast between a judgement about my experience and one about a material object, in terms of the former being less open to error than the latter, is all that is meant by talk of inference here, it is hard to see what objection there could be. But equally, nothing would have been done to show that we do not directly perceive lamps. As yet no reason has been given to suppose that we always experience intermediaries, such as impressions or sense data, and never things in the world themselves. Similarly, the fact we can misperceive or hallucinate does not show that we have to think of ourselves in such circumstances as really seeing a mental impression of a bent stick or a sense datum of a pink rat, rather than as being in a state of mind in which we are taking a straight stick for bent or in which we are actually perceiving nothing at all. If we decline to speak of seeing sense data in these cases, the temptation to think that a non-illusory perception of, say, my lamp really consists of seeing a lamp-like impression directly and then inferring that it is caused by a lamp will be correspondingly weakened.

To many, however, talk of inference in the context of perception inevitably suggests the following picture. Our experiences are at most 'messages' from the objects we regard as composing the external world, messages which have been transformed by the circumstances of perception and by our perceptual apparatus itself. From a phenomenological point of view (how they appear) there is no difference between a veridical message, a misleading message (an illusion, like a 'bent' stick in water) or an experience which is actually no message at all (because the result of an hallucination). It is only in the light of subsequent analysing and sifting of these messages that we are able to make such distinctions. Thus, from a number of lamp-like messages, visual and tactile, I infer that there really is a lamp on the table. But if my inference is not confirmed by future messages confirming that there is a lamp there (for example, messages to the effect that some other person is himself having lamp-like messages, or that I myself receive further lamp-like messages later on) then I will begin to wonder at the correctness of my original inference, and may come to the conclusion that it was in some way mistaken. In fact, on this view, the very notion of an enduring external object is seen as being built up through recognizing that there are perceptions on the basis of which I can successfully predict that I will in certain circumstances have future experiences of similar sorts. These perceptions which are taken to amount to perceptions of objects are then naturally regarded as messages from those objects or 'sense data' emanating from them.

This picture with its suggestion that we infer conclusions about the existence and nature of objects on the basis of experimental data separable from, but none the less caused by, those objects is one that has been subjected to devastating criticism by Ayer himself. For the clear implication of the picture is that the objects themselves are not observed by us. They lie behind the sense data, which are what we really perceive. Now, what qualities are these unobservable objects supposed to have? Obviously they cannot have any of the qualities we do see, such as colour or shape, for then we would be able to observe something of the object itself and not all of what we perceive would be clearly distinguishable from it. So these objects which cause our perceptions have no observable qualities; they themselves are completely unobservable. Now, while we are accustomed from science to talk of unobservable objects, the unobservable objects referred to are regarded as being part of the same world or spatio-temporal system to which the things we do observe belong and continuous with them. It is because of this that we can give them positions and times in the space and time of observable physical objects and so identify them. But, on the view we are considering, none of the objects which supposedly cause our perceptions are themselves perceived, nor are any of their properties. Nor is any part of the world external to us to which they belong. Both they and their world, including their space and time, are regarded as beyond the reach of our perceptions, in another realm altogether, while all we have access to is the world of our perceptions. But, if this is so, and the causes of our perceptions are, as Ayer puts it, unobservable occupants of an unobservable space, we should have no means of identifying them or locating them, except presumably as the merely inferred causes of our perceptions. But is is quite empty to speak of a cause which we can neither identify nor say anything about except that it causes a certain type of effect. We are really doing no more than referring once more to the effect itself; we are in no sense explaining the effect, for which independent identification of and evidence for the alleged cause are required. But it is just this independence of identification that is lacking, and necessarily lacking, if we introduce physical objects as the inferred causes of our perceptions. We may contrast this case with the unobservable objects of physics, which are both located in particular regions of our space and time, and postulated as the causes of several different types of effect, and hence as identifiable independently of any one of the types of effect they are taken to cause.

The conclusion is that if, as is surely reasonable, we want at some stage in our account of the world to speak of physical objects as the causes of at least some of our perceptions, we cannot do this by assuming that the perceptions are in some sense prior and the objects only secondary or inferred. We have to begin by assuming that we are in contact with objects and perceiving them as they are, so as to identify them, prior to investigating their causal role in our perceptions and the causal mechanisms of perception generally. The 'message' picture is thus misguided in its implication regarding the essential unperceivability and unknowability of the objects that cause the 'messages', for it makes it impossible to identify the supposed causes of our perceptions independently of the perceptions they are supposed to cause. Objects, then, must be perceived directly if we are to have grounds for speaking of them as the causes of our perceptions. Indeed, we will be in a position to regard some perceptions as illusory and due to abnormal circumstances only given a body of unquestioned perceptual knowledge from which to identify the deviant perceptions as such. We can still be realists about our perceptions, then, without naïvely accepting that everything is just as it appears.

Rejecting the idea that we can introduce physical objects as the causes of our perceptions, however, does not mean that there is nothing more to be said about the relationship between perceptions and objects. One reaction at this point might be to say that, in fact, we are not in touch with objects at all, either directly or mediately; that all that really exists is ideas or sensations. Talk of objects and other people, on this view, would be simply a shorthand way of referring to groups of types of sensations which tended to go in regular conjunction with each other, and not a reference to some cause of the sensations 'behind' them, as it were.

Before considering whether objects can be regarded as constructions from sensations in this way, it is worth noting how idealism – the idea that the world is no more than ideas – is a natural consequence of extreme forms of empiricism. Historically, empiricism is the idea that experience is the only route to knowledge, and the denial that we are born with innate knowledge or have any direct purely intellectual access to truths about either this world or any other. Whatever we know, according to the empiricists, is derived from the experiences we have from the time of our birth onwards, a view summed up in the medieval slogan that nothing is in the mind that was not first in the senses. Taking the senses to be the means whereby any knowledge is gained, it is but a short step to the assertion that all we can really know is sensory experience itself. In empiricism medium (experience) thus becomes the message itself. As John Locke, the empiricist and critic of innate ideas, put it in 1689, 'knowledge is founded on and employed about our ideas only',[4] a nice example of the conflation of the medium and the message. It is true that for Locke not all ideas were sensory experiences; he included in his concept of an idea notions derived from reflection on the internal operations of our minds, such things as perception, thought, memory, reason and will. Nevertheless, it is easy to see how both the ideas derived from sense experience and the ideas of reflection can come to seem like no more than different aspects of the experiential show, continually passing before the mind of the perceiving subject. Hume, in 1739, had no qualms about lumping them all together and began his *Treatise of Human Nature* with the words

All the perceptions of the human mind resolve themselves into two distinct kinds, which I shall call Impressions and Ideas . . .

and he goes on to speak of impressions as 'all our sensations, passions and emotions' and of ideas as 'the faint images of these in thinking and reasoning'. A large part of Hume's philosophical project can be seen as the attempt to show how the things we ordinarily believe about enduring physical objects, laws of nature, selves and the rest are (or are not) analysable in terms of the immediate and fleeting impressions that are present to our minds and the 'faint images' we get of them in thinking and reasoning; as is well known, Hume's conclusions on these matters are coloured by a degree of scepticism, due to the vivid realization he had that the impressions that we or any other observers have fall far short of justifying even our ordinary common-sense picture of the world, with its enduring objects, causal forces and persisting selves, let alone the more recondite claims of natural science.

Two consequences of the concentration on immediate experience we find in Locke and Hume can be drawn immediately. The first consequence was one admitted by Locke himself, and it must be said that his way of dealing with it in Bk IV of his *Essay* is not very convincing. The problem is that if the mind perceives nothing but its own ideas, how can we be sure that its ideas represent things accurately? Locke's reply is simply to appeal to the supposed inability of the mind to create its own ideas, and to assert that the things which cause our simple ideas (or sensations) do so in such a way that the idea in our mind of, for example, whiteness or bitterness, exactly answers to 'that power which is in any body to produce it there'. In addition to the doubts that we have already raised about the 'message' theory of perception, it is quite gratuitous on Locke's part to suppose that our ideas give us any sort of accurate knowledge of the unknown thing or things that cause them (and even more to claim, as he does, that some of our ideas exactly resemble qualities in the things that produce them). These are things he simply cannot know without some way of comparing the ideas with their supposed causes and it is just this ability to get at the causes independently of our ideas of them that is ruled out by his claim that all we know directly is our ideas. This indeed is simply another aspect of the problem we had with the 'message' picture of sense data, and reinforces our conclusion that taking experiences as the primary stuff of the world makes thinking of objects as the causes of those experiences incoherent.

A second consequence of the claim that all we know directly is our ideas concerns the viability of communication through language. The problem pointed to here will, in the end, prove a major stumbling block for the alternative empiricist view of objects, that they are constructions out of sensory experience. It would appear to be the case, on Locke's view, that when I use a certain word, say 'blue', I am referring in the first instance to some content of my mind, and that when you use the same term you are referring to something in your mind. In each case what is being referred to is an experience private to each of us, and so we will have no means of knowing whether what is referred to by my use of 'blue' bears any resemblance to what is referred to by your use of the same term. Language, then, is subject to an ineradicable and un-decidable ambiguity, and its efficacy as a means of genuine communication is called into question.

One could, of course, accept these consequences of Lockean empiricism; that we can have no real knowledge of things and no genuine communication with other people. (Indeed, it has yet to be shown, on Lockean principles, that we would have any grounds for speaking of other people apart from certain people-like sensations we may have.) These thoughts push one very strongly in the direction of a solipsistic idealism, a fact Bishop Berkeley exploited in his criticisms of Locke. If I take my own ideas as my philosophical starting point, I am likely to conclude that I have no grounds for a belief in anything else at all. For on this view, things are inaccessible and communication with others an illusion.

Solipsism (the theory that there is nothing in the world other than myself or my ideas) exposes in an interesting way some of the limits and possibilities of philosophical argumentation. The solipsist is not going to be moved at all by someone else's claim to exist, any more than Dr Johnson effectively replied to idealism by kicking a stone. The other one's claim is simply part of the solipsist's experience, while Johnson's pain or sensation of hardness is just one more mental impression. Theories such as solipsism and idealism are just not open to straightforward refuta-tion by appeal to the deliverances of common sense. For what they are doing is to reinterpret those deliverances systematically, and in so doing they begin by taking those deliverances into account.

Nevertheless, solipsism can be shown to be a position of some futility. In the first place, one can know that anyone else who asserts that the world is *his* idea is wrong. For, in addition to his ideas, there are also my ideas, which, by definition, cannot be his. Hence the world is not just *his* idea. Then, and perhaps more fundamentally, in the second place, against the thought that the world is *my* idea, I can come to realize that that thought on its own has no practical value whatever in helping me to put any order into the experiences that make up what I am supposing to be my world. For that, I have perforce to use the theories and beliefs of science and common sense, in which what I am regarding as simply 'my' experiences are interpreted as simply one facet of a public and material world of things and people apart from me which existed before my birth and which will continue to exist after my death. In actually coping with my own experiences, my solipsism will have to rely on a set of terms and beliefs which entail the falsity of solipsism. Even though the solipsist can reinterpret these terms solipsistically, the fact that in understanding and manipulating his own experiences he has no genuinely solipsistic alternative (which does not mention physical objects, and other existences apart from his own experiences) to the theories of science and common sense suggests strongly that his reinterpretation of those theories is uncalled for.

In this case, as in others we shall look at, we take it that the case for the existence of entities of a certain type is strengthened if theories implying the existence of such entities are the only ones actually formulated which allow for the explanation and prediction of experiences of a certain type. Of course, this means that our philosophical and metaphysical conclusions are in part dependent on the theories and beliefs human beings have actually managed to come up with in dealing with their experiences. We are thus basing some of our arguments on the possibly chance fact that people have not devised theories of different types. But this dependence of philosophy on chance aspects of science and other human theorizing is only an aspect of our denial that philosophy is not and cannot be prior to our positive theories about the world and how it functions.

The case against both full-blooded solipsism and the more guarded phenomenalist claim, that one's own experiences are to be regarded as the primary stuff of the world and physical objects and other people in some way constructed out of experience, can also be advanced on the grounds that a world view which does not allow for the existence of a world of enduring objects or other significant regularities regarded as independent of and not constructed out of or inferred from experience will be unable to allow a subject to bring his own experiences under descriptive categories. It would not just be that I could not communicate with others; I could not effectively communicate with myself. In calling some sensory experience of mine 'blue' or 'bitter', say, I am saying that it is like other experiences of mine which I am disposed to call 'blue' or 'bitter'. How do I know that I am using the terms in question (whether vocalized or not) in the same way on a present occasion as on past or future occasions? This question does not simply concern my accuracy in thinking of a present or past sense datum as blue. It concerns my grasp of the significance of the term 'blue', for my grasp of the significance of a term and my meaningful use of it, even if one used only privately by myself, depends on my using it with the same sense on different occasions; and it is this which I am looking for assurances on. It will not do here to say that I remember that my present sensation, which I am calling 'blue', is like other ones I called 'blue' in the past. The reason for this is not because in saying this I am using my memory to check my past use of 'blue'. Memories of one sort and another are going to be involved in any checking process of any sort. The reason is rather because, in attempting to justify my present use of 'blue' by appeal to a memory of things I described as 'blue' in the past, I am actually appealing to my present use of 'blue' to justify itself, for my present use of 'blue' consists in the claim that I have called qualitatively similar things 'blue' in the past, and this claim is nothing other than an appeal to my memory of things I described as 'blue' in the past. It is for this reason that Ludwig Wittgenstein, to whom this so-called 'private language' argument is due, says that attempting to check my present use of a word describing my own sensations by my memory of previous sensations I called by the same term is like buying a second copy of a newspaper to check some item I read in my first copy of the same paper.[5] He understands this argument as undermining any attempt, such as that implicit in the writings of Locke or Hume, to base languages or schemes of classification primarily on experiences private to individual subjects, and to treat external objects and other people as constructs out of or inferences from private experiences. In fact, Wittgenstein's own position is, as we shall see in Chapter 3, like that of the American philosopher John Dewey to treat both language and knowledge as essentially social, involving a community of mutually interacting and correcting persons. A shift of emphasis from the individual's private experience to the world of public activity and discourse has in fact been a marked feature of philosophy in the twentieth century.

Whether or not one accepts the Wittgenstein–Dewey insistence on language and classification as requiring a shared form of life, Wittgenstein's private-language argument does point to a problem for any metaphysical scheme taking sensory experience as basic, for the categorization of sensory experience is not like the categorization of objects that are assumed to endure relatively unchanged from one time to another. If I am in doubt as to what is meant by a term like 'red' or 'magenta' or as to whether a particular object is red or magenta, if I am in the world of unchanging objects I can return to some standard exemplar of the colour, such as a colour chart, and effect the necessary reminders or comparisons. (Of course I will in such a case be using my memory that such and such an object is my exemplar, but the memory that an object of a certain sort is a standard case of red or magenta is not the same as my memory of what red or magenta looked like, so this would not be buying two copies of the same paper to check each against the other.) But this kind of comparison or reminder is just what is not available in the case of fleeting experiences. I can't keep my original experience of red filed away for future reference, and this does indeed have the consequence that judgements relating present experiences to qualities of previous experiences are simply untestable. There seems to be no difference between such a judgement and an arbitrary decree that my present experience is like some past one, which is Wittgenstein's point. As Wittgenstein puts it, whatever seems to be right is right in this case; whereas any objective inquiry requires that we make a distinction in our judgements between what is right and what merely seems to be right.

In *The Structure of Appearance* Nelson Goodman, a philosopher by no means hostile to phenomenalism, or the attempt to construct a world out of sensory experience, states that what he calls quale-recognition (what we have been calling the categorization of sensory experience) is a matter of decree, but he adds that decrees on sensory presentations can be revoked in a non-arbitrary way under certain circumstances:

> For example, suppose that I (perversely) decree that the colour quale presented by a (red) apple now is the same as that presented by the (blue) sky yesterday noon. Then I cannot very well also maintain both the following (natural) statements: (1) that the quale now presented by the sky is the same as that presented by it yesterday noon, and (2) that the quale presented by the apple now is very different from the quale presented by the sky now.[6]

The conclusion is presumably that I would be persuaded by (1) and (2) to give up my original 'perverse' decree, and that this would be a reasonable move in the circumstances, but it is quite obvious that the only reason for holding (1) and claims like (1) is that there are objects which both endure through time and have similar appearances at different times. Premises like (1) in fact appear to be essential to any scheme of classification of experience, which neither relies on memory for the fixing of its categories of classification in the way objected to by Wittgenstein, nor results in the issuing of arbitrary and rationally unjustifiable decrees. Only with assumptions such as that made in (1) can we have any independent check on our classifications of sensory experience or on the constancy of our terminology.

Goodman himself in fact makes no claims regarding the priority of phenomenalistic systems over physicalistic ones which take for granted the existence of physical objects and regularities. Not only is he prepared, as we have seen, to refer to a physicalistic system to assess judgements on quale recognition, but he is also sceptical that we have any basis for claiming that what we *really* perceive are sense data (moving patches of red) rather than things (cardinal birds in trees) or vice versa. Certainly, experience does not come to us neatly and definitely packaged in either way to the exclusion of the other. As a rule, we do not make inferences from noticed features of our experiences to the existence of objects. Indeed, if we want to adopt the phenomenological point of view, and concentrate on the content of our sensory fields to the exclusion of the things we are perceiving, we have to make a conscious effort of abstraction from the things we are perceiving to isolate the experiences themselves, and in many cases the experiential judgements we might make in practice are less certain than physical-object judgements. (For example, I can be much more confident that I am seeing a house than I can about the amount of space it takes up in my visual field.) On the other hand, as we have seen, the truth of particular perceptual judgements (what I see) about things does rest on the truth of some more guarded judgements about our experiential states (what I seem to see), and the relationships between these more guarded judgements and judgements about the objects we are taking our experiences to be experiences of are certainly of interest, and we shall return to this in our chapter on epistemology.

But in investigating these relationships it is important not to fall into the trap of thinking that we never perceive objects. Even if we say that, relative to our stream of experience, objects are posits, transcending our experiences in time and space, this does not mean that what we properly perceive are only intermediaries, sense data or whatever. We directly perceive objects, even if at any one time we perceive only temporal or spatial parts of them, or even if we do not always perceive them accurately. Neither the adoption of the phenomenalistic approach nor the realization that objects exist apart from and beyond our experiences of them require that we say that we do not really perceive objects. In the same way, the fact that in hallucinations we may believe that we are perceiving objects, when in fact we are perceiving nothing external to ourselves at all, does not by itself show what we never perceive objects directly. At most it would show that judging whether we are really perceiving an object or hallucinating may require that we take into account data beyond those available in the experiences in question. For example, we may want to consider the way the experience connects with other experiences, with our beliefs and expectations about the way things behave, and so on.

A particular experience of ours can be regarded as both an item in a stream of consciousness and as an experience of an object, and it may be fruitful in investigating the relationships between experience and the world to follow the lead of Ayer and Goodman and, for the purposes of philosophical analysis, to take the stream of experience as the stuff out of which our world picture with its distinctions into private and public, subjective and objective, is constructed. But if the line of argument followed here is correct, it would be quite wrong to regard such a construction as anything other than a philosophical fiction or abstraction for the purpose of illuminating the connections that may exist between our perceptions and the world, something to be undertaken only once we have a picture of ourselves existing and moving about in an external world manifesting in itself significant regularity and in direct perceptual contact with it. For only against a background of such a world can we develop a vocabulary or classificatory scheme to apply to our experiences, while, if we take experience to be the stuff of the world, the route to the world is for ever closed. Without assuming things, then, or at least a world behaving in regular ways independently of us, and the certainty of some of our judgements about that world, we can neither classify our experiences nor break out of them. Even the solipsist and the idealist will probably require that we attempt to do the former of these things but, if we can do it successfully, we will already have transcended the limits implied by these doctrines.

The assumption of a world apart from us also makes it possible to see how we could form a conception of an objective space and time, for we could introduce units of spatial and temporal measurement by reference to the perceived positions and motions of re-identifiable and stable objects, and locate positions in space by reference to unmoving and re-encounterable objects. It is hard to see how the phenomenalist, with only his fleeting and private sensory fields, might do any of these things with any sense of consistency. Indeed, it cannot be said that phenomenalist attempts to reconstruct our talk of a public world, with its objects, people and objective space and time out of the experiences of each individual subject have generally been regarded as successful. It is common, for example, in phenomenalistic analyses to think of objects in terms of the experiences different observers would have in specified spatiotemporal circumstances. But clearly the phenomenalist cannot assume other observers and a common space and time. These too would have to be given a phenomenalist analysis, which could be started in principle from the position of each subject. And then, even if we were able to show how all my talk of objects and other people were analysable in terms of projections from my experiences, and their talk of objects, including presumably me, analysable in terms of their experiences, it would remain quite obscure why the experiences of different experiencers coincide, as they so clearly do. That we were all experiencing the same objects in the same world in different ways would be the obvious and natural explanation of something otherwise totally mysterious.

Realism and Scientific Theory

In the previous section, I have argued that we cannot hope to order or categorize our experiences except on the assumption that they are experiences of a relatively stable world independent of us. We cannot, then, regard the world as simply inferred from or constructed out of experience, and ought to adopt a realistic attitude to it; that is to say, we should regard it as having a real existence apart from our experiences of it.

To say this, however, does not mean that any particular view of the world is either guaranteed or sacrosanct. Our most primitive view of the world is indeed that which sees it in common-sense terms, as including numbers of fairly stable and enduring three-dimensional objects existing independently of our perceptions of them. What I have suggested is that it is wrong to see the common-sense picture as being secondary in any sense to a sense-datum version of the world. But, it may be felt, even if it cannot be undermined by philosophical argumentation designed to establish the primacy of sense data, it may quite properly be undermined in other ways.

For one thing, there is a lot of vagueness in talk of the common-sense picture of the world. Just what is included in this? Dogs and cats, trees and ponds, houses and cars, no doubt, or no doubt if we are talking about a western European street scene in 1983. But what about witches and familiars, astrological influences and magnetic fields, psychoses and moral wickedness? The answer seems to be that it all depends whose common sense you are talking about. A hundred years ago, it is doubtful whether cars would have been part of anyone's common-sense picture of the world, and we could imagine tribes for whom dogs or cats were not part of the language, but who had no doubts about the existence of witches or who they were.

The fact is, of course, that what counts as commonsensical is dependent on the beliefs current in a society at the time in question, and these will always include elements rejected at other times and places. In societies where there is a scientific tradition, there will often be a gap between scientific theory and popular belief, to such an extent that common sense may be thought of as simply the worn-out deposit of a previous science. It is, indeed, the impact of scientific theory on our primitive conceptions of the world that is here at issue. For while we have argued that the notion of a stable world is required for any coherent ordering of experience at all, and hence that we cannot regard our primitive picture of the world as replaceable by a scheme, such as a purely sensory one, which lacks the assumption of a world with some degree of objective stability and regularity (which is marked in our world by enduring macroscopic objects), none of this shows that our primitive view of the world cannot be replaced by some other set of theories which postulate objects and regularities rather different from the ones presupposed in our ordinary interaction with the world. Indeed, it might be urged, this is just what is proposed by modern science, where, following the well-known 'two-tables' theory of Eddington, we are asked to think of the familiar solid and substantial table of ordinary experience as really being 'mostly emptiness'; it is, scientifically speaking, a collection of rapidly moving and invisible electric charges separated by enormous relative distances, insubstantial, and possessing neither colours nor textures.[7]

Apart from a dogmatic decision in its favour, we can argue in favour of the scientific world view and against the primitive common-sense one as follows. Naïve realism may be defined as the view that the world is just as it seems in immediate and uncontaminated experience. As such, however, it is clearly untenable. Apart from doubts about the possibility of experience that is not affected by expectations and ideas, we all know from everyday experience that things are often not just as they seem. Science can be regarded as continuing this process of correction of first impressions, in proving to us for example that the moon does not follow the walker over the rooftops or increase in size when near the horizon, or that the stars are not really tiny pinpricks in the sky. More advanced discoveries in physics, such as those referred to by Eddington, simply continue this process of correction of first impressions somewhat further, coming up with more radical corrections, telling us, for example, that the table we perceive as solid and coloured is not really solid and coloured at all, but mostly empty space thinly populated with colourless particles and unobservable forces. Once we admit the untenability of naïve realism, we implicitly admit the need for a surer touchstone of reality.

Science is just this touchstone, a position gained by virtue of its systematic and quantitative researches into phenomena and the causes of phenomena.

While admitting that naïve realism is open to criticism, we must be careful in considering claims advanced on behalf of science not to cut away the ground on which we (and science) stand. It is quite true that the physicist's version of the table is strange, even outlandish, from the point of view of common sense. But before accepting that it simply refutes the common-sense version, we must consider why the physicist's version is acceptable. It is acceptable (if it is) only because it follows from certain acceptable theories in physics concerning the nature of objects like the table in front of me. These theories in their turn need to be shown to be acceptable, and this can only be because they have consequences which are observable and true. A theory about the underlying structure of matter would have no claim to acceptability at all if it did not come up with true predictions about the observable behaviour of observable things. So if physicists tell us that everything we know and believe about observable things is false, they will in effect be depriving their own theories of the grounds on which they rest.

In fact, despite Eddington, there is no reason why the theories of physics should be regarded as standing in total opposition to our common-sense beliefs about the world. The 'physicist's table' ought to be regarded as the same table as the one I am writing on, for the simple reason that all that the talk about congeries of electric charges is doing is to give an account of the microstructure needed to produce the macroscopic table I see and write on with the particular appearance it presents to us. It is true that, in the scientific account, some aspects of the table, in particular its colour, are taken to be the result of the operations of colourless particles on our visual receptors. But what is meant by saying this? It does not mean that if *per impossibile* we could see the particles we would see them as colourless, for colour is a pervasive feature of our visual perception. Everything we see, we see as having some colour or other, so there is no question that if we could see the table *as it really is* we would see it as colourless. Nor should one conclude from the pervasiveness of colour in our vision that the 'real' table, being colourless, is not observable at all (which would once again make the 'real' an unobservable occupant of an unobservable space, with all the problems that would raise). All that properly follows from the assertion that material things are in themselves colourless, and that colour is due to our perception of objects, is that science affords us grounds for making a distinction between those properties of objects which are intrinsic to them or ascribed to them in scientific theories, and those that are dependent in part on our manner of perceiving them, a distinction aptly characterized by Michael Dummett as one between an absolute and a relative form of description.[8] The point of the distinction would be to suggest that creatures with quite different sensibilities might be able to agree on the characteristics attributed to things by the absolute form of description without having to understand what was implied by the relative form of description.

There would only be a contradiction between the accounts of science and common sense if the physicist's table and the table of common sense were held to be colourless and spatially discontinuous at the same level of matter and observation, whereas, in fact, the claim being made is that something colourless and discontinuous at the fine observer-independent level of microstructure can still truly appear to observers as continuous and coloured at the grosser, macroscopic level. The physicist's account thus in a certain sense explains what we observe – how the microphysical objects in conjunction with our sensory apparatus come to look as they do to us – and this is the aim even in the cases which can plausibly be said to show that there is actually something false in our first impression. Thus it is not enough for an astronomer simply to assert that the stars or the moon are not as they seem; ideally he will be able to explain why uncountable masses of very large and very light bodies look very faint in the night sky and do not fill the whole sky with their light, why the moon looks different at the horizon from how it looks at the zenith, and so on. But both in correcting our first impressions and in making his distinctions between the intrinsic properties of objects and those relative to our means of perceiving them, the scientist will have to appeal to 'first' impressions of ours as the evidence for the theories he is basing his corrections and explanations on. It is not open to the scientist to propose a wholesale revision of our common-sense level of observation if he wants his theories to retain any degree of acceptability for us.

For us – the last two words of the previous paragraph point to what may seem an unfortunate and arbitrary restriction on the scope of natural science. Science we might hope will tell us how the world really is, independently of human limitations and viewpoints, and we have seen how it might do this both in correcting our first impressions of how things are, and in drawing distinctions between the absolute and relative properties of objects. But we have to remember that science is a human activity, an activity by which human beings investigate nature. No science could be acceptable to us which transcended our powers to assess its correctness. Our assessments of a theory's acceptability are necessarily conditioned by the observational and recognitional powers we have. This fact of nature, itself matter for scientific investigation and research into the evolution of human perceptual apparatuses, may seem unfortunate to those hoping totally to transcend human perspectives, but it can hardly be regarded as arbitrary. After all, from what other point of view would we have human beings judge?

What I have been suggesting in this section is that our judgements about what is true and false in the world are, as a fact of nature (and in part for good evolutionary reasons), tied down to the schemes of theory and observation with which we are born and which are in the first language we learn.* Science can correct and modify these first impressions, but only up to a point, up to that point in fact where the truth of science is still being assessed on the basis of and with respect to those first impressions, for it is through them that we first learn to talk about the world and to relate to it. Stepping right outside this picture would be like being born again, perhaps even as a non-human in so far as our first impressions are part of our evolutionary inheritance. But, apart from the psychological and social impossibility of such a fresh start, the new world picture we thus reached would have no tendency to show that human first impressions were false, except in so far as the new picture could be interpreted in terms of the old. But the possibility of a translation of this sort entails that enough of the beliefs implicit in the new scheme are similar enough to those of the old for, as Donald Davidson has insisted, in translating the words of another we are also attributing beliefs, hopes and desires to him and hence speculating about his actions, and this understanding of another's mind and behaviour must be done so as to make him seem rational, again, to us.[9] The more peculiar and inconsistent we make him seem in his behaviour and his beliefs, the less we understand him, until we come to the point at which we have to say that because he is apparently acting so peculiarly in the light of the beliefs and desires we are attributing to him and of what ought to seem obvious to him in the circumstances he is in, we do not understand him at all. At that point, it is time to start reconsidering our attributions of attitude to him and our translation of his talk. The corrections between translatability of speech and agreement in judgement would seem to apply just as much in the case where I am schizophrenically trying to map

*The physicist Richard Feynman writes that you can find out whether the consequences of a scientific theory are true or false only if you can translate the theory's claims into 'the blacks of copper and glass that you are going to do the experiment with'. (*The Character of Physical Law*, London, 1965, pp. 55–6.)

two world views of my own on to each other as when I try to unravel the words and thoughts of some alien. Recognizing disagreements in belief requires having enough agreements in belief to translate or understand the words and deeds of my opponent. This line of thought simply serves to reinforce from another direction the extent to which our first, largely banal and for us largely uncontroversial picture of the world has to remain the starting point from which its own competitors and critics are judged. This can be said even without postulating any universal or essential body of common-sense knowledge, because it is consistent with each human group having a somewhat different set of initial assumptions and beliefs in dealing with the world. Nevertheless, each group is afloat on its own boat, which it can modify only plank by plank, whether the modifications are suggested by meetings with alien groups or by scientific developments within its own culture.

Abstract Objects

Things and their appearances certainly form part of the common-sense picture of the world. Though interesting and difficult philosophical questions can be raised about them, the ordinary man is in no doubt that there are such things. Where he might be naturally rather more sceptical is in the claim – typically philosophical – that there are abstract objects over and above those particular things that can be experienced in the material world. How can there be such things? What does saying that they exist amount to? On what grounds are they postulated? This section will sketch and assess the reasons philosophers have advanced for thinking that universals such as redness exist, apart from instances of red things and that numbers exist.

Against common-sense scepticism about abstract objects, one could, following Rudolf Carnap, attempt to defuse the whole issue by saying that questions of existence are properly to be thought of as internal to a particular subject matter or area of discourse.[10] Thus, if we want to know whether numbers exist, we simply ask a mathematician whether in his work he speaks of such things: clearly he does, so numbers exist. Similarly, in ordinary speech we talk of the colour red being louder than green. So red and green exist as abstract qualities over and above red and green things. Equally if, in economics, reference is made to inflationary trends, then inflationary trends exist. Of course, saying that each of these types of things exist is not to say that they have the same type of existence as spatiotemporal objects which also exist, but they exist in their own way, as defined by the conditions for existence for objects of that type.

Questions of existence, on this view, simply raise issues within areas of discourse. Can we employ a given area of discourse without referring to electrons, say, or numbers? The so-called external question, as to whether we are prepared to engage in a particular language game at all, is not to be regarded as decidable by seeing whether entities of particular types exist, for in attempting to see whether or not something exists we will have to use the criteria for existence from a particular type of inquiry. Thus, it would be entirely inappropriate to deny the existence of numbers simply on the grounds that we had never seen or touched any. What we need to do is to judge an area of discourse as a whole, in terms of its usefulness for our life in some general sense and this, in Carnap's view, is to be regarded as a matter of policy rather than of straightforward proof. He regards attempts to decide directly on questions of existence from outside the relevant area of discourse as meaningless. This sort of attitude to questions of existence can also be found in Wittgenstein's later philosophy, with its picture of human activity being divided into self-contained language games, and in Quine's assertion that what we should regard as existing is to be determined by those myths we have found most efficacious in working the flux of experience into manageable shape, and that in principle there is no reason why the Homeric gods might not have proved as efficacious as physical objects, as well as in Carnap's distinction between internal and external questions.

The demand that questions of existence be regarded as relative to areas of discourse can be a useful corrective against the dogmatism – typically materialistic – that only what can be seen and touched is to be admitted as existing. As we shall see, much of the prejudice against abstract objects, whether lay or philosophical, is motivated by the thought that sensory experience provides the only sure touchstone of reality. Nevertheless, the characterization of existential questions as, properly speaking, internal questions cannot be regarded as satisfactory. For one thing, it is far too tolerant and non-discriminatory. The scientifically minded philosopher might be happy with the existence of numbers, but he would presumably be less happy with witches or angels, both of which might be allowed to exist on internal grounds, witches being internal to the language game of magic and angels to that of religion. While magic might, conceivably, be ruled out as a separate area of discourse, even by someone adopting the Carnapian distinction, on the grounds that magic and its entities actually appeal to the same criteria as science and common sense (but fail where science succeeds) and so do not really form a separate area of discourse, the position of religion is rather different. Adherents of religion, if they are at all sophisticated, usually begin by claiming that religion and its beings are not to be judged by scientific standards; they are realities of a different sort altogether. Treating the assessment of religion, in the Carnap vein, as a matter of policy is far too vague. It is by no means clear that religious myths have been less efficacious than scientific ones in coping with experience (efficacious with respect to what, one feels like asking). What we seek in adopting a policy with regard to religion is precisely some reasons for or against the belief in the existence of religious entities. If they exist, a very different policy might be advisable than if they do not exist.

Then, secondly, treating questions of existence as straightforwardly internal does scant justice to the rather complex issues involved in many metaphysical disputes which are hardly to be settled by seeing whether some conceptual framework does or does not make room for them. We have already seen this in the case of phenomenalism and solipsism, where talk of objects and the external world is regarded as the starting point for a reduction. Equally, in the case of abstract objects, what is at issue is not whether they are *mentioned* in sentences in mathematics or ordinary discourse. It is how those sentences are to be understood that is at issue; in particular, it is whether in deciding the truth or falsity of the sentences in question we have to identify some abstract object and see whether something or other is true of it. The claim of the opponent of abstract objects will be that, in deciding whether the blueness of the sky is darker than that of the sea or that $2 + 2 = 4$, we have no need to assume the existence of something called blueness, aside from individual instances of blue, or of a number 2, aside from actual pairs of objects or human calculating processes. An intriguing and linking feature of these two questions is that the notion of a class turns out to be crucial to both.

The so-called problem of universals is one of the oldest questions in philosophy. Much of Ancient Greek thought was concerned with the ways in which identity and similarity could be discerned underlying the multiplicity of phenomena. At some points it is hard to distinguish early physical speculation about the basic ingredients of matter from the more philosophical questions as to the grounds on which we are able to make judgements of similarity at all. What I have called the philosophical question may be stated like this: in cases of applying general or universal terms to particular things, two or more different objects, events or actions are being classified by us as examples of the same type of thing. In order to make this classification or grouping together of different things, we must be disregarding the respects in which the different cases are actually different (and hence two, not one). What is it that entitles us so to disregard the essential differences between things and say that some things are really to be grouped together under some general or universal term? As is well known, Plato's answer to this question involved postulating an ideal world, non-physical, outside space and time, in which the forms (or Forms) of things were laid up. Two instances of beauty-on-earth or redness-on-earth or two dogs-on-earth were properly to be regarded as beautiful or red or doggish because of their relationship to the really existing Universal, to the Form of Beauty or the Form of Dog. What Plato thought the nature of the relationship between earthly things and the Forms was is extremely hard to unravel. Sometimes he speaks of it in quasi-mystical terms, as one of participation, and sometimes more mundanely, in terms of copying or resemblance. But, however it is conceived, the Platonic account of universals is one which would analyse any meaningful discrimination we make in our experience as being meaningful in virtue of its implicit reference to an ideal Form or Universal, outside space and time and sensory experience, something abstract in other words, though for Plato abstractness of this sort was an existential virtue rather than an enfeeblement. However, the Platonic account suffers from a fatal flaw, which was actually recognized by Plato himself, in the dialogue *Parmenides* (131-2). An ideal Form or abstract Universal is postulated to explain and justify our grouping together of two earthly objects, dogs, let us say. But if their both being related to this Form explains and justifies our claim that Bonzo and Fido are both dogs, what explains and justifies the relationship between Bonzo and the Ideal Dog and between Fido and the Ideal Dog? Are we not going to be led to postulate yet another Form to account for the relationship between any worldly dog and the Ideal Dog; and then another one to account for the relationship between the Ideal Dog and this new Form, and so on forever? This difficulty, known since antiquity as the 'third-man argument', is going to bedevil any theory which, like Plato's, attempts to explain universal predication by appeal to yet another particular. For the particular in question (in Plato's case the Ideal Form) will always itself need to be recognized as an example of doggishness or beauty or whatever, which would appear to require yet another Form to which it is related. But that too will require to be recognized as a dog or beautiful, and so an infinite regress is generated.

Plato held that our grouping things together under universal or general ideas was due to our apprehension of something as real as the particular things we perceive around us. Aristotle, while accepting the third-man argument, was also convinced that there is or ought to be more to our schemes of classification than our own choices or points of view. For him the reality of universals consisted in the possession by particulars of essences, common to all members of a given type or species. This connected with his scientific world view in two ways. First, individual things were regarded as striving to fulfil the essence that was inside them; the behaviour of things was thus to be seen and explained in essentially goal-directed or teleological terms and it is the adoption of a teleological viewpoint that is the most characteristic feature of Aristotelian science. Second, the aim of science was seen as the classifica-tion of things into their natural kinds and the subdivisions thereof by our intuiting their essences. Aristotle's esteem for teleological explanations in the sciences is not now shared by many. His essentialism regarding natural kinds, however, has recently found influential supporters, as we shall see, and there is certainly something right in his hope that in the classificatory schemes with which we group and individuate things in the natural world we are governed by the actual nature of those things, as revealed by natural science. However, it cannot be said that as an explanation of our use of general terms his theory is any more successful than Plato's. It would be quite implausible to suppose that our actual grouping of dogs and tables together is because we perceive in each individual dog or table some identical thing or essence, especially when for many of our classificatory concepts we would be hard put to say just what (if anything) each individual instance had in common with all the others. Aristotle's talk of intuition in this context is hardly illuminating, especially if it is supposed to tell us how we should ideally group and classify things, for even in the case of the idealized natural kinds recog-nized in chemistry or biology, say, such as iron or ungulates, that a specific grouping is thought to constitute a natural kind is not to be verified by intuition, but is owing to its explanatory role in the relevant theory (which is how present-day essentialists conceive of their natural kinds).

The accounts given by Plato and Aristotle of universals are often called realistic, but passivist would perhaps be a better characterization for, in attempting to underline the objectivity of our classificatory schemes, they fail to account for the role played in forming them by us, through our perceptual faculties, our language, our interests and our theories. One can, of course, view the formation or construction of our classificatory schemes in a more or less passive light, and there is a tendency among empiricist philosophers of the seventeenth and eighteenth centuries to see our general ideas being more or less foisted on an otherwise empty mind by regular encounters in experience of like things. After so many encounters with furry, barking, four-legged creatures, we will eventually 'abstract' the idea of dog. But against the tendency to regard the abstraction of general ideas from particular experiences as forced on us by experience, it must be pointed out that in order to see different experiences as repetitions of one another, we must already be concentrating on those specific features of them which would make them appear similar and ignoring the countless others in which they are different. Moreover, in registering experience at all, we must be dividing it up and analysing according to some schemes of classification, putting two shades of brown together, for example, and not with some other colour. Doubtless to a dog, the world would look very different, and might be populated with quite different types of object. These considerations combine to suggest that any grouping together of things must start from some prior tendency of the organism doing the grouping to react to particular types of stimuli, and to group particular types of things together and not with other things. This implies that at the basis of our use of universal terms are certain tendencies on our part, some learned, some inborn, to react to experience in specific ways. Universals are initially to be sought in us, rather than in some ideal world or even in the essences of things in this world (although we might hope, as a scientific ideal, to bring our initial schemes of classification into line with significant structural properties of things, rather than with their superficial appearances).

We can credit most animals with the possession of inborn tendencies to react to and group together certain types of stimuli – for example, certain colours or certain shapes. Conditioning shows that some types of animal can be taught new types of response. But human cognition, although based on reactive tendencies, seems to go beyond this. We do not simply react to red things, or to dogs; we also have explicit ideas about what redness is, about what dogs are, and about how they are related to other colours and other animals. How is this more intellectual capacity to be thought of? Locke spoke in this context of our possession of general ideas, abstracted by the mind from its ideas of particular things to 'become general representatives of all of the same kind'[11] and gives as an example our abstracting of the idea of whiteness from today's observation of chalk or snow and makes it stand for all examples of whiteness, including yesterday's perception of milk and, no doubt, tomorrow's of a shark's tooth. While Locke does not do what some of his critics say he did, and hold that abstracting a general idea of table was like forming an image of a somewhat skeletal table with no determinate properties whatever (an impossible image!), his thinking of the general ideas as mental particulars does lay him open to a version of the third-man argument. For what makes this particular idea the idea of a table? Other tables are tables by virtue of being related to it, but what makes it stand for tables? In any case, it is extremely unclear that there is any particular idea in my mind that stands for my general idea of money, or murder, or multiplication. And even where I might plausibly be said to have some introspectible mental particular connected with a general idea, as in the case of whiteness or warmth, there is nothing to ensure that my representative of whiteness is the same as anyone else's. Yet, we do, apparently, succeed in communicating about white things and warmth and money and murder and multiplication, which would be hard to explain if in talking about these things we were really referring to private mental particulars. Rather than base our account of universality in elusive ideas, private to each person, perhaps we would do better to go straight to language and concentrate on our use of universal terms.

According to those philosophers known as nominalists, language is what gives us the idea that there are such things as universals. It is through language that we group sets of particular objects and particular properties under some general heading which is explicit, and the grouping itself becomes more than a disposition to respond in similar ways to stimuli perceived as similar due to the particular ways our perceptual faculties sift the world. The world itself is either a particular or a complex of particulars. There is nothing universal in it (or out of it). That there are general things, according to the nominalist, is only an illusion foisted on us by our tendency to group things together under general terms in our talk about the world. While such groupings may be based in resemblances between things, either ones we perceive or ones revealed in natural science, they remain groupings of particular objects, and it would be quite wrong to see them as any more than collections of individuals brought together by human activity under general terms. As we have already suggested, there is more than a grain of truth in seeing universals in terms of human sorting activity, but does this entail the nominalist conclusion that nothing but particulars exist? What, actually, does nominalism amount to? According to Goodman, it is 'an inability to understand how a class, which does not differ in content from the sum of its members, can yet be an entity distinct from that sum'.[12] The failure to accept this principle will, in Goodman's view, lead to a universe bloated with classes, and classes of classes, and classes of classes of classes, and so on *ad infinitum*. For Goodman, there is no difference of entity without difference of content; thus no difference between the state of Utah, the acres that make it up or the class of its counties; no difference between the two shoes I am wearing, the class consisting of these shoes, the class consisting of the class consisting of these two shoes, the class consisting of the class consisting of . . ., and so on. In fact, we should drop all this spurious talk of classes altogether and stick with individuals. We may apply what general terms we like to individuals. Thus, Hume is a philosopher, Russell is a philosopher, Quine is a philosopher, but there is no class of philosophers over and above the individuals composing it. All that is involved in such talk is the individuals who are philosophers, the resemblance between them in respect of their profession, and the human ability to describe individuals in general terms based on such resemblances.

Nominalism of this sort may seem to deal with the problem of universals, at least as traditionally conceived, by focusing on language, but there is more than a suspicion that in language itself the very same problem arises all over again. For in my speaking of Hume as a philosopher and my writing the same thing and in someone else's utterance to the same effect, we recognize an occurrence of the word 'philosopher'. But we have here three very different particulars; how is it that we see these three particulars each as tokens of the same type? The Platonist will say that it is because each token is a token of an abstract universal meaning that underlies all particular utterances of 'philosopher', the conceptualist that each is a mark of the similar ideas in our minds, the Aristotelian that there is some essence common to each physical event. None of these replies is illuminating, but neither, it must be said, is the nominalist's. For the nominalist, the type–token distinction can have no ultimate validity, for it involves regarding each inscribed or uttered token of, say, 'philosopher' as an example of something inherently general, the word 'philosopher'. If we are prepared to admit classes, the natural thing here would be to see the words of a language as classes of the individual instances of the words in speech and writing, and to explain the sameness of function and meaning of these different and different-looking instances in terms of their membership of the class (which is what, in effect, is being said when different 'philosopher'-tokens are seen as tokens of the type or word 'philosopher'). But Goodman, quite consistently, refuses to think of words in this way, as being classes of utterance or inscription-tokens. For him, each occurrence of 'Paris' in an utterance or inscription is a separate word[13] and it is left unclear why in *some* cases the differences in shape or sound pattern between two 'words' is to be regarded as unimportant and the two 'words' thought of as the same, and in other cases not. Appeal to language explains some of our generalizing abilities without having to invoke Platonic universals, Lockean ideas or the intuition of Aristotelian essences; but language itself is a structure whose operation seems easiest to account for in terms of a recognition on our part that words are classes of word-occurrences, and that word-occurrences have the sense they do because they are seen as belonging to the class in question. The abstract notion of a class of word-occurrences plays a crucial role in our understanding of particular occurrences of words in utterances and inscriptions, and cannot simply be reduced to the sum of actual word-occurrences; this is both because those word-occurrences are understood by reference to the abstract word they are instances of, and because we envisage the word as having the same sense in sentences that might have been uttered, but were not, or in sentences that have not yet been uttered. Consideration of language thus leads us to distinguish between the actual utterances people make and the abstract system (which includes the notion of a word as a class of word-occurrences) which guides actual utterance. (This is roughly the distinction made by the linguist Saussure between *parole* (individual speech) and *langue* (the abstract system which guides individual speech). The notion of a word, I am suggesting, belongs to *langue* rather than to *parole*.)

So, if in language we have to admit the existence of abstract classes logically distinct from spatiotemporal individuals, can there be any harm in thinking of abstract classes of other sorts, logically distinct from the individuals that make them up, if the postulation of such things is required by a particular form of activity? Goodman's fears about indefinite generation of classes of classes of classes are unwarranted if we restrict our talk of classes to those that actually perform some explanatory role. In this sense, there may be reason for thinking even of pairs of shoes, as well as of individual shoes. As we will see in the final chapter, there are strong reasons for thinking of social objects, such as armies and, despite Goodman, states, as logically distinct from their constituent individual members. Moreoever, when we turn to mathematics – undeniably the most powerful tool available to the scientist – we find that an abstract notion of a class is the most natural way to account for talk of number.

Since the work of Gottlob Frege, around the turn of the century, it has been common to think of numbers as classes of classes. The point of doing this for Frege was originally to show that arithmetic could be based on pure logic, together with the harmless-looking notion of a class or set ('any collection of definite well-distinguished objects of thought'), and so given a foundation which would not seem arbitrary. The underlying thought in Frege's definitions of numbers was that two collections of objects are equal in number if there is a one-to-one correspondence between the members of one and that of the other. A given number can then be defined in terms of classes of classes with as many members as a given class. Thus, the number 4 will be the class of all classes equal in number to the class of Brahms's symphonies. But this definition of 4, while correct, is not one guaranteed by logic; Brahms might have written another symphony or one fewer or none at all. However, there is at least one class whose size is guaranteed by logic, and that is the class of all things not identical to themselves (for which $x \neq x$). As there are no such things, this class contains no members, so we can define 0 as the class of all classes with as many members as the class whose members are not self-identical. Two classes with the same members are the same class, so there will only be one class containing no members (or null class), and this allows us to define 1 as the class of all classes with the same number of members as the class of null classes. 2 can now be defined as the class of all classes with as many members as the class containing 1 and 0; 3 as the class of all classes with as many members as the class containing 2, 1 and 0, and so on. It is clear that in these definitions of numbers we are referring to abstract things: the classes of classes which are said to constitute the various numbers.

Frege's grand project, of reducing mathematics to logic, failed, as is well known. One reason for this was that the intuitive notion of a class, whereby any grouping of objects one could contemplate could be regarded as forming a class, turned out to be far from harmless and to lead to contradictions. (Russell's paradoxical class was the class of all classes which do not belong to themselves: is this class a member of itself? If it is, it is not; but if it is not, it is!) The repairs that had to be made to the notion of a class to avoid these contradictions take one beyond pure logic, and there are different accounts of just what the repairs should be. Nevertheless, thinking of numbers in terms of counting procedures (pairing off one group of individuals with another, and taking a set of sounds or marks to stand for and measure the counting) is what underlies the accounts of number in terms of classes of classes, and there is surely something right about that. Whatever else we want to say about numbers, one fundamental truth is that our grasp of the notion of number is based in our practice of counting the individuals in given groups. However, we cannot therefore suppose that we can eliminate abstract objects from mathematics in favour of actual enumerations of individuals. Apart from the fact that we regard the actual signs we use ('2', 'II', 'two', etc.) as tokens of the abstract type '2', in speaking of the number 2 we are not speaking of all the pairs of objects we have actually counted, or even of all the pairs of objects we might count off from now to the end of time. We are speaking, as the definition suggests, of the class of *all* classes of pairs, and this class is certainly more extensive than anything human beings could count. Only in this way could the definition be sufficiently general, for in arithmetic we want to say, for example, that the sum of any two single individuals whatever, whether we actually count them or not, is two. So the number 2 refers not to the class of actually enumerated pairs, but to something far more abstract. It is, of course, precisely the abstractness of mathematics that makes it so widely applicable.

However, even if we are naturally pushed into regarding a number such as 2 in terms of the class of all classes of a certain sort, and hence to an admission of classes, there is a major divergence of opinion among mathematicians about how far one should allow the extension of mathematical notions beyond our actual processes of counting. The definition of 2 as the class of all classes of pairs might seem like a harmless and indeed necessary extension of our actual sorting of objects into pairs, but what about extending numerical notions vertically, so to speak, as well as horizontally? It is indeed a fundamental thought in arithmetic that every number has a successor, yet it is hardly conceivable that anyone should actually count a set consisting of 197,319,214 individuals, and certainly not with any assurance of correctness. Nevertheless, we do have ways of recognizing and calculating such sums. Nobody would be surprised to be told that it was the population of the USSR, but it might be wrong, and it can be checked by means that seem to be simple extensions of our counting practices. And we can, if we want, calculate and manipulate even larger numbers by further extensions of the mechanisms we are quite sure of, addition, multiplication and the like. Where, however, there are problems of a more philosophical sort is when mathematicians start speaking of numbers which are not just unimaginably high, but of infinite numbers, and infinite sets larger than each other.

Philosophers and mathematicians of the so-called constructivist camp will simply reject such talk outright, saying that we have no right to speak of such things. A completed infinity is a contradiction in terms; moreover we should in general refrain from making statements about

objects, such as infinite sets, which we could neither construct nor recognize. (We could perceive only that a set was unending, not that it
was actually infinite.) Against this view, the majority opinion among
mathematical logicians will point out that certain branches of mathematics, including classical analysis, require the postulation of infinite
sets, adding that this is good enough reason for accepting their existence.
Ontology here would be seen as determined by the demands of an area
of discourse, rather than by any feeling that human recognitional powers
and abilities should determine the limits of our language.

Actually, the dispute over the existence or non-existence of infinite
classes reflects and highlights a deep divergence on the nature of
mathematics and its objects between what are called Platonists and their
constructivist opponents. What is not in dispute is that an infinite set
is not something we can construct or recognize in any direct way. So,
if we think of such things as actually existing, we would be implying
that there are mathematical truths and objects with an objective existence
beyond our constructions and calculations. This, indeed, is how the
Platonist does conceive of mathematics, not merely as a realm of abstract
but still humanly created constructions, but as a world of abstract
objects and structures which we have not created, and which determine
whether or not our calculations are true or false, whether we are aware
of this or not.

In favour of Platonism in mathematics, we can point to the sense of
necessity involved in reaching a proof and in the surprising results often
achieved in mathematics, which might suggest we are dealing with an
objective realm we observe in some way, rather than with a tool for
calculating with which we construct and manipulate according to our
convenience. Against this, empirically minded philosophers will point to
the differences between mathematics and sensory observation. Computa-
tion is quite unlike observation, nor has any Platonist succeeded in explaining just how we are supposed to 'see' the world of pure numbers. Certainly numbers do not have any causal effect on our sensory apparatus
like objects in the physical world. The necessity of mathematics derives
not from the Platonic existence of mathematical objects, such as numbers,
in another world, but from our adoption of certain axioms as starting
points and of certain rules to determine the admissible transformations
from one mathematical statement to another. The surprise we might feel
in the results of our calculations is simply due to the fact that we do
not always know what consequences our initial choices and constructions
might have. In this respect, there is no difference between the invention of a

mathematical system having unexpected consequences and a drug having unwanted side-effects. Moreover, if one studies the history of mathematics, one often sees mathematicians tampering with their initial axioms if they are unable to prove the conclusions they want. The idea of mathematics as a smooth, one-way transition from axioms and rules of inference to proofs sometimes inverts the actual process of mathematical discovery.

However, a so-called formalist account of mathematics in terms of rule-directed transformations of axioms is open to difficulties of its own. In the first place, how are the axioms and transformation rules to be thought of? They can be regarded as simply uninterpreted strings of signs and rules for manipulating such signs, which would have the advantage that we would no longer need to ask what numbers are or whether they require the postulation of classes of classes. But this would leave considerations governing the choice of the axioms and rules quite obscure, it would sever the link we have insisted on between mathematics and human calculating practices, and it would also make the applicability of mathematical systems to the real world even more mysterious than it is. If, on the other hand, we regard mathematical axioms and rules as statements of some sort rather than as meaningless strings of signs, the questions of their truth or falsity arises. To say that it is obviously or self-evidently true that, for example, each member has a successor is, of course, to invite questions as to what it is that makes the axiom self-evident, thus opening the door a little to Platonistic thoughts. Similarly, as we shall see at the end of Chapter 3, not all the rules involved in inferring and calculating can be regarded as adopted by convention. Finally, purely formalistic accounts of mathematics identify mathematic truth with provability: a mathematic truth just is a formula which is either an axiom or follows from an axiom by an admissible transformation. There are, however, problems with this from within mathematics itself. Not only are there mathematical statements (such as Goldbach's conjecture and Fermat's last theorem) which mathematicians are convinced are true, but which they have no idea how to derive as proofs, but Kurt Gödel proved in his first incompleteness theorem in 1930 that any formal arithmetical system contains a statement which is true, but unprovable within that system. This result certainly undermines the formalist hope that mathematical truth might turn out to be a property which all the true members of a deductive system derive from the premises of the system.

It cannot be said that any of the main philosophical positions of abstract objects is without difficulty. There may be a natural resistance to admitting the existence of abstract objects, and a desire to dispense with any notion of a class apart from its members, born of a common-sensical intuition that only spatiotemporal individuals are truly real. Nominalism – the idea that there are only individual things and the names we group them under – can seem attractive until it is realized that the most natural way of accounting for linguistic terms is in terms of universals of a more abstract type. The nominalist might object that the accept-ance of any notion of a class, logically distinct from its members, opens the way for a teeming host of new entities, many of which are different from each other only in name. But, as we have suggested, some may not be, particularly in social activity and mathematics; in any case, the proliferation of classes of classes and classes of classes of classes and so on can be made to seem quite innocuous once one realizes what is involved. It is not like saying that there are hosts of angels surrounding each person. Mathematics naturally invites notions of abstract objects and classes, though whether we should accept the existence of infinite sets remains highly disputed; it is fair to say, however, that the balance of mathematical opinion is in their favour despite the philosophical problems involved.

Identity and Individuation

The question as to just what it is that makes something the same thing through its changing history was, like that concerning universals, one of the preoccupations of the early Greek philosophers; indeed, as we shall see, the problems of identity and universality are closely connected.

Everybody has heard of the problem Heraclitus had with stepping in the same river twice. I step in the Scamander today and I step in it tomorrow. Yet what I step in tomorrow will be different from what I stepped in today. The actual stuff I step in today will have flowed into the Aegean Sea and been dispersed and mixed with other bits of water long before I go to the river bank tomorrow. So how can I step in the same thing today and tomorrow? The problem may seem to be one peculiar to rivers, but rivers are only a dramatic case of the general fact of change. My own body, the table I write on, my pen – all these things are changing in various ways all the time, at both microscopic and macroscopic levels. So what is it that persists through change? In virtue of what are we entitled to speak of something remaining the same thing through all the changes it undergoes?

Reflections on Heraclitus' river suggest that any answer to these ques-tions will involve saying something about the ways in which objects are specified or sorted. Thus, while I do not step into the same collection of molecules of water two days running, I may step into the same river. What makes something the same river has to do with source and course, and not with bits of water. Equally, to speak of my body is not to speak of a particular collection of cells at one instant in time, but of an organism that grows and changes and eventually corrupts; what makes it a single organism is to do with continuity and organization of its cellular composition, not with the sameness of its constituent cells from one time to another.

The ways we sort things in the world, then, determine the meaning of our judgements of identity. It would be a misunderstanding of what is meant by 'river' or 'body' to object to a claim that this is the same river or that the same body as what was observed on a previous occasion on the grounds that what we had were different bits of water or different cells. Indeed, one could go further and say that judgements of sameness and difference are empty or indeterminate unless we specify (or are able to specify) the respect in which the candidates for sameness or difference are being judged. Am I stepping into the same thing today as yesterday? Same river, yes; same water, no. This example might suggest that some one thing could be the same in one respect and different in another, but in fact it does no such thing. This is simply an illusion foisted on us by the harmless-looking word 'thing'. In pointing to something occupying a position in space and time and asking whether it is the same thing that occupied some other position previously, I am actually asking nothing unless I specify or am being understood to intend some type of thing in my pointing. Once it is unambiguously understood what thing it is I am asking about, it will become clear that it is not one single thing that is the same in one respect and different in another. It is not the one river that is the same in respect of being a river and different in respect of being two different localized bits of water, for the river is not a localized bit of water (or even two localized bits of water).

My pointing to something, then, is sufficient to raise significant questions of identity and difference regarding what I am pointing at, or even – what amounts to the same thing – sufficient to determine just what it is I am pointing at only when it is clear under what type of concept I am doing the pointing. Am I pointing at what is before me in terms of its being part of a large-scale geographical feature, in terms of material constitution, or of colour, or temperature, or in terms of what? In simply pointing, I could be gesturing at any (or at none) of these things, all of which are before me, all of which are different types of things; and it is in so far as different types of thing, and hence different things, are being pointed at that what looks like a single pointing at what is incorrectly regarded as one thing allows different answers to the question, 'Is this the same as that?'

From the previous two paragraphs, two important conclusions suggest themselves. The first is that any genuine individuation of a physical object (as opposed to an indeterminate pointing) requires either the actual use of a general or universal concept, under which the object is individuated or sorted,* or at least the anticipation that one will be able at a later stage to formulate an appropriate concept marking off the boundaries of the object in space and time. Concepts used to individuate objects in this way are often called sortal concepts, and the sortal concept used in a particular case will – unless it is hopelessly vague – suggest the criteria for individuation, counting and re-identifying members of the class in question. The second conclusion follows from the idea that an object, once individuated, will not prove to be the same thing as something picked out on another occasion in one respect but not in another, and that supposed counter-examples to this 'absoluteness' of identity arise because of failure either to specify unambiguously the ways in which the objects in question are being individuated (in much the same way as our difficulty with Heraclitus' river), or to distinguish what a thing is (my body) from what it is constituted of at some time (a collection of cells).[14] Given the absoluteness of identity, we can assert with some confidence that if two objects are identical then there is no property that one has, that the other will not have. This fundamental principle concerning identity is often called Leibniz's law, although in fact it was known long before Leibniz, and is to be distinguished from Leibniz's own more characteristic and more controversial principle, to the effect that any two things that are indiscernible are in fact identical.

Questions of sameness and difference, then, can be significantly raised only when there is a question of something being individuated under some sortal concept. On the significance of this fact, there is a deep division between philosophers. On the one hand, there are those who, like Aristotle, regard at least some of our sortal concepts as individuating objects in such a way that certain properties are then to be regarded as belonging to those objects necessarily, in view of their essential natures. On the other hand, there are those who, like Quine and Ayer, fail to

---

*One will have done this even if one miscategorizes what one perceives, as when a pebble is mistaken for a fish; but the thing has been individuated because it has been picked out as a fish.

understand how individual things could have any properties necessarily. They analyse any necessity that arises from saying that, say, if Jones is a man, then he is necessarily a rational animal, in terms not of what has to be the case with this particular object (Jones) before us, but from the definition of the concept 'man', which we are applying, rightly or wrongly, to that object. On this view, while we can ask what properties it is necessary for an object to have in order to be a thing of such and such a kind or to fall under the concept in question, it makes no sense to think of any individual thing necessarily being such and such or necessarily having such and such properties. It follows, further, on the anti-essentialist view that necessity attaches only to the way things are described (is only *de dicto*) and not to things in themselves (never *de re*), and that what properties we regard as essential to an object, rather than merely accidental, depend entirely on the way we specify it. Thus, to adapt an example of Quine's, 9 is necessarily equal to 3 × 3, but not necessarily equal to the number of the planets, though the number of planets is 9.[15] Necessity, on Quine's view, attaches only to sentences, and then only to particular ways of referring to things, the point being that, while anyone who understands what is meant by '3 × 3' can be brought to see that it could not but be equal to 9, the same is not true of the phrase 'the number of the planets'; although this latter phrase happens to refer to 9, this is a matter of empirical discovery, only realized when research into the solar system had revealed the existence of Pluto (and, presumably, the non-existence of any other planets).

There would appear currently to be two main ways of arguing from considerations concerning identity for the essentialist view that some properties at least attach necessarily to objects. The first, and more restricted, argument is a self-conscious revival of Aristotelian essentialism, and has been eloquently advanced by Wiggins in *Sameness and Substance*. On this view, the sortal concepts which we use to individuate members of natural kinds (or types of things found in nature) are not and are not intended to be invented by us at whim. We hope, and it seems plausible to suppose, that concepts such as 'tiger', 'whale' and 'hydrogen atom', while in a sense human constructions, at the same time reveal types of thing with their own principles of activity or functioning. It is because of the types in question having their own functioning in this way that we are able to pick out individual examples of them from the rest of reality, under concepts which determine their identity and persistence conditions through time. The sortal concepts we use to demarcate natural things actually presuppose that there is some ultimate physical constitution (or essence) underlying our natural-kind terms which explains the functioning and activity of the individuals in question. Wiggins now argues that the existence of, say, a man is regarded by us as dependent on the individual in question having that constitution (call it G) and that we predicate 'man' of the individual by virtue of an indirect reference to this (possibly unknown) G. Hence we can say that if x is a man, he necessarily has this constitution G. Moreover, there is no principle of individuation (conditions for existence and persistence), other than that given by the concept 'man' or one equivalent to 'man' in respect of such conditions, which enables us to pick out individual men as discrete individuals, so there is a sense in which anything that is a man is necessarily a man. (Being identified in this way is essential to *it* being identified as an individual at all.) So anything that is a man cannot but be a man and hence G as well.

Wiggins sees this type of essentialism as ruling out the nominalist view that whatever something identified as Peter can do, something identified in some other way could also do, or, indeed, anything whatever could do.[16] In a way, he is trying to forge a sense of natural necessity which is stronger than that given by seeing causality in terms of simple natural regularity in the world. (See our next section.) On Wiggins's view, it seems that things don't just happen to behave regularly as they do – they have to. Indeed, he remarks that where properties (like the G-constitution of men) are fixed to their bearers by virtue of their being inherent in the individuation of them, the *de re* 'must of causal inflexibility ... passes over into an inflexibility that is conceptual (though only loosely speaking logical)'.[17] It is only loosely speaking logical because there is nothing within the concept 'man' itself to entail the truth of 'whatever is a man is necessarily G'. As we shall see again, advocates of *de re* necessity are arguing for a type of necessity that is not purely logical. But against Wiggins's attempt to erect an essentialist necessity of this sort (and against analogous attempts by Putnam, Kripke and others to derive essentialist conclusions from an examination of the workings of natural-kind terms), it is worth remarking that there is no conceptual necessity at all for anything having the manifest properties we associate with our use of the term 'man' to have a G-constitution. Whatever this G-constitution might turn out to be, this may be most simply a feature of the present organization of matter on this planet. Other laws might have obtained and might indeed obtain elsewhere so as to produce creatures indistinguishable from men, except at the micro-constitutional level. Whether or not these creatures would in some metaphysical sense *be* men (and Putnam, as we shall see, argues that they would not be), it would not follow from the fact that we individuated them under the sortal concept 'man', in virtue of their manifest properties, that they had to have G-consitutions. Indeed, there seems no reason to suppose that identifying an object in a certain way entails that it *has* to behave or be constituted in a particular way. We may have well-founded beliefs that natural objects picked out under certain concepts will resemble other natural objects similarly individuated, but there is no more necessity about these resemblances being borne out in individual cases than attach to scientific theories generally, in which it is generally admitted that the next example of an x we come across might turn out to be different and behave differently from all the other x's we have seen. In the case of human artefacts, individuating an object as a car, say, may lead us to have well-founded expectations about its origins, performance and structure, but no more necessity can be milked out of this concerning these expectations than is given by the evidence from our past experience that things that look like this generally behave like that. The problem for anyone who wants to derive a type of necessity concerning the properties or constitution of individuals individuated under particular sortal concepts is to explain how this necessity can amount to more than saying that in the past similar-looking things tended to behave or be like that.

The second way in which a version of essentialism might be defended by appeal to considerations concerning identity has even more surprising consequences than the modified Aristotelianism we have just been considering. For it would entail that if, for example, a heavenly body is referred to at one time as 'the evening star' (or 'Hesperus') and at another time as 'the morning star' (or 'Phosphorus') then, if it should turn out that actually these are different ways of referring to the same thing (Venus, perhaps), it is necessarily the case that Hesperus is Phosphorus and that both of them are Venus. The argument, originally formulated by Ruth Barcan Marcus, derives from two axioms. The first is the proposition that everything is necessarily identical with itself, while the second is Leibniz's law (if two objects are identical, they have all their properties in common). Using Hesperus and Phosphorus to illustrate the point, we first say that Hesperus is necessarily identical with itself (or Hesperus); then, as Hesperus is identical with Phosphorus, Phosphorus has all the properties of Hesperus. These include the property of being necessarily identical with Hesperus, so Phosphorus is not only identical with Hesperus, but necessarily identical to it. But surely, one feels, it is not in any sense necessary that the planet we observe in the evening is the same as the one we see in the morning. It might easily have been another heavenly body altogether that we noticed in the evening, perhaps not even a planet at all.

If we want to block the idea that all identities are logically necessary via the Barcan proof, and hold on to the common-sense idea that the number of the planets might not have been nine, or that Dickens might not have been Boz or water not H_2O, then we will have to attack one of the steps in the proof. Perhaps, following Ayer, the simplest thing to do is to query the idea that being necessarily identical with itself is a genuine property of anything, ascribable to things independently of the way they are specified.[18] Thus, while it is true and necessarily true that Hesperus is Hesperus because here the same thing is being picked out twice in the same way, it will not be necessarily true that Hesperus is Phosphorus, because the name 'Phosphorus' does not have the same sense as 'Hesperus'. Phosphorus would be necessarily identical with Hesperus only if the name 'Phosphorus' had the same sense as 'Hesperus', and clearly they do not, as people can understand both names perfectly well without realizing that they refer to the same thing.

We shall return to the way in which proper names have sense in Chapter 3, but, in concluding this section on identity, we can say that individuating things and deciding when two things are really the same involve dividing the world up by means of sortal concepts which pick out individuals and determine the conditions under which things will be regarded as identical. Certain conditional necessities may follow from our use of these sortal concepts, in such a way that if something is a man, then it is necessarily an animal, although one should be wary of resting too much on this. Concepts may change in response to changing circumstances. In an age of plastic surgery and organ replacement, we may come to call beings made largely of synthetic materials men. But even if there is something about the concept 'man' that currently precludes our calling any non-animalian being a man, any necessity that follows from this is due to our understanding of the concept. This in turn, as well as the connections between the manifest conditions in which we apply the concepts and the unobserved structure and future behaviour of the individual things we apply the concepts to, may well be the outcome of repeated experience. But the fact that experience has led us to have certain expectations of things we are inclined to classify in certain ways in no way guarantees that the next thing we classify under one of these well-grounded sortal concepts will necessarily be correctly classified, or, what amounts to the same thing, actually turn out to have the expected constitution or future behaviour. The world could change, things could change, and, if they did, our classifications with all their conditional necessities and well-grounded expectations could well let us down.

Causality and Determinism

The notion of cause is basic to our picture of the world. We could hardly act so as to bring about our intentions unless we had some idea of how to achieve effects in the physical world, and this means having an idea of what is likely to cause the effects we want. Since the seventeenth century, science has itself often been seen as the attempt to manipulate nature, which means precisely discovering and exploiting causal regularities in nature. While this is undoubtedly too narrow a characterization of science, as science often seeks explanations for natural phenomena with no immediate technological application in mind, technology is clearly an important aspect of science and the one to which it owes much of its prestige in the popular mind. Moreover, the type of explanation sought in science is the uncovering of causes; we explain a phenomenon when we describe how it is caused.

No satisfactory philosophical account of causality should ignore these perfectly obvious observations. Nevertheless, there are radically different ways of accounting for them, depending on the way causality is conceived. On the one hand, there are those who think of nature as governed by underlying and unobservable forces or powers; events are linked by the necessities arising from these forces, and objects are determined in their natures by the basic powers or potentialities of matter. This view, which has some affinity with the essentialism considered in the previous section, is perhaps closer to the common-sense picture of the world and causality than its reductionist rival, the main argument for which points to the lack of any direct evidence we have for unobservable forces or powers existing in nature. Not surprisingly, one of its most persuasive advocates is the empiricist Hume, who characteristically begins his analysis of causality by asking just what the evidence is for speaking of two events as causally connected. Hume writes:

> Suppose two objects to be presented to us, of which the one is the cause and the other the effect; 'tis plain, that from the simple consideration of one, or both these objects we shall never perceive the tie, by which they are united, or be able certainly to pronounce, that there is a connexion between them.[19]

The conclusion Hume derives from this is that when we speak of a causal connection between two events we are not to think that there is some *unobservable* link which forces the effect to follow the cause. Indeed, not only can no such link be ascertained, but from a single case of an event of one type following an event of another type we would never have any reason to speak of a causal connection at all. What grounds and justifies our talk of causality is the realization that there are regularities in nature, such that events of one type are always followed by events of another sort. Indeed, all that is meant by talk of causality in a single case, where we say that *A* has caused *B*, is that we have previously perceived events like *A* regularly conjoined with events like *B* and that we expect to find similar conjunctions in the future.

Hume's own account of the nature of the conjunctions between events of one type and events of another which ground talk of causality has been criticized on various counts. For example, he talks of objects rather than events as being causally related. Also, he requires, in some places at least, that objects causally related be spatially next to each other, thus ruling out causal action at a distance. Further he holds that causal relations between types of event, if they obtain at all, must always obtain, whereas certainly in common usage we speak of causes and effects (such as smoking and cancer) which are not invariably linked. Finally, in his treatments of causality he tends to suggest that our minds are in some unexplained way forced to postulate that there is a necessary causal connection between things we have observed to be regularly conjoined in the past. An elegant statement of a Humean position on causality, purged of these questionable elements, is that of F. P. Ramsey:

> The world, or rather that part of it with which we are acquainted, exhibits as we must all agree a good deal of regularity of succession. I contend that over and above that it exhibits no feature called causal necessity, but that we make sentences called causal laws from which (i.e. having made them) we proceed to actions and propositions connected with them in a certain way, and say that a fact asserted in a proposition which is an instance of a causal law is a case of causal necessity.[20]

The dispute between Humeans and non-Humeans on causality is fundamentally on whether there is any more to causality than 'regularity of succession'.

One objection to the Humean view is to assert that we all know from our experience of willing our actions that there is such a thing as a natural necessity, because we feel it when we cause our limbs to move. Against this, it could be questioned whether we do feel any such thing. Do we not just move our arm? Is there anything which *forces* our arm to move, anything experienced linking the decision and the movement? Even if there were, however, it is doubtful whether appeal to human action at this point would help the anti-Humean much, unless he wanted to say that nature itself was full of quasi-personal agents, causal connections being the executing of their edicts. Further, as Ayer has stressed, observing or in some other way isolating the supposedly necessitating link between a cause and an effect would not really get to the heart of the Humean position.[21] Hume's position should not really be seen in terms of a merely empirical failure to observe any forces or powers in nature. Indeed, against Hume it might be suggested that sometimes we do; we do feel the wind that slows us down, the blow that knocks us flat, and it might be the case that with electron microscopes and the like we could see something describable as the 'communication of forces' in cases of gravity or of magnetism. Hume's point is rather that, even given perception of the forceful link, we want to know why the effect has to follow. What is there about the blow that means I must fall down? Worlds are certainly describable in which people do not fall when hit, in which electrical activity does not bring about effects of attraction and repulsion, and so on; science fiction is made of such stuff. There appears to be nothing in the force that necessitates the effect. In particular, there is nothing in the force that means that the next time it occurs the effect has to follow, and, as we mentioned at the start of the section, causal relations are of interest very largely because of their importance in the future prediction and manipulation of nature. The Humean attitude to causality is not that we can never perceive microscopic or other links between macroscopic causes and effects, but that there is nothing in the cause (or in any intermediary links) that mean the effect has to follow; there is in short nothing more to causality than the regular succession of causes and effects, however much we may 'feel' a force or isolate microscopic intermediaries. What Hume is doing here is to point to the relationship between the so-called problem of induction and talk of causality. This problem arises from the impossibility, clearly demonstrated by Hume (which we will examine in Chapter 2), of showing that the future has to resemble the past in any particular respect. Hume's opponent on causality, by talking of necessary connections between causes and effects, is really saying that, given a cause, the effect cannot but follow, but without showing why a causal connection that has obtained in the past has to obtain once more in this case.

The anti-Humean (or causal realist, as I will call him), however, has one powerful consideration in favour of his belief that there is more to talk of causality than the good deal of regularity of succession mentioned by Ramsey. For there can be a good deal of regularity of succession without our being in the least inclined to speak of causality. Philosophers often speak here of a distinction between a merely accidental generalization in which things just happen in our experience to be conjoined, and a genuinely universal law, in which the conjunction is not just due to haphazard features of our experience but reflects a structural regularity in nature itself. An example of an accidental generalization might be that all antelopes in the wild die before the age of twenty. This, it might be said, has nothing to do with the nature of antelopes, but is just owing to the pervasive but avoidable presence of predators wherever they happen to live in the wild. In an antelopean eden, it would not be the case, and is, in any event, not the case in zoos. Now it might be said that this is a merely accidental generalization because being restricted to the wild it is not a genuinely universal statement. The genuine universal 'all antelopes die before the age of twenty', is not even true. However, we can think of unrestrictedly universal statements which may well be true but which, even if they were, we would still regard as accidental and not law-like. Hempel has proposed as an example 'all bodies consisting of pure gold have a mass of less than 100,000 kilograms'.[22] The question is whether the Humean has any grounds for the natural claim one would make about statements such as this, that they do not reflect genuine causal impossibilities. The causal realist wants to say that there is a sense of causal possibility and impossibility which is not reducible to statements about regularities of succession, which is why the admission that there are generalizations which are true but 'merely accidental' is a strong point in his favour.

The distinction between a causal regularity and one that is merely accidental can be further illustrated by the fact that statements regarded as expressing causal laws are held to support conditional statements whose antecedents are unfulfilled (so-called counterfactual conditionals), whereas this is not the case with merely accidental generalization. Thus, we would regard it as true that if I had put my pen into the furnace, it would have melted, while we would not regard it as true that if we were to fire together two bodies of pure gold each weighing 60,000 kilograms they would not fuse to form one gold body of more than 100,000 kilograms. The latter counterfactual statement is rejected as false because there is in our current physics and chemistry no law against such fusion, even though no such fusion has ever been attempted nor in all probability ever will be. But that no such fusion has never taken place is taken to be a merely accidental generalization even if this remains the case until the end of time. What makes a generalization accidental rather than an expression of a law is that we are nevertheless prepared to envisage situations in which, without any change in the basic processes of nature, we would expect to find the generalization falsified, even though for other reasons the envisaged situation is regarded as highly unlikely. We project or extend law-like generalizations to cover imaginary situations in other worlds similar in structure to our own, while for purely accidental generalizations we admit imaginary situations in such worlds in which they would not obtain. So we are prepared to accept that in a world, such as ours, where someone attempted to fire the two massive gold bodies of our example, he would produce a gold body of more than 100,000 kilograms in mass.

The trouble with any account of the differences between generalizations of law and those of accidental fact of the sort just offered is that it relies on the existence of just the distinction it is trying to explain. It speaks – counterfactually – of what people would do or find in imaginary or counterfactual situations[23] and we have already seen that deciding on the truth or falsity of counterfactuals depends on the availability of just the distinction between laws and accidental generalizations which we are trying to explain. Moreover, the explanation assumes that we, the rejecters or accepters of the counterfactuals in question, are already able to deploy the distinction between laws expressing basic processes of nature and statements of mere chance regularity, because this is the basis of our present decisions on these imaginary cases. What, otherwise, makes us so sure that the discovery of gold bodies of 60,000 kilograms in mass and their fusion would not in themselves constitute changes in some basic process of nature?

For a Humean, this conclusion should be unsettling, because it suggests that there is something in our conceptual apparatus which allows us to think of some regularities as evidence for basic processes of nature, and others as evidence for no such thing, and that there is nothing in the facts of regularity of succession which can motivate or ground the distinction. The position of the causal realist is that we can and do envisage cases in which generalizations about regularities hold without exception, but which we do not regard as supporting any counterfactuals, because the regularities in question are not based in causally necessary connections between the types of event regularly conjoined in our experience.

The problem for the Humean here is to explain what he bases his distinction on without invoking any idea of natural necessity. One possible line of approach for him is to say that we should not take regularities of succession in isolation from each other, and to claim that the problem seems worse for him than it is because of a tendency to concentrate in these discussions on particular cases of causal connections. The reason for regarding the accidental generalization about the non-existence of large amounts of pure gold as just that is that such bodies are not ruled out by what we regard as the basic laws of physics and chemistry, and we count regularities as basic laws when they appear to be very pervasive indeed, and connect with other similarly pervasive regularities. Hempel sums the situation up in this way:

> Thus, whether a statement of universal form counts as a law will depend in part upon the scientific theories accepted at the time ... even if [a statement of universal form] is empirically well confirmed and presumably true in fact, it will not qualify as a law if it rules out certain hypothetical occurrences (such as the fusion of two gold bodies with a resulting mass of more than 100,000 kilograms ...) which an accepted theory qualifies as possible.[24]

So universal causal laws (or statements which, though not universal, we regard as expressing causal connections) will be based on those regularities of succession which we regard as the basis of our picture of how the world works.

Does this then mean, as Ayer puts it, that in a case of causal connection *propter hoc* adds nothing to *post hoc*?[25] Ayer goes on to answer his question by saying in effect that causal sequences are no different from sequences we regard as accidental regularities at the level of primary fact. It is just that we are prepared to project generalizations based on what we are regarding as causal sequences into imaginary or counterfactual cases. 'Cause and effect', he says 'have their place only in our imaginative arrangements and extensions of [the] primary facts.' One would have to object to this if, as we have done, one had claimed that even the classification of sensory data required the postulation of physical systems exhibiting a fair degree of stability, for this is tantamount to crediting those systems, or at least some of the entities in them, with causal powers. This is certainly the case with the enduring three-dimensional material objects of our own world. If these are what form the primary facts,* then causal beliefs about their behaviour and properties are part of the primary facts, and cannot be so easily dispatched to the realm of imaginative arrangements and extensions.

---

*Ayer himself sees the primary system and the primary facts rather differently. The primary system for him is restricted to assertions to the effect that such and such an observable property is located at a particular time and place, and he sees the rest of our world picture as constructed out of such assertions. My argument at the end of section on 'Things and Appearances' was intended to suggest an important sense in which a primary system such as Ayer's would not really be primary.

Nevertheless, even if causal beliefs were present and necessarily present in our world picture right from the start, it would not show that the realist is right about there being physical necessities in the world over and above our perceptions of regularity in the world. All it would show is that we could not form any picture of the world or of our experience at all unless we were able from the start to see the world as consisting of entities which exhibited perceptible regularities of some sort. It would not show that these regularities had to be as we perceived them, or that they might not change in various ways. The causal realist and the essentialist of the last section are right in so far as they stress the ways in which crediting stable things with enduring properties and projecting those beliefs into the future and into imaginary situations are central to our pictures of the world. But they are surely open to criticism, in so far as in talking of necessity, whether causal or physical, they imply that the next thing that happens could not be other than it is, or other than what we think it will be. For this would amount to a failure to recognize the problem of induction for what it is. But if this is not what is meant by talk of necessity, it is hard to see how it adds anything to the fact – admitted by Humeans – that the world of our experience is pervaded through and through by regularities of succession.

Saying that our world is pervaded through and through by regularities of succession naturally raises the question of determinism. Determinism has traditionally been seen as the belief that there is no occurrence which is not the result of a prior set of conditions which are such that, given those conditions, the occurrence could not but occur. To writers in the Humean tradition, this formulation has unacceptable implications of natural necessity, yet Hume and many of his followers regarded themselves as determinists. In any case, it does not bring out the connection which certainly exists in people's minds now between determinism and the growth of natural science. Science seems to many people to reveal the world as operating according to regularities (described in statements called laws of nature) in such a way that for any event, if we knew the relevant laws and the relevant conditions obtaining prior to that event, we would be able to predict the occurrence of the event before it actually happened. This indeed is the point of Laplace's famous intelligence or demon:

We ought to regard the present state of the universe as the effect of its ante-cedent state and the cause of the state to follow. An intelligence knowing, at a given instant of time, all forces by which nature is animated and all things of which the universe consists, would be able to comprehend the actions of the largest bodies of the world and those of the lightest atoms in one single formula, provided his intellect were sufficiently powerful to subject all data to analysis; to him, nothing would be uncertain, both past and future would be present to his eyes. The human mind in the perfection it has been able to give astronomy affords a feeble outline of such an intelligence.[26]

It will be noted that this formulation is consistent with either a Humean or a causal realist view of causality, because the emphasis is not on the way in which the causal connection works, but on the predictability of events by means of knowledge of scientific laws.

Of course, no determinist of a Laplacean variety claims the knowledge attributed to the demon, nor, if he is wise, will he claim that such knowledge might at some definite point in the future be available to human beings. For most occurrences there would be no point in having such knowledge anyway; we are hardly likely to waste the time and money needed to develop the means of predicting the precise fall of each leaf from the tree I can see from my window simply to appear to satisfy the demands of what is, after all, a purely philosophical theory. What the determinist is really claiming is that there is in nature no such thing as chance. Everything that happens is conceived of as happening in the regular and predictable way things happen in physics textbooks,* where, for example, we are given a formula which enables us to calculate the precise degree of expansion when we apply specified amounts of heat over specified times to metal objects of specified masses.

It will be clear that whether we are Humeans or realists about causality, there is no theoretical reason for supposing that the universe must be like that. The factors which bring particular events about (or which precede them on the Humean view) need not be such that we can truly say that a similar set of factors will produce an exactly similar result next time round, let alone throughout the whole of space and time. Universes which bobble irregularly in either small-scale or large-scale ways are certainly not inconceivable. What the determinist is claiming is that any unpredictable bobbling we imagine we perceive is really a factor of our ignorance; if we knew all the laws and all the factors operative at any region of space and time we would see that what appeared to us to be chance was actually regular and precise and predictable.

A significant aspect of the dispute between determinists and indeter-

---

*But not in reality. The philosopher and experimentalist C. S. Peirce noted that even the most refined measurements and comparisons in the laboratory 'fall behind the accuracy of bank accounts' and that the determinations of physical constants 'are about on a par with an upholsterer's measurements of carpets and curtains'. (*Collected Papers*, Cambridge, Mass., 1931–5, Vol. VI, p. 35.)

minists is that, even when tied down to something as specific as the all-pervasiveness of laws of nature, it is essentially undecidable. Even if the determinist is immensely successful in devising universal theories to predict as many actual occurrences as you like, we will be able to check only a tiny fraction of all the occurrences covered by those theories. We would never be able to say with certainty that these theories cover all space and time. In fact, of course, the boot is on the other foot. Aside from reservations of the sort expressed by Peirce about the accuracy of measurement (and hence of prediction) even in the laboratory, large parts of contemporary physics do not even attempt to predict individual occurrences. The best that can be done in many areas appears to be to offer theories which say that certain proportions of given populations of certain particles will behave in such and such a way, but there seems to be no way of saying just what any individual particle will do. Faced with the presence of these so-called statistical theories, and at the most basic level of matter too, the determinist is reduced to saying that if we knew more and had better theories, the apparent randomness would be revealed as due to our stupidity and ignorance; God, at any rate, does not play dice. (This was Einstein's position.)

So neither determinism nor indeterminism is open to conclusive proof or disproof. One might still say that determinism is a useful methodological postulate. We should not be satisfied with merely statistical theories, and should strive for theories promising completely precise predictions. Whether this advice is always useful is open to question, as in many cases, such as town planning and insurance, predictions of tendencies within populations are just what is wanted. It is in virtue of an observed tendency among smokers rather than of an absolutely universal rule that we are able to speak in general terms of smoking being a cause of cancer. This does not necessarily mean, though, that when a particular smoker, Jones, contracted cancer the events that constituted his smoking only partially or in some random way brought about his cancer. The events that constituted *his* smoking may well have brought about his cancer without any qualification, even though smoking alone may not bring about cancer unless the smoker has a particular physical constitution. But the events that constituted Jones's smoking were cases of a person of that particular physical constitution smoking. We have, as Davidson has shown in his paper 'Causal Relations',[27] in speaking of particular events or series of events causing other events, to distinguish between the event or events which were the cause and our descriptions of the event or events, which may be incomplete descriptions of the event or events from the point of view of a full causal explanation or even irrelevant from that point of view. From the point of view of a full causal explanation, we may, as Davidson does, require a description of the cause in a form from which we can deduce from a true and exceptionless universal law, to the effect that whenever there are events of that type there will be such and such an effect, that there will in this case be such an effect. So a complete description of the cause of Jones contracting cancer may require us to speak of a series of smokings by a person of such and such a constitution in such and such circumstances. We may, of course, be quite unable to do this, but this entails neither that his smoking did not cause his cancer (for his smoking was a smoking of the relevant type) nor that there is no such complete description of his smoking (smoking by a person of such and such type in such and such circumstances, etc., etc.). Moreover, the exceptionless laws may be so complicated to frame and difficult to apply that for all practical purposes it is better to stick with incomplete descriptions of the causes, under which it is not invariably true that the effect follows. (Smoking usually causes cancer.) A full-blooded determinist, however, will continue to hold that, whatever the impracticalities involved, all events can be described in such a way that they will be covered by true and exceptionless universal laws. Determinism no doubt answers to a deep need in us for explanations in which nothing is left unpredictable or chancy. But there can be no presumption that chance is actually eliminable.

Some may object to our discussion of determinism on the grounds that it takes too restricted a version of determinism in linking it to natural science in the way we have, and that what determinism really says is that every event has a cause, or even that everything that happens has a sufficient reason for its happening. The trouble with these formulations is that they are ambiguous. If by cause or sufficient reason here one means that every event has or is preceded by that without which it could not come about, then the claims are true, but vacuous. It is only when one starts to specify through science or in some other way what would count as a cause or a sufficient reason that one is saying anything at all, but then what one is saying will probably be false. After all, something, be it God or the universe as a whole, would appear to require nothing to precede it or to bring it about, so in at least one case it would appear that the cause or sufficient reason would be nothing at all. But, even restricting determinism to happenings within the universe, it is not self-evidently true that things cannot come about at least in part by chance, in such a way that there is nothing in the present state of a particular set-up or anywhere else which determines what its next state will be. The dispute between determinism and indeterminism, while still undecidable, takes on some substance when it is viewed as a dispute properly about the availability or otherwise of deterministic theories in science, theories, that is, that give substance to the belief that for every observable difference of outcome from two apparently similar set-ups in the universe, there must have been some real difference between the initial set-ups. What one decides about the truth of determinism will depend in part on the success science has in evolving deterministic theories, although, as we shall see in Chapter 4, special problems arise when we consider the relationships between human action and determinism.

Time and the 'Myth' of the Passage

It is no doubt possible to imagine the universe and its history as a four-dimensional space–time manifold. Physical objects and persons are space–time 'worms', extended in all dimensions in the manifold. The positions of these worms in space–time determine their velocity, mass, position and time relative to each other. Tense can be eliminated from this model of reality; we can say simply that each thing or person extends or is (tenselessly) at or through such and such points in the manifold. This spatializing of time is, as Quine points out, a natural consequence of relativity theory, but what he calls 'the idea of paraphrasing tensed sentences into terms of eternal relations of things to times' was clear enough before Einstein.[28] We can, then, regard the world and the things in it as from a vantage point which is in effect outside time. We can see how things are interrelated to each other temporally, one earlier, one later, and we can do this without regarding some events as having disappeared irrevocably into the past and others as not yet in existence. We can regard all events, past, present and future, as all present in some tenseless now. In place of the ever-diminishing thinness of the perceived or experienced present, the scientific world view gives us a temporally thick world in which past, present and future are but aspects of the perspective from which an observer inside the world perceives or describes events earlier, contemporaneous and later relative to his position in the manifold. Thus, the Battle of Hastings is (tenselessly) at Hastings at 1066, Beethoven is (tenselessly) in various parts of Europe from 1770 to 1827, what I call next year's Derby is (tenselessly) at Epsom at June 1984 while I am (tenselessly) writing this in Ham at 19 April 1983, and this fact determines whether these other things are in my past, present or future as I write. There is in principle no difference between events spatially distant from where I am now and those temporally distant, only, says Quine, a tiresome bias in our ordinary language treatment of time. 'Relations of date are exalted grammatically as relations of position, weight and colour are not.'[29] It is, in fact, an illusion to think of time changing or of us moving through time. Time changes no more than space, being only an aspect of the siting of events and things in the manifold. Nor do events change in time, nor do we travel in time. All that happens is that events have specific temporal positions, and some things, such as people, are regarded as being extended in time as well as in space. Time itself does not pass, nor do we pass through it, except as a metaphorical way of expressing our wormlike extension through the manifold.

Although proponents of the timeless view of the world in which past, present and future tenses are eliminated in favour of a tenseless 'is' would not necessarily admit the connection, there is in fact a close connection between their thesis that the passage of time is a myth and that of the British philosopher J. M. McTaggart who, in a famous article in 1908, attempted to show that time is unreal.[30] McTaggart's strategy is first to distinguish two ways of talking about time and then to show that one of those ways leads to contradiction, while the other fails to do justice to our intuitions concerning the passing of time. We have, according to McTaggart, the A-series, according to which events are ordered with respect to their being past, present and future, and the B-series according to which events are ordered in terms of being earlier or later than each other. The B-series (essentially what we have in the tenseless view of time) tells us how events are temporally related to each other, but implies nothing about the passage of time, or the way in which the same event is successively future, present and past. Yet this successiveness is the essence of time, the manner in which, as Augustine puts it in his *Confessions* (Bk XI), the past no longer is, the future is not yet and the present appears to be an ever-vanishing extensionless point, having no duration of itself (for that would imply that bits of it were past or future or both). These facts can only be expressed by means of tenses, by the A-series, in other words.

According to McTaggart, however, the A-series is irretrievably contradictory. The same event cannot be past, present and future. These are incompatible predicates, yet they are true of every event. Of course, what will be said in response to this is that what applies to every event at any one moment are not the simple predicates 'past', 'present' and 'future', but more complex predicates. Thus an event which is happening now is present in the present, future in the past and past in the future. But, according to McTaggart, if we use these more complex predicates, it is actually the case that all nine predicates of this type apply to every event, not just three of them, and some of these will be mutually contradictory. For example, when an event is past in the present it is not future in the present. We can, it is true, avoid this contradiction by saying that it is in the past that the event is future in the present, and that it is in the present that it is past in the present, but this further duplication of 'past', 'present' and 'future' yields twenty-seven new predicates, some of which are again mutually incompatible, yet all of which at some time or other apply to each event. In fact, as Dummett has pointed out, on this new level developed to remove the contradictions of the lower levels of predicates, there will be predicates equivalent to simple past (past in the present in the present), present (present in the present in the present) and future (future in the present in the present), and the same will be true of every higher level of predicates we devise to remove contradictions in lower levels.[31] So the original contradiction reappears at every attempt to remove it, and McTaggart's proof is vindicated against this type of objection, unless one regards an infinitely regressive explanation of apparently straightforward concepts as adequate.

Most people who consider McTaggart's argument regard it as resting on a failure to attend to the way in which the truth of certain sentences depends on the circumstances of their utterance. This is certainly true of tensed sentences, but other elements of language such as personal pronouns and positional adverbs have the same effect. 'I am close to you, but far from him' depends for its truth on who is speaking to whom, as well as on the time of utterance. When we realize that tenses indicate that the sentences in which they occur have to be judged in terms of their circumstances of utterance, we will see that it is wrong to think of an event being just past, present or future. It is past, present or future only in relation to the now in which a statement about it is being uttered. But, as we have just seen, a similar thing is true of personal pronouns and spatial adverbs. Couldn't a McTaggart-style assault be mounted on them, on 'I' or 'you' for example, because everyone can be called 'I' and 'you' (though only 'I' by himself and 'you' by another)? Dummett regards it as significant that McTaggart shows no inclination to extend his argument to personal pronouns or to spatial expressions, such as 'here' and 'there' or 'near' or 'far', whose contribution to the sense of utterances depends intimately on where or by whom they are uttered. In Dummett's view, the difference between talk about time, on the one hand, and reference to one's position or to the utterer of sentences, on the other, is that we can say everything that needs to be said about people or about spatial positions without using expressions whose sense depends on the individual doing the speaking, or his or her position. Whether Dummett is right on this regarding space and person, it is certainly not the case with time, and this is what is involved in McTaggart's denial that the A-series can be explained in terms of the B-series. What is missing from the B-series is just that sense of something happening *now* which is so central to our intuition of time, and we cannot get that into the picture without using expressions from the A-series. To identify the observer's sense of now with a certain position in the time dimension would, as Dummett puts it, simply make him part of the region observed, and we could still ask what is happening now for someone observing that region.

The B-series – what is provided by what I have been calling the scientific world view – can only give a static picture of reality. Everything that happens can be described in it, except, of course, our sense of the passing of time. This is why philosophers who espouse the scientific world view tend to speak of the 'myth' of the passage of time, and it is the passage of time that, in McTaggart's view, is unreal. But, of course, it is not. Dispensable it may be from some points of view, but even if we decide that our perception of the changing of things in time is inherently sub-jective and that relations between things are not really in the A-series or Augustinian sense temporal at all, our apprehension of things is itself temporal: that is to say, it changes, and in it, what was present is lost in the past, while what will be present is in the not-yet of the future. There is, then, a way in which the idea that time is unreal is self-refuting, for even if we chose to regard ourselves as space–time worms extended through certain points of space and time, there is no denying that our experience is of ourselves moving and changing through the world, and not simply extended in it. To adopt a metaphor of Dummett's, regarding life histories as worms extended in space and time is like seeing the road without seeing the traveller moving down it.[32] But seeing the movement involves the observer conceiving himself in terms of a transition from future through the present to the past, for that is just what perception of change consists in.

Admitting that tensed judgements can be made and assessed only relative to the now of the person making the judgements does mean that there is no single correct description of the world in terms of the A-series because from moment to moment there will be changes of tense in the statements describing various events. McTaggart's proof rests on treating A-series predicates as if they are timelessly true, and this seems an elementary mistake. That they are not timelessly true is why scientifically minded writers prefer to conceive the world in terms of B-series judgements where there is no such relativity.* However, as we have suggested, our own perspective on the world is a temporal one, and limited by that fact. From that perspective, the past is inaccessible and so, in a different way, is the future. As regards the past, we naturally favour a picture in which every statement about the past is either definitely true or definitely false. But the fact remains that there are many statements about the remote (or even the not so remote past) for which there is not the least likelihood of our ever being able to determine truth or falsity, and whose actual truth or falsity it is difficult to see making any difference to us in any case. We certainly feel that there must have been some definite number of hairs on Julius Caesar's head the day he crossed the Rubicon, but it is hard to see what this belief amounts to other than a payment of lip-service to the reality of the past. Belief in the determinate reality of the past is doubtless reinforced by B-series thinking in which there is no sense of the past being lost, but, from our point of view at least, that is just what things past are. Travel into the past is a conceptual impossibility, for it would entail the ability to get into a time machine at midday today and in five minutes, say, being both at 12:05 today and at some time several hundred years ago. The problem for the realist about the past is to say what the point is of speaking of the actual definite reality of a past realm that is inaccessible in this way. On the other hand, the countervailing idea – that the past exists or is real only in so far as there are or could be traces of the effects of past happenings in the present or the future – is one that most people find so repugnant as to be almost offensive, not, of course, that that is in itself any argument against it.

The dispute between those who assert the full reality of the past, meaning by that that there is something which makes any judgements about the past either definitely true or definitely false, however undecidable it is in practice, and those who say that we are entitled to think of the past as real only in so far as we have or could obtain some evidence in favour of the truth or falsity of particular statements about the past is an aspect of a much deeper dispute in contemporary philosophy. This

*A similar relativity, of course, obtains in the case of judgements about what *I* am doing, what is going on *here*, and so on.

is the dispute between those who construe our linguistic practices as entitling us to think of statements as definitely true or false even though we have no means of confirming even partially either their truth or falsity, and those who find it hard to distinguish a reality which impinges on us in no way at all from a fiction. Certainly we have no way of distinguishing in terms of truth or probability between a number of competing and mutually contradictory statements concerning the state of Caesar's head on that famous morning. What is the cash value of hammering on the table and insisting that one or other of them must be *the* correct one? On the other hand, it may, with some plausibility, be urged that thinking in a fully realistic way about the past is itself just part and parcel of that thinking of the world as manifesting that stability and regularity apart from our perception of it which we took to be required for any stable classification of experience.

Questioning the reality of the past does not, of course, imply that we can actually alter what has already happened in the past. Is the future similarly fixed, or is it to some degree open to us to affect the future course of events? We have already seen that physical determinism is by no means obviously true, but the fatalistic belief that what happens is fated now to happen, whatever steps we take to prevent it, does not require support from physical determinism (nor, indeed, as we shall see in Chapter 4, is it obvious that physical determinism actually has this consequence, for even if we and the consequences of our actions are determined in various ways, what we do and what happens may still depend on our choices). Nor does thinking of objects and people as space–time worms necessarily entail that we cannot now affect the future, because adopting a timeless perspective on the world does not in itself say how the things we are regarding timelessly actually come about; in other words a timeless perspective could be adopted as a rational reconstruction of events which unfold through an open future, although if there were anyone (such as God) who now really sees from a perspective outside time what I am going to do tomorrow, it is hard to see how I am anything but fated to do it, which is presumably what those who believe in predestination have in mind. There is, however, a famous line of thought, dating back to Aristotle in his *de Interpretatione*, Ch. IX, which has appeared to many to establish the truth of fatalism on the basis of far less disputable premises than the foreknowledge of God or specific interpretations of physics.

As Aristotle's own argument and even his conclusion are matters of great controversy, I will present the fatalist case in my own version. The fatalist first appeals to the belief that future-tense statements are definitely true or definitely false in the present. It is important to realize that the argument does not depend on our knowing which, but only on the supposition that (to use Aristotle's own example) 'There will be a sea-battle tomorrow' is now either true or false. Whichever it is, it is now. But if it is true now, then the sea-battle cannot but happen tomorrow, while if it is false now, then the sea-battle cannot happen tomorrow. So, whether the sea-battle happens tomorrow or not, it happens, as Aristotle puts it, of necessity. Another way of putting the point would be to say that if it is the case now that the sea-battle will happen (or not happen) tomorrow, then it has to happen (or not happen); its happening (or not happening)· is thus something laid up now, and we have to conclude that there is, in that case, nothing we can do now to prevent it (or bring it about).

Some, including probably Aristotle himself, have reacted to this argument by asserting the common-sense view that tomorrow's possible sea-battle can still be prevented or brought about by steps we take between now and tomorrow, and going on to locate the source of the problem in the argument's premise to the effect that 'There will be a sea-battle' is actually true or false now, or that it is the case now that there will or will not be a sea-battle tomorrow. But denying that future-tense statements are either true or false in the present is itself highly counter to common sense; we certainly believe that a sea-battle either will or will not take place tomorrow, that one or other of the appropriate statements is true now, and that this belief will be vindicated by the way tomorrow's occurrence or non-occurrence of a sea-battle, whichever it is, will permit us to say which of the statements made today about tomorrow's battle was true today. So, if the argument is valid, we have either to accept fatalism or give up the idea that future-tense statements are either true or false in the present in which they are made.

But the argument is not valid. Both versions we have considered rest on misreading truisms. The truisms are, respectively, that it is necessarily the case that if 'There will be a sea-battle tomorrow' is true (false), then there will (will not) be a sea-battle, and, necessarily, if it is the case now that there will (will not) be a sea-battle tomorrow, there will (will not) be a sea-battle tomorrow.

What is truistic and necessarily the case is, in each case, the whole conditional: 'If "There will be a sea-battle tomorrow" is true, then there will be a sea-battle tomorrow'; 'If it is the case now that there will be a sea-battle tomorrow, then there will be a sea-battle tomorrow.' But the argument removes the qualifying 'necessarily the case' from its correct position outside the conditionals, to an incorrect and misleading position inside the conditional, making it seem as if there is something necessary or fated about the consequent of each conditional (necessary that there will (or will not) be a sea-battle). From the truistic and necessarily true conditionals, nothing properly follows about the fatedness or otherwise of sea-battles or anything else. So it seems that we can go on thinking of future-tense statements as true or false when they are made, without having to embrace fatalism.

It might be suggested that Aristotle could not have been guilty of so crude a fallacy as the one just exposed. In other words, the argument I have just refuted could not possibly have been his argument. This may indeed be the case; his 'sea-battle' passage is, as I have already said, notoriously hard to interpret. He *could* be saying something like this. We assign truth or falsity to some future-tense statements in the first instance because we are able (pretty well) to verify them at the time of utterance (because of our knowledge of regularities in nature, and so on). We then extend this practice to statements, like the one about tomorrow's sea-battle case, which we are not able here and now to verify or falsify, saying that the statement in question is now either true or false, and this has the possibly misleading consequence that we come to believe that there is something we could now discover which would show whether the event will or will not happen. In other words, acceptance of the determinacy of the truth-value of future-tense statements depends on broadly deterministic assumptions about the present existence of factors which are now causally determining future events. So those, such as Aristotle and the Polish logician Lukasiewicz, who want to withhold truth-values from at least some future-tense statements are really rejecting determinism with respect to the events those statements are about, and concluding that, because there is nothing discoverable now which would make those statements true or false, we cannot legitimately say they are true or false.

In response to a suggestion of this sort, I do not see how our present ability to discover the truth-values of statements about the future has any special bearing on their actually being either true or false. Or at least, if we think it does have a bearing on the matter, we will then have to say that many other types of statement which we are not in a position to prove or disprove are not either true or false as well, such as statements about universal natural laws, statements about the remote past, statements about God, and so on. If we envisage ourselves as living in a fully objective world, apart from ourselves and our ability to find out about it, a price we pay will be to admit that statements describing events in that world can be true or false quite independently of anything we might know or ever be in a position to discover, and saying this has nothing to do with physical determinism. A world could be objective in this sense, without being totally deterministic. In fact, whether we regard all future-tense statements as determinately true or false, or whether we predicate truth or falsity only of those statements which we envisage ourselves as one day being in a position to confirm or deny, at least in part, will presumably depend on considerations analogous to those governing our attitude to the reality of the past. But these considerations are, as I have already remarked, not based in features peculiar to time or to judgements about time. What they are based in we will examine at greater length in Chapter 3.

The Claims of Religion

Vast amounts have been written and spoken about religion, and certainly no serious person can avoid taking up some position on the claims of at least some religions, whereas it is not obviously the case that a well-educated person needs to have formed a view on some of the other topics we have been considering. Nevertheless, the philosophical issues involved in assessing religious claims can, I think, be indicated fairly briefly. I shall consider here two issues, first the attempt to establish religious claims by appeal to religious experience, and secondly the more familiar philosophical routes to the existence of God by appeal to certain familiar arguments.

Whatever else religion is, it is not a theory. For most religious believers the most important indicators of the truth of their belief come from their religious experience. Such experience can take many forms; there are those ecstatic mystical trances and contemplative suspensions of the sense of time and everyday reality, coupled with an overwhelming sense of the presence of something spiritual, which are not all that common, but which many believers claim to have experienced at least occasionally in their lives. Then there are the far more common feelings of guilt, forgiveness, security and so on, which believers characteristically interpret as relating to the supernatural, as well as those feelings of warmth, companionship and uplift which many experience during communal religious services. The differences between all these different types of experience are not to be minimized or overlooked, but the same question arises in the case of each of them: to what extent do such feelings objectively support belief in a deity or some other supernatural force?

Subjectively, there can be no doubt of their power. Indeed, a fairly typical attitude even among reflective religious thinkers is to claim that to those who have had religious experience any speculative or verbal proof of the existence of God is unnecessary, while to those who have not had such experiences any argument will fail to carry conviction. Moreover, many people have changed their lives in dramatic and unexpected ways, as a result of having had a religious experience, and been led to heroic feats of self-sacrifice and asceticism. But, of course, none of this is enough to establish that what religious believers believe as a result of their experiences is actually true. Something more than conviction and sincerity is needed here, particularly when one takes a long-term historical view of religious behaviour and sees the numerous recorded instances of people being led astray factually by what they conceived of as religious experience; the history of Christianity alone is full of cases of apparently inspired figures claiming on the basis of their experiences to foresee the imminent founding of a heaven on earth, from the apostolic times right down to the tragic events at Jonestown in our own day, and who is in a position to doubt the sincerity of many of these would-be prophets? The Catholic Church was traditionally extremely wise to treat claims to religious experience with a great deal of initial suspicion.

The fact is that religious experience lacks just those features of ordinary experience which allow us to conceive the latter as supporting a picture of an objective world. In earlier sections, we have seen how there is a sense in which our picture of the external world transcends our experiences of it, how it is a world composed of objects which exist while unperceived and which have properties not directly manifested in experience. Nevertheless, our experiences do support this picture in a number of ways. The belief that my current visual experience, say, includes my seeing a table in front of me allows me to predict that I will have specific experiences of touch and hearing if I strike what I see with my fist, that I will (in all probability) re-encounter the table if I return to where it is now located, and that other observers will have experiences appropriate to there being a table where I am now, and will thus be able to corroborate my ideas about my seeing a table at the moment. Our picture of the world as consisting of such things as tables and other enduring physical objects is thus supported by the way that picture enables us to predict the future experiences of ourselves and others, and by the way these predictions are, in the overwhelming number of instances, confirmed.

So our physical-object picture of the world, and its more sophisticated

ramifications in scientific theory receive some degree of experiential confirmation from the way they successfully enable us to project a high degree
of regularity, predictability and mutual support in our own experiences,
and in the experiences others have. These features of ordinary sensory
experience are almost entirely lacking in the case of religious experiences:
the latter are not regular, nor are they predictable, nor do they connect
with the deliverances of other senses, nor is there any significant measure
of agreement between religious believers about what it is that they are
perceiving. If religious experience was indeed a window on to a wider
and more inclusive world (as William James puts it), we would expect
some of these conditions to be fulfilled, particularly perhaps the last. Lack
of regularity and predictability in religious experience and lack of connections with other types of experience, while depriving those experiences
of the probative power of ordinary sensory experience, might perhaps
be overlooked on the grounds that the object or objects of religious
experience cannot be expected to reveal themselves to men in the same
way as physical objects or persons do; but it is very hard for the non-
believer to understand how there could be genuine experiences both of
the Virgin Mary and of the Lord Krishna, belonging as these figures do
to mutually incompatible systems of belief, and even more to conceive
how such radically different experiences and systems could somehow be
brought into harmony, as revelations of one underlying reality.

Actually, religious experience is often declared by those having it to
have no clear cognitive content in itself. It is often regarded as a transport, a suspension of all processes of thought and perception. In the light
of this, it is not surprising that believers from different religious
traditions report on their experiences in the terms appropriate to their
own particular religious traditions. But, equally, if the experiences themselves are indeterminate in content, they are even less of a support for
specific religious beliefs, particularly when one realizes that indeterminate
feelings of well-being, or anxiety, or elation, or of oneness with nature
are also experienced by non-believers. The believer will naturally say that
the non-believer is actually having religious experiences without being
aware of the fact, but, while this would be entirely reasonable from his
point of view, the onus is very much on him to show why the non-believer
should interpret his experiences religiously. Unfortunately for him, the
types of reason open to us to justify speaking of ordinary sensory experiences as experiences of tables, other people and so on are just not
available in the religious case, because religious experiences are neither
as widely shared nor as consistent and predictable as ordinary sensory

experiences. If they were, then belief in a supernatural being might well be on the same footing as belief in physical objects. But, for whatever reason, this is not so. If the religious believer wants to justify his belief in any way, he will have to appeal to facts other than his experiences. Should such an appeal prove successful, his regarding his religious experiences as experiences of the divine may well be reasonable, though the difficulty religious authorities have in sifting what they regard as true from false consolations ought to sound a cautionary note: this internal difficulty is itself an aspect of the difficulty we have uncovered in assessing claims based purely on religious experiences, owing to their indeterminacy and irregularity.

If the basis of religious belief cannot be religious experience taken at face value it must be something more reflective, and naturally a large number of arguments have been advanced to prove the existence of something worthy of worship. Not all the arguments actually point in the same direction, but this should not occasion surprise given that there are present in men's minds at least two quite different and apparently incompatible concepts of deity. On the one hand, there is the idea that God is something beyond all attributes and determinations, pure being whose very essence is to exist, and whose purity and self-explanatoriness would be contaminated were God to have any definite characteristics. If God had particular characteristics one could ask why the *fons et origo* of all particular beings had these characteristics, rather than others, and why it was closer in nature to some created things rather than others. On the other hand, there is the idea that God is a person of great power, wisdom and love, with definite attributes and entering into developing relationships with his creatures. He is the active designer of the universe, its judge and perhaps its redeemer too. Defenders of the first view of the godhead would say that worshipping a super-personal God of this sort is akin to idolatry; the reply is that a God beyond attributes, pure being, is an idea of such sublime emptiness as to be intellectually equivalent to the idea of pure nothingness.

While I think it is clear that God cannot be both pure being and a living person, it would be a mistake to think that some religions hold first to one concept and others to the other. In practice, all the major religious traditions encompass both concepts, though it may be true that Hinduism places more stress on the first, with its idea of the world as an emanation from the emptiness of Brahman, while the God of the Christian Bible corresponds more to the second idea. Sometimes, as in the case of Aquinas, both views can be found in a single thinker, co-existing in an uneasy dialectic. Despite examples of this sort, a major problem right at the outset for religious thinkers is to clarify the nature of the God they are proposing, and to explain how their particular conception of the divine does the work required of it: if they favour pure being, how can this explain anything? If they favour a more personal God, how this can be the end to all explanation questioning religious thinkers are usually hoping for?

Of the most familiar proofs of the existence of God, the ontological argument would appear to be emphasizing the God who is pure being, whose essence or nature is simply to exist, while the arguments from cause and design point naturally in the direction of an active, personal Creator. The ontological argument is often given as the most notorious example of speculative metaphysics, for it appears to be an attempt to prove the existence of something, in this case God, by reasoning alone. As such, empirically minded philosophers tend to reject it out of hand, for empiricism is precisely the claim that we can acquire no genuine factual knowledge except through the senses. The ontological argument, by contrast, postulates a concept of God which, it is claimed, we only have to think about to see that it must be instantiated. The concept is that of a being (which, for simplicity, we shall call God), more perfect than which nothing can be imagined. Now the crux of the argument is that however this most perfect imaginable being is conceived, it must be conceived of as actually existing, because if it did not exist, it would always be possible to imagine a being similar to this merely imaginary being which actually existed and so was yet more perfect than the imaginary God. The claim is, in short, that a non-existing most perfect imaginable being would be something self-contradictory: an existing most perfect imaginable being would be yet more perfect. So, once we think of God as the most perfect imaginable being, we see that he cannot but exist.

Existence, then, is a necessary part of God's perfection. This can be seen by merely thinking about God. Hence, if we can think about God, God must exist.

There have been many attempts to repudiate this line of thought since it was first formulated explicitly by Anselm in the eleventh century. Many of the objections are themselves suspect, and we should certainly beware of too facile an acceptance of any of them simply because we do not like the argument. Perhaps the simplest thing to say here, which may well be the thought underlying many of the objections, is to agree with Anselm that existence is indeed a necessary part of God's perfection, but to point out that saying that in no way entails that God actually exists. A non-existent God would not be a perfect being, but then neither would a non-existent island be a perfect island, or a non-existent unicorn a perfect unicorn or indeed a unicorn at all. So, if Anselm wants, we can write existence into the definition of God, and agree that a non-existent being, however perfect in conception, would not in fact be the most perfect imaginable being (or God). Only an actually existing God would be that. But, it does not follow from any of this that there is an actually existing God, or that the idea of the most perfect imaginable being is actually instantiated anywhere, any more than saying that only existing unicorns would satisfy the concept of a unicorn entails that there are actually existing unicorns. What Anselm has drawn attention to in the ontological argument is that only something existing can satisfy the concept of God, but, while this is true, its power to make us think that God's existence follows from his concept diminishes once we realize that something similar is the case with all other concepts, and that we can no more imagine a non-existing unicorn or a non-existing man than a non-existing perfect being. For, like perfect beings, anything that is a man or a unicorn exists; but it remains for us to discover whether each or any of them exist in fact.

Some recent writers, notably Charles Hartshorne and Norman Malcolm, have suggested that what Anselm was really getting at in the ontological argument was not the ultimately ineffective move of writing existence into the concept of God, but rather the connection between the perfection we impute to God and a certain type of existence. A true God, on this view, would be eternal and self-sufficient; he would not depend for his existence on other things or on chance factors. He would have a different type of existence from all contingent and created things. While thoughts of this sort may well be in Anselm's writings and are undoubtedly part of many people's concept of God, I cannot see that anything like the ontological argument can be derived from them. For thinking that God would have to be eternal and in some way self-sufficient in no way shows on its own that there actually is a God, or that a universe lacking such a being would be an absurdity. To show that needs more than the mere thought of God as eternal and self-sufficient and, as this is just what is attempted in the arguments from cause and design, we will now leave the ontological argument and turn to them.

The intuition behind the various versions of the argument from cause (or cosmological argument, as it is often called) is that nothing happens without a sufficient reason for its happening. This intuition is, as remarked earlier, true if taken in a trivial sense. Obviously, whatever happens must be preceded by whatever conditions are requisite for its happening. But this does not preclude the possibility of there being nothing at all requisite for something's existing or coming into being. The cosmological argument appears, at first sight, to want to interpret the principle of sufficient reason so as to preclude things coming about without prior conditions. For the argument says first that there is nothing in the world which is uncaused. If we take a rather wide view of cause, so as to allow the individually unpredictable but statistically regular events of sub-atomic physics to count as examples of caused happenings, then it is probably true that there are no uncaused events in the universe. The next step in the argument is to say, correctly, that the notion of something causing itself is an absurdity (for that would imply that it existed or happened prior to itself). The universe itself consists of things and events which are caused and require causes, so it is plausible to think of the universe as a whole as requiring a cause. This cause of the universe as a whole is interpreted as something quite other, which is unlike any worldly cause in being an uncaused cause, somehow containing in itself the ground of its own existence, and this, says Aquinas, is what all men call God.

One's first reaction to this line of thought is to notice that the God of the cosmological argument does not require any cause or condition of its own existence. The principle of sufficient reason in God's own case points to God's self-sufficiency of existence. So the first problem for the cosmological arguer is to explain the way in which God can be an uncaused cause without in effect becoming a counter-example to the very principle which initially motivated the argument. At this point, some defenders of the cosomological argument will maintain that God's self-sufficiency is due to his essence or nature in some sense being to exist. But if this line is pursued, the argument quickly becomes indistinguishable from the ontological argument and open to its problems.

A more promising line of approach for the cosmological argument has been suggested by Richard Swinburne.[33] It is to concede that wherever we start, with the world or with God, we are going to be left with an unexplained and inexplicable datum: the sheer existence of matter or of God. But to claim that, given we are going to have a sheer unexplained starting point anyway, seeing God as this starting point is less repugnant to what we know about the world than having brute facts about matter and its behaviour as the ultimate beginning of things as they are now. Central to this line of thought is the idea that there is something more simple and intellectually satisfying about an explanation of complex facts

(which the world and its contents and laws undoubtedly are) which cul-
minates in an act of will of a simple being (God) than one which leaves
a set of complex facts (such as the Big Bang and what happened there-
after) as the point beyond which we can get no further in our quest
for understanding. At this point, I think we are very much left with a
decision between competing intuitions of probability, and nothing much
to base them on. The trouble is that we just do not know what is likely
or unlikely in the formation and creation of universes. True, within our
explanatory schemes we do not like being left with unexplained complexes
of fact and law, but the case we are considering is a rather special one,
where we are not asking about things and events within the universe
for which further intra-universal explanations could be forthcoming. We
are asking about what, in the agreement of both parties in the dispute,
are being regarded as the ultimate facts and laws of the universe. Can
they simply be, as brute facts? We have no samples of other universes
to know whether such things are likely or not. The theist, of course,
finds material facts and laws as always crying out for further explanation,
and this is certainly not an unreasonable demand. But whether his own
explanation of them is any more satisfactory than the atheistic one of
brute material facts is open to question. As J. L. Mackie has argued in
response to Swinburne, in our own experience at least, we do not en-
counter disembodied spirits producing large-scale material facts by sheer
acts of will.[34]

The theist might hope at this point to strengthen his case, or indeed
to reformulate his position entirely, by an appeal to the existence of order
in the universe. Order, he will say, is a type of design, and design requires
a designer. We see in animals and human beings the ordering of parts,
such as limbs and organs, which have a function in the whole organism.
The parts themselves are not intelligent beings; so they must have been
so ordered by some creative intelligence. This type of thinking is typically
pre-Darwinian in that it fails to recognize the probability of evolution
of order in organisms arising randomly and spontaneously through the
operation of environmental selection on developments in earlier organisms. While Darwinism is somewhat disputed, it cannot be denied that
subsequent discoveries in genetics, which have revealed the nature of
genetic material and of the randomness of change within it, have vastly
strengthened the probability that a Darwinian type of evolution has
obtained in the living realm, that in some way or other the organisms
we now find in the world are the result of natural selection on random
genetic mutations in earlier species. We do not need to postulate an

intelligent designer to account for the adaptiveness and ordering of parts which we find in living things. Strictly speaking, of course, we never did need to postulate any such thing, as it was always open to atheists to claim that animals and men had come about by non-intelligent processes (and Epicurus and Hume had claimed just this without manifest incoherence), but the theory of evolution and recent genetic discoveries have given us a plausible account of the mechanisms through which living species might have developed without the guiding hand of a designer.

But the argument from design does not simply point to the order and adaptiveness we find in living things. It is a remarkable fact that what we know of the physical processes of the universe reveals them as, by and large, highly ordered on the basis of a comparatively small number of physical laws. Is this not something that cries out for explanation in terms of a designer? It is no good replying to this that any universe that held together at all would have to have some sort of order, because this argument is claiming that there is a very great deal of order in this universe through all space and time as far as we know, and that this is what has to be explained. Nor is it enough to say that any universe human beings could live in and observe is bound to have a lot of order in it. While this may well be true, what the argument is focusing on is the need for an explanation for the existence of a universe of just the type we are actually living in.

As with the cosmological argument, we reach an impasse at this point, largely because we have no idea as to what is likely or unlikely in the case of universes and Gods. Is it likely that a highly ordered universe including human observers exists uncaused? Is it likely that a disembodied spirit could have brought such a thing about? And even if we conclude that neither of these things is very likely in itself, does that rule out the possibility that either of them might actually be the case? How might such questions be decided? Theist and atheist are both left with questions that they should find puzzling, perhaps as puzzling as the problems their explanations were designed to solve. To suggest, as we have done here, that the claims of religion cannot be settled by appeal to experience or to the arguments we have considered is not to say that the atheist has solutions to any of the ultimate puzzles about existence either.

Chapter Two

Epistemology

What we are concerned with in epistemology is in showing what the grounds are which we have for thinking that our beliefs about the world are true. The crucial problem which faces anyone who considers this question in any depth is that we cannot simply compare our beliefs with the world or with elements of the world. We have no direct access to the world: all our observation of the world and of things in it rests on categorizations and assumptions we impose on what we are observing, on beliefs of ours, in other words. When I judge that something is the case, even as simple as that there is a table in front of me, I am assuming all sorts of things that go beyond what is immediately evident; I am assuming that my own senses are normal and conditions of observation are currently normal, that what is before me has certain ways of behaving, that I am entitled to use a scheme of classification in which tables and such-like things figure, and so on. If I restrict my judgements to my own current sensory experience saying, for example, that there is a blue patch now before my eyes, I will still be saying that what I am now experiencing is similar to other experiences I have classified as blue in the past, and this assumes that my memory of such things is reliable. Classifying sensory data in this way may well also require the assumption that there is an external world manifesting a significant degree of regularity, as I suggested in Chapter 1; it certainly assumes that I am a continuously existing subject of experience with a reliable memory, and none of this can be just read off from my current experience. Access to experience or to the world which is pure and 'uncontaminated' by assumptions, such as those mentioned here, would be access which was totally unarticulated and uninformative, and from which no picture of the world or of experience could emerge.

The lack of direct experiential access to the world, combined with a growing realization of the way in which our more theoretical beliefs about the world are far from conclusively supported by our observational levels of judgement, has led a number of philosophers to question whether there is any sense in which we are entitled to think that our beliefs about the world are true or justified. Whether we accept this pessimistic conclusion or not, epistemologists nowadays are much concerned with debating whether one is driven to it by realizing that we cannot step outside our view of the world in order to compare beliefs of ours directly with it. All we can do is to compare some of our judgements with others, and the question is whether this entails that we cannot properly speak of truth in connection with our beliefs at all. Before discussing this question in detail, it will be necessary to clarify our ideas about truth.

Truth

A definition of truth, which is correct and which has dominated epistemological discussion ever since, was given by Aristotle in his *Metaphysics* (1011b, 25–8)

> To say of what is that it is not, or what is not that it is, is false, while to say of what is that it is, or what is not that it is not, is true.

One desirable feature of the Aristotelian definition is that it implies that sayings or statements are what truth and falsity are primarily properties of. Compared to elusive mental objects, such as ideas or beliefs, statements are concrete occurrences. If we want to think of beliefs as being true or false, there is a gain in clarity and accessibility in thinking of a belief in terms of the statement that would count as expressing it.

The problems with the Aristotelian account of truth begin when one attempts to say just what it is for a statement to say of what is that it is. Truth, on this view, appears to be a relation obtaining between some statements (or writings) and some states of affairs in the world. But just what is this relation? And how does it differ from the relation which obtains between false utterances or inscriptions and the world? Even if we could hold up the world or bits of it for direct inspection, how are we to think of a set of sounds or marks as expressing or describing it? At this point, philosophers have found it irresistibly tempting to indulge in metaphor. True statements, but not false ones, correspond to or picture reality (or bits of it, called facts or states of affairs). The trouble is that the metaphors are broken-backed. How can a statement – something linguistic – correspond to a fact or a state of affairs? Certainly, it cannot be a replica of a state of affairs, nor does it fit with it in the way a nut might be said to correspond with a bolt. Further, even if we could make some sense of a simple affirmative factual statement (such as 'the cat is on the mat') corresponding to some discrete and identifiable state of affairs on the floor before us, there are considerable problems with knowing just what it is other types of statement are supposed to correspond to. What, for example, of negative statements, that something is not the case, or does not exist? Are they supposed to correspond to states of affairs that do not exist, or to the absence in the world of something? And what of counterfactual statements, to the effect that if something that had not happened had happened, then something else would have followed – for example, if Napoleon had won the Battle of Waterloo, then he would not have been exiled a second time? What is the state of affairs that that is supposed to correspond to? And what of universal statements, or mathematical and moral statements? Are there universal facts, and mathematical and moral ones too?

If there are problems with the nature of the correspondence relation, and with the things true statements are supposed to correspond to, there are even greater problems with the idea of statements picturing reality. A statement cannot be said to picture a state of affairs in any but the most attenuated way. Statements lack just those visible qualities of similarity in shape, line and hue that seem to constitute the life-likeness of pictures. I say 'seem to' here, because many have questioned whether the actual similarities between pictures and things even in respect of line, shape and hue are actually greater than the dissimilarities in the same respects; and whether in fact there is not a great deal of convention and learning involved in our reading even a photograph as an accurate and life-like representation of something in the world. If this is the case, then our conception of picturing itself stands in need of clarification, and can hardly be invoked to throw light on what it is that makes a true statement true. Perhaps what is needed is not a picture theory of language, but a general theory of representation, though beyond saying that any object such as a sentence or a picture that represents any state of affairs in the world will have to be regarded as fulfilling the dual functions of referring to something or things in the world and of conveying something about how those things are, it is unclear that any such general theory could say anything very useful.

Of course, what the correspondence and picture theories of truth are concerned to defend is the idea that truth depends on the way things are in the world, and not on the way we look at things or conceptualize reality, or on what satisfies us in some way. They are firmly realistic theories in the sense that they would deny any suggestion that truth depends on us in any way, but the problems they have in specifying what it is in the world that true statements correspond to or picture has led some to the conclusion that the states of affairs or facts which they take to be the worldly end of the correspondence relation are simply shadowy reflections of statements we regard as true for other reasons, rather than as genuinely mind-independent realities. Although I shall suggest in Chapter 3 (especially p. 197) that this is not necessarily so, it is not altogether easy to avoid the impression that in talking of true statements corresponding to facts or states of affairs in the world, one is implicitly relying on the absurd idea that we can pick out bits of an un-conceptualized reality to compare our statements with. (This idea is absurd, because once we have picked out a bit of reality, we have conceptualized it.) Problems of this sort with correspondence views of truth have led some philosophers to attempt apparently quite different approaches to the question of truth. Of these different approaches, the most familiar go under the name of the pragmatist and coherence theories of truth. Both are easy to object to; nevertheless each contains more than a grain of the truth about what we call truth, though the objections are largely based on an insistence that what we call truth may not actually be the truth.

The pragmatist theory, which is usually associated with the American philosophers C. S. Peirce, William James and John Dewey, is concerned to stress the connection there undoubtedly is between the truth of statements and their practical applicability or their working for us. The underlying intuition is that any significant statement, if true, must make some difference to the world which we or our successors will be able to make out. More specifically, with the American pragmatists, truth was always seen in terms of what would solve a problem, remove a perplexity, resolve a frustration. In this way, in addition to depriving mere verbalizing of candidacy for truth or falsity, James and Dewey, at least, hoped to develop a notion of truth that would extend into areas such as morality and mathematics, which we do ordinarily regard as containing truths, and which present special difficulties for correspondence theories (for what things in the world do the truths of these disciplines correspond to?).

Naturally, a lot is going to hang on just how practical applicability is conceived. William James was rightly criticized by Bertrand Russell for incautiously taking the truth of certain religious propositions to consist in the satisfaction and comfort they brought to believers. Furthermore, it is easy to give examples of cases such as the use of pre-Copernican astronomy in navigation where outworn and provably false theories still apparently have practical usefulness, though a sophisticated pragmatist should not have too much difficulty in accounting for such cases.

Peirce was a sophisticated exponent of pragmatism. For him, truth consisted in what worked in the sense of being acceptable to scientists in the long run – 'the opinion which is fated to be ultimately agreed to by all who investigate'.[1] Concentrating on this version of pragmatism will enable us to see what really separates pragmatism and its opponents. The opponent of pragmatism will maintain that the acceptability of statements, however informed and long term, can never constitute truth; that human powers are not such as to guarantee truth even in their most conscientious employment; and that, over and above human fallibility, there are many truths which will forever escape us.

The dispute between pragmatists and their opponents may then seem to be one centring on optimism or pessimism regarding human powers of investigation, but this would be misleading. Peirce and Dewey were both fully committed to fallibilism. That is, they both believed that the possibility of error can never be completely ruled out, even from judgements about our current sensory experience. Revisability is an inherent property of human cognition. How does this square with the identification of truth with ultimate acceptability? The answer, I think, must lie not in attributing to Peirce a naïve optimism regarding science, that is plainly inconsistent with his professed fallibilism, but rather in considering what sense – or difference to experience – there could possibly be in withholding the accolade of truth from a scientific theory that satisfied all the criteria we adopt for calling a theory true – that its observational consequences turn out as predicted, that it is consistent with other theories we accept, that it is simple, wide-ranging, and so on. That, in other words, it satisfies what Hilary Putnam refers to as all the operational constraints.[2] If we follow Putnam here, we will be taken straight back to the point about knowledge and truth made at the start of this chapter: that we have no direct access to the world, except through those theories and judgements that satisfy the 'operational constraints' on such theories and judgements, including, of course, the operational constraint of conforming to our best available perceptual evidence. Given that the world, apart from our various judgements and theories on it, is an empty term, Putnam concludes that 'the supposition that even an "ideal" theory (from a pragmatic point of view) might *really* be false appears to collapse into *unintelligibility*'.[3]

All this is interestingly and importantly quite consistent with fallibilism, and with whatever degree of pessimism about human powers you like. For there is no reason to suppose that any interesting theory we have or are likely to have does or will satisfy all the operational constraints. In particular, no theory in science ever appears to be at once accurate in all its predictions and simple enough or comprehensive enough to satisfy fully enough the goals of scientific inquiry or even of utility. Big theories tend to lack accuracy, while little theories and judgements restricted to our present perceptions lack interest and general applicability. The pragmatist theory of truth can (and perhaps should) be understood as suggesting that there would be no point in not calling something true that satisfied all our aims in inquiry, although one does not need to conclude from this that in practice anything very interesting or grand could be called conclusively true on this version. In fact, of course, what would be called true would be just those things we are inclined to call true as it is, just those things we think we have good reason for believing. The non-pragmatist will continue to say that nevertheless, even after all our best efforts, this does not mean that they are true; the pragmatist will insist that, regarding those things we call true in the long term, this is a merely verbal manoeuvre, a distinction without a significant difference.

The coherence theory of truth is often thought of as the property of system-building metaphysicians, that what is true is what fits into the system and what squares with its presuppositions and dynamics. Such coherentist systems are often criticized on the grounds that the relation of coherence involved is never clarified, but appears to depend on the feelings and hunches of the system's builder. In Hegel's system, for example, it is quite obscure why becoming is the logical outcome of the opposition between what is and what is not, or why eyeless, colourless sculpture was, as Hegel claimed, a particularly appropriate manifestation of objective spirit in classical Greece. (In fact, it wasn't; classical sculptures were painted, including their eyes.) Nevertheless, a far more interesting version of the coherence theory of truth can be extracted from strictly empiricist premises, which turns out to be pretty close to the sophisticated version of pragmatism we have just been considering.

This view sees sets of beliefs as forming an interlocking system and truth as being a property attributable to statements in virtue of their belonging to the best or preferred system of beliefs. Systems here are regarded as being governed by nothing more mysterious than the normal relations of implication and contradiction which we find in elementary logic; whereby, for example, a scientific theory allows us to deduce a prediction that something will happen, and what actually happens may be seen as contradicting the prediction if it turns out not in accord with it. At the lowest level of such a system are statements recording sensory observations, while at intermediate stages are statements of more theoretical content, such as those saying which perceptions are to be regarded as normal and which abnormal, and also general theories about the behaviour of specific types of object. At higher levels still, there will be the most basic laws of physics, while the highest level of all will be occupied by statements which tell us how to derive statements at lower levels from other statements, mathematical or logical or definitional transformations. (The highest level will, in other words, be occupied by the mathematics, logic and dictionary of the system.)

It will be clear that our own picture of the world, in its ascent from statements recording basic observations about chairs and tables to the laws of nuclear physics, forms a system of the sort here envisaged, although there may be doubts as to the overall consistency of our actual system, due to the way many of our preferred scientific theories are known to suffer from observational counter-evidence, which we are also disposed to accept. The coherence theory of truth, then, might say that a statement that was part of our current beliefs was true if it could be envisaged as belonging to a system similar to ours, but without its inconsistencies. The problem with this as a theory of truth, however, is that consistency in a system of statements is quite easily achieved. We can simply take our present (inconsistent) system and delete one of every pair of inconsistent statements. If an observation statement was inconsistent with a theoretical one, for example, we could simply delete the observational one (or the theoretical one). The drawback of this approach, though, is obvious. We might have equally strong reasons for wanting to hold both statements true, the observational one because it appeared to be obviously true according to our sensory evidence, and the theoretical one because of its usefulness in leading to all sorts of other predictions. Consistency is not our only aim in constructing a picture of the world, and it can be too cheaply bought. We need further guidance as to when and when not to accept statements, other than that they fit in with other statements.

A further objection that is often made to the coherence theory of truth is that it is possible to imagine different systems of statements which are internally consistent and which are equally acceptable for all practical purposes, but which contain mutually contradictory statements. Let us suppose, what might have been the case, that Newtonian physics and

Einsteinian physics are equally good in predicting the course of nature. Then, in an Einsteinian system (S_1) we might find the statement 'the length of an object is relative to its velocity relative to an observer', whereas a statement contradicting this would presumably be found in a Newtonian system (S_2). Does this mean that we have to say that the statement is true in S_1 but false in S_2 and that truth is relative to systems? Many would regard this as a conclusive objection to the coherence theory of truth, for surely whether a statement is true or not depends on the facts and not on the systems we are using to interpret those facts. Despite this objection, there is, in fact, a profound insight embodied in this seemingly implausible consequence of the coherence theory of truth, namely, that the empirical data available to us from the world do not determine our theories about the world. We shall see this in more detail shortly; for now I shall simply state that two theories about the world may agree totally in respect of observational predictions (and may actually share a level of description), but disagree at the theoretical level, in the sense of providing mutually inconsistent accounts of how the observed data came about. To see what is at issue here, we may, for the sake of argument, assume further that the competing explanations do just as well on simplicity, comprehensiveness and other operational constraints. Pragmatically and empirically the two accounts are just as good, so there would be no conclusive reason for preferring one system to the other. The opponent of the pragmatist and coherence views of truth (which at this point are merging) will say that one or other of the theories must be true, that the world must be one way or the other. The reply will be to ask what difference insisting on this makes, and to say that, so long as we relativize truth to systems and we realize which system we are talking in, not only is there no harm in saying that the same theoretical statement may be true in one system and false in another, but that this is just what we should say, because the lesson to be learned from the coherence theory of truth is that statements, particularly at more theoretical levels, take their meaning (and hence their truth or falsity) from their relationships with other statements which they are connected to, and not from any direct comparison with a raw, conceptually uncontaminated experience. We shall return to this point at the end of the chapter.

In saying that the truth of a statement consists in its having some special property (such as pragmatic applicability or coherence), pragmatist and coherence theories may seem to fall foul of a major insight embodied in the Aristotelian definition – that is, of the equivalence between saying that a statement A is true and simply asserting that statement. If A is true, then so is 'A is true', and *vice versa*. Ayer concluded from this equivalence in truth of A and 'A is true' that 'the terms "true" and "false" connote nothing, but function in [a] sentence simply as marks of assertion and denial'.[4] Yet, it might be objected, the pragmatist theory of truth would appear to be saying that a true statement is one that works in some way, the coherence theory that it coheres with other statements, the correspondence theory that it pictures some fact in some way. They all seem to be saying that more is involved in calling a statement true than in merely asserting it. But is this so? To answer this, we will need to examine theories of truth which make an equivalence of 'A is true' and A their starting point. One such theory was formulated by F. P. Ramsey in his article 'Facts and Propositions'.[5] In Ramsey's view, as in Ayer's, saying that it is true that A is exactly the same as saying that A, and to think any more is involved is mere linguistic muddle. For this reason, his theory is sometimes known as the redundancy theory of truth.

The equivalence suggested in the redundancy theory between asserting a statement and asserting that it is true is correct at least to the extent that the one assertion cannot be true and the other false, and recognition of this fact must be a constraint on any satisfactory account of truth. An account of truth which works consciously within this constraint is the so-called semantic theory of truth, developed in the 1930s by the Polish logician Alfred Tarski. The motivations behind Tarski's own work are somewhat technical and logical. His own truth definitions are worked out for certain formal languages, and he himself expressed doubts as to the possibility of formulating similar definitions for natural languages such as English. Waiving these doubts, however, his idea was that a truth definition should enable us to state, for any sentence of the language for which truth was being defined, the condition which would have to obtain for that sentence to be true. Now if English is the language for which truth is being defined, the truth definition will enable us to deduce that, for example,

(1) 'Snow is white' is true if and only if snow is white.

It is important to realize that (1) is not the truth definition we are after, but at most a minute part of it, because 'snow is white' is only one of the infinite number of sentences that can be formulated in English. Because we cannot list an infinite number of sentences, we cannot regard the truth definition as actually being composed of lists of sentences like (1). It might also be said that (1) is quite uninteresting, and so, even if we could list all the sentences like (1) for English, our work would be entirely trivial. This would perhaps be true if we were giving our truth definition for English in English as in (1), though the thing would appear less trivial if we were giving, say, a truth definition for English in German:

(2) 'Snow is white' *ist wahr wenn und nur wenn Schnee weiss ist.*

Nevertheless a degree of triviality about (1) and even about (2) is central to Tarski's work, for it follows from the redundancy theory that any truth definition that did not yield equivalences such as those in (1) and (2) would be hopelessly wrong. Our truth definition should certainly not yield anything like

(3) 'Snow is white' is true if and only if grass is green.

Tarski interprets the redundancy theory of truth as constraining any adequate definition of truth to yield sentences like (1) and (2) in which the truth conditions for sentences turn out to be just those sentences themselves, where we are working in the language for which we are defining truth, or their translations, as in cases like (2).

What then could conceivably be interesting in a Tarskian account of truth? The main interest will lie not in its yield, but in the route it takes to produce sentences like (1) and (2) and which never leads to anything like (3). Because of the infinity of sentences in English, what will have to be done will be to break whole sentences into their component words and phrases, and to show how these words and phrases, together with rules of construction, combine to give the whole sentences in which they can figure the truth conditions they have. In other words the truth definition will show on the basis of a finite stock of words and constructions how the significant parts of sentences contribute to the meanings of an infinite number of whole sentences, and this task is neither easy, nor trivial, if, indeed, it is possible at all. At the same time, it may be questioned what light executing it would throw on truth, rather than on the workings of various different languages, especially as a different truth definition will be required for each language, while truth is surely a notion which has the same function and meaning for all languages.

We shall have more to say about the philosophical significance of Tarski's work in Chapter 3. But what is worth noticing here is that accepting the insights involved in the redundancy theory and in the formal apparatus of Tarski's work does not enable us to decide on the issues separating pragmatist and coherence theorists and their realist opponents. The objection raised earlier to various substantive theories of truth, on the grounds that they appeared to deny the equivalence between asserting A and asserting 'A is true', is not actually sound. The equivalence in truth or falsity between the two does not show that nothing more could be meant by the truth predicate. There is no reason why the supporters of any of the more substantive theories should deny that a statement is true if and only if it is assertible. They can all agree, and indeed should all agree, that if A is assertible, then so is 'A is true', that 'snow is white' is true, if and only if snow is white, and vice versa, and so on, for all the sentences of our language. The point is that each theorist of truth, while accepting these equivalences, will regard *each* side of the equivalence in his own way. The pragmatist will interpret the assertibility of 'snow is white' in terms of the differences this assertion makes to experience, the coherentist in terms of its position in his favoured system of sentences, the correspondence theorist in terms of its correspondence to some mind-independent fact out there in the world, quite apart from any experiential or systemic import, and in the same way, each theorist will interpret what is being said when we say that 'snow is white' is true. In other words, each theorist will deny that, at least from his point of view, applicability or coherence or correspondence has nothing to do with the assertion of 'snow is white'. Purely formal considerations about truth are powerless to settle what makes statements true or assertible, which is why both the redundancy theory and Tarski's theory are sometimes said to be philosophically neutral. As far as epistemology goes, what we now have to do is to examine knowledge and our entitlement to claims to know. In doing this, we will find that there is something futile in thinking that what we know is achieved by direct access to a mind-independent reality, which would suggest that a naïve correspondence view of truth, at least, is likely to be able to give us little guidance in our actual inquiries and researches.

Knowledge: Its Definition and Nature

In saying that someone knows something, we generally intend to imply that what is known is believed by the person on good grounds and that the belief is true. The intention is to exclude things from knowledge which a person believes, but without any good reason, and things which a person believes, but which turn out to be false. A definition of knowledge, then, can be offered along the following lines. For some subject X and some proposition or statement A, X knows that A if and only if

  (i) X believes that A;
  (ii) A is true;
  (iii) X has good grounds for believing A.

We will now consider each of these clauses in turn.

The first clause of the definition and the type of knowledge being defined seems to take knowledge as a matter of belief in statements. Yet we often speak of knowledge which is not linguistic in this sort of way. We speak of people knowing other people or places, and of people knowing how to do things, like swimming or riding a bicycle. In fact, philosophers have developed some semi-technical jargon to deal with these other types of knowledge. Knowing a person or a place through personal experience, in distinction to knowing a fact through some verbal account, has sometimes been called knowledge by acquaintance as opposed to knowledge by description. It could indeed be argued that something like knowledge by acquaintance is prior to knowledge by description, because understanding, say, that buses in Paris are green involves acquaintance with greenness and the other qualities that go to make up the concepts of a bus and Paris. Certainly it is true that understanding some of the terms of a language involves being able to pick out examples that satisfy those terms, and it is hard to see how one could do this in at least some cases without having been acquainted with examples of the things the terms refer to, though clearly one does not have to have met in one's own experience cases exemplifying all the terms one could recognize instances of, were one to be confronted with one. Despite the admitted primacy of some sort of knowledge by acquaintance over knowledge by description, what often interests us in epistemology, however, is the justification of our beliefs about things with which we are not directly acquainted and obviously this means concentrating on knowledge by description. Even when we are speaking about our knowledge of things with which we are personally acquainted, what we are primarily interested in will be the relationship between the statements with which we express that knowledge and the personal experience we take as justifying those statements. Indeed, one could regard one of the main tasks of epistemology as the investigation of the relationships between statements of belief and the experiences that might justify those statements.

Practical knowledge, as opposed to theoretical knowledge, is usually called knowing how as opposed to knowing that. Knowing how need not involve any verbal capacity; one does not need to speak about what one is doing in order to be able to swim, nor is knowing a lot of facts about (say) swimming the same as knowing how to swim. All this should be sufficiently obvious, though not so obvious but of some importance is the fact that being able to speak a language is itself fundamentally a matter of knowing how. You cannot endlessly explain what you mean by words in other words, or you would never break out of the circle of language. At some points, you must simply recognize that a certain sentence is true, or a certain term satisfied, and this is a recognitional ability, or an example of knowing how. Nevertheless, despite the importance of knowing how, we shall restrict ourselves to an examination of knowing that in this chapter, where we are considering the relationships between statements and the evidence that there might be for them.

A further query about the first clause of the definition might be its emphasis on the psychology of knowers. Is all knowledge believed by individuals? Is there not a sense in which we speak of the knowledge laid up in books, libraries and even computers, which may not actually be believed (or known) by anyone? There may indeed be such a sense and anyone who wants to bring this sort of knowledge into the compass of our discussion can change the definition so as to accommodate it. At the same time, there seem to be some advantages to keeping in mind the fact that knowledge is part of the human world, something used by human beings and determining their actions, and our first clause brings this out. As to whether there can be unconscious human knowledge, things that I might know without believing them, as such a supposition would presumably be justified in terms of my acting on a certain proposition *as if* I consciously knew it, and hence parasitic on the notion of conscious knowledge, there are definite advantages in clarifying the conditions for fully conscious knowledge – as spelt out in the definition – in the first instance.

Without then denying the importance of knowledge which does not have statements for its object, we shall continue to concentrate on the type of knowledge which involves belief in statements. What, then, of the second clause of the definition which states that the statement had to be true for it to be a candidate for knowledge? Don't we often speak of the 'knowledge' of past times, including in that phrase many things which we now know to be false, such as the once widely current belief that the earth is flat? The answer is that we do, and that there are indeed uses of the term 'knowledge' which would include falsehoods as well as truths. But, as our interest in epistemology is in true belief and the conditions for that, we will simply stipulate that we are here taking knowledge in the sense that it involves true belief, and that what we say is an attempt to elucidate that undoubtedly important notion. Whether or not we ever have good grounds for talking about knowledge in that sense is precisely what epistemology is about.

This brings us on to the third and most puzzling clause of the definition, that knowledge involves belief for which the believer has good grounds. The point of this clause is to distinguish between cases of belief which, while true, is not well founded, and cases of knowledge proper. Thus a man might believe that a horse called African Prince is going to win the 3:30 at Kempton Park because he met a friend that day who had just returned from Nigeria, and whose name was Prince. Even when African Prince came in lengths ahead of the rest of the field, we would hardly say that this man's hunch, however firmly and vehemently he had held it, amounted to knowledge prior to the event. The grounds for the hunch were just not related to African Prince's victory in the right way. On the other hand, had our punter inside information that the rest of the field was going to be drugged on the morning of the race, we might well agree that he knew that his horse would win. He was in the possession of information which justified his belief, or which gave him the right to claim that he knew that African Prince would win.

It is not difficult to see the point of the third clause in cases like the one just considered. The difficulty is in formulating this clause in such a way as not to include cases that are not cases of knowledge and exclude cases which are cases of knowledge. That clauses like the third clause would allow some beliefs to count as knowledge which are not cases of knowledge at all is apparent once it is realized that a man can have good grounds for holding some sentence A to be true, but that A, while true, is not true for the reasons the man thinks it is, even though the reasons are good ones for the belief. An example of this sort of thing might be an extension of the African Prince case, where our punter knew about the drugging conspiracy. Let us suppose that those nobbling the horses were unknowingly using a substance that was quite harmless to horses because of some mix-up in the pharmaceutical works, and had no effect on the performance of the runners at all. African Prince just won! Of course, the grounds or evidence which we are saying justified our punter's belief in African Prince's forthcoming victory (knowledge of the conspiracy) would not in this case be *conclusive* proof of the belief, but they surely would be good enough to justify a claim to knowledge if the conspiracy had worked. As we shall see, restricting cases of knowledge to cases where we have conclusive or fully probative evidence for what we believe will leave us with a very slim and uninteresting concept of knowledge.

Although the third clause lets in cases which are not really knowledge at all, there is a persistent hope that some tightening up of the clause might exclude these cases, without losing sight of the point of the clause.

A more fundamental problem, however, is whether any such clause is a necessary condition for knowledge. Do people have to have grounds or evidence or reasons for everything they know? There has been some discussion in the philosophical literature as to whether people cannot sometimes just know; they are certain in their minds about certain things, and are consistently right about them, but are quite unable to explain or justify their beliefs other than by saying that they know. An example of this type of thing might be the wife who always knows when her husband has been philandering. It is tempting to explain this sort of case in terms of cues picked up subconsciously by the wife from her husband's manner, and certainly there might be an explanation of her coming to have the belief in such a way. But we need to distinguish here between what causes someone to have a belief and what might count as reasons for it. My love for my child might explain my belief in her intelligence, but it is not a reason justifying the belief (even if the belief is true and even if I could easily find good reasons). Sometimes what causes a belief is also a good or justifying reason for it, as when I believe African Prince will win at Kempton because I have seen him win on several earlier occasions. We might also feel that some causal link between the knower and what he knows is necessary for knowledge. The reason the punter who had knowledge of the drugging conspiracy did not know that African Prince would win was because there was (in fact) no causal connection between the conspiracy and the horse's victory. We could also explain the undeceived wife's knowledge of her husband's infidelity in causal terms, by saying that her title to knowledge here is because her belief is caused by unconscious perception of various cues which, were they at the conscious level, would give her good reasons for her belief. So a causal analysis of knowing might fill some of the gaps in traditional accounts of knowledge.

But one should not be too sanguine about what can be achieved by causal analyses, for it is not the case that any causal chain linking a belief I have with some event or with some sufficient cause of the event of which I have knowledge will actually give me knowledge of that event. The causal chains have to be of the appropriate sort, containing things which would, if spelled out, actually justify the belief, and excluding things that would rule out talking of knowledge. Thus, to give an example considered by Marshall Swain, my belief that I am seeing a sheep in a field may be caused by the presence of a sheep, but in the following way: a real sheep causes a televisual image, which I mistake for a real sheep.[6] Despite the causal chain linking my belief to what I think I am perceiving, we would not speak of knowledge here. The causal chain linking my belief to the event I have the belief about has to be a causal chain that actually gives me good reason and no bad reasons for my belief. So in developing causal accounts of knowing we still have to specify the types of reasons which are to be counted as good or knowledge producing reasons for beliefs. More generally, it is unclear how many items of knowledge, about the future, say, or about general regularities in nature, can be fully cashed out in causal terms. What causes our beliefs in such cases is presumably often far short of constituting sufficient causes of future events, let alone of general regularities in nature. Unexpected changes in nature can upset all our beliefs about the future, and about nature in general; yet in many such cases, even where the causes of our beliefs may not be strictly speaking sufficient causes of what we believe, in that there are many other factors necessary to produce the future event or to bring about the general regularity beyond those which cause our belief, we still want to talk about knowledge when our beliefs are confirmed. So causal accounts of knowledge may tell us something about the conditions under which a person might be in a position to claim knowledge, specifically that a person knows only if facts that justify a given belief play a causal role in that person's having the belief, but they cannot tell us what should be counted as knowledge in the first place or when reasons are to be regarded as justifying or not. This, I think, is admitted by Alvin Goldman when, in his pioneering work on the causal account of knowledge, he says that he will assume that one is warranted in inferring that all men are mortal from observations of particular deaths.[7] Traditional epistemologists will wonder about the acceptability of this inference. Causal theorists appear to take that for granted, and try to deal with the different question as to when a particular individual may claim knowledge of the general truth, by saying that he may do so if his belief in the general truth is brought about in some way by occurrences of particular deaths.

What I now want to suggest, however, is that whatever might be said about the causal genesis of our knowledge and beliefs, there are many things we know for which we have no justifying reasons or grounds; if this is so, a revision of the third clause in our definition of knowledge will be called for, to allow for cases where people are entitled to think of certain beliefs as knowledge, but for which neither they nor anyone else has grounds.

In the first place, it is worth remarking that much of what we – I mean, you and I – know, we could not justify at all if pressed. Probably most of us would be very hard put to prove in any way that the earth goes round the sun, yet this is certainly something that is generally known. Although I suggested earlier that we should not underestimate the extent to which knowledge is a human institution, we should no more overlook the significance of its being a social institution, and the divisions of labour there are in it. Often the only reason we can give for a belief we are claiming as knowledge is that some experts hold it to be so; often enough we would be hard put to say who the experts in question were, or what sort of evidence might found their particular field of expertise. So the social dimensions of knowledge enable each one of us to claim as knowledge beliefs whose grounds we are quite hazy about. Far from being a disadvantage, this sharing of knowledge ought to be reckoned as one of the great benefits of human society (as well as a warning to any would-be Descartes who thinks that he can re-establish the whole of knowledge by his own researches).

The social aspect of knowledge does not entirely invalidate the third clause, even from an individual point of view, provided we are prepared to count reliance on experts as good grounds for our beliefs. But what I now want to suggest is that many of our beliefs are both known and groundless. Take first my belief that I am currently sitting at a table and writing. Do I have grounds for this? It might be said that my grounds are my beliefs about current feelings of pressure on my hand and my bottom, my current visual data, and so on. Some may doubt that these beliefs are in fact better founded than my belief in these circumstances about my writing at the table. (It is important to note the qualification 'in these circumstances'; one could perhaps think of circumstances in which I would need to check my sensory states in order to confirm that I really was writing at a table.) Presumably if one belief is to serve as grounds for another, it must be the more certain of the two, and, despite Ayer's point noted in Chapter 1, that in strict logic any judgement about physical objects can be false despite the truth of any statement you like about my present sensations, it is far from clear that in practice, in the world in which we live and with our theories and knowledge about it, we actually regard statements about things as always less certain than the corresponding statements about perceptions. Thus, it might be said, if in these circumstances I doubt the proposition that I am writing at a table, I will in effect be calling into doubt everything I have come to accept about the external world and my perception of it. If I am doubting all of that, why should I place any more reliance on my understanding of the meanings of the words I use to make statements about my perceptions?

We do not need to answer this question at this stage, because even if we decide that statements about my current perceptions can serve as grounds for my belief that I am currently sitting at a table and writing, we are left with those statements, and what could possibly serve as grounds for their truth? It is true that doubting their truth would be tantamount to calling into question my grasp of the terms I use to describe my sensations and my understanding of the conditions in which I am to regard myself as having sensations of such and such a type, but saying this is hardly to give grounds for the individual statements in question because what would be required would be a proof that my understanding was correct in these cases. It seems that whether we regard physical object talk or sensation talk as the most basic level of description, we are going to be left with sets of statements for which no grounds can be given. The most that can be said about them is that our system of knowledge is such that in certain circumstances we regard ourselves as simply entitled to assert them. We regard them as simply, or what is sometimes called barely true, that is, not true in virtue of anything else that grounds them. At most an indirect justification can be given of them, in terms of the success of the whole system they support in predicting and controlling experience.

If we are going to be unable to give grounds for the most particular things we know, the same seems true of the most general things. Take, for example, the proposition that the world has existed for a long time. We can hardly adduce as evidence for that statements about Caesar and Alexander, for they presuppose its truth and hence cannot stand as a proof of it. A sceptic about the age of the world would presumably reinterpret all the appearances of age in the world, and even our memories, as actually quite recent occurrences, misinterpreted by us as evidence of age. (Philip Gosse did just this in attempting to reconcile geological evidence of the age of the world with his belief in creation at 4004 BC.) The position here is rather similar to that we encountered in considering solipsism in Chapter 1. All that can be said is to give the sort of indirect proof we suggested there to the effect that our actual system for dealing with experience (the only one in contention) contains statements which imply the existence of an ancient external world, and that the sceptic must give positive reasons for his unnatural reinterpretation of these statements if (as he undoubtedly will) he continues to use them.

We are gradually moving away from the individualistic, atomistic account of knowledge suggested by the traditional philosophical definition of knowledge, in which each knower will ideally have reasons for what he knows. This is being replaced by a view of knowledge as a socially constructed systematic body of statements, with no absolute foundations. One such account will be examined in the remainder of this section.

A distinction that is often made in connection with knowledge is that between truths of reason and truths of fact. Truths of reason are supposed to be those things we know have to be the case, without observation or empirical investigation, while truths of fact are supposed to be made true by states of affairs in the world which could conceivably have been otherwise. The basis of truths of reason is, of course, a problem for empiricists, who doubt the existence of knowledge which does not come through the senses. Nevertheless, empiricists have sometimes proposed their own version of truths of reason in terms of what are called analytic statements: statements which are true by virtue of meaning alone. Often included in the category of analytic statements are propositions of logic and mathematics, whose truth is held to follow from the meanings of the terms involved and the rules used to manipulate them. (Thus '$2 + 2 = 4$' is true because of the meanings we have assigned to '2' '4' and '$=$', and the rules governing the addition operation.) Truths of fact are held to be expressed in synthetic statements, whose truth or falsity is dependent on the existence or non-existence of particular states of affairs in the world.

The empiricist suspicion of the idea that there are truths of reason which are neither logical nor definitional seems justified. The problem is that the claim that something is a substantive truth of reason will be based in appeal to its self-evidence, and self-evidence is a notoriously relative property. What is self-evident to one person is far from self-evident to another, and what is obvious in one age is mere superstition in another. Thus, Descartes thought it self-evident that there could be no physical action over distance. Every physical event had to involve contact between bodies, even if those bodies were invisible or diminishingly small. This is hardly an unreasonable assumption, but it is an assumption which scientists since Descartes's time have found unhelpful. Now the idea that there are forces acting between bodies that are spatially distant is one to which we have become accustomed, and it no longer seems contrary to reason or self-evidence. Our common-sense conceptions of the world, which empiricists claim are what form our intuitions of self-evidence, have come under increasing fire from physics since the formulation of the special theory of relativity in 1905. Aside from changes in concepts as a result of scientific developments, we have already seen that obvious-seeming principles such as the principle of sufficient reason and the principle that every event has a cause are, on examination, far from obvious as to either their truth or their meaning.

If the idea that there are substantive truths of reason is one which seems suspect, the notion that there are truths of fact, which depend simply on the way things are in the world, can seem equally the result of an uncritical approach to knowledge. Indeed, the idea that there are statements whose truth depends simply on the existence or non-existence of states of affairs in the world to which they refer (and in terms of which their meaning is given) is the second of the dogmas attacked by Quine in his famous article 'Two Dogmas of Empiricism'.[8]

Quine sees the idea that each factual (or synthetic) statement can be confirmed or falsified in isolation from the system of statements in which it figures as the natural descendant of the reductionist idea that statements about the world can be analysed ultimately into statements about experience (and the obverse of the idea, which he also wants to reject, that analytic statements, including those of logic and mathematics, are true or false by virtue of meaning alone, and independently of the way things are in the world). Against the idea that factual statements are made true or false purely in virtue of the existence or non-existence of states of affairs to which they are supposed to correspond (and equally against a similar thesis in terms of experiences rather than states of affairs), Quine proposes a generalization of a thesis originally argued by the French philosopher Pierre Duhem in connection with scientific theories. Duhem's point is that scientific theories are never confirmed or falsified by their observational consequences taken in isolation, or, more accurately, that scientific theories do not have observational consequences on their own. The point can be illustrated by considering what actually happens when a well-entrenched scientific theory is faced by counter-evidence. An appropriate example is given by the events that led, in 1846, to the discovery of the planet Neptune. Until 1846, Uranus was the outermost known planet, but its actual orbit was known to deviate considerably from the orbit it was predicted to have by applying Newtonian principles to the relevant facts concerning the planet itself and the behaviour of Saturn, Jupiter and the Sun. The scientific reaction to this apparent disconfirmation of Newtonian principles was not to regard the principles as falsified, but rather to explain the problem away by postulating a hitherto unknown factor as the cause of the problem. It was argued that Saturn, Jupiter and the Sun were not the only factors impinging on Uranus; there was also another planet in the vicinity of

Uranus, pulling its orbit out of its predicted course. And so, of course, it proved; a triumph for Newtonian principles and all concerned!

Several lessons can be drawn from this story. First, in making predictions about Uranus's orbit, observers could not simply apply Newton's laws. They had to make observations and measurements of the set-up in which Uranus figured. As will be clear from the example, the observations in this case included determining facts about Uranus itself and other planets, no straightforward task in itself, but requiring the application of other highly theoretical principles. So any 'error' in Uranus's orbit could, quite logically, have been attributed to mistakes in determining these initial conditions. Although this is not what happened in this case, there are many analogous cases in which this course is taken. Then, secondly, any theory-based prediction of natural events will necessarily be made on the assumption that, in determining the initial conditions, all the relevant conditions have been taken into account. This was the assumption which was challenged when Neptune was postulated, correctly as it turned out. But even had Neptune not been discovered, there would have been nothing in itself illogical or unscientific had the scientists involved postulated some other interfering factor causing the deviations of the observed orbit from the predicted one. The assumption that all the relevant factors have been taken into account is quite open-ended. Failure of prediction can always be accounted for by denying that they have, and when the theory on which one is working has proved highly successful, this might often be the best course to take with problems. Finally, thirdly, problems in scientific prediction can be accounted for by denying or questioning the observations which seem to be causing the trouble. When the observations themselves are highly theoretical interpretations of data, which is very often the case, there can be no reason in principle against this course.

The lesson which we can derive from Duhem is that a scientific theory never makes a prediction of some specific event (and hence is never confirmed or falsified by a specific event), except in conjunction with many other theories and assumptions; particularly important are the theories involved in determining the initial conditions and the final outcome, and the assumption that one has taken into account all the relevant factors. Quine draws the conclusion that:

> Our statements about the external world face the tribunal of sense experience not individually but only as a corporate body.[9]

Is he justified in drawing such a general and all-embracing holism from what might be felt to be considerations drawn from examples and problems peculiar to theoretical science?

A defence of Quine's holism could be mounted along the following lines. While we might regard some of our beliefs, for example those about immediate experience or our immediate physical environment, as pretty close to the basic facts of experience, they actually depend for their accept-ability on non-basic theoretical assumptions; assumptions, that is to say, about our use of the terms involved, about the correctness of the memories involved in the use of those terms, about perception and standard con-ditions of observation, and so on. So 'basic' statements are dependent for their acceptability on other non-basic assumptions. When we come to more theoretical statements, the Duhemian argument applies directly, and it is easy to see that the relationship between theories and observa-tions is not a simple one. Even where the relevant predictions are couched in terms pretty close to those of our 'basic' statements about experience or ordinary objects, the relevance of such basic statements to the theory depends on assuming that the observations are normal and non-hallucinatory in various ways, as well as on dating and locating them, so assumptions about the coordinating of the spatiotemporal framework involved are also going to enter in. Statements about the past quite clearly depend for their testing on holistically integrating and check-ing one person's memories with those of others, with dating mechanisms, with other types of evidence, such as historical records, architectural and archaeological remains, geological data, radio-carbon dating, and on checking these types of evidence among themselves. Over and above accepting particular statements and theories as reliable, our whole system of beliefs will be held together by statements of meaning, of mathematics and of logic which allow us to move from one statement to another, and to see statements as mutually incompatible; by replacing a statement with, say, the word 'bachelor' in it with a similar one with the phrase 'un-married man' in place of 'bachelor'; by transforming various statements of numerical quantity into others more convenient for specific purposes; and finally, and most importantly, by allowing us to conclude that a given statement or statements imply some other statement, or to see that some statement rules out some other statement. These definitional, mathe-matical and logical statements form the interconnecting links in our system of knowledge, but should not in Quine's view be regarded as standing outside the system, in some privileged position immune from empirical challenge or criticism.

Quine sums up his holism as follows:

Any statement can be held true come what may, if we make drastic enough adjustments elsewhere in the system. Even a statement very close to the [experiential] periphery can be held true in the face of recalcitrant experience by pleading hallucination or by amending certain statements of the kind called logical laws. Conversely, by the same token, no statement is immune to revision. Revision even of the logical law of excluded middle has been proposed as a means of simplifying quantum mechanics; and what difference is there in principle between such a shift and the shift whereby Kepler superseded Ptolemy, or Einstein Newton, or Darwin Aristotle?[10]

Experience thus impinges on the system as a whole. While it is more likely directly to determine our attitude to some statements (observation or basic statements) so that we change them immediately in response to experience, we may defend particular observation statements in the face of experience (by pleading hallucination, say), if they appear to contradict some theory we want to hold on to because of its general usefulness in helping us to cope with experience, although, of course, doing this may necessitate some alterations in our theories of perception. No change at one point in our system is entirely without its ramifications in other parts. On the whole, we seek to minimize upset to the system as a whole (and here, Quine's views link with both pragmatist and coherence theories of truth). However, under considerable and conflicting experiential and theoretic pressure, we may even contemplate revisions to logical laws – those very statements which determine just when one statement is to be regarded as contradicting another. Changing a logical law in this way is not to be considered lightly. Precisely because it governs inference within the system as a whole, the effect of such a change will be very wide-ranging indeed.

A holistic view of knowledge may initially seem wrong in two particular respects. First, playing fast and loose with the logic and definitional apparatus of the system may be regarded as tantamount to demolishing the very notion of system which makes holism initially plausible and attractive. Without our terms and our logic being firm and clear at the outset, it will be unclear just what is meant by any statement at all. Indeed, by changing fundamental logical principles, such as the law of non-contradiction, we could hold on to any theory and any combination of other theories and counter-evidence, even if, on our original logical principles, the two were patently inconsistent. Just what effect experience is to have on any belief of ours will always be left in doubt, and this is hardly different from having no belief at all. But, despite some of Quine's own words, the holist need not totally abandon the distinction between logical and definitional statements on the one hand, and a more empirical level of statements on the other. For any particular experiment at any particular time, he can regard logic and meaning as fixed. What he will see his holism as committing him to is simply a denial that changes in logic and meaning may never be made in response to empirical pressures, a denial, in other words that logic and meaning are totally trans-empirical, matters of reason quite divorced from fact. So long as the changes that are made are clearly signalled beforehand, there is no reason why his system of knowledge should collapse into an incoherent and featureless pile of statements, the sense of any one of which is indeterminate and perpetually shifting because of changes he may decide to make in other beliefs.

Then, secondly, holism will be found unacceptable by those who think there is an observational or experiential basis to knowledge, in which statements are made true or false by particular experiences in isolation from more theoretical beliefs and assumptions. We have already said enough on this, but, even if what we have said is unconvincing, the Duhem argument shows that a degree of holism regarding our more theoretical beliefs is inescapable.

What now would be left of the distinction between truths of reason and truths of fact? The answer would be: very little of philosophical interest. Simple everyday definitions would perhaps be regarded as prior to experience and immune to foreseeable revision, at least where little of interest hangs on them. (But we should be careful of pronouncing in advance just where interest might lie; it is not hard to imagine the apparently trivial definition of 'bachelor' becoming an issue of sexual politics.) Logical laws and the more complex definitions of science such as those of 'force' in physics (which, of course, has changed since Newton) or of 'water' in chemistry would be regarded as conventions or postulates adopted for the purposes of inquiry, neither discovered by pure reason, uninfluenced by experience nor in any deep sense prior to experience. It will be said they are adopted precisely because of their usefulness in promoting the discovery and transmission of truths and this is, in the broadest sense, a factual matter. Revision of logical rules and definitional starting points would be expected when the rules or definitions one is starting with lead to an inability to deal with new or recalcitrant experiences. The differences between logical laws and definitions, on the one hand, and ordinary factual statements about desks being in front of me, and so on, on the other, is that the former, but not the latter, would never be abandoned (or adopted) as a result of just one experience or observation. But this would only be a matter of degree with general theories of science occupying a position somewhat between the two extremes. Holism of this sort gains credibility because in science, at least, definitions are often regarded as part of the theory in which they are presented and acceptable in so far as the theory itself is. On the other hand, as we shall see in the final section of Chapter 3, following Quine himself, there are powerful reasons for not regarding every principle of argument and inference as revisable. The most basic ones have to be prior to any specific thought or inquiry, including, of course, inquiry into logic itself.

Scepticism, Justification and Evolution

Scepticism of a philosophical sort is typically directed at whole classes of statement. This is precisely why it is hard to respond to. Instead of asking what grounds we have for believing that, say, the Achaeans were ever at Troy, the sceptic questions our entitlement to any beliefs about the past at all, and similarly with our beliefs about the external world in general, about regularity in that world, and about the reliability of our senses, and so on. Often, though, the strategy is to focus on something known to be doubtful, such as the Trojan war, and then to suggest that weaknesses in that case may actually be far more widespread than we think. Thus, Descartes on dreaming:

> How often has it happened to me that in the night I dreamt that I found myself in this particular place, that I was dressed and seated near the fire, whilst in reality I was lying undressed in bed! At this moment it does indeed seem to me that it is with eyes awake that I am looking at this paper; that this head which I move is not asleep, that it is deliberately and of set purpose that I extend my hand and perceive it; what happens in sleep does not appear so clear nor so distinct as does all this. But in thinking over this I remind myself that on many occasions I have in sleep been deceived by similar illusions, and in dwelling carefully on this reflection I see so manifestly that there are no certain indications by which we may clearly distinguish wakefulness from sleep that I am lost in astonishment. And my astonishment is such that it is almost capable of persuading me that I now dream.[11]

Part of Descartes's complex and subtle argument appears to be that past blunders concerning dreaming and waking suggest that we have no certain grounds for making the distinction between the two states.

A reply to this part of the argument would be to say that if Descartes's point depends on the recognition of past blunders, then he must have just what he claims to be unsure about, namely, a means of demarcating sleeping from waking. Of course, it may turn out that the means in question is not something that would enable us to identify with certainty whether a particular state of ours was one of waking or dreaming in isolation from other memories, beliefs and assumptions. Indeed, there is something incoherent about the search for a conclusive criterion enabling us infallibly and immediately to distinguish waking from dreaming states, because, even if it made sense to talk of applying a criterion while dreaming, which some have questioned, there could never be any guarantee that we might not simply be dreaming that such a criterion was on any given occasion being correctly applied. The infuriating thing about the dreaming argument is that whatever we propose as a means of distinguishing waking from dreaming, we can never rule out the possibility that we might simply be dreaming that we are applying it. After all, in the past we have been deceived into thinking that we had made sure that we were awake, when in fact we were dreaming ...

Descartes's own position on dreaming is not easy to unravel, but there are hints in the *Meditations* and elsewhere that he was not really interested in discovering a criterion for infallibly telling whether one is awake or dreaming, while one is dreaming.[12] Indeed, later on in the *First Meditation* he goes on to suggest that even if we were dreaming, there are some things we might still have a right to be sure of, because even within a dream their self-evidence would be apparent, though might we not only be dreaming their apparent self-evidence, one feels like asking. Leaving this last question aside, however, it could be argued that what Descartes was (or ought to have been) looking for were the marks by which we might rationally judge certain experiences to be reliable guides to the external world. The relevance of dreaming and waking to this project is that we know from past experience that dreaming experiences are unreliable. But why should I regard waking experiences of physical objects as reliable if there are no marks to distinguish waking from dreaming experiences? Are there, in fact, any marks present in one's experience when one is awake, which make it rational to accept it as veridical, while rejecting dreaming experiences as illusions?

Indeed there are, as Descartes himself argues at the end of the *Sixth Meditation* (although he is less than candid about the existence of such an argument in the *First Meditation*):

At present I find a very notable difference between [sleeping and waking], inasmuch as our memory can never connect our dreams one with the other, or with the whole course of our lives, as it unites events which happen to us while we are awake. And, as a matter of fact, if someone, while I was awake, quite suddenly appeared to me and disappeared as fast as do the images which I see in sleep, so that I could not know from whence the form came nor whither it went, it would not be without reason that I should deem it a spectre or a phantom formed by my brain (and similar to those which I form in sleep), rather than a real man.[13]

He goes on to say that when he can connect current perceptions with those that occurred in the rest of his life, he can rest assured that he is waking rather than sleeping. Perhaps what he should have said here was that he can be assured that his perceptions are reliable, and that for this it is in a way irrelevant whether he is awake or asleep; what he actually says looks like an attempt to answer the incoherent demand for an open-and-shut test of current wakefulness. But the most important remark of all is the conclusion:

> I ought in no wise to doubt the truth of such matters [i.e. my perceptions] if, after having called up all my senses, my memory, and my understanding, to examine them, nothing is brought to evidence by any one of them which is repugnant to what is set forth by the others.

Descartes thus anticipated Quinean holism by over 300 years, avoiding the empiricist trap of taking sensory evidence as either the only or indeed the main source of empirical knowledge, by giving due weight to the operations of memory and understanding in building up our picture of the world.

The sceptic, as I remarked at the start of this section, tries to spread doubt around whole areas of discourse, about the past, or external reality, or one's waking state, and he often does this by fixing on the weakness of our reasons for individual beliefs in the offending class, taken in isolation. That his manoeuvre has some sense to it often emerges when people try to respond to the sceptic by presenting examples of supposedly incorrigible truths; but if these truths have any interest at all, the sceptic is usually able to show that true they may be, but fully provable they are not. You say that you are seated on a chair, but chairs are human artefacts. How can you be sure that it was made in a factory or a workshop? That, if it is a chair, it is not going to disappear in the next minute or two. How can you be sure of that? Moreover, your own perceptions of it could be mistaken in various ways; such things happen. Also, are you sure that this is what other English speakers would call a chair? Might you not have forgotten the correct sense of the word? The obvious reply to these doubts and questions is that we can carry out tests to settle each of them in turn, but this will not satisfy the determined sceptic, because further doubts can be raised concerning the results of the tests.

In any case, testing necessarily comes to an end at certain points, as we have already seen. In the end we will always be left at a point at which we simply have the conviction that we are judging correctly, using words correctly, understanding others correctly, forming expectations for the future correctly, and it is difficult to see how every imaginable doubt as to the truth of this conviction can be totally ruled out. You might just be a brain in a vat, wired up by some scientist to have all these thoughts and convictions! (This is the contemporary analogue of Descartes' evil deceiving demon, similarly manipulating our thoughts and convictions from outside.)

However, I do not think that we should regard any of this as a vindication of scepticism, except in the emptiest sense. We have already seen in Chapter 1 in considering the classifying of experiences, which is perhaps the most guarded form of judgement, that assumptions concerning the reliability of memory and of a stable world apart from us underlie our continuing and successful use of descriptive terms. People can certainly raise doubts about memory in general and about the assumption that we live and will continue to live in a stable world which are difficult to answer directly. Any proof that my memory is reliable is going to involve appeal to the memories of others and to other data that assume that human beings have reliable knowledge of the past; there seems no route to a general proof that memories are in general reliable. Equally, we cannot prove that the world is and will continue to be stable by appeal to past experience of stability. Not only does this rely on memory, but it completely fails to meet the sceptic's point, which is precisely to question the justification for thinking that past experience is a good guide to the future. (This is the so-called problem of induction.) It must be conceded to the sceptic that, just as there are no conclusive arguments to refute solipsism or to show that our beliefs about what happened in the past are by and large true, so there is no way of showing that the stability we experience in the world is either very widespread or likely to continue for any length of time in the future. Indeed, it may not; we might suddenly find ourselves in a totally different sort of world, quite unable to cope because of a general mismatch between our expectations and the environment.

But lack of conclusive disproofs of scepticism in various areas does not show that scepticism is necessarily a good policy to adopt. In fact, with regard to the fundamental assumptions that our perceptions are somewhat reliable, that our memories and beliefs about the past are not totally misguided and that our world does and will continue to manifest regularities apart from our perceptions of it and of a sort recognizable by us, scepticism would appear to be a hopeless policy, and one that can be presumed to have been shown to have been a hopeless policy in the past. The reason I say this is because of the way assumptions about memory and perception of a stable world are required as the basis of attempts to describe and categorize what we experience, and because of the way we may be presumed to be having some success in doing this, given that we are in fact able without obvious contradiction or absurdity to think of ourselves as forming a coherent picture of the world, and as having succeeded in stumbling on the means to pick out regularities that actually pertain and have pertained.

Wittgenstein in some lectures he gave on sense data and private experience in the early 1930s brings out well the dependence of schemes of classification and the assurances of memory on stability in the world:

We learn the word 'red' under particular circumstances. Certain objects are usually red, and keep their colours. Most people agree with us in our colour judgments. Suppose all this changes: I see blood, unaccountably sometimes one, sometimes another colour, and the people around me make different statements. But couldn't I in all this chaos retain my meaning of 'red', 'blue', etc., although I couldn't now make myself understood to anyone? Samples, e.g., would all constantly change their colour – 'or does it only seem so to me?' 'Now am I mad or did I really call this "red" yesterday?'[14]

In fact, from our own subjective point of view, it would be hard to distinguish a situation in which the world became chaotic (at least from the point of view of our expectations of it) and one in which our own memory and perceptual faculties started to go wildly wrong. In both cases a breakdown of our ability to categorize what we perceived could be expected, given that this ability depends on enough stability in what we perceive to give us confidence that we are continuing to categorize the same types of experience in the same way.

Scepticism of a radical sort, extending to scepticism about the existence of a stable world apart from us and about the reliability of any of our memories, would then leave us without a workable scheme of classification for what was left to us, the momentary subjective experiences the sceptic claims are all we can really be sure about. This is why a radical scepticism is a poor policy to adopt, at least if one is interested in any sort of description or categorization of what one experiences. Like the ultimate sceptical doctrine, that there is no truth, scepticism concerning these assumptions is going to leave the sceptic with precious little to say, and if, like the sceptics of Roman times, someone were to regard silence as epistemologically golden, we could point out that we are interested in action as well as in words, and that we need classificatory theories in order to choose future actions and to judge their reasonableness.

Moreover, it would be hard for the sceptic to deny that we do at least appear to succeed in describing and predicting things. His line of attack is to claim that we do so without firm foundations, or without foundations firm enough to make the thing rational. Moreover, there is no guarantee that our expectations about the world and our environment will not be blown apart in the next instant. In examining sceptical arguments, we may well be led to conclude that there is truth in much of this. There is a definite sense in which our knowledge is without foundations, in which reasons for beliefs give out without the beliefs being self-evident beyond all possibility of doubt. (I am writing at my desk, but I just might be dreaming.) Certainly any or all of our expectations regarding the future could fail us. But we should not conclude that the success of the sceptic in showing a certain groundlessness to our beliefs and our expectations is the same as showing that it is irrational to hold them.

In the first place, the raising and entertaining of doubts are themselves activities which we first understand and which can be seen as being rational or irrational against the background of our accepted standards of knowledge and belief. Thus, it is rational to entertain doubts about the Trojan war because the evidence for it is somewhat weak compared with, say, the evidence for the Battle of Austerlitz. Equally, after a drugged sleep, it might be reasonable to wonder whether conversations I seem to remember having were real or dreamt. The sort of total scepticism implied by the brain in the vat hypothesis or the hypothesis that I am being deceived by an evil spirit does not meet these standards of rationality. There is no reason to suppose that these things might be the case, only an inability to rule out their impossibility with total certainty. The sceptic is, in fact, equating lack of total disproof with a doubt that it might be reasonable to entertain.

Moreover, I could and would go on making my judgements about the comparative credibility of such things as the Trojan war and the table in front of me, as I always have done, even if I was in some way a brain in a vat, so long as the course of my experiences followed the sorts of regularities experienced in the past. What would it mean, saying that I was a brain in a vat in these circumstances? Certainly it would not mean that I was like what within my experience I perceived as a brain in a vat on the shelf of some laboratory. I can see that I am not like that; unlike that thing, I move about, etc. What would it mean, applying the words 'I am a brain in a vat' to myself, given that all the tests of brain-in-a-vathood, which I understand within my experience as establishing that something is a brain in a vat, would fail in my own case? Or, to put the same point another way, there is something verging on meaninglessness in a hypothesis (such as the one that I am continually deceived by the manipulations on my brain of some scientist or evil spirit) that makes no difference whatever to experience or to the actual judgements I make. One wonders what the *significance* (let alone the rationality) could be of denying that I was an embodied person sitting on a chair if all the tests I take to establish whether I was really sitting on a chair suggest that I am.

The brain in a vat hypothesis is really only an extreme form of what is involved in scepticism about the external world and about memory. For if we are totally deceived in thinking that we are ourselves fairly stable embodied beings in a world which has been fairly regular and stable in our experience, we must be something else, such as a brain in a vat. But what would denying that we are such beings in such a world amount to, given that everything we know and believe, and all the mutual support and confirmation within our knowledge and beliefs, suggests that we are? At the very least, it raises a question as to whether the sceptic might not in the end have to be understood as denying that we are embodied beings in a stable world in some strange metaphysical sense that is still consistent with most of our judgements about chairs, tables, other people and so on being true, because the most natural explanation of our experiences, including of course our experience of recalling that we have been proved to be correct countless times in the past when we have judged something to be a chair or a table or another person (because of its appropriate subsequent behaviour), is simply that these judgements are true. These judgements are (in the main) true; so long as our senses, our memory and our understanding continue in their interactions to corroborate most of our judgements about what we experience, by subsequently confirming the expectations we engender of things presently perceived on the basis of past experience and this indirectly confirming the correctness of our memories as well as of our expectations for the future, it would be merely perverse to deny the rationality of believing these judgements to be true.

Where a degree of scepticism is in place is over induction. For, even if we agree that we have good reasons for supposing that our experiences and memories have been reliable up to now, there seems no hope of a proof that they are going to continue to be reliable in the future. There is no way of showing that the world might not change in such a way as to refute our most deeply ingrained beliefs about its regularities and stability. Past successes with our beliefs give no proof of their future success, unless we are assuming that the future will resemble the past, but this is just what the sceptic thinks we have no reason to assume.

The sceptic is correct in his premise. There could be no proof that the future had to resemble the past in any respect that did not run the risk of empirical disproof. But it does not follow from this that it would be a reasonable policy not to act on those theories and beliefs which have served us well in the past. In the first place, many of the beliefs we have about the things we are currently perceiving are not only confirmed by past evidence, they also have implications for the future behaviour of those things. Then, secondly, as we have continually emphasized, our schemes of classification depend for their viability on stability in the world. Our past experience of success with them, while not proof of their future certainty, is nevertheless an indication that they are genuine regularities in the world as it at present is and as it has been for some time. They are thus well-founded beliefs, better founded than a belief in some new type of regularity that is merely postulated now for the first time and may reflect nothing of the actual course of events. Of course, there is no guarantee that the world might not change so radically that any or all of our well-founded expectations let us down. But no policy regarding our theories or beliefs could protect us if such a catastrophe occurred, so it should not be thought an objection to a policy that it cannot do this. What we need are means of investigation which will enable us to uncover any regularities in the world that really do exist and the more basic and far-reaching the ones we uncover the better, to safeguard against basing our lives on short-term, local ones. In this way we may hope to avoid the fate of the chicken, mentioned by Bertrand Russell, who got an unpleasant shock on the day her own hitherto regular break-fast was replaced by an instance of the altogether more sinister regularity by which chickens become food for human beings. It is surely rational to seek to uncover the most far-reaching regularities there are in the world, and then to base our activity on the theories we come up with in doing this.

The conscious and explicit search for the wide-ranging regularities in the universe is part of what is undertaken in the natural sciences, and we will consider some of the philosophical issues raised by natural science in the next section. But most of our beliefs and expectations regarding the world are not the product of science or of conscious reflection at all. Indeed, if we see ourselves as part of nature, an evolutionary product, then much of our picture of the world must be seen as part of our evolutionary inheritance, in so far as it is based on what is delivered to us by our perceptual faculties and by our instinctive reactions to our environment. Of what relevance to scepticism and epistemology are such evolutionary considerations?

To clear away misunderstandings at the start, it is necessary to say that no biological data about the adaptation of the faculties and reactions of a species to its environment can guarantee that the means by which the species has survived will ensure its survival in the future. The ecological niche to which it is adapted may change, and this can happen without any change in large-scale regularities in the world. A species whose survival depends on the continued fulfilment of its instinctual expectations by the environment will be unlikely to survive substantial changes in its environment. Nevertheless, on the assumption of stability in one's ecological niche, evolution can tell us something about the way we generalize on the basis of past experience.

The problem of induction is often posed as if it were the search for a justification of the procedure of generalizing on regularities in past experience. But, as Goodman has shown, this distorts what is really at issue by grossly undercharacterizing the problem.[15] For the regularities in past experience can be generalized and projected into the future in any number of ways, yet we would immediately reject many of them as invalid. To give Goodman's own by now famous example, our past experience that all emeralds we have observed up to now are green supports the generalization that all emeralds are green. But, if we introduce a new term 'grue', where a thing is grue if examined before AD 2000 and found to be green, or is not so examined and is blue, then exactly the same evidence that supports my saying, in 1983, that all emeralds are green, also and equally supports my saying, in 1983, that all emeralds are grue. Yet these two generalizations are conflicting, and will lead to different predictions concerning the appearance of emeralds observed only after AD 2000. (A grue emerald first examined after 2000 will be what we call 'blue'.) Now, there have been many attempts to uncover something spurious in Goodman's example. The most obvious of these is to say that 'grue' is an unnatural sort of predicate, containing as it does a time reference. The reply to this is to say that for those to whom talk of 'grue' (and corresponding 'bleen') is natural, our 'green' and 'blue' will have to be explained in temporal terms. ('Green' = 'if examined before

AD 2000 and found to be grue, or if examined after AD 2000 and found to be bleen'.) While this reply does meet the objection, and other objections to the legitimacy of the predicate 'grue' can also be met, over-concentration on 'grue' misses the substance of Goodman's point, which is simply that we can generalize about the evidence we have at any time in many different ways, and which can actually be made by other examples. Thus, Ayer points out that my finding ninety-nine green balls in a bag of 100 balls confirms the hypothesis that all the balls in the bag are green; but equally, it confirms the hypothesis that ninety-nine of the balls are green and one is not green.[16]

In his lecture on the new riddle of induction, Goodman said:

> Every word you have heard me say has occurred prior to the final sentence of this lecture: but that does not, I hope, create any expectation that every word you will hear me say will be prior to that sentence.

And, after stating that regularity in greenness confirms the prediction of further cases of green emeralds, whereas regularity in grueness does not confirm anything, he concludes:

> To say that valid predictions are those based on past regularities, without being able to say *which* regularities, is thus quite pointless. Regularities are where you find them, and you can find them anywhere.[17]

I am told that octopuses recognize shapes that we do not perceive naturally at all. This means that they group things together and can presumably be regarded as generalizing about them in a way that would seem bizarre to us. Perception of similarity and subsequent generalization on the basis of regularities among things grouped in virtue of perceived similarities is clearly highly dependent on what seem to be natural groupings to the perceivers in question. There is no reason to suppose that there is anything inherently impossible in other creatures sorting and generalizing about the world in ways that seem highly artificial to us. Perhaps on other planets there are even speakers of a 'grue'-'bleen' language: this might even appear reasonable to us if, on that planet, classes of objects such as emeralds and rubies appeared to have what we would regard as different colours depending on the time they were first examined.

It is in recognition of these facts and of the problem of explaining why we project some regularities in experience into the future and not others (and so regard some hypotheses as being confirmed and others equally compatible with the same evidence as not confirmed) that Quine, in his paper 'Natural Kinds', speaks of us and all other animals being born with innate standards of similarity.[18] These quality spacings, as he puts it, are what enable us to recognize a red circle as being more similar to a pink ellipse than to a blue triangle. We can assume that the quality spaces of other members of the same species will be, by and large, similar to ours, and so similar presentations (for example, of yellow things) will be grouped and described similarly (as yellow things) by other speakers of our language. This, Quine points out, is itself a type of induction. We expect that our own use of 'yellow' will match our neighbour's, but the dice in this case are somewhat loaded in our favour, because of our sharing of similar quality spaces (though this does not completely prevent mistakes and misunderstandings at all levels of language use). But when we make inductions about the future behaviour of non-human objects on the basis of the regularities we have picked out, we are doing something far more risky. As he puts it, we are supposing 'that our quality space matches that of the cosmos';[19] in other words we are assuming that nature will continue to perform so as to reproduce what we have picked out as regularities.

What we are doing is risky, clearly, but we do notice that in the past our subjective spacing of qualities has not led us completely astray. We do pick out groupings and regularities that seem accurate reflections of the way nature works and which are themselves based in fairly stable and enduring properties of objects, which, as I suggested earlier, is a necessary condition of our being able to learn and use a property-term with any degree of stability. Isn't there something here that itself needs explanation? According to Quine, Darwinian natural selection does give a plausible partial explanation:

> If people's innate spacing of qualities is a gene-linked trait, then the spacing that has made for the most successful inductions will have tended to predominate through natural selection. Creatures inveterately wrong in their inductions have a pathetic but praiseworthy tendency to die before reproducing their kind.[20]

The picture we are given is one of the environment selecting those genetically based perceptions of similarity and regularity which help most towards the survival of the species in question, in leading them to make the best inductions from their point of view.

Creatures, such as human beings, who can go beyond their genetic inheritance in their interaction with the environment can develop theories which may modify their original sense of similarity, suggesting previously unperceived regularities to be a better basis for inductions than perceptually obvious ones. This, in effect, is what happens in science. Colour, undeniably important at the food-gathering level, in science is displaced in favour of similarities leading to inductions which are more accurate and wider-ranging than those based on colour classifications. We also begin to get a sense, itself inductively based, of what types of regularity are likely to be properly projectible into the future. This enables us to rule out a predicate like 'grue' from the start, as being highly unlikely to feature in correct theories. We 'know' now on the basis of such a sense that 'all emeralds are grue' is false, though this will not be strictly proved until AD 2000. Indeed, an important element in our system of knowledge is the way we assign degrees of probability to new theories prior to any actual testing, which is another way of looking at Goodman's new riddle of induction. Without this ability we would have no way now of choosing between 'all emeralds are green' and 'all emeralds are grue'; though, if *per impossibile* they did turn out after AD 2000 to be grue rather than green this would, of course, have a catastrophic effect on our whole approach to knowledge and the world.

In 'Natural Kinds', then, Quine argues that natural selection has given mankind both a set of perceptual quality spaces, with which to sift the data of experience, and the ingenuity to rise above our original classifications and inductions. Nevertheless, for Quine, there remains something unsatisfactory about the result, because our new classifications and inductions still appear to be based on the fact that, relative to some point of view, some things are found more similar to each other than to other things, and grouped together. Quine objects to the relativity and subjectivity implied in a grouping based on a standard of similarity, because things are only similar in a relative way. There is no absolute standard of similarity, however much particular standards of similarity are entrenched in our genes or reinforced by the environment. Quine suggests that we rise above subjectivity of similarity only when we get to a stage in a science in which we can regard elements in the science as being similar to the extent that they are interchangeable parts of the cosmic machine; this drive to reduce things to their elements is, of course, as Quine recognizes, something that has been dominant in science since Greek times, going from early atomic theory, through theories of elementary particles, to the hills of space–time.

Despite Quine's wish to dispense with unanalysed notions of similarity, it is doubtful that we can dispense with them altogether. This is partly for the reason given in Chapter 1 (p. 37), that the findings of theoretical science must be regarded as testable in terms of more familiar notions. If we are adopting an evolutionary perspective, we can now see why this has to be so. For we are a part of nature, in a particular ecological niche and with particular perceptual structures. It is hard to see how even theoretical science can completely divorce any thoughts we entertain seriously as to the nature of the world completely from our own position in nature and our viewpoint on it. This may seem a limitation of our thought, unavoidable though it is, though, from another point of view, it would appear to be what keeps our theories genuinely empirical.

Some may doubt the relevance of anything inspired by evolutionary considerations to epistemology. After all, success in the battle for survival up to now offers no permanent justification or guarantee of survival to what has been selected. This complaint assumes that the aim of epistemology is, or ought to be, the final justification of our knowledge claims. But we have seen a number of reasons for supposing such justification to be impossible. We cannot get outside our theories and beliefs to compare them with an uncontaminated reality. Moreover, none of our theories or beliefs is totally self-verifying, nor can they survive ingenious sceptical attacks unscathed. But if we take our corpus of theories and beliefs as a datum, much of philosophical interest can be gleaned. We can now see how the various levels of beliefs relate to each other, and to the impact of experience; how changes in one level have effects on other levels; how our system as a whole is mutually supportive, and how corroborations of beliefs in one area (for example, about the future) might also be corroborations of beliefs in other areas (for example, about the past, in our selections of prior probability standards); and how piecemeal improvements might be made by increasing the smoothness and accuracy of the system as a whole. To this study, further facts from a study of evolution might add the following: an idea of the mechanisms by which our initial perceptions and reactions to the world, with their various inductive implications, have been selected; evidence that the indirectness of the impact of experience on our consciously formulated theories might be paralleled by a similar indirectness in the evolution of our perceptual apparatus, where once again there is no question of any simple 'fit' of a newly mutated organ directly in contact with a raw nature, but rather a picture of a new evolutionary 'try' having to fit in with existing organic systems, and being tested by nature through its contribution to such a system; a partial vindication of the deliverances of our senses as being the result of natural selection though the previous point should be borne in mind – there is good reason to think that the eye gives us many distorted images of reality as the price for the immeasurable benefit it accords us in giving us clear and readily decipherable impressions, well suited to most of our survival needs, including the need to make quick and definite decisions; the suggestion that we are subjects seeking survival in a real world, with our theories and beliefs shaped by interactions with that real world; and finally, some idea of the limitations of our knowledge and the ways in which we might partially transcend these limitations. Evolutionary theory is, of course, part of our body of knowledge, and not more certain than any other part. It cannot be used to provide a foundation for our perceptual or common-sense beliefs.* The use of evolutionary theory to throw light on our knowledge in the way suggested here – by means of description and explanation of our knowledge processes – is simply an instance of our taking seriously the idea that there is no first philosophy, that philosophy itself is a matter of drawing on and comparing what we learn in other fields of human inquiry.

Truth and Relativism in Science

Much of these two first chapters has concerned the status of scientific theories, and their relation to common sense. Nevertheless, in closing this chapter on epistemology there are some problems which arise particularly vividly in the case of scientific theory, and which are worth considering directly. The problems in question are all to do with the lack of any direct or definite proof or disproof of the truth of scientific theories, and the resulting absence of a decision procedure, enabling us to choose with any degree of certainty between competing theories. Some have taken these findings to establish that science is, despite its claims, not a rational procedure, and that its success in convincing us that it is owes more to ideological and economic forces, and a resulting science fetishism, than to any real validity in its theories or procedures. What I will say in this section can be read as a qualified rebuttal of this conclusion, but before tackling the detailed problem involved in justifying the theories of science, it is worth making some general points.

Science, since the sixteenth century, provides us with an amazing example of knowledge growing, however this growth is seen – as a steady increase in knowledge, or as a series of revolutions and counter-revolutions – and whatever we might think of the human effects and technological applications of this growth. But the growth is clearly there, and visible to all in its applications. Science, secondly, is highly

---

*I argue this point more fully in my contribution to the 1984 Aristotelian Society Symposium on evolutionary epistemology (*Supplementary Proceedings of the Aristotelian Society*, Vol. LVIII, pp. 193–217).

institutionalized. From this it derives much of its great strength, in the division of labour and consequent specialization thereby permitted, as well as mutual criticism and cross-checking. Institutionalization and specialization are also a source of weakness for science, although it could be argued that the weaknesses are actually strengths in the long term, in that a strong institutional framework is necessary for the critical co-operative enterprise science is. We all know something of the life of institutions, and the way they impose conformity, suppress criticism and throw out dissenters. This sort of thing is no doubt part of science, as much as it is part of a religion, part of an army and part of a corporation. Much of the strength of recent criticisms of science is very probably due to the success science has had up till recently in concealing this as part of its sociological and institutional nature. Nevertheless, the irrational and conformist aspects of institutional life are strongly mitigated in the case of science itself, by the way results in science are cross-checked and replicated institutionally, by the way scientific facts are outside the whim and control of investigators, and, above all, by the way intellectual honesty and criticism are themselves high institutional values in science (even if by no means always adhered to). A philosophical examination of science should certainly take into account both the growth of knowledge in science and the existence and nature of the institutional aspect of science. The hope would be for a philosophy of science that would go some way to explaining the reasons for the growth of knowledge in science and for the particular values institutionalized in science.

Science aims at theories which can be regarded as explaining natural phenomena. More precisely, in science we are looking for theories which tell us about the causation of phenomena, and, as we have already seen, there is something implicitly general in talk about causality. Scientific theories thus aim in the first instance at generality, explaining some particular effect by showing it to be caused by some other phenomenon, or, in other words, that the two types of phenomena concerned go together as an example of general regularity in nature. Thus, the type of explanation desired in science will not necessarily explain a particular effect by putting it in terms of something more familiar or more readily intelligible. Indeed, the general regularity, of which we see a particular and rather familiar event being an instance, may require description in terms of entities that are highly theoretical from the point of view of common sense, such as electrons, or mass, or gravity. Common-sense analogies or models may help us to formulate the explanations used in science, as when we see gas in terms of clouds of molecules, or talk of an electron having spin, but the adequacy of a scientific explanation is judged in terms of its accuracy and power in predicting all phenomena of the type it is introduced to explain.

To consider a simple example, we may notice that metal bars expand on being heated. We may then generalize on the basis of what we have observed, claiming that the cause of the expansion is the application of heat, and produce a formula relating the rate of expansion to the mass of the bar and the amount it is heated. This formula will be adequate if it turns out to enable us to predict correctly the amount of expansion of all the metal bars we come across in the future, and we will, in this way, have explained our original observations by showing them to be instances of some general regularity.

However, we may feel that this explanation is neither wide enough nor deep enough. It is not wide enough, because, dealing only with the behaviour of metal bars, it does not tell us anything about other heat phenomena. Nor is it very deep: it does not say anything about the inner states of the metal bars which cause them to expand on being heated. As yet our theory only offers a causal regularity that heating causes expansion, but it does not explain the underlying causal processes. We may hope to widen and deepen our original simple generalization by developing a theory of heat, which will both say what heat is at the micro-structural level and apply to all heat phenomena. Thinking of heat as increased molecular motion is designed to do both these things, though, once again, this will be adequate as an explanation of particular examples of heat only if the theory as to what heat is is expressed in such a way as to enable us to predict the various phenomena associated with heat (such as metallic expansion) and to do so accurately.

Our example, though a simple one, does bring out the way that scientific theories have to be general in form, the way that they have to lead to correct predictions of particular occurrences, and the way that scientists seek theories that show more and more superficially different types of event as being examples of underlying similarities and regularities. The rationale for this last point is not simply the beauty and utility of such a demonstration. It is also that if a very general theory of this type turns out to succeed in many different types of test, we have some indication that what is being described in the theory is a genuine regularity in nature and not simply a merely accidental or local coincidence we have stumbled on. We have already stressed (p. 26) that significant talk of causes should enable us to identify the causal mechanisms independently of the phenomena that they are originally invoked to explain. This condition is met even by our low-level generalization about the expansion of metal bars, for their expansion is identifiable quite independently of observing them being heated. Similarly, we must presume that molecular motion is detectable in bodies independently of our observing heat being applied to them, otherwise we would be explaining or adding nothing to our understanding of the causal mechanisms underlying heat phenomena by introducing talk of molecular motion (and this would still be the case even if, as is apparently true in this example, for theoretical purposes scientists eventually come to identify heat with molecular motion*). Obviously, though, the wider and more general a scientific theory is the more testable it will be and the more chance we will have of discovering if it is inaccurate in one or other of its applications.

The generality of scientific theories precludes our establishing their truth. Even in the case of the metal bars being heated, we can only examine a small and insignificant proportion of the total number of actual cases. There are, moreover, many counterfactual implications of such a theory (about what would have happened had someone applied heat to this bar on some occasion when they did not do so), which cannot be tested directly. Nor can we declare a general theory probable without making highly risky assumptions. We can examine only a tiny proportion (an infinitesimally small one) of all the cases covered by the general theories, which are intended to apply over the whole of space and time as part of their claim to be describing genuine regularities in nature; even if we could examine a significant proportion of cases in a given domain, say ninety out of a population of one hundred objects, we can only have confidence that the ninety-first case is not likely to upset our expectations based on the previous ninety if we have reason to think that our sample is representative of the remainder. In nature, such confidence has often been shown to be misplaced, however rational and unavoidable forming beliefs on such a basis might be. So, because of their generality we cannot verify scientific theories or even be sure that they are probable with anything like mathematical certainty.

Some, notably Sir Karl Popper and his followers, have hoped to avoid the difficulties inherent in attempting to prove or justify scientific theories, by emphasizing their falsifiability. Precisely because of the universality of what is claimed in a theory which states that all phenomena of a certain class have such and such characteristics, one counter-

---

*This identification actually has the curious effect of making it merely contingent that heat gives rise to sensations of heat, for it is surely conceivable that molecular motion might not have had this effect on us.

example will serve to show that the theory is false. What scientists should attempt to do is to submit their theories to the most stringent testing possible, and indeed to formulate theories which are extremely likely to be false through the precision of their predictions and their improbability relative to what we already know. (Popper's own favourite example here[21] is Einstein's special theory of relativity, which in 1905 made the extremely unlikely claim that light was bent by heavy bodies, a claim which could not be tested until a total eclipse of the sun in 1919.) Theories with high testability will probably be weeded out quickly, if false. Scientific knowledge grows by doing just this in a conscious effort to imitate natural selection. Those theories that survive severe testing can be retained, but in an entirely provisional spirit, because their survival of tests should not be thought of as positive proof or confirmation, owing to the problem of induction. Rationality, on this view, in science and elsewhere, is constituted by the critical approach, in which there is no justification, but only falsification, and the honest attempt to uncover erroneous theories and replace them with something better.

The Popperian replacement in epistemology of justification with the critical approach may mean that we can by-pass the problems involved in any sort of empirical justification, but as a philosophy to live by it can hardly be regarded as satisfactory. In the first place, whatever Popper and his followers call it, there is only a verbal difference between regarding it as rational to retain and act on those theories that have survived severe testing, and regarding those theories as in some sense confirmed. If they are not confirmed in some sense, how can it be rational to act on them? We can say this without thinking of confirmation in terms of a theory being proved or being assigned a definite probability, once we accept that confirming a theory has as much to do with its efficacy and fit with our other theories and the rest of our beliefs, as it has to do with a direct confrontation with a raw, uninterpreted nature.

Then, secondly, and this is the more important point, it is not easy to falsify a scientific theory. Theories are not simply confronted with counter-evidence and immediately revealed as therefore false. We have seen this in considering the Quine–Duhem hypothesis (pp. 106 ff.), and do not need to go over this ground again, except to underline the way in which all our observations are themselves impregnated with our concepts and our expectations, because much has been made of this by critics of the Popperian view of science. These critics, notably T. S. Kuhn in his book *The Structure of Scientific Revolutions*,[22] have pointed out the extent to which scientists do in fact protect their theories against falsification, and also the way in which the favoured theory of a period in the history of science tends to affect the way in which investigators see the data, again with the effect of immunizing the theory against criticism.

Kuhn's own central concept for understanding the history and development of science is that of a paradigm, a complex and many-sided notion, but whose basic point is clear enough. Scientists are normally guided in their day-to-day work by the currently accepted paradigm, which, among other things, encapsulates the current basic ideas about the subject matter, determines the methods of research to be used and questions to be raised, and organizes the forms or *Gestalten* under which the data under investigation are viewed. (Kuhn often speaks of scientists with different paradigms seeing the data differently. Aristotelians looked at swinging stones and *saw* constrained fall where Galileans *saw* pendula. Priestley saw dephlogisticated air where Lavoisier saw oxygen.) The paradigm, then, determines theory, method and, above all, perception. Without a paradigm determining these aspects of inquiry, there is no science, hardly even naïve fact-collecting. But the paradigm-imbued nature of science means that science itself is in some large measure non-rational, particularly at points of crisis, where a new paradigm is set against an old one. This is partly because we can never conclusively verify or falsify a paradigm, for the sorts of reasons we have already considered, but, above all, because of the way people operating within different paradigms talk across each other. This is not just psychological; it is because of the way the paradigm determines the data being dealt with, so there is no paradigm-independent observation on which genuine comparisons can be based. Instead, a change from one paradigm to another is like a religious conversion, or a *Gestalt*-switch. Scales fall from the eyes, and

the scientist who embraces a new paradigm is like the man wearing inverting lenses. Confronting the same constellation of objects as before and knowing that he does so, he nevertheless finds them transformed through and through in many of their details.[23]

For this reason, we are precluded from saying what seems natural in many cases of scientific change, namely, that the new theory (or paradigm, if you like) explains the data better than its predecessor; for Kuhn, there is an absence of fixed or stable data, and only a paradigm-guided interpretation of the data, because of which we inevitably look at the data in a way that favours our own paradigm. Each protagonist, in a dispute between competing paradigms, can look at things only from his own point of view, but in doing this he will be unable to see things from his opponent's point of view. Because of the absence of fixed or stable data, there can be no mutual comparison or translation of paradigms in terms which would not assume the correctness and point of view of one of the competitors: 'the proponents of competing paradigms practice their trades in different worlds ... practicing in different worlds, the two groups of scientists see different things when they look from the same point in the same direction'.[24]

Most of what Kuhn says is true. Science is guided by basic theoretical and methodological assumptions that are treated as immune from criticism. If it were not, progress could never be made, because we only find out what is in a theory by seeing how it can deal with counter-evidence. (Remember the case of Uranus and Neptune.) Furthermore, observations are conditioned by our schemes of classification and expectation. Theories are not compared directly with nature, nor do our observations give us uninterpreted access to nature. The main point on which Kuhn is open to question is in his assumption that, in a mature science, the observational level is totally determined by classificatory schemes which are themselves part of a scientific paradigm. In everyday laboratory work, of course, they may well be. Only someone trained in the theoretical and practical assumptions of the work can 'read' what they see in microscopes as bacteria and the like, or see flashes on screens as evidence of sub-atomic particles. But, in a wider context, this point does not hold. We rightly expect scientific theories to have some ultimate applicability to the world of everyday observation, even if this is as attenuated an application as the seeing of certain patterns of light in the reflector of a telescope. Without such applications, however, the essential connection between the theories of science and our evolutionarily assured point of contact with the world will be lost.

Once the possibility of a type of observation independent of scientific paradigms is admitted, it also becomes possible to compare competing paradigms with respect to their performance in explaining the same data. Curiously, this possibility is implicit even in Kuhn's own example of the merits of the pendulum and constrained-fall accounts of the swinging stone, for we can observe and identify the swinging stone in these terms, without having to see it as either a pendulum or a case of constrained fall. Once we do this, we can ask the sorts of questions scientists do ask in comparing theories: which leads to new discoveries, which needs less protection against counter-evidence, which is more general, which is more integrated with other acceptable theories, which is simpler, and so on.

Even if the answers to these questions point in different directions, or are themselves indeterminate on some occasions, the possibility of raising them and answering them suggests that paradigm choice is not necessarily the non-rational switch of point of view Kuhn sometimes makes it out to be.

Relativism and the idea that we might each be imprisoned in our various conceptual schemes with no hope of a truly unbiased and rational assessment of competing claims to truth or knowledge or even of understanding them is obviously what underlies Kuhn's paradigm-centred analysis of science, and the reason why people find Kuhn so interesting, and react so violently for or against him. Relativism itself appears to be either a liberation from the shackles of authority and thought control (despite its stress on our mental imprisonment in a paradigm), or a doctrine of sublime and self-refuting irresponsibility. (Can one consistently be relativistic about one's own relativism? It all depends on one's point of view!) At any rate, these wordgames aside, at first sight relativism seems a heady doctrine and deciding on it the most important question there is for epistemology. But, on further reflection, the very considerations which give rise to the communication-breakdown version of relativism we are considering – the way all observation and experience is necessarily conditioned by our categories and expectations – turn out to reveal that type of relativism itself as a paper tiger.

If we did have a grip on the notion of an uninterpreted reality in the sense that such a notion actually played an effective role in our judgements and decisions, then there might be something in Kuhn's claim that there could be alternative and equally good conceptual schemes for dealing with the world with no rational way of choosing between them because of their incommensurability or lack of mutual translatability. But, although, despite Kuhn, we can be sure that there is only one world, we cannot stand above the world and people's sets of beliefs and declare that two different sets of beliefs amount to radically different, but alternative and equally valid conceptual schemes. The dualism between a conceptual scheme and a content (such as the world or experience) which the scheme organizes or fits, which is implied by such a doctrine, is not, in the end, tenable, as Davidson has argued in 'On the Very Idea of a Conceptual Scheme'.[25] The reason is that speaking of conceptual schemes fitting the totality of experience or the world or the facts (or anything you like) amounts to no more than saying that the sentences or statements going to make up the schemes in question are true (or largely true, as Davidson says, to allow for sharers of the same scheme to differ on details). Now, as we have suggested at the start of this chapter, our understanding of the notion of truth for a given language depends on our ability to state in our own language the conditions under which specific sentences of that language are true. This means neither more nor less than the ability to translate those sentences. But, of course, if we can translate them or, even more, if they are already expressed in our own language (or conceptual scheme), our language already contains the resources to express the other scheme. So the supposedly alternative, but incommensurable conceptual scheme is either something we can express in our own terms and go on to assess as we assess any other truth claims, or something to which we have no idea how to apply the notions of truth, or of fitting the facts, or experience or anything else, and hence have no grounds for considering as a candidate for the accolade 'alternative way of fitting experience'.

What Davidson's argument suggests is that there is something vacuous in entertaining the idea that there might be alternative, but untranslatable conceptual schemes. To speak of people having alternative beliefs, we must be able to understand, and hence to translate those beliefs. And as Davidson has suggested in many places, understanding another person's beliefs enough to be sure we disagree with him itself entails quite substantial amounts of agreement with him. Meaningful disagreement depends on agreement at many points, because meaningful disagreement implies at least that we understand what our opponent is saying. But understanding his words is part of a process of understanding him; attributing to him beliefs and intentions which make some sort of sense, given what we know of him and what he is in a position to know. In understanding others, as Davidson puts it, 'Charity is forced on us; whether we like it or not ... we must count them right on most matters'.[26] Of course, we do this sort of adjusting all the time in our dealings with others; if someone says something that seems flagrantly absurd, such as that there is a hippopotamus in the fridge, we realize after a while of observing our interlocutor and his behaviour that in his dialect 'hippopotamus' is a word for an orange.

So the radical thesis, suggested by Kuhn, that we are all locked in our own point of view on the world, and hence cannot compare ours with anyone else's equally valid point of view, fails. We could never be in a position to judge that others had concepts radically different from our own, as Davidson puts it. There are simply the sentences we hold true and the objects and states of affairs we are thereby committed to, and we cannot but assume in the main somewhat similar commitments on the part of others we are able to envisage as speaking a language or having beliefs, because envisaging them in this way involves understanding them, and this can be done only on a basis of general agreement.

But the general agreement on beliefs postulated by Davidson does not show that we are necessarily in a position to decide between incompatible theories about the world whose net effect in terms of common experiential or observational expectations is the same. The considerations adduced by Davidson against the sort of incommensurability between scientific theories proposed by Kuhn will not help us in deciding between theories which are translatable and commensurable, but which do equally well (or badly) in prediction and explanation of some given set of data which can be picked out and described in terms independent of both theories. Because of the general under-determination of theory by data in science, such possibilities are not to be dismissed lightly. It is perfectly possible that two theories could make exactly the same testable predictions, yet make incompatible claims about those bits of reality which are not regarded as directly accessible to observation or experiment. I have suggested a hypothetical example earlier (pp. 93-4); in the last chapter of *Meaning and the Moral Sciences* Putnam has developed an example of Goodman's making the same point. We are asked to imagine a universe consisting of a straight line. Now we know that there are two ways of looking at straight lines, one in which the line is made up of infinities of infinitely small parts (or points) and one in which there are only finitely extended line segments. These two stories can be shown to yield equivalent descriptions. Points can be analysed as constructions out of converging line segments, while line segments can be seen as constructions of points. Whatever we want to say about lines (and hence about this world) can be said in terms of either story, except what the line (or world) actually is! It *must* be one thing or the other, we feel, but what it is (basically points or basically extended segments) remains undecidable.

Scientific theories can be regarded as doing for our multi-dimensional world what each of our two stories did for the linear world, and it needs little imagination to realize that similar conundrums could arise in the big world. One response to this situation is to adopt an instrumentalist view of scientific theory, that is, to treat the inner or non-observational core of theories as non-referring, and to regard theories as simply instruments for predicting observable events. All talk of entities we cannot directly observe is simply a fiction, just a bridge enabling us to move from one observable event to another. There are a number of objections to a purely instrumental view of science, of which two are worth mentioning here. In the first place, it seems to depend on a clear distinction between what is observable and what is theoretical in science, which will not bear examination, even though, for purposes of testing between theories, we regard some data, such as the swinging stone, as our observational base, relative to higher levels of theory. Are we to regard all the theory-dependent data we observe in optical telescopes and microscopes as fictional? But if we allow these data as real and genuinely observed – and it seems absurd not to, given that telescopes and microscopes are only extensions of our ordinary sensory faculties – then why not allow in data which are yielded by only slightly more theoretical means, say, by electron microscopes or radio telescopes? This process of extending what is observed as opposed to what is merely postulated seems to admit of no natural end, but even apart from this, the instrumentalist assumption that what is given to us in our senses is itself directly observed and simply and unquestionably there in nature is open to question. If theories mentioning unobservable forces and particles help us to cope with experience by leading to true predictions, at other levels of experience, why not, as Davidson's argument implied, simply accept it as true, for in the end we accept what is implied by our observational levels of experience as true on very similar grounds (that it contributes to a coherent and credible picture of the world)?

This brings us to the second and more general objection to instrumentalism. Science, we regard as being simply the systematic continuation of the process of investigation into the world begun with our gene-linked expectations and sensory experience. Our senses and the world picture they reveal 'work'; so what they tell us we regard as real. Equally, if scientific theories work, we should regard what they tell us as true. Moreover, if a scientific theory with great predictive power and accuracy is not true, its success must be totally mysterious. It will be claimed that a realistic view of scientific theory – that scientific theories are to be regarded as telling us about the underlying structure of the world, and do indeed sometimes do so – explains the actual success of scientific theory in a way that an instrumentalist view cannot hope to.

This defence of a realistic attitude to scientific theory, however, itself raises two difficult problems. First, the history of science is at least a bit like Kuhn's picture of it; a progression through fairly large-scale revolutions. A Newtonian in the nineteenth century might fairly confidently and fairly rationally have deployed the argument of the last paragraph to defend the truth and reality of a Newtonian world picture as at least a good approximation to the way things are. But how much of the inner mechanism of the Newtonian world picture remains? Relativity and subsequent theories give us the true Newtonian observational predictions, but how much else remains? A serious realism about scientific theory will have to show how science in some sense preserves the explanations as well as the true predictions of outworn but partially successful paradigms. Moreover, the one lesson to be learnt from the history of science is that no theory or paradigm ever holds the field for ever, which might make us uneasy about too confidently advancing realistic claims for our own current theories.

It would no doubt be said that what should actually make us more uneasy about advancing claims for our own current theories than the reason just given is that they do not actually yield true predictions in all cases. But even if they did, this would still not get round the fundamental problem for realism in science raised by the possibility of alternative theories yielding equivalent descriptions. Are there really points or really just line segments? Are there really fields of force in the universe or just particles acting at a distance? It is important to notice that this problem would arise even if we did not actually have alternatives, for the problem is due to the under-determination of theory by data, not to the existence of actual competitors. It might be said that we need not worry about it, because we are never likely actually to have one theory that satisfies all the requirements or operational constraints of scientific theories, let alone two. As Putnam himself suggested (cf. p. 91 above), if a theory satisfies all the operational constraints on theories, saying that it might *really* be false verges on the unintelligible. Some might also, though perhaps unwisely, take some heart from the thought that a theory that fits in with our observations and our intuitions about simplicity and credibility has some evolutionary backing, in that our senses and intuitions have presumably been developed through our interaction with nature. On the other hand, none of this rules out the theoretical possibility of alternative versions of the world and their theoretical possibility is all that is needed to make the point that no one version of the world is forced on us by the data alone. If we accept that talk of a version fitting the world or satisfying the operational constraints amounts to saying that the theory in question is true, can there be alternative true descriptions of the world? If so we see from yet another angle that at the level of theoretical science the significance of a sentence and its truth must be assessed relative to the theory and system in which it figures, rather than in isolation in direct comparison with the world. Have we now reached a position in which the very inaccessibility of the world except through our theories and observations means that we have to entertain the possibility not, it is true, of untranslatable and incommensurable conceptual schemes and different worlds, but of different and, at a deep level, incompatible versions of the one world, all with an equal title to truth? There just is no way to judge theories except relative to other beliefs and any given set of beliefs will be consistent with differing theoretical accounts of the phenomena that make those beliefs acceptable. Nevertheless, this does not show that there might not be something about the world, way beyond our powers of observation, which makes one of those accounts actually false. I have argued throughout for the existence of a world apart from our experience of it, and will suggest (pp. 196–7) that we need a verification-independent theory of truth and meaning to account for the workings of our language. How far, though, this realism should be pursued into the theoretical outreaches of science, into saying that empirically equivalent but mutually inconsistent explanations of the same data cannot all equally truly represent the one world, remains one of the most difficult questions confronting epistemologists and philosophers of science.

Chapter Three

Logic and Language

Philosophers are interested in the twin topics of logic and language because they are interested in human thought and its relationship to the world. Language is the vehicle for human thought *par excellence*. Logic is the systematic inquiry into argument and inference; and thought, if it is to be rational, relies on argument and inference. A philosophical interest in language will have overlaps with that of a linguist, but will be oriented rather differently. Linguists will be interested in the structure of particular languages, and in comparisons between different languages. A philosopher may well take a particular language, such as English, as the focus of his study. But he will not be interested in the details of English, except in so far as these details throw light on the general conditions any language and its speakers will have to fulfil in order to say and communicate things of various sorts about the world and, ultimately, to have thoughts of particular sorts about the world. Equally, while philosophers will be interested in the formal presentations of particular types of inference which are to be found in the study of logic, their particular focus of interest will be on the conclusions that might be drawn from such formalizations about human language and thought.

In this chapter I will begin by saying a little about logic, as it is currently understood by philosophers. I will then examine how the notions of naming and predication which arise in logic might be applied to natural language, before going on to consider various influential ideas on what is involved in understanding a natural language, and the place of rules or conventions in language and argument.

Logic

Logic has always had a central role in philosophy. The reason for this is that logic is, among other things, the study of valid argument; philosophy is essentially argumentative, relying as it does on discriminations between good and bad arguments.

Valid arguments are those in which the truth of the conclusion of a set of premises is guaranteed by the truth of those premises. Thus, it follows from

(1) All men are mortal

and

(2) Socrates is a man

that

(3) Socrates is mortal.

There is no set of circumstances in which (1) and (2) could be true and (3) false.

Valid arguments do not need to have true conclusions. One of the premises might be false, or even ridiculous. For example,

(4) All pigs can fly

(5) Jemima is a pig

therefore,

(6) Jemima can fly.

The validity of this argument consists in the fact that if (4) and (5) are true, then (6) cannot be false. Because of the validity of the argument, we know that if the conclusion is false, then one or more of the premises is false too.

If valid arguments can sometimes have false conclusions, true conclusions can sometimes appear as the conclusions of invalid arguments. For example, someone might invalidly infer from

(7) All pigs are mortal

and

(8) All animals are mortal

that

(9) All pigs are animals.

That this argument is invalid becomes clear if in (8) we replace 'animals' with 'fish'. 'All fish are mortal' is both true and similar in form to 'All animals are mortal', but the conclusion of this new argument, 'All pigs are fish' is false. An argument of the type (7)–(9) does not always produce a true conclusion from true premises.

Logicians attempt to make explicit what the validity of valid arguments consists in. In the two examples of valid arguments just considered, it may seem obvious that there is a common structure or form running through the two arguments, which accounts for the validity of the arguments. The common form might be represented schematically as

(10) All *S* are *P*

(11) *A* is *S*

hence,

(12) *A* is *P*

Any set of sentences with this structure would constitute a valid argument. Logic confines attention to those arguments that are valid in virtue of specific formal or structural relationships between the sentences that constitute the premises and conclusions of the arguments.

In order to study these formal-logical relationships between sentences, logicians replace those parts of sentences whose content is not directly relevant to the validity or invalidity of the types of argument being examined with symbols, which mark schematically the pattern of occurrence of those parts. If the symbolic schemata (10)–(12) correctly represent the form of the arguments in (1)–(3) and (4)–(6), we would be saying that the bits about pigs and men, flight and mortality are irrelevant to the validity of the arguments involved.

Extending this idea logicians have found it useful to invent artificial formal languages in which to study inference. The advantage of this procedure is that in a formal language, all the underlying rules and interpretations can be made explicit and the notion of proof for that language can be stated as a set of formal, quasi-mathematical rules. Moreover, it can be useful, and simpler, to concentrate on certain aspects of language for a time, in abstraction from other elements present in actual speech. The disadvantage of the study of formal language from the point of view of attempting to understand the thoughts and arguments expressible in a natural language are that a formal language will inevitably be simpler than a natural language in various respects, so that a question is bound to arise concerning whether the formal language really represents the thoughts in which we are ultimately interested.

Formal logic dates from the time of Aristotle, but modern logic and the use of artificial languages in logic really began with the work of Gottlob Frege (1848–1925). Frege's approach to logic still forms the basis of our present understanding of the subject, and, as we shall see, his analysis of the structure of sentences has carried over into the philosophy of language.

We can begin by briefly considering what is known as the logic of propositions. This is the study of those arguments whose validity depends on units of thought (or language) no smaller than a proposition (or sentence). We will thus be considering, among other things, relationships which obtain between compound propositions or sentences, and the simpler sentences from which they are made up. For example,

(13) John came to tea and Mary left
can be seen as the result of conjoining

(14) John came to tea

and

(15) Mary left.

If we represent (14) by '*p*' and (15) by '*q*' and use '&' as the symbol for conjunction, we could represent (13) as

(16) *p* & *q*.

Propositional logic deals with the ways in which whole sentences can be joined by what are called sentence (or sentential) connectives, such as 'and', 'if ... then ...', 'either ... or ...', and so on. 'Not', when applied to a whole sentence, is also a sentential connective.

In addition to dealing with whole sentences, propositional logic as conceived by Frege operates on the assumption that every sentence is either true or false. Thus, if some sentence '*p*' is true, its negation 'not-*p*' (usually written '-*p*') will be false, but if '*p*' is not true, then '-*p*' will be true. The possibility of a sentence being neither true nor false is not allowed for in so-called classical logic, although logicians have subsequently worked on systems in which sentences not regarded as being definitely either true or false are allowed for.

It is possible to devise formal languages to represent the ways in which complex sentences can be constructed out of simple ones. One such language might consist of

   (i)   symbols for sentences: *p*, *q*, *r*, *s*, ...,
   (ii) symbols for connectives: -, &, v, →, ≡,
   (iii) brackets: ( ).

Brackets are for punctuating complex sentences. On the significance of the connectives, '-*p*' corresponds to 'not-*p*', and '*p* & *q*' to '*p* and *q*', as we have already seen. '*p* v *q*' will mean 'either *p* or *q* or both'. '*p* → *q*' has no precise ordinary language equivalent; although it is called the material conditional, and sometimes read as 'if *p*, then *q*', it is more accurately read as 'either not-*p* or *q* or both'. '*p* ≡ *q*'. is the material biconditional, and sometimes read as '*p* if and only if *q*'. In fact its sense is that if '*p*' is true so is '*q*', and if '*p*' is false, so is '*q*', that '*p*' and '*q*' have the same 'truth-value', in other words.

It is natural to ask why we are working with this somewhat unfamiliar set of connectives. (Actually, we could work with only '-' and '→', because all the others mentioned (and others not here listed) can be defined taking '-' and '→' as primitive.* Nevertheless, the ones listed are the ones commonly used in logic, while not all ordinary language sen-

---

*The sets consisting of '&' and '-', and of 'v' and '-', can also be used as primitive, and so can others, consisting of connectives not mentioned here.

tential connectives are regarded as desirable.) The reason for the choice of connectives is that classical propositional logic assumes what is called truth-functionality. That is to say, it deals only with those sentences whose truth or falsity (or what Frege called their truth-value) is wholly determined by the truth and falsity of component sentences. (13) is truth-functional; its truth-value depends entirely on the truth-values of (14) and (15).

A sentence that is not truth-functional is

(17) John believes Mary will come.

The truth-value of (17) is not determined one way or the other by the truth-value of the component

(18) Mary will come.

John could still believe that Mary will come whether it is true that she will come or not.

Generally speaking, sentences expressing people's pyschological attitudes (hopes, fears, beliefs, etc.) are non-truth-functional. So are most ordinary language uses of 'if ... then ...'. For example,

(19) If the bomb goes up tomorrow, then we will all be killed

and

(20) If Alpha Centauri explodes tomorrow, then we will all be killed.

Let us assume the antecedent sentences in both cases are false; we will still want to say that while (19) is true, (20) is false. Something other than the truth-values of the component sentences in (19) and (20), then, are determining their truth-values, something about particular causal relationships, presumably. Other important contexts which are not truth-functional involve the use of such modifiers as 'necessarily' and 'possibly'. To say that the truth of some sentence is necessary or possible is not at all the same thing as to say that it is true or false. In a sentence stating that it is necessarily true that all bachelors are male, we can discern the simpler sentence

(21) All bachelors are male.

But though the more complex 'It is necessarily true that all bachelors are male' is true, this is not simply due to the fact that (21) is true. After all,

(22) All creatures with hearts are creatures with kidneys

is true, but not necessarily true.

Different logics have to be developed to deal with non-truth-functional contexts. Nevertheless, classical propositional logic can cope with every genuinely truth-functional mode of connection of sentences. Not only that, but classical propositional logic has the important logical properties of being consistent, complete and decidable. This I will now explain.

We begin with a formal language similar to the one outlined in clauses (i)–(iii) above, but including only one sentence symbol, 'p' and a dash (') to generate infinitely many different sentence symbols, 'p'', 'p''', 'p'''', etc., and only two connectives, '$-$' and '$\rightarrow$'. Assume we know nothing about the significance of the connectives, such as the fact mentioned earlier that '$-p$' is true just when 'p' is false. What we will have now is a purely formal language, call it P, with no interpretation. We can now specify a set of axioms and rules of inference for this language. The axioms will be simply strings of symbols, such as

(23) $p' \rightarrow (p'' \rightarrow p')$

We will specify which strings of symbols are to count as axioms by means of specific axiom-schemata, which will signify that any string of symbols of a given form is to be regarded as an axiom. We can express an axiom-schema saying that if 'A', 'B' and 'C' represent formulas of P, then the following is an axiom-schema

(24) A $\rightarrow$ (B$\rightarrow$A)

From (24), it is easy to see that (23) is an axiom. Our other two axiom-schemata will be

(25) (A$\rightarrow$ (B$\rightarrow$C)) $\rightarrow$ ((A$\rightarrow$B) $\rightarrow$ (A$\rightarrow$C))

and

(26) ($-$A$\rightarrow$$-$B) $\rightarrow$ (B$\rightarrow$A)

Our system actually needs just one rule of inference, namely, if A and B are formulas of P, then B is an immediate consequence of any pair of formulas A and A$\rightarrow$B. The formal calculus that results from applying this rule of inference and the three axiom-schemata (24)–(26) to P will be called PS.

A proof in PS will be a string of formulas of P, such that each one is either an axiom, or a consequence of two preceding formulas in the string by the rule of inference. A theorem of PS will be the last formula of any proof.

The formal system PS is consistent, and this can be proved. By this, I mean that it can be shown that if we can derive A as a theorem of PS, then $-$A will not be so derivable. Remember however that we have not yet given any interpretation of the language P, even to its sentential connectives, '$-$' and '$\rightarrow$'. All that can be meant so far by talk of the consistency of PS is that the property of being a theorem in PS cannot be possessed by a formula $-$A if it is possessed by A. In order to see why the consistency of PS is important, and what talk of its completeness means, we will have to move from the purely syntactic approach of specifying formal rules for the manipulation of strings of symbols to the semantic level.

The language *P* and its formulas have so far been treated as meaning-less. The truth of a given formula or its meaning have not been in question. The definitions given of proof and theorem made no reference to truth, nor were the axioms presented as self-evident truths or anything of that sort. It would, indeed, have been quite wrong to do so, because the connectives had been given no interpretation; we did not specify the circumstances in which formulas of the form A→B or even –A were to be regarded as true or false. As they are meaningless strings of symbols, we could, of course, give any number of different interpretations to the elements of *P*, but the semantics we will now give corresponds to that I gave informally in first introducing the connectives.

Semantics is basically a matter of specifying the conditions under which a so far uninterpreted formula is to be regarded as true or false. We will now read a formula of the form –A as true if and only if A is false, and one of the form A→B as true if and only if either A is false or B is true. We can represent the semantics for A→B by means of a 'truth table', in which the various possible truth and falsity combinations for A and B are shown to determine the truth of the whole formula:

A	→	B
T	T	T
T	F	F
F	T	T
F	T	F

The first horizontal line of 'T's and 'F's says that when A and B are both true (signified by the 'T's directly below A and B), the formula A→B is true, the second that when A is true and B false, A→B is false, and so on.

Under the interpretation just given for the connectives, we find that the rule of inference of *PS* transmits truth from premises A and A→B to conclusion B, and that the three axiom-schemata (24)–(26) will always yield truths, whatever combinations of truth-values the component sentences have. This can be shown by means of truth tables; for example, for (24):

A	→	(B	→	A)
T	T	T	T	T
T	T	F	T	T
F	T	T	F	F
F	T	F	T	F

(The vertical column of 'T's under the *first* arrow gives the truth-values of the whole formula for the various truth/falsity possibilities of A and

B. In working out a truth table, one starts with the bits in brackets first, here (B→A), and leaves the unbracketed parts to the end.) When a formula comes out true on every possible truth combination of its components (i.e. when there are all 'T's in the last vertical column to be worked out) it is called logically valid, or, in the case of the propositional calculus, tautologous. It means, in effect, that this combination of symbols will always turn out true. So the axioms (24)–(26) are tautologies. From the tautologous nature of the axioms and the truth-preserving nature of the rule of inference, it follows pretty directly that, on our interpretation, *PS* will not yield both a formula and its negation as theorems, since both could not be tautologous. *PS* will thus be semantically 'sound', on our interpretation. But it will also be consistent, according to our earlier (syntactic) definition of consistency. We will have shown that for no formula A of *P* can both A and −A be theorems of *PS*. (All theorems of *PS* have a certain property (true on our interpretation), while A and −A cannot both have that property.)

It is possible to give a purely syntactic proof of the consistency of *PS*, without using interpretations of the symbols of *P* (or so-called model-theoretic means). Instead of assigning truth-values to our sentences and giving truth tables to the connectives, we could assign uninterpreted '1's and '0's where we had previously put 'T's and 'F's respectively. Thus we could give a table for the symbol '−':

A	−A
1	0
0	1

Syntactic 'tautologyhood' would be when the final column in a 1–0 table for a formula had all '1's in it. We would then be able to show as in our semantic proof of consistency that all the axioms and theorems were syntactic tautologies, and that from our table for '−', if any formula A is a syntactic tautology (always has '1' associated with it), −A will not be (it will have '0' associated with it). So −A cannot be a theorem. Hence *PS* is consistent. This syntactic proof of consistency obviously apes the model-theoretic proof; clearly our main philosophical interest in proving a system's consistency rests on its model-theoretical implications.

Completeness in a formal system has a number of senses. Syntactically, it is often held to mean that for each formula A in a system, either A or −A is a theorem. In this sense *PS* is not complete; '*p*'→*p*'' ', for example, is not a theorem, nor is '−(*p*'→*p*'')', although it is complete in another syntactic sense, namely, that no unprovable formula can be added to its axiom-schemata without inconsistency. But the philosophically interesting sense of completeness will be the semantic one. This is that every tautology or logically valid formula of the propositional calculus is derivable as a theorem from our axioms and rule of inference. This can be proved in a number of ways, though the proofs are not easy, and I will not even attempt to sketch them here.

A third important feature of the propositional calculus, in addition to its consistency and completeness, is that it is decidable. It is, in other words, possible to decide whether any formula of *P* follows as a theorem from the axioms and rule of inference of *PS*. We cannot necessarily do this directly – the formula might be too complicated and our minds too obtuse to derive it step by step as a theorem – but the truth-table method does provide a mechanical method for analysing all the possible truth combinations within a given formula, and establishing, for each combination, whether it is true or not, and hence whether a formula is tautologous or not. So the 'tautologyhood' and hence 'theoremhood' in *PS* of any formula of *P* can be revealed by its truth table.

Although I initially treated *P* as a purely formal language and *PS* is to be regarded as uninterpreted, the philosophical interest of *P* and *PS* is presumably due to their applicability to natural languages through interpreting the symbols. Frege, in his pioneering work on the sentential connectives, treated them as indicating the circumstances in which given compound sentences are to be regarded as true or false. Thus, for example, the symbol '&' as in 'p' & p''' (equivalent to the primitive '$- (p' \rightarrow -p'')$') would mean that 'p' & p''' was true if and only if 'p''' was true and 'p''' was true; in other words, '&' means 'and'. The axioms Frege actually worked with, or some other suitable set, such as the simpler ones deriving from (24)–(26), would be chosen in part because they seemed self-evident enough when interpreted in the normal way. Wittgenstein, on the other hand, in his *Tractatus Logico-Philosophicus*, preferred to base propositional logic on truth tables – a method to whose development he contributed – rather than on axioms, not only because truth tables provided a mechanical method for deciding whether or not a proposition was a logical truth, but also because they did away with the implication that some logical truths, in being treated as axioms, were more basic or obvious than others. A further important point emerges clearly from the use of truth tables, and that is the way that logical truths such as (24) are true, whatever the truth-values of the constituent propositions. They are true, in other words, in all possible worlds. By contrast, in an empirical or factual proposition, one whose truth or falsity depends on the way the real world is, in which a world is put together experimentally, as Wittgenstein put it, a state of affairs is indicated which is true in some possible world, but not in all possible worlds, and not necessarily in this one. This would come out in the truth table for such a proposition in which the final column of truth-values would include a mixture of 'T's and 'F's.

Whatever the comparative merits of the axiomatic formalization of the propositional calculus as opposed to the truth-table approach, it is clear that we need something stronger than a system of propositional logic if we are to hope to account for more than a tiny fraction of the arguments of ordinary discourse. Not even the validity of syllogisms (1)–(3) and (4)–(6) can be made apparent so long as our analysis stays on the level of complete sentences. Frege's mathematization of logic, however, continued into the internal structure of sentences, and it was here above all that he made a distinctive advance over all previous logical systems, which had concentrated on the grammatical subject–predicate form of sentences, assimilating sentences of the form

(27) Jones is bald

(28) Some philosopher is bald

and

(29) All philosophers are bald.

Subject–predicate logic also had problems in dealing with expressions of generality, such as 'someone', 'no one' and 'everyone', particularly when there was more than one in a sentence, as in

(30) Everyone loves someone.

Frege's approach to predication showed a huge difference in form between (27), on the one hand, and (28) and (29), on the other, despite their grammatical similarity. His insight enabled him to solve the problems regarding expressions of generality which had vexed logicians since the time of Aristotle.

According to Frege, and to classical logic subsequent to Frege, when we say that Jones is bald, as in (27), what we are doing is predicating the incomplete expression (or predicate, in the logical sense) '— is bald' of the individual named by 'Jones'. Whether (27) is true or false will depend on whether Jones does or does not have the property indicated by the predicate (or satisfy that predicate). Using a typical notation for modern predicate logic, we can symbolize the proper name 'Jones' by 'a', and the predicate '— is bald' by 'F' and write (27) as

(31) Fa

When we come to (28), (29) and (30), however, there is no individual being picked out by name. In these cases, Frege will see one or more logical predicates being applied to the whole universe of particular individuals, so as to make assertions to the effect that some or all members of that universe satisfy the predicate or predicates in question. What (28) says is that in our universe (or domain) of individuals, there is or exists some individual that satisfies the predicate '— is a philosopher' and also satisfies the predicate '— is bald'. (29) on the other hand, on the Fregean analysis, says that in our domain of individuals any object satisfies the predicate '— is bald'.

In symbolic notation, we can write what is called the existential quantifier – the device by which we indicate that some individual, x, exists in our domain that satisfies some predicate thus: '$(\exists x)$'. Assuming our domain is the domain of people, 'Some people are bald' will then come out as '$(\exists x) Fx$', to be read as 'There is some individual x, such that x is bald'. The universal quantifier, 'everything x is such that ...' is written '(x)', so 'Everyone is bald' will be '$(x) Fx$', 'Every individual x is such that x is bald'. Using this notation for quantifiers, and symbolizing '— is a philosopher' by 'G', we can write (28) as

$\quad$ (32) $(\exists x) (Gx \,\&\, Fx)$

and (29) as

$\quad$ (33) $(x) (Gx \rightarrow Fx)$

It might be asked why (33) is conditional in form, 'everything x is such that *if* x is G, x is F'. The reason is that the sense of (29) is not that every individual in our universe is both a philosopher and bald (which is what '$(x) (Gx \,\&\, Fx)$' would say), but only that anything that is a philosopher is also bald. This thought is captured by (33). (33) does not say that anything actually is a philosopher. If we wanted to assert that as well, and we may feel that this is part of the English (29), we would have to add a clause to that effect ('$(\exists x) Gx$').

In (32) and (33), and in my informal expositions of the quantifiers, we have been speaking of the individual(s) x such that ..., and of all individuals x such that ... The 'x' in these expressions, or so-called variable, has not really played a role so far, and what is expressed by the quantifiers in (32) and (33) could have been achieved without use of a variable. The point of using variables emerges, though, when we turn to sentences like (30), in which we are saying that one group of individuals in our domain satisfies one condition, while another group, not necessarily the same, satisfies another. In (30) we have a relational term, or two-place predicate, 'loves'. In 'John loves Mary' John loves and Mary is loved, but it is not necessarily the case that John is loved or that Mary loves or even, if these contingencies obtain, that John is loved by Mary. So who is doing the loving and who is loved makes a difference.

In (30), we are not saying that everybody loves everybody, or even that somebody (not even Princess Diana) is loved by everybody. In order to bring out what is involved in (30), the Fregean analysis will have to use two quantifiers, to express 'everybody' and 'somebody', respectively, and two different variables in conjunction with each quantifier to show which quantifier applies to which bit of the loving relationship. Informally, and assuming that our domain is the domain of people, we could express (30) by saying that for all individuals x, there is some individual y, such that x loves y. If we take 'R——' to symbolize 'loves' (where the first blank is the space for the lover and the second for the loved), (30) will come out as

(34) $(x)(\exists y) Rxy$

If we wanted to say that somebody is loved by everybody, this would be expressed by

(35) $(\exists y)(x) Rxy$

The relative position of the quantifiers is thus important; the earlier quantifiers are read as governing the later ones. In (34) the condition of loving somebody is being predicated of everybody, while in (35) there is someone whom it is true that everyone loves.

A formal language for predicate logic will, then, add variables, quantifiers and predicate letters to the elements of the propositional calculus. Names may also be added, and normally are, though they are for formal purposes in principle replaceable in the predicate calculus. This can be done either by replacing occurrences of a name ('Socrates') by some predicate uniquely true of Socrates ('— is a hemlock-drinking Athenian philosopher'), or by introducing a symbol for identity ('=') and transforming a sentence such as a 'Socrates is wise' into 'There exists an individual x, such that x is identical with Socrates and x is wise'. '— is identical with Socrates' ('= Socrates') will be treated here like a predicate such as '— is wise'. As we shall see in the next section, however, we cannot apply a language to the world and dispense totally with devices denoting specific individuals in the world, nor are names actually understood as equivalent to descriptions.

Predicate logic can be formalized by means of its own axioms, and the interpretation of its symbols can be given by means of a formal semantics, specifying rigorously the contributions the various elements of the language (such as quantifiers, variables, predicates, names and connectives) make to the truth or falsity of whole sentences. Thus, for example, we will be told that '$(x)Fx$' is true on the interpretation if and only if every object in the domain has the property ascribed to it by

'*F*', that '*Fa*' is true if and only if the object denoted by '*a*' has the property ascribed to it by '*F*', and so on. An important assumption within predicate logic, known as the principle of extensionality, is that when an individual is referred to by means of some singular term, such as a name or a description, replacing that singular term with some other singular term which also refers to the same individual will not alter the truth-value of any sentence in which the original term appears. Schematically, extensionality may be stated as implying that if '... *a* ...' and '*a* = *b*' are true, then so is '... *b* ...', where '*a*' and '*b*' are names or descriptions of the same individual. Extensionality plays a similar role in predicate logic to truth-functionality in propositional logic, which may be stated as implying that if '... *p* ...' and '*p* ≡ *q*' are true, then so is '... *q* ...', where '*p*' and '*q*' are propositions or sentences.

Extensionality tells us, for example, that if 'Socrates is wise' is true and Socrates is the Master of Plato, then 'The Master of Plato is wise' must also be true. But this substituting of terms that refer to the same individual without changing the truth-values of the relevant sentences does not hold good when we are talking about people's beliefs or about logical or mathematical necessities. Jones believes that $3 \times 3 = 9$ and it is also necessarily true that $3 \times 3 = 9$. But even though 'The number of planets in the solar system = 9' is true, Jones may not know this and so fail to believe that $3 \times 3 = $ the number of planets, nor is it necessarily the case that $3 \times 3 = $ the number of the planets. The axiom systems for predicate logic can be shown to be consistent and complete, but there is no method for predicate logic comparable to truth tables, and there is no mechanical way of telling whether an arbitrary formula in the predicate calculus is a theorem or not (though there are methods for deciding whether certain specific types of formulas are theorems or not).

Logic may be the study of argument, but it remains a difficult matter to decide how far the propositional and predicate logics throw light on the thoughts which underlie the use of natural languages, and the arguments expressible in those languages. There are at least three aspects to this question. First there is the extent to which the interpretations given of the connectives and of names, predicates, variables and the rest correspond to anything in ordinary language. I hope to have shown already that there are connections in these areas that can profitably be drawn, and in succeeding sections we will examine in more detail what is involved in naming expressions and in predication, in so far as we find examples of such things in ordinary language. There is no doubt, though, that philosophers interested in uncovering the thoughts expressible in natural languages have been strongly influenced by the concepts Frege and his successors have used in developing formal logic and have sought to analyse ordinary speech in terms of similar structures.

But, and this is a second major problem for the application of formal logic to natural languages, there are of course many idioms of ordinary language, and hence possibilities of thought and argument, that are not captured by Fregean logic. We have already seen how that logic applies only to truth-functional and extensional contexts and constructions, and it is an open question as to whether to deal with other types of context by expanding our logical syntax to include in it non-extensional operators and contexts, such as 'necessarily' or 'believes', or whether to keep the strict Fregean syntax, and try to capture the problematic notions by means of an expanded ontology. Some, taking the latter course, have hoped to account for the logic of modality (possibility, necessity and impossibility) by developing the notion of possible worlds. A necessary truth will be one that is true in all possible worlds, a statement that is possibly true, one that is true in some possible worlds, and one that is impossible, one that is false in all possible worlds. It has been suggested that the logic of statements of psychological attitude, belief and the like, and of causal necessity, could also be illuminated by talk of possible worlds. If I believe A, then A is true in all possible worlds consistent with my beliefs, while statements of causal law are those which are true in all worlds similar in structure to our own, but not in worlds different in structure. The notion of a possible world used in these developments stems from Leibniz's view of a necessary truth as one which is true in all possible worlds and of a contingent truth as true only in some or one of the worlds God could have created. Thus, '$3 \times 3 = 9$' is true in all possible worlds, whereas, 'The number of planets in the solar system $= 9$' is not. The advantage of possible-world analyses of the classes of statements just considered is that we dispense with talk of what is necessarily or contingently true, or believed or hoped to be true in various ways, in favour of what simply is true in various possible worlds. So saying '$3 \times 3 = 9$' is necessarily true means that '$3 \times 3 = 9$' is true in all possible worlds. By contrast, saying that there might not have been nine planets means that there are some possible worlds in which the solar system has more than or less than nine planets. The statements that go to describe the various possible worlds considered will be regarded as operating truth-functionally, and extensionally, and thus brought within the scope of Fregean analyses by an extensionalizing of syntax. On the other hand, the nature and existence of possible worlds and of the individuals in them, and of their relationships to the individuals in this, the actual, world are matters of dispute, and, further, it is not clear that possible-worlds idioms always succeed in illuminating the logic of the areas of discourse in question. Certainly there is no general consensus among philosophers and logicians that possible-world analyses succeed or even what form they should take.

In 1967, Donald Davidson spoke of Frege's 'massive contribution' to understanding the logic of our language, but went on to list 'a few' of the areas where Fregean analyses in terms of names, predicates, quantifiers, variables and truth-functional connectives did not do the job: these included counterfactuals, statements about probabilities and causal relations, statements attributing psychological attitudes, mass terms (like 'fire', 'water', 'snow'), verbs of action and adverbs.[1] Davidson has himself attempted to clarify the logic of certain adverbial constructions and in closing this section on logic, it would be worth looking briefly at this attempt, as it illustrates both the limitations of the analysis of sentences in terms of predicates satisfied by individuals such as objects or persons, and has interesting metaphysical consequences.

The problem with the adverbial expressions Davidson considers is seen by him as really a problem about the logical form of action sentences, and the inferences we can draw from them. Davidson's own example (which like most of the other examples in the rest of this section is taken from his *Essays on Actions and Events*,[2] particularly Chapters 6–8) is about one Jones, who butters a piece of toast, slowly, deliberately, in the bathroom, with a knife, at midnight. People familiar with the Fregean style will tend to regard a sentence describing this event as being decomposable into the name 'Jones' and predicate, '— buttered a piece of toast, slowly, deliberately, in the bathroom, with a knife, at midnight'. Or '*F*' for short. An immediate drawback with this analysis is that we would regard the sentence 'Jones buttered a piece of toast' as being a logical consequence of our original sentence, but this fact is obscured by treating '*F*' as a single undecomposable predicate. '— buttered a piece of toast' would have to be regarded as another predicate altogether, represented, say, by '*G*', and the fact that '*F*' was in essence but an adverbial modification of '*G*' would be obscured. A second problem, though connected to the first, is that as every adverbial modification of a given predicate would be a new predicate altogether, and as there are endless possible such modifications, it becomes quite obscure as to how we ever learn a natural language, such as English, in which we can and do easily modify verbs by adverbs and adverbial phrases.

Davidson's solution to this problem involves taking events as well as things as basic particulars, and regarding them as having properties. Thus 'Shem kicked Shaun' will come out as:

(36) (∃x) (Kicked (Shem, Shaun) x)

(or something approximating to 'There is an event x, such that x is a kicking of Shem by Shaun'). The inferential connection which exists between 'Shem kicked Shaun' and 'Shem kicked Shaun in the knee' would be brought out in the analysis of the second sentence as

(37) (∃x) (Kicked (Shem, Shaun, x) & In (the knee, x)

On such a reading (37) formally entails (36), in the same way that we could infer '(∃x) Fx' from '(∃x)Fx & Gx'.

A consequence of Davidson's analysis of verbal constructions is that we have to recognize a basic ontological category of events, and this raises the question of how we might individuate events. The event that was a kicking of Shaun by Shem might also have been an insulting of Shem by Shaun. That is not too difficult to accept, but was it also the start of the family feud, the manifestation of Shem's hitherto latent sibling rivalry, the first thing of note to happen at Rachael's wedding reception, and so on? How do we decide such questions? Moreover, events, unlike the concrete individuals we are familiar with in space and time, often appear to be difficult to pin down in space and time. Is the Battle of Borodino an event, and if so, when and where did it begin and end? Or is it a lot of smaller events, as Tolstoy insisted? Perhaps these difficulties should not be exaggerated. After all, we speak happily of large-scale individuals such as nations, composed of multitudes of smaller individuals, such as persons. Just as the criteria of individuation for nations are different from and in some ways vaguer than those for persons, so those for battles are different from and possibly vaguer than those for individual strikings, orderings, woundings, firings, killings and so on. Davidson's own proposal is that we say that an event is the same under one description as it is under some other descriptions if the causes and effects are the same. So we can identify Shem's kicking of Shaun at a given time with Shaun's being insulted at that time and very possibly with the start of the family feud, and so on. The event that was a kicking of Shaun by Shem had the same causes and the same effects as the event that was an insulting of Shaun by Shem (even though what made the kicking an insult rather than a bit of harmless horseplay may have had its roots in Shaun's over-sensitive personality), and, similarly, it was the start of the feud (though for it to be the start of the feud it had to be an event in a certain family's tortuous history).

Although the causal criterion may enable us to settle some of the questions involved in individuating events, the fact that events are here being individuated through their causes and their effects demonstrates the extent to which Davidson's proposal makes events metaphysically fundamental. For causes and effects are themselves, at least in a vast number of cases, events. (The kicking was caused by a heavy-handed remark, and brought on another event, a heavy-handed blow, and so on.) Davidson can avoid a charge of crude circularity here, as Mark Platts has pointed out, by showing that while the identification and re-identification – and hence the identity – of material objects depends on locating them spatio-temporally, our spatiotemporal framework itself rests on our identification and re-identification of other material objects.[3] This type of circularity is inevitable, given that material objects are admitted as a basic category of particulars, irreducible to anything else, and Davidson could claim the same for events. Indeed, he would presumably wish to do so; so this is a way of bringing out the extent of his commitment to events as basic, which is also, incidentally, implicit in his analysis of causal relations (cf. above, p. 68).

Davidson's event analysis may show us how to deal with Jones's buttering of the toast, so long as it was in the bathroom and at midnight and with a knife, but what about its being slow and deliberate? The trouble with 'slow' is that, like 'big' or 'clever', it is an attributive adjective. A slow plane may nevertheless be a fast mode of transport; a slow buttering of the toast may still involve fast movements of the hand. So things and events are not fast or slow in themselves, but only relative to descriptions, and this is a problem for Davidson's analysis because he does not want two predicates, one for buttering and another for buttering slowly. Of perhaps more general importance is Jones's deliberate buttering, for Davidson denies that doing an action deliberately or intentionally is to do it in a particular way, or to mark out a manner of doing it. It is rather to see the event in question as an action of an agent, having a special relation to the agent's beliefs and attitudes, and this is something we will explore further in Chapter 4, although it is worth remarking here that putting matters like this gives rise to the problem that while an agent may intend something under one description, he will not necessarily intend it under another. Thus, although Oedipus intentionally killed the rude old man at the crossroads, he did not intentionally kill his father. So the event that was a killing of his father was a direct product of his beliefs and attitudes only so far as it was a killing of a rude old man, and we have somehow to block the inference from 'Oedipus intentionally killed the rude old man' to 'Oedipus intentionally killed his father', even though there was but one killing and one event.

I hope, in this section on logic, to have given an idea of the type of logical analysis of language which has been current in philosophy since Frege's momentous innovations and discoveries, and to have illustrated some of its strengths as well as some of the areas which it cannot deal with; we have also noted some counter-proposals and examined some of their metaphysical consequences. Logic, indeed, is not metaphysically neutral but may well reveal the types of thing various forms of thought and argument commit us to. However, before going on to examine how the logical notions of naming and denoting objects and of predication might be applied to our everyday thought and talk about the world, I will mention the third type of problem raised by the application of Fregean logical techniques to everyday speech. These techniques regard the meanings of whole sentences as constructed in a rule-governed way from their parts, and analysable in terms of the contributions the parts make to the sense of the wholes. Language, on this view, is like a logical or mathematical structure, and in understanding it we are, in a way, showing an implicit grasp of the rules underlying its operation, rules which could in principle be made explicit. But, as we shall see in the closing section of this chapter, there are those who would regard such an analysis of language as totally inappropriate to the complexities and nuances of even the simplest everyday talk, and hold that the meanings of everyday utterances derive from the contexts in which they are uttered rather than from any abstract rules determining the meanings and implications of their parts, in abstraction from those contexts.

Naming and Referring

In speaking about the world, we are concerned to say how things are in the world. This may involve us in making assertions of a general kind, which pick out no individuals. These are the sorts of assertions whose sense is captured by means of quantifiers, such as assertions of the sort that there exist brown bears in the universe, or that whenever a heavy body is dropped near the earth, it falls. But these general assertions would appear to need testing by assertions of another, and perhaps more fundamental type, assertions in which reference is made to a specific individual as having such and such a general property. Any language adequate to our purposes in speaking about the world is going to have to enable us to pick out and speak about individual things in the world. This was, of course, recognized by Frege right at the start of his analysis of subject–predicate sentences. The sentence 'Caesar conquered Gaul' was thus analysed as attributing the potentially generalizable property of Gaul-conquering to the unique individual we know as Caesar. Both the generality of the predicate and the uniqueness of reference are essential for the meaning of the sentence. If Gaul-conquering were not a generalizable property, we would be saying nothing *about* Caesar; if, on the other hand, the name 'Caesar' did not denote a unique individual for us, it would be unclear just who Gaul-conquering was being predicated of.

Other than by means of pointing or using a demonstrative, such as 'this', neither of which would be of any use if an object distant from us in space or time, such as Caesar, were the intended reference of some statement of ours, there seem to be two distinct ways of referring to a specific individual. We can either use the individual's proper name (such as 'Gaius Julius Caesar') or we can use a description which picks out the individual in virtue of its uniquely referring to the individual. Thus, I could refer uniquely to Caesar by speaking of the author of *De Bello Gallico*, but not by speaking of the consul for 59 BC. (Caesar was not the only consul in 59 BC.) On the face of it, names and unique descriptions pick out individuals in rather different ways. A description, even though it refers to someone uniquely, and even if such singularity is part of it, as in '*the* Queen of England' or 'the tallest man in England' does so by virtue of the individual picked out having certain properties. We understand the description when we understand what those properties are and the individual concerned is seen as the possessor of those properties. Moreover we could understand the expression 'the Queen of England' without knowing who the Queen was. There is thus a sense in which even some uniquely identifying descriptions consist of properties which could apply to individuals different from the one they in fact apply to. Involved in a description, then, will be a property or complex of properties and where the description is uniquely identifying, the bearer of the property will be regarded as identifiable through the properties in question and our seeing them exemplified by the given individual in question. A proper name, however, looks, on the face of it, quite different. There does not appear to be any attribution of a definite property to Gaius Julius Caesar by his being called 'Caesar'. People who identify Caesar as Caesar do not do so in virtue of his having some specific property, which anyone who understands the name will know is the relevant identifying property, nor do we think of the name 'Caesar', when used to refer to Caesar, as possibly picking out someone other than Caesar. It looks tempting to conclude that, whereas a description has a sense as well as a reference in that it attributes properties to the individual it refers to, a name has only a reference. A name simply stands for its bearer, but does not indicate anything that the bearer is or any property that it possesses.

The idea that proper names are simply marks or sounds whose sole function is to represent the thing they name, in contrast to descriptions (such as 'the Queen of England' or 'the author of *De Bello Gallico*') which tell us something about the individual referred to, is one that has been heavily attacked by Frege, especially in his celebrated article 'On Sense and Reference'.[4] The main argument advanced there against the idea that proper names simply refer to their bearers and otherwise have no sense or meaning is that if this were so, an identity statement in which an object named in one way were said to be the same object as something designated by another name could never represent a discovery for somebody who understood both these names, for, on this view, understanding a name could be neither more nor less than unmediated grasp of what it referred to. Yet this is far from being the case. Imagine a traveller in an unexplored region seeing an impressive mountain on the southern horizon, which he calls 'Afla'. (I am using the Afla–Ateb example, which Frege developed in a letter, rather than the morning star–evening star example that is used in 'Sense and Reference' because of the natural, but mistaken, tendency people have of treating 'morning star' and 'evening star' as descriptions rather than as names.) Another traveller sometime later in another part of the region sees a very different-looking mountain to the northwest and calls it 'Ateb'. People at first think that two mountains have been discovered, and it is only much later that it is realized – discovered – that Afla is Ateb and that the belief that they were different was based on errors and distortions in the original accounts. Yet, if understanding what 'Afla' meant was equivalent to a bare knowledge of what it referred to, in understanding 'Afla' one would have to know of the object it referred to that it was the reference, and similarly for 'Ateb'. So, in understanding each name, we would realize straight-away that 'Afla' and 'Ateb' were merely typographically different signs for the same thing. In fact, on Frege's view, in understanding a proper name one never has bare knowledge of the thing it refers to in this way. Under a name, an object is always presented in a specific way, which is why there can be informative statements asserting the identity of the one bearer of two different names, such as 'Ateb = Afla', which do not simply have the force of '$a = a$'. In attributing what he calls sense to proper names (sense = mode of presentation of what is designated), Frege is effectively denying that we have a simple or unmediated knowledge of the thing named in understanding a name. We always know the thing named as identified or picked out in a particular way, which is why we can make discoveries about identities, and why we can on occasion fail to realize when we are using two names for the same thing that we are doing just that, because we do not realize that the two routes indicated by the two names actually converge on the same object.

It is hard to resist Frege's argument, although Russell was at one time drawn to do so by means of the heroic manoeuvre of denying that what we recognize as proper names in ordinary language are names in the logical sense.[5] Russell in effect agreed with Frege about our ordinary-language use of proper names, that they did have sense and that we could fail to realize what they referred to when it was presented to us under another name or another description. But he insisted that we must at some point be able to refer to spatiotemporal particulars directly without approaching them via a sense. The only candidates he could find for such a role, where one simply knew the particular one was naming in its entirety, without its being presented to us in any particular way, and whose name, as he puts it, simply stood for the 'thing', were the data of immediate sensory experience, for which questions of identity over time or of presentation from different points of view hardly arose. And the only way in which one could name such things without thinking of them in some specific way was by means of the demonstratives 'this' and 'that'. 'This' and 'that' used of sensory data then became the only 'logically' proper names for Russell, whose sense, as Dummett puts it, 'shrinks down to reference'.[6] Frege's argument that the proper names of ordinary language have sense is, as I have said, hard to resist. The question is, what conclusions is it proper to draw from this fact?

According to Russell, the proper names that we commonly use are really abbreviations for descriptions, and he goes on to say that when we use the word 'Socrates' our thought may be rendered by some such phrase as 'the Master of Plato' or 'the philosopher who drank the hemlock'. On a description view of proper names, the sense of the name would be the phrase or some set of phrases conveying the description we associate with the name. It would be via this description or set of descriptions that the name refers to its bearer – the individual Socrates, in this case – and the same distinction between the sense and reference would be available in the case of names as it is in the case of actual descriptions, such as 'the Master of Plato'. (The reference of a name as I am using 'reference' here is the thing the name picks out. Confusingly, this is some-times rendered as 'referent' in English, and even more confusingly Frege's German term for it, *Bedeutung*, is conventionally rendered as 'meaning' in English.)

The idea that proper names are disguised or shorthand descriptions, whose sense is the associated description, solves the problem about the identity of things named. Two names for the same thing may well have two different associated descriptions, so we may well unknowingly use two names for the same thing. Unfortunately for this view, however, the description theory of proper names is open to some formidable objec-tions, several of which have been put forcibly by Saul Kripke in his *Naming and Necessity*.[7]

Kripke actually discusses a version of the description theory of names which at first sight seems a good bit more plausible than the one we have been considering thus far. For it is fairly obviously not the case, as Russell himself realized, that proper names in common use have a single description or a clearly defined set of descriptions associated with them which all those who use the name to refer to the same person understand and agree on. Different users of the same name will tend to identify the bearer of the name in different ways, according to their knowledge of the person. Moreover, even where everybody does pretty automatically think certain thoughts when a particular proper name is used, it could well be the case that the person named in actual fact failed to satisfy the description. Moses, to take an example, might not have led the Israelites out of Egypt. It could, for all we know, have been Aaron who did that. But we would not want to say if that turned out to be so that, when we had used the name 'Moses' in the past, we were really referring to Aaron, because the name 'Moses' was simply shorthand for 'whoever led the Israelites out of Egypt'. We would not want to say that because there are other things we think Moses did, which we could still appeal to in identifying him, even if it turned out he was not the person who led the Israelites out of Egypt.

Repairs to the description theory can be made to remedy these defects, but the cost of the repairs turns out to be rather high. We can say that for each user of a given name there must be a cluster of descriptions associated with that name, most of which or enough of which are satisfied by a unique individual, who is then the bearer of the name. If there is no one single person who actually is picked out by the cluster of descriptions in this way, then that name fails to refer. In other words, if it turned out that there was no single individual who did most of the things Moses is believed by us to have done, then we will have to conclude that Moses did not exist. Further, if he did exist, then, according to Kripke, we will have to say that 'Moses satisfies most of the cluster of descriptions we are using to identify him' expresses a necessary truth (for he would not be Moses if he did not). We can get round the lack of a common cluster of descriptions associated by all users of some name, by taking the sense of the name in public use to be constituted by some sort of pooling of the description clusters of the various users of the name, although this has the obvious drawback that the full sense of the name might be known by no speaker of the language. *Prima facie* this would seem to be a strong objection to any such proposal, given that the notion of the sense of a name was originally introduced to explain something about the way names were actually used and understood. We could simply accept that in ordinary language different speakers may well have different senses for the same name, and say, as Frege and Russell do, that this may be tolerated in a natural, unscientific language, so long as the different senses still refer to the same individual, but saying no more than this leaves the common use of proper names unexplained.

Let us, however, consider the description cluster view as simply giving the sense of a name for the individual speakers who associate a given cluster with a particular name, and leave aside for now problems that arise from other speakers having other clusters. On this view, it appears to follow that, say, it is a necessary truth that Aristotle, understood by us to be the teacher of Alexander, the inventor of syllogistic logic and the greatest philosopher of antiquity since Plato, is those things, for the name 'Aristotle' is simply an abbreviation for this cluster of descriptions. This Kripke regards as fundamentally wrong, arguing that Aristotle – the man we call 'Aristotle' – might have done none of these things, and might have stayed at home in Stagira and never have become a philosopher at all. Even if we weaken the description theory so that the descriptions we attach to a name are simply regarded as the means by which we identify the bearer of the name, its implications are wrong, according to Kripke. He engages in fantasies concerning individuals whose names have come to be regarded as pretty well synonymous with the discoveries they are credited with. The name 'Gödel', for example, would conjure up for most philosophers, at any rate, his proof of the incompleteness of arithmetic, and perhaps not much else. Does it follow, then, that when we use the name 'Gödel' we are actually referring to whoever discovered the incompleteness of arithmetic, even if Kurt Gödel was not actually the discoverer of the proof, but a plagiarist of the work of some individual, completely unknown in the philosophical world, called, let us say, 'Schmidt'? In speaking of Gödel, understood by me to be the discoverer of the proof, would I really be referring to Schmidt?

Kripke clearly expects us to answer 'no' to this question, and also to reject the idea that Aristotle necessarily taught Alexander or that Gödel necessarily discovered his famous proof. On the latter point, Kripke is certainly right. Both Aristotle and Gödel might have died in infancy. Even if we use their achievements to pick them out in the actual world, we conceive the individual so identified in the actual world as possibly having had a different history that might never have brought him to these achievements. Where Kripke is far less convincing, however, is in his claim that the description theory of names has any such implication. While it is true that on the description theory there is a sense in which Gödel could not have failed to be the discoverer of the incompleteness proof (if that is the description associated with the name 'Gödel'), this is the same sense in which it is necessarily true and, indeed, tautologous that the discoverer of the proof is the discoverer of the proof. In the case of the description, however, there is another sense in which the person who is actually and correctly identified as the discoverer of the proof might have failed to make the discovery. So it is both necessarily true that the discoverer of the proof was the discoverer of the proof, and true that the discoverer of the proof might not have discovered the proof!

In fact, of course, we have to sort out an ambiguity here in what is being said, between saying that it is possible that the person who actually discovered the proof might not have discovered the proof, and saying that it is possible that there is someone who satisfies the description 'the discoverer of the proof' who is not the discoverer of the proof. It is only in this latter impossible sense that the discoverer of the proof is necessarily the discoverer of the proof, and this does not rule out the possibility that the description might not have applied to the person to whom it does actually apply. If the name 'Gödel' is being taken as an abbreviation for the description 'discoverer of the proof' it is hard to see why the same possibility (of its not applying to the individual actually picked out by it) does not arise in the case of the name as well.

So the description theory does not imply that there is anything necessary about Gödel's career, but does it mean that in using the name 'Gödel', I might, in some circumstances, really be referring to Schmidt? Before attempting to answer this question, it is worth bringing out what is surely a crucial point in this connection, namely that although we, as users of a name might associate only one thing (and possibly even something false) about the intended reference of the name, we would accept that persons and places (the typical bearers of ordinary-language proper names) are in fact identifiable by many other means than those available to us at any one time, and we would regard the correct use of a given name as being sustained so as to refer to its proper reference by one of these other means, including other descriptions, even though we could not supply them. We would regard these means as being, at least in principle, suppliable by others in the linguistic community. The institution of using proper names, as well as knowledge, depends on a reliance on the labour of others. So, the fact that we knew that 'Gödel' was the name of a human being of the twentieth century would lead us to expect that he was identifiable in ways other than as the discoverer of the incompleteness proof, and the conventions underlying this expectation would probably lead us to say, if Kripke's story were true, that we had been wrong in saying that Gödel had discovered the incompleteness proof, and not that we had really been referring to Schmidt all the time. (The situation would be different if *all* we knew about Gödel was that he was whatever discovered the proof: but this is not all – we know he is a human being and all that that implies.) As A. J. Ayer says, our reliance on the description 'discoverer of the incompleteness' proof 'poses' for us a person 'who is known to be identifiable in other ways and is therefore not confined to that pose'.[8] We can thus tolerate the idea that an individual with a certain name may not have done the one thing we associate with that name, as in the Gödel fantasy. Indeed, tolerating such an idea is actually part of what our use of proper names consists in.

Kripke himself attempts to give an alternative account or picture, as he calls it, of the use of proper names, in which there is no reliance on users of a proper name being in possession of a set of descriptions. According to him, proper names are rigid designators, by which he means that they designate the same individual in every possible world in which it exists, in contrast to non-rigid designators, such as some descriptions, which do not. Thus the description 'the President of the US in 1970' actually designates Richard Nixon, but it could have designated Hubert Humphrey or someone else, while retaining the same sense. In some other possible world Humphrey was US President in 1970. But the name 'Richard Nixon' designates the same individual in every possible world. But who is that, given that any of the details of Nixon's career might have been different? The answer to this question is determined in Kripke's view by the origin of the individual and the history of the name. A name is given to an individual by an initial 'baptism' and later users of the name use it with the intention of referring to whoever was baptized with the name. The link between someone distant from the baptism and the baptism is forged by later users of the name picking it up from earlier users and intending to comply with the initial use, so there is a causal–intentional chain from the baptism outward. The baptism may take place either by means of pointing, which is more usual, or by some description by which the reference is fixed. But if a description fixes the reference, this does not mean that the description gives the sense of the name. It is only the way the individual is picked out. Now, if we take a human baptism, an individual is named, but even if the individual is only a few days old there are aspects of its history that could have been different. He or she could even have been given a different name. The individual our name 'Richard Nixon' names across all possible worlds is, in Kripke's view, the individual who had the same parents as the actual Richard Nixon, and who came from the same fertilized egg – even if that individual had been born somewhere else, not called Richard, etc., etc. Indeed, we can now see in Kripke a further motivation beyond the Barcan proof for the claim that identities between co-referring proper names are necessary (cf. above, p. 58). The individual baptized 'Tully' and the individual baptized 'Cicero' are the same in all possible worlds, because those names rigidly designate the same individual, defined as such in terms of its origin. If we want to block this conclusion, we will have to give an account of proper names in which the notion of sense has a role to play.

Kripke's picture of proper names is part of a wider attempt to account for reference by appeal to facts about the world, rather than by invoking quasi-psychological appeals to descriptions people might mentally associate with their use of names. We shall see shortly that there has been an analogous attempt to account for the reference of natural-kind words, such as 'gold' or 'tiger', without appeal to the thoughts that people might have in connection with these terms. Kripke takes the reference of proper names to be determined by initial baptism and subsequent causal links between the baptizers and other speakers. But his picture suffers from three major defects. First, speakers in a causal chain can all intend to use a name correctly, and yet fail to do so, because of some mistake at some point in the chain. Thus, the land initially baptized 'Madagascar' was actually part of the African mainland. The European sailors who applied the name to the island simply mistook what their African informants were referring to. Does it follow that practically all our statements about Madagascar are thereby false, as referring to the mainland and not to the island? It seems rather that what we actually refer to by a name is determined in part by what we think we are referring to; in this case, an island. If this is so, what is the relevance of facts about initial baptisms, causal chains, etc., to what we actually refer to? Kripke says of this sort of case that

the phenomenon is perhaps roughly explicable in terms of the predominantly social character of proper names ... we use names to communicate with other speakers in a common language.[9]

He is certainly right about the social character of proper names, and emphasizing this may well enable a description theorist of names to avoid having to say, implausibly, that every user of a name has to know a fully identifying description of the bearer of the name. What Kripke's response to the Madagascar type of case leaves entirely open is the possibility that the social character of proper names might be based on adequate identifying descriptions of the bearer of the name being possessed somewhere in the community, and I can say this even though I do not believe in fact that there is any such requirement in our use of proper names.

A second problem with Kripke's account is that it would make referring to someone through a proper name too easy. Let us suppose, following an example of Gareth Evans, that I simply hear a name in bar-room conversation, say 'Louis XIII', and know nothing about French history, or even that the name referred to a king in the seventeenth century.[10] But on Kripke's view, assuming that I intended to use the name in the same way as the person I heard using it, and he was part of an appropriate causal chain going back to the initial baptism, then I would be referring to Louis XIII, even though I had no idea who he was, or when or where he existed.

The third problem with Kripke's account of proper names is that it appears to rule out asking what, say, Kafka might have been like had he not been Jewish. Kripke wants our use of a proper name to be anchored to its bearer's actual origin, but this seems quite arbitrary. So long as we tie our use of a name to some part of the bearer's actual history, we can surely make whatever speculative changes we like. Kripke's picture enables us to envisage given individuals being cut off in infancy, and there can be no objection to this; but why is origin so important? Can we not, equally intelligibly, envisage an individual as arriving at some point at his later history from a different starting point? (Here, and elsewhere in this section, I am indebted to A. J. Ayer's 'Identity and Reference'.) In a way, this is one aspect of the more general problem one has in thinking of the same individuals existing in different possible worlds, for one needs some account of the respects in which an individual can be different in life history in different possible worlds, while still remaining the same individual. Kripke's answer may be as good as any other, but it does have some counter-intuitive consequences.

I have tried to show how the description theory of names might be defended against certain objections, and also how Kripke's picture of naming is vulnerable. But it does not follow from this that the description theory is correct, and, indeed, I do not think it is. Names are not abbreviations for descriptions. At the most basic level, this can be shown by the fact that if we ask for the meaning or sense of a proper name, say 'Richard Nixon', what we want is to be told who this person is, and this will be done by any suitable manner of indicating the person. No specific description is asked for; some indeed may be quite useless for the purpose – if, for example, I said, correctly let us suppose, that Nixon is the man with exactly 117,125 hairs on his head. Further, I can show who is meant without any description at all (for example, by pointing). As Gareth Evans puts it, in asking about what a speaker is referring to, by name or by pointing, the hearer

> ... always confronts just one question, 'Which object does the speaker mean?' – not two questions, 'Which object does the speaker mean?' and 'How am I intended to think of it?'[11]

There are an indefinite number of ways any given object can be thought of, and communication about an object by way of naming or pointing, between speaker and hearer can succeed without them both thinking of it in the same way.

Where, then, does this leave the Fregean problems about identity sentences? What is left of the notion of the sense of a proper name if, as we now seem to be saying, a proper name is not to be construed as a type of description? We have to hold on to two principles here. The first is that an utterance such as 'Afla is the same as Ateb' can be informative in the way 'Afla is the same as Afla' could never be. We need the notion of a proper name's having sense in order to preserve this truth. The second, seemingly destructive of any full-blooded doctrine of the sense of proper names, is that speakers of a language can use proper names quite correctly even to the extent of identifying their bearers or being related to them in a host of different ways, and even, on occasion, without having the slightest idea of how they recognized the bearer. (Perhaps this last type of case is actually what happens in the most common and homely use of proper names, when we use them to refer to people we are well acquainted with.)

A most ingenious way out of this apparent impasse has been suggested by John McDowell in 'On the Sense and Reference of a Proper Name'.[12] McDowell is concerned to show how we should state a theory, knowledge of which would enable anyone to understand a language. In the case of proper names, he suggests that the right thing to say is that someone knowing that, say,

(N) 'Richard Nixon' stands for Richard Nixon

knows the meaning of 'Richard Nixon'. In other words, if we were to use (N) in order to describe the behaviour of someone who had the name 'Richard Nixon' in his vocabulary, and to use similar clauses for the other proper names in his vocabulary, we would be able to make sense of his use of those proper names. (The speakers of the language are not required to have explicit knowledge of (N) or anything like it. The theory McDowell is interested in constructing is one that would enable someone reflectively and systematically to make sense of what native speakers say and understand unreflectively. (N) and similar clauses fixing the sense of the terms of the language are, on this view, part of the means by which an interpreter of the speech of native speakers of a language could systematically infer from an input of initially uninterpreted sound, what it is those speakers are saying, what they are doing, believing and intending by means of their words in the actual utterances they make.)

McDowell sees a clause such as (N) as preserving the sense–reference distinction in the way it describes the meaning of a name, because, while knowing the reference of a name involves acquaintance with that object (= *connaître*), knowing the sense of a name involves knowledge of a truth (= *savoir*). In saying that someone theorizing about English knows a clause such as (N), we are attributing to that person knowledge of a truth, and so we can say that what they know is the sense of 'Richard Nixon', rather than its reference (whom they would probably not know anyway).

Clauses such as (N) will reveal why we as theorists and the speakers whose behaviour is being described by means of clauses such as (N) can make discoveries about identities between bearers of different names. 'Afla' and 'Ateb' will have different clauses and if we know only these clauses we would have to discover that the names in fact refer to the same thing. This, combined with the fact that a person's use in his speech of 'Afla' may well be quite different from his use of 'Ateb', is enough to suggest that, in contrast to 'Afla = Afla', there is nothing tautologous about 'Afla = Ateb'. If the world had been different in only one respect from the world of our example, people might have used the terms rather like they do in our example, thinking they are referring to two mountains, and really referring to two mountains. Nevertheless, it will be felt that (N)-type clauses impute too little knowledge for knowledge of the sense of a name, and can be too cheaply known. Won't anyone who knows merely that 'Richard Nixon' is a proper name know that 'Richard Nixon' stands for Richard Nixon or behave in a way describable in terms of a clause like (N). McDowell's answer to this is to insist that we would use a clause like (N) in describing the linguistic capacity actually possessed by a given speaker only if he or she 'showed an ability to use the name, or respond intelligently (with understanding) to uses of the name on the part of others, in speech acts construable as being about [the former President]'.[13] Although, as will become apparent, McDowell shares much of Kripke's hostility to psychologistic accounts of proper names – those in terms of what speakers associate mentally with the uses of their words – he avoids the problem Kripke's picture had through its stress on the initial baptism of an object with a name. Our use of 'Madagascar' is not construable as being about the African mainland, but only as being about Madagascar. In other words, (N) will be used in a description of his or her behaviour only if he or she is able to use the name appropriately. Similarly, a mere mouthing of (N) on the part of a theorist of the language would not enable him to understand the name, because a mere mouthing of (N) could not be described as knowledge that 'Richard Nixon' stands for Richard Nixon.

McDowell concedes that anyone who knew – beyond merely mouthing sounds – that 'Richard Nixon' stands for Richard Nixon or behaved in a way describable by (N) would undoubtedly have some beliefs about Nixon, on the basis of which he can use the sounds 'Richard Nixon' to express in his talk his various attitudes to that person; equally having some beliefs about him would be part of what the intelligent response to uses of the name on the part of others would consist in. He could not have bare knowledge of the object or person referred to. But these beliefs need not amount to anything like an explicit description full enough to identify the bearer of the name, nor need they be the same from speaker to speaker. McDowell regards any attempt to require that some specific mental content, such as a description, be had by anyone who knows the sense of a proper name as not only a falsification of our actual (successful) use of proper names, but also part of a deep and persistent temptation to psychologize about language. Instead of seeing linguistic behaviour for what it is, a multiple interaction between speakers and the world and other speakers, and seeing the philosophical task as being to describe what that behaviour is, we are tempted by the chimera of the ultimately incoherent goal of explaining *in words* to someone who has no language how he might acquire language, specifically, by getting him to acquire mental mechanisms which would guarantee the link between words and things. In the case of proper names, this means fixing in the mind the descriptive pictures associated with the name. But the possession of such a picture or its counterpart in words is not only frequently not present when someone is able satisfactorily to use a name, but even if it were, it would not by itself secure an attachment between a name and a bearer.

One fundamental reason for saying this is that one's mind could be full of the 'right' images or words, to go with a given object, yet one could nevertheless in one's speech and behaviour fail to refer to that object. One could just not be speaking about *it*; one might not be in the right sort of contact with *it* to be in a position to refer to it. To see this point, we could imagine another world in another part of the universe just like this one, and twin-earth human beings whose heads were full of the same sorts of thoughts as ours. Nevertheless, the speech of a twin-earth duplicate of myself could not be described by means of a clause such as (*N*) ' 'Richard Nixon' stands for Richard Nixon' for he would have no knowledge of Richard Nixon, but only of the twin-earth Richard Nixon duplicate, and so he would not be in a position to use any term to stand for Richard Nixon.

It may, further, be the case that, as Colin McGinn has put it,

an accurate description of the phenomenological content of an experience will employ only *general* terms to specify how the experience represents the world.[14]

We often regard our thoughts and other experiences as being thoughts about particular individuals in the world, but on McGinn's account we are able to do this because we are in direct causal and perceptual contact with some of those particulars, and we locate other individuals by reference to a single spatiotemporal framework in which we and the rest of the individuals we refer to live and move.

This inherent generality of experience may also be part of what Wittgenstein was referring to when he said 'If God had looked into our minds, he would not have been able to see there whom we were speaking of.'[15] Looking into our minds alone, he would not have been able to see who and what we were in contact with, and so who or what we were speaking and thinking of. There is, as we will see in the final section of this chapter, a further aspect to Wittgenstein's hostility to mentalistic or psychologistic explanations of language, and that is that any image or thought can be interpreted or applied to the world in more than one way. So it is no use appealing to thoughts or images to settle what a speaker means by his words, or to explain how he is able to mean what he does by them. We should, on the contrary, eschew psychologistic inquiries about meanings, and see the role a man's words play in his life and how they link with his actions and those surrounding him.

The contrast between psychologistic and realistic accounts of the meaning of proper names is perhaps brought out most clearly in the way that the two accounts deal with names which actually fail to refer, such as 'Mumbo-Jumbo'. As McDowell points out, the psychologistic account will give the sense of 'Mumbo-Jumbo' in terms of some description, such as 'the controller of the winds'; its sense would be just like the sense of any other proper name, the only difference being that in this case the sense doesn't take us anywhere. But believing, as we do, that there is no such person, it is not open to us to devise an N-type clause for 'Mumbo-Jumbo'. 'Mumbo-Jumbo' does not and cannot stand for Mumbo-Jumbo, because there is no Mumbo-Jumbo. Nor, given that we do not believe in Mumbo-Jumbo, can we explain the behaviour of someone who speaks of Mumbo-Jumbo in terms of beliefs or other attitudes he has concerning Mumbo-Jumbo. Again, this is because there is no such being for our speaker to have attitudes to. The realist position here is derived from the general premise that what one says and believes is not constituted solely by what is in one's mind, and that, in contrast to theories which would analyse meaning in terms of the mental states or contents of speakers of the language, it makes all the difference in the world to what one is doing when one is using a name, if the name happens to refer to nothing real. If there is no Mumbo-Jumbo, one cannot have thoughts about Mumbo-Jumbo or refer to Mumbo-Jumbo. The most one can do is to manifest by one's words or behaviour one's false belief that one (wrongly) thinks there is something corresponding to the description 'controller of the winds'. It is a consequence, and not a totally implausible consequence, of the anti-psychologist line in philosophy that one can in this way be mistaken about the actual content of one's thoughts and the actual sense of one's words. When you think you are talking and thinking about Mumbo-Jumbo, you are actually talking and thinking about nothing, although of course you will be having thoughts and images of various sorts passing through your head. The sense of one's referring words and thoughts is thus crucially affected by the existence or non-existence of objects corresponding to those thoughts. It is crucially in the difference between the way we would explain what it is someone is doing when a name he uses does refer and the way we would have to explain what he is doing when he uses a bearerless name. In the first case the right thing, and the only right thing, to say is that he uses 'Nixon' to stand for Nixon. In the second case we will have to say that by 'Mumbo-Jumbo' he is signalling his belief that there is someone who does this and that, and explaining what this belief amounts to may well be difficult and indecisive, in the same sort of way as it is hard to give any correct community-wide account of descriptions associated with proper names that do refer.

The idea that there is a great difference between proper names and other directly referring terms on the one hand, and definite descriptions on the other, is one that was basic to Russell's philosophy, and was the motivation behind one of his greatest contributions to philosophy. Russell's contention was that while a sentence containing a definite description, such as

(1) The King of France is bald

had a clear sense, this was not the case where a sentence included a name for which there was no clear descriptive condition for something being its reference, such as

(2) Slawkenburgius was wise.

(1) has a clear sense, precisely because we perfectly well understand what it would be for someone to be the King of France, even though there is no such person, while (2) as a whole lacks sense because there is no person answering to the name 'Slawkenburgius'. (That Russell actually analysed most of the proper names of ordinary language as abbreviated descriptions complicates the picture, but does not affect the underlying point that if there are any names or other terms whose function is to denote an individual particular without any definite description of that individual being given to us, the sense of sentences containing such terms which in fact denote no individual will be lacking entirely.)

Russell's analysis of definite descriptions such as 'The King of France' was extremely ingenious as well as being arguably philosophically epoch-making.

According to Russell,

(1) The King of France is bald

is not to be construed as being about the King of France, in the same way as (2) may be said to be about Slawkenburgius. If it were, (1) would suffer from the same sort of problems as (2), there being no King of France. What (1) actually consists of is an existential claim, 'There is a king of France', a uniqueness claim, 'There is not more than one king of France', and an additional predication, 'Whatever is king of France is bald'. The upshot of the analysis is to allow us to regard (1) as fully meaningful, but false, because the first of its three subdivisions, while being perfectly intelligible, is false.

The reason for saying that Russell's theory of descriptions was epoch-making is because it suggested dramatically and graphically that the logical structure of a sentence might be quite different from its surface structure or even its grammatical structure. (1) stood revealed as something quite other than the simple subject–predicate sentence it appeared, and quite different in form from a sentence like (2). The theory of descriptions seemed at least in the view of Wittgenstein to open the way for logical inquiries into the nature of language, which would reveal 'enormously complicated' tacit conventions, on which the understanding of ordinary language depended.[16]

What, though, of a sentence like (2) on a Russellian analysis? Russell's position was sharp and straightforward. A genuine proper name which failed to refer would render any sentence in which it occurred meaningless. The corollary of this position was that any apparent proper name which did not refer, and which did not render sentences in which it occurred meaningless, was not a proper name at all, but a disguised description. We have spent long enough considering objections to this view, and we have suggested reasons for thinking that the use of a bearerless proper name, by someone whose discourse or language we are trying to fathom, is going to give us problems in understanding the utterances involved.* Admittedly, these reasons are not conclusive, and are based on the point, which some may still contest, that the sense of a proper name is not to be given by a specific description or cluster of descriptions, but by mentioning the individual named.

The defender of the description theory of proper names will continue to insist that however much the descriptions normally associated with

---

*Unless, that is, the name is really being used as simply shorthand for some description as when newspapers use a term like 'the Ripper' to stand for 'the person who committed those horrible murders'. But this is not the usual case with proper names, which should be clear enough by now. The normal use of proper names is based on the assumption that a name will still refer to the individual named even though any, or in some cases all, of the descriptions normally associated with our use of the name are untrue of that individual.

a given name are untrue of the bearer of the name, the name still attaches to the bearer via some description which somebody knew at some time, possibly at the individual's baptism with his or her name. Thus it might seem that a *rapprochement* could be effected between Kripke's picture of naming and description theories, but this would, I think, be to misunderstand what underlies (or ought to underlie) opposition to description theories. The underlying objection to description theories of naming is the point, already mentioned, that if everything is identified by description, we run the risk of, as Evans puts it, 'the whole system of identification failing to be tied down to a unique set of objects',[17] because of those same descriptions theoretically being satisfiable by other sets of qualitatively indistinguishable objects. So somewhere in our language, even if it is not in proper names, there must be terms in which there is a demonstrative or referring element, which is independent of and irreducible to any descriptive element that may be involved. This is why it has seemed worthwhile to examine and defend the thesis that the sense of proper names is to be given by reference to the individuals they stand for, rather than via any description that might be associated with them. But even if this is wrong, and some version of the description theory is correct for ordinary proper names, as Russell thought, there must be some terms (such as 'this', 'that', 'I', 'you') whose sense in a given context is given by picking out non-descriptively the individuals they are being used to signify.

Accepting the existence of terms functioning demonstratively in this way, are we then able to avoid the conclusions of the previous chapter and to think of some objects in the world as ready-made, and simply given to us independently of any categorization or scheme of classification? Even more, would acceptance of a theory of proper names which sees their sense as being established and maintained in some sort of causal and perceptual interaction between the objects named and the users of the name permit us to repopulate the world with self-identifying objects known and picked out without any human seeing at all? According to Hilary Putnam, this is just what it means; he says that theories of reference in which the reference of terms is fixed by the world rather than by anything psychological or 'inside the head' are a modern reversion to medieval essentialism in which there were types of thing out there in the world, independent of human classification, the difference being that, in the medieval context, this realism was backed up by a psychology in which God had so arranged things that the mind was able correctly to abstract the substantial forms or essences of the things in the world. Putnam's objection to any such view is that we have no such God-guaranteed access to the essence of the world and that how we conceive the world is not the only way even ideally rational beings might conceive it.[18]

It is not clear that an account of language in which the use of proper names and demonstrative terms is seen to depend on direct causal perceptual interactions between at least some of the users of those terms and the objects to which the terms refer need amount to a repudiation of the epistemological problems alluded to by Putnam, or to an acceptance of the view that the world comes to us in ready-made packages. In the first place, the individuals demonstratively identified by naming or by terms such as 'this' or 'that' are still picked out as individuals of such and such a type. Demonstrative identification presupposes particular ways of carving up the world (into people, animals, human artefacts, etc.) even where it does not rest on those doing the identifying being in possession of identifying descriptions of the things individuated. Nothing that has been said so far entails that demonstrative reference to individuals in the world requires no human input into the way we carve up the world into those individuals. It commits us neither to a world of self-identifying objects, nor to the qualitatively empty 'this' and 'that' of Russell's logical atomism.

Then secondly, against Putnam's suggestion that any causal theory of reference implies a view of the world as already parcelled up without human ways of sensing we have to consider once more what can be expected from philosophy of language. To repeat what we have already said, neither philosophy of language nor anything else can transcend or stand outside our (I mean mine and yours) words and thoughts, and show us how these words and thoughts connect with an epistemologically uncontaminated world. What philosophy of language can do is to show from within our language and our world how the parts of the sentences we speak go to make up the truth conditions of those sentences and, more generally, how those sentences can be regarded as featuring in speech acts we can intelligibly be supposed to be engaging in, given our dealings with our environment.

The implications of this understanding of the philosophy of language become clearer when we suppose ourselves to be doing the same thing for someone else's speech, perhaps the speech of a 'native' speaking a very different language from ours. Whereas in the 'home' case, because the proper names we use are the names of just those individuals we believe to exist, we will always understand our own use of proper names in terms of clauses like (N) in which the sense of a name is given by simply mentioning in the very same terms the object named, in the case of the native we will have to try to find an understanding of his proper names which will map those names on to individuals we can pick out and which we imagine the native to be in a position to refer to. Of course, in many cases this will present us with no difficulty. We learn simultaneously that a given individual is, say, Chukwu and the sense of 'Chukwu'. But 'Mumbo-Jumbo' presented us with problems, precisely because we do not believe that any such individual is to be found. We, at least, cannot *use* the name 'Mumbo-Jumbo' to explain someone else's understanding of the name, because for us the name has no use. This, it seems to me, demonstrates the 'internal' or non-transcendent nature of philosophy of language. What we learn about the reference of names and the interaction between objects and speakers from the philosophy of language is necessarily and firmly internal to our picture of the world. It is not and cannot be a short-cut solution to the deep problems of epistemology alluded to by Putnam, but within our picture of the world, there can surely be no objection to speaking of the way speakers might get into a position to refer to objects and the causal and perceptual relations and connections that might obtain between objects and speakers, so as to enable speakers to refer to those objects. Although, of course, I have argued that it would be quite misleading to suggest that these causal relations are themselves part of the sense of a name, they might well be part of the evidence on which we say that someone is using a name with such and such a sense. That the objects featuring in such an account will be just those we regard ourselves as being able to identify should make it clear that in giving such an account we do not hope to avoid any problems concerned with the epistemological standing of those objects.

General Terms

The distinction between sense and reference was introduced here in the context of proper names, but something analogous can with at least equal reason be applied to predicates or general terms. A general term, such as 'bachelor', is true of a certain class of individuals in the world, but it does not, indeed could not, simply or barely pick out the members of the class. It picks them out in virtue of their possessing certain properties, in this case, their being male and unmarried. These properties, the route by which we get to the individuals we are calling 'bachelors', is the sense of the term, and so we have just the same sense–reference distinction as in the case of proper names. (A terminological point, the class of all entities of which a predicate or general term is true is often known as its 'extension', while the sense or meaning of a general term is sometimes called its 'intension'.)

Armed with the distinction between the sense of a general term and its reference, philosophers have gone on to distinguish between two types of truths, analytic truths, which are true by virtue of the senses or meanings of the terms involved, and synthetic truths, whose truth depends on the way things are in the world. The contrast is between 'All bachelors are unmarried' (analytic, because of the senses of 'bachelor' and 'unmarried') and 'All bachelors are sowing their wild oats' (synthetic, its truth dependent on the behaviour of the individuals in question; perhaps it is false anyway. We'll just have to go out and look !).

Despite the initial plausibility of the analytic–synthetic distinction, it will be clear from Chapter 2 that, in Quine's view, its very existence is called into question. It is, in his view, one of the two dogmas of empiricism. The way he attempts to undermine it is to show that we cannot explain the idea of a sentence being analytic or true by virtue of meaning except by invoking other notions which he regards as equally in need of analysis and defence, such as synonymy (sameness of meaning). Thus 'All bachelors are unmarried' is analytically true because 'bachelor' and 'unmarried man' are synonymous. Quine then shows what was never really in doubt, that two terms are not synonymous just because they are co-extensive, even though in extensional contexts we can substitute co-extensive terms without altering the truth-value of the whole sentence. Thus, it so happens that creatures with hearts are just those creatures that have kidneys, and, except where people's beliefs and other propositional attitudes are concerned or except where we are speaking of what is necessarily true, or of what might have been, but isn't, whatever is true of creatures with hearts is true of creatures with kidneys. (There are just the same individuals in both classes, and obviously they have the same properties.) But, clearly, 'creatures with hearts' does not mean the same as 'creatures with kidneys'. Sameness of meaning would obtain only if the result of any interchange were necessarily equivalent, as with substituting 'unmarried man' for 'bachelor', but according to Quine the notion of necessity itself requires explanation in terms of analyticity. So, in trying to explain what analyticity amounts to we travel quickly through related notions, such as synonymy and necessity, straight back to where we started.

Does this mean that we have to abandon the whole idea of analysis in terms of meaning? What Quine is in effect doing is to demand that meaning notions (such as analytic and synonymous) be explained in terms of other types of concept altogether and claiming incomprehension when this cannot be done. Perhaps we should not be surprised that a reductive analysis of such notions cannot be given, and perhaps it does not matter anyway. While it is true that there are borderline cases where we are not sure that some statement is analytic or synthetic, such as 'Everything green is extended' – and Quine makes some play with this – there is no doubt that the truth of hosts of statements like 'All bachelors are unmarried' appears to follow directly from the meanings of the terms involved, while equally large numbers of statement are true or false in virtue of the way the world is. It may be perverse to deny the reality of a distinction that can be made with such certainty in so many cases, even if we cannot explain the distinction according to some imposed standard of explanation. Moreover, communication through language demands that we understand what speakers and hearers take to follow from words, at least in normal cases. Just as successful communication requires that we know in advance what logical inferences can be drawn from a man's words, so we require to know the connections which obtain between his words and other words by virtue of meaning.

However, even if we can defend some part of the idea of analyticity against Quine's frontal attack on it in 'Two Dogmas of Empiricism', this does not imply that any substantive problems about the nature of reality either in philosophy or elsewhere can be solved by invoking it. As already mentioned in Chapter 2, statements which, for the purposes of some inquiry we regard as true by definition or by virtue of meaning, are not to be regarded as uninfluenced by empirical facts, natural or social, or forever unalterable in response to new discoveries or social change. Indeed, the study of the meanings people attach at various times to concepts in science and to social concepts can tell us a lot about them and their knowledge of the world. But it is unclear that *these* meanings will need special philosophical training or gifts to uncover, or that they will not make themselves available to ordinary speakers of the language and ordinary lexicographers.

We now need to go beyond the facts that our understanding of our predicates is governed by meaning rules and that these meaning rules can change and develop, and consider some of their implications. How is our understanding of predicates governed by meaning rules? One answer, somewhat akin to the description theory of proper names, is to say that the meaning rules determine what things fall under a predicate by giving us sets of conditions which determine what these things are.*

If we take as our example the definition of 'bachelor' as 'unmarried man'; anything that is unmarried and a man will be a bachelor. The model is of explicit sense determining reference. But, even if this works for this case, there are many concepts for which we would be quite unable to give such a straightforwardly explicit and uncontroversial definition. (Consider 'money'.) Sense in these cases is something apparently far more elusive. Furthermore, even in science, where we often find explicit definitions of terms, these definitions tend to be summaries of current theory, and to change, even in extension. That is to say, with advances in scientific knowledge things that might at one time have safely fallen within the then current definition of, say, 'gold', may turn out not to be gold at all. Maybe some Mycenaean 'gold' turned out not to have the atomic number 79. But, if what a predicate term, or concept, meant was determined by its definition, then when the definition changes, doesn't the concept change too? So if the ancients and ourselves define 'gold' differently, we do not really mean the same thing by the term, and we are in error when we think they were wrong to classify something as gold which fitted their definition, but not ours. It *was* gold for them; we just mean something different by the term and apply it in different circumstances.

This, however, seems a preposterous thing to say; what we want to say here is that we have made a discovery about gold and that the ancients were just wrong about it. (If the gold case does not convince, consider a case like that of multiple sclerosis, where we apply a term to a set of symptoms we believe connected, before knowing what exactly we are talking about, in the expectation that at some time in the future we will discover what the underlying cause is. If we are successful, and even if, as seems probable, some things now thought of as cases of multiple sclerosis would be revealed as cases of something else, surely it would be correct to say that we had made an important discovery about multiple sclerosis, and not merely that a term was now being used differently.) So there appear to be two connected reasons for denying that anything like an explicit definition or set of criterial conditions is needed to secure the reference of predicates or general terms. Many of them can be applied in the absence of any such thing, and even where there is such a thing and it does

---

* These conditions might be thought of as giving the essence of the things falling under the term, or they might simply lay down the external conditions (or criteria) in which we think the term properly applied. The difference between essentialist definitions and criterial or operational ones is important, but what follows would apply equally to both.

demarcate a number of things as falling under the predicate, we want to be able to say that the definition can in fact be wrong about what the reference of the predicate really is.

What seems to be happening in the case of predicates is very similar to what happened in the case of proper names. An account of predication which sees it in terms of 'meanings in the head' either fails to operate at all in some cases or, in others, saddles us with false information about the things the predicate really applies to.

Hilary Putnam has argued that it is particularly in the case of natural-kind terms (i.e. names for such things as natural substances, species and physical magnitudes) that the model of sense determining reference via an analytic definition is inappropriate. In its place, he proposes an account of natural-kind terms very similar to that proposed by Kripke for proper names. In Putnam's view our use of a word such as 'gold' or 'lemon' or 'water' depends on our having certain standard examples (or what he calls 'paradigms'). These examples are picked out as paradigms because they fulfil our initial stereotype for the stuff, for example, that a lemon is yellow, bitter, etc. What makes something actually gold, or a lemon or water is its having the same nature as paradigms, and this means, in the state of current physical theory, the same atomic composition, which we hold to determine the law-like behaviour of a substance. This analysis of the meaning of 'lemon', say, allows us to count as lemons things which do not have the manifest properties of our paradigms and which do not fulfil our initial stereotype. Equally, something indistinguishable in respect of manifest properties from water – in taste, colour, thirst-quenchability, washing power, etc. – would not be water if it did not have the chemical structure H_2O. To bring this point home, Putnam indulges in fantasies about a twin earth and twin-earthians whose so-called 'water', though identical in all other aspects to ours, happens, on analysis, to have the chemical composition XYZ. Their 'water' would not be water, according to Putnam, and we would have been wrong in calling it 'water', and this is still how things would have stood even had the chemical analysis not have been invented and everyone involved incorrectly referred to twin-earthian XYZ as 'water'.

The point of Putnam's view of natural-kind terms is to insist that their extension

is not fixed by a set of criteria laid down in advance, but is, in part, *fixed by the world.* There are *objective laws* obeyed by multiple sclerosis, by gold, by horses, by electricity; and what it is rational to include in these classes will depend on what those laws turn out to be.[19]

The analogy with Kripke's analysis of proper names is that in both cases objective factors (for names origin and history, for natural kinds atomic structure) are the decisive determinants of reference. The analogy is reinforced by Kripke's insistence that if water is H_2O, then it is necessarily H_2O, which is only another way of saying that twin-earth 'water' is not water. Putnam is, incidentally, prepared to extend his account of natural kinds to deal with some aspects of our talk about artefacts, claiming, for example, that pencils could not (logically could not) be organisms. For him, a twin earth in which pencil-like organisms just grew would not contain pencils, because pencils (what we pick out as pencils) are artefacts by nature, and not organisms.[20]

Putnam sees his theory of the functioning natural-kind terms as a rehabilitation of an essentialist view of natural kinds, although it is not easy to square it with his later attacks on 'ready-made' worlds. The things natural-kind terms refer to (and in that sense what natural-kind terms mean) have basic natures, and things belong to a given kind if they have the same nature as the things included in our paradigm. In other words, natural-kind terms are rigid designators, designating rigidly things with the structure of the things we pick out in our paradigm cases.

The connection with Wiggins's view of essence should be clear enough; in Chapter 1 (pp. 57–8 above) I suggested some reservations about the view of natural necessity Wiggins was drawn to. What we now have to examine is the plausibility of the Putnam–Kripke account of the functioning of natural-kind terms, and its possible extension into the world of artefacts.

A. J. Ayer has pointed out that a critical step in Putnam's argument is the claim that 'what is and always has been meant by the English word "water", and its counterparts in other languages, is anything that has this microstructure (that is, the microstructure of paradigm cases of water), whatever its manifest properties may be' and that nothing else, however similar its manifest properties may be to water, is water. But, as Ayer points out, the claim that what is meant by 'water' is just what has the microstructure H_2O is simply false, and we do not have to have recourse to possible worlds to see this:

Suppose that in some part of this world we came upon stuff which had the chemical composition H_2O but did not have the properties of falling as rain, allaying thirst, quenching fire and so forth, perhaps even failed to appear in liquid form. I certainly should not call it 'water' and should be surprised if the majority of English speakers did so either.[21]

Conversely, suppose we discovered some stuff which had all the manifest properties of water, and which we had always called 'water' (such as the stuff that comes out of my tap at home), actually has a slightly different structure from H_2O – and tap water may after all the treatment it gets – we would be most unlikely to stop calling it 'water', though, of course, for chemical purposes we would have to distinguish it from H_2O.*

So, the Putnam–Kripke analysis of natural-kind words entails a departure from our actual usage, in that we do not tie such terms so strictly to whatever discoveries about microstructure might turn up. So we still have our original problems with the sense and reference of general terms, that sense seems necessary, but elusive in many cases, and that reference alone is insufficient for meaning.

In what we have said so far, I have been assuming that we have a fairly clear idea of what sort of thing is being referred to when we hear a term such as 'rabbit' or 'lemon' used, even if we are unable to give a precise set of determining conditions and believe that it is at least possible that we might alter what we believe should fall in the class in question. However, this is an assumption that we are by no means entitled to take for granted, at least if Quine is right about ontological relativity and the indeterminacy of translation. Quine introduces his ideas on reference by means of an extended thought experiment in 'radical' translation.[22] His underlying thesis is that the truth conditions of whole sentences fail to determine what it is their parts are about; that is to say, we can know all there is to be known about the circumstances in which particular sentences of a given language will be assented to by speakers of that language without being able to tell what things those speakers are referring to.

The radical translation story might be seen as a device to get us to concentrate on the thinness of the observable and behavioural basis of language, compared to the thickness of the theoretical commitments of any language regarding the types of things there are in the world. In part, Quine sees his point as arising from the under-determination of theory by data, something we have already encountered several times, but, in addition to that, and crucially, from the fact that the data in question are the data available to us as hearers of another's speech, and the other's speech the theory we are trying to scrutinize.

Radical translation occurs when we, as anthropologists, try to fathom the speech of some native tribe, without the aid of interpreters, and when

* The position being criticized here is 'early' Putnam. In 'The Meaning of "Meaning"' (p. 233 – see notes), he wrote 'it isn't logically possible that water isn't H_2O'. In *Realism and Reason* (p. 63 – see notes) he says it is!

that speech has no connections with any language we know. In such circumstances, the data available to us will consist simply in observations we make of the speech behaviour of the natives and the surrounding circumstances. After a while, we manage to pick out the native signs for assent and dissent, and to isolate a number of sentences whose utterance appears to depend on the natives noticing certain specific, but transitory features of their environment which are assented to only in these circumstances and dissented from on other occasions. Call these sentences observation sentences, an example of which might be the single-word sentence 'Gavagai' which is assented to when and only when there are rabbits in the native's perceptual environment, and dissented from otherwise. Of course, it will be a fallible hypothesis on our part that 'Gavagai' is so connected to rabbits, but one which we can test, and which, Quine says, provokes only the normal inductive uncertainties. Let us suppose that our hypothesis about 'Gavagai' is correct; that it is an observation sentence, equivalent in use to the English observation sentence 'Lo, a rabbit!' Here we have two sentences which are what Quine calls stimulus-synonymous, that is, provoked by the same sets of stimuli – and whose meaning is very closely tied down to occurrent stimulation (unlike sentences such as '$2 + 2 = 4$' or 'Yesterday was fine' which might be assented to in a vast variety of stimulus conditions). Can we, even in the case of 'Gavagai' and 'Lo, a rabbit', conclude that the terms 'gavagai' and 'rabbit' are coextensive terms, terms true of the same things? According to Quine, that is just what we cannot do:

> For, consider 'gavagai'. Who knows but what the objects to which this term applies are not rabbits after all, but mere stages, or brief temporal segments of rabbits? In either event the stimulus situations that prompt assent to 'Gavagai' would be the same as for 'Rabbit'. Or perhaps the objects to which 'gavagai' applies are all and sundry undetached parts of rabbits; again the stimulus meaning would register no difference. When from sameness of stimulus meanings of 'Gavagai' and 'Rabbit' the linguist leaps to the conclusion that a gavagai is a whole enduring rabbit, he is just taking for granted that the native is enough like us to have a brief general term for rabbits and no brief general term for rabbit stages or parts.[23]

Quine goes on to say that the native could equally be using 'gavagai' as a mass term like 'water' to refer to the single though disconnected portion of the world that consists of rabbits, or even as naming the platonic universal rabbithood: 'Point to a rabbit and you have pointed to a stage of a rabbit, to an integral part of a rabbit, ... and to where rabbithood is manifested.' We could, of course, start asking further questions like 'Is there one gavagai here or two?' or 'Is this the same gavagai as that?' but this will not help us to solve our problem as to which of the various alternative readings of 'gavagai' are correct, because they could systematically reinterpret the notions of sameness and difference, oneness and diversity, so as to mask any difference between 'gavagai' and 'rabbit'. Thus, when we think we are asking 'Is this the same gavagai as that?' what we say could have the sense for the native of 'Are these stages of the same gavagai-series?'

Quine construes the indeterminacy of translation as ruling out any talk of *the* correct translation of the native speech. The reason for this is that so many different translation schemes are compatible with all the evidence available to the radical translator that there is no sense in claiming that, as he puts it, there is 'an objective matter to be right or wrong about'.[24] What will be done, and all that can be done is to map the native speech as best we can in the most natural-seeming way on to our own. (This is the part of the general presumption that the point of translation is to make the behaviour of others intelligible to the translators.) But we should not expect the mapping always to be exact or decisive, and we must remember that, in doing the mapping, we are making the native usage seem natural to us.[25] There are, in Quine's view, other incompatible ways of doing it, and, ultimately, no fact of the matter to declare one way or another as being the right one. Does indeterminacy of translation, and the resulting indecision as to what is being spoken of, carry over into the case of speakers of one's own language? Quine says that even though we can imagine different speakers of the same language coming to their language by different individual histories, 'if two speakers match in all dispositions to verbal behaviour there is no sense in imagining semantic differences between them'.[26] In other words, there is no sense in imagining that, in using the term 'rabbit', I mean 'rabbit part' where you mean 'rabbit', if I speak English and talk about rabbits just like you, and deny that I intend my words to refer to rabbit parts. To suppose that I did would seem a crazy sort of mentalism, that behind my words and behaviour there could be something quite different from what is behind yours, even if there are no behaviourally detectable differences between us. Quine does nevertheless flirt, on occasion, with an indeterminacy of translation obtaining between speakers of the same language.

Perhaps the real moral of speculation about what someone really means, independently of relativization to some scheme of translation, is that if we try to take the terms of a language in abstraction from translational schemes or of mapping on to themselves, we will indeed get crazy results. If we take the true sentences of our language, they will clearly be made true if the terms in them ('cat', 'mat', etc.) refer to the things in the world that they speak of (cats, mats, etc.). But there will be re-interpretations of the predicates that make the same sentences true, without anything in the world being different. 'Cat' could refer to cat stages, or instances of cathood, or cat parts, and, provided we reinterpret other bits of language appropriately, our true sentences will still come out true. Putnam has argued further that we could have even more way-out reinterpretations, in which, say, all the true sentences we have apparently about cats come out true in the same circumstances even if we take 'cat' to refer to cherries.[27] Of course, wholesale reinterpretations of other bits of the language will be needed, and this is really the point. If we begin by treating our language or some other language as something un-interpreted, in which all we know are the truth conditions of various sentences, there are many interpretations of the terms of those sentences which would have the same sentences coming out true, even though some of the interpretations might appear very odd indeed. The moral of all this is that we should begin by doing no such thing. If we know anything about our language, we know that 'cat' refers to cats and not to cat stages, cat parts, cathood or cherries. When we try to interpret another language, we have to begin with our language, and how the world is presented in it. We cannot expect the world, on its own, to determine the reference of our terms, or those of another language, for us.

What we have to do is to start by assuming the interpretation (of the world) already given in our understanding of our language. What justifies us in saying that the sense of 'cat' is cat, rather than any of the other possibilities we have mentioned, is not the way of the world, but the way we already understand our language (and the world). For our own langu-age, then, we are going to be back to saying things like we said of the name 'Richard Nixon', that is, the sense of 'cat' will be given by a clause which says: 'cat' refers to an object x if and only if x is a cat. Of course, this clause will properly be used to interpret the behaviour only of someone who used the word 'cat' to speak about cats. As with proper names, mere assent to such a clause would not show that anyone actually understood what 'cat' meant. So, anyone who understands what 'cat' means will undoubtedly have some beliefs about cats, and some of these beliefs will agree with some of ours, but what we need to avoid is insisting that anyone who understands the sense of 'cat' has to have any specific beliefs which are to be taken as necessary for anyone to be speaking about a cat. I want to be able to say that the people who thought that cats were divine still spoke about cats with some word of theirs, and that we, as translators, should still be able to translate that word as 'cat', while saying that a lot of their beliefs about cats were false. (The agreement in belief that is the basis of translation does not, of course, rule out quite considerable divergencies of belief, particularly at what might be called non-observational levels.)

It might be felt that a theory of sense should tell us something more interesting than that 'Richard Nixon' stands for Richard Nixon, or that 'cat' refers to an object *x* if and only if *x* is a cat. Indeed, the objection would go on, all that such clauses will be doing will be to construct translation functions, which is quite trivial when we are giving the sense of terms of a language in that language itself.* The reply to this objection begins from the impossibility of explaining a language non-linguistically, and goes on to point out that in the explanations of the terms 'Richard Nixon' and 'cat' we are not mentioning more terms but using the name 'Richard Nixon' and the general term 'cat' to state relationships between a name and a man and a general term and certain animals respectively. We are not translating terms into other terms. Nevertheless, in our explanations, we are using the very terms being explained, it is true, in order to explain what those terms refer to. In defence of this procedure we can stress the unavailability of an unconceptualized world, and the fact that we are attempting an account of language in terms of language. Indeed, the very notion of reference, crucial as it undoubtedly is to our thoughts about language, about what we are doing when we speak about Nixon or the cat on the mat, is itself a notion internal to our language and the view of the world it brings with it.

The suspicion is that theorists of reference too often hope to stand outside ourselves and our language, and to speak of what we are doing when we refer to things as if from some non-linguistic, non-conceptual perspective. They seem to be telling us that if we have the right pictures in our minds we will get to the right objects, or that if our words are caused by objects in the right way we will succeed in referring to them, over-looking the fact that the objects we get to or the objects we envisage as causing our words are already objects conceptualized by us through our language.

Once we realize this, it becomes clear that at least some of our explana-tions of the sense of terms will have to be repetitive in the way that our

---

*One must be careful not to overstate this objection. Our explanations of the logical constants and the quantifiers do not involve simply repeating the same terms in the explanation, but rather explain how the truth of sentences containing such devices depend systematically on the fulfilment of other conditions.

cat clause is. We can, it is true, explain 'bachelor' in terms of 'unmarried man', but what we are doing here is to explain one of the terms of our language in terms of others. At some point, when we are talking of our own language, self-mapping is going to be inevitable, and it is surely better to recognize this from the start, rather than indulge the hope that the sense of every expression can be explained in terms that do not ultimately bring us back to it.

If we can't state non-linguistically and non-repetitively what either the sense or references of the terms of our language are, what is the point of a theory of language which deals in notions like sense and reference? The answer must be that these notions, like the more general notion of meaning itself, are simply posits which are used in inferring in a systematic way from their words the speech acts we regard speakers of a language as engaging in. It is because we regard a speaker of a language as being in a position to refer to certain things in a certain way (because say, of his theoretical knowledge about those things, or because he is causally or perceptually acquainted with those things) that we are able to interpret his words in speech acts of his as an expression of specific beliefs or desires he has, relating to such people as Richard Nixon, and such animals as cats. From the other side, we regard his speech and the words he uses as evidence that he is in a position to refer to those things in a certain way. The theory of language in which we speak of such things as sense and reference, and of meaning more generally, is thus part of a larger project of understanding the speech and hence the propositional attitudes and psychology of others, and this is perhaps the deepest reason for being content with the apparently trivial explanations of sense and reference we get in dealing with our own language, for these explanations are precisely appropriate to the purpose of allowing us to understand the speech of others. Nothing more is needed for this purpose. Apart from all the other objections to richer accounts of sense, whether these are in terms of descriptive beliefs in the heads of speakers, or of causal relationships between speakers and initial baptisms of objects, such accounts invariably make false claims about the knowledge of speakers or their relationship to what they speak about. The account of meaning given here is empirically based, in that we will only be able to say that speakers are using words with given senses if their behaviour, beliefs and causal-perceptual situation generally makes this plausible. The mistake of richer theories of meaning, employing some notion of descriptive sense or of sense being constituted by specific causal relationships between speakers and things, is that they try to make facts about speakers part of the meaning of their words, rather than seeing them as part of the evidence for attributing specific meanings to their words.

Understanding Language

We have seen that a philosophical theory of language ought to enable us to give a systematic account of the utterances of speakers in such a way that those utterances can plausibly be represented as speech acts expressive of psychological attitudes on the part of speakers, speech acts such as asserting, ordering, questioning, pleading, and so on. So far we have been tacitly assuming that the possibility of engaging in a particular speech act with a particular force presupposes that the sense and reference of the words that are used are already fixed. In other words, someone can use the words 'Shut the door!' to express his desire that the door be shut, because the speaker and hopefully the hearer already understand the meaning of 'door', 'shut', etc. But it might be felt, particularly in view of the account of sense offered in the last two sections, that to put things this way round is precisely to reverse the true order of things and that what we should do is to analyse sentence meaning in terms of the intentions with which a speaker utters his words, rather than in terms of the meanings the elements of the sentences might be thought to have prior to or independently of their use in particular speech acts. Such a suggestion can be extracted from a number of papers on the subject of meaning by H. P. Grice, especially 'Meaning',[28] 'Utterer's Meanings and Intentions',[29] and 'Utterer's Meaning, Sentence-Meaning, and Word-Meaning'.[30]

Grice opens his paper on 'Meaning' by distinguishing between cases of what he calls 'natural' meaning from cases of 'non-natural' meaning (referred to as meaning *nn*). Into the first category fall such things as:

1. Those spots meant measles.
2. The recent budget means we shall have a hard year.

Meaning *nn* would be cases like:

3. Those three rings on the bell (of the bus) mean the bus is full.

or

4. The remark 'Smith couldn't get on without his trouble and strife' means in rhyming slang that Smith found his wife indispensable.

The distinction between natural meaning and meaning *nn* should be clear enough from these examples, but a few aspects of it are worth underlining. Only in the case of natural meaning does it follow from '*x* means *p*' that *p*. With meaning *nn* – as in (3) – the agent producing the sign may be mistaken or lying. Indeed only with meaning *nn* is there any implication that an agent is meaning anything. In (1) there is no suggestion that anybody meant anything, while in (2) even if somebody (the Chancellor) meant something by the budget, there is no implication that what he meant was that we should have a hard year.

Having established his distinction, Grice concentrates entirely on meaning *nn*. He begins by rejecting accounts of meaning *nn* in terms of the power of something I do to cause a reaction or belief in others. Thus, my putting on a tail-coat might make people believe I was going to a dance, but this is not an instance of my meaning (in either sense) that I was going to a dance. Equally, my saying 'Jones is a professional basketball player' would probably make most people believe that Jones is tall, but this is hardly part of the meaning of the utterance and no rule of meaning would be violated by talk of short professional basketball players.*

In contrast to attempts to explain meaning *nn* in causal terms, Grice takes intention and the recognition of intentions to be central. He also takes the individual act or utterance as the basic datum to be explained. To say that some speech act or utterance A means *nn* something timelessly (or in general) is, for Grice, simply to say that individuals generally intend to use A (or, more accurately, tokens of type A) to produce reactions of some general type in their hearers. One basic criticism of Grice's account will be to question whether such generalized meaning-types (such as words and sentences) can be accounted for in terms of the use utterers have made of the tokens involved on specific occasions, but before we go into this we must bring out Grice's particular insight regarding meaning *nn*, and this may be done by taking his own example of a case where we do not have a generalizable sign.

The example is of my showing Mr X a drawing I have done of Mr Y making amorous advances to Mrs X. This Grice regards as being a genuine case of meaning *nn*. For what we have here is my intending to produce a belief (about Mr Y and Mrs X) in my audience (Mr X) by means of my act (showing the drawing to Mr X) *and by Mr X's recognition that I do have such an intention.*

This last clause is Grice's particular insight: the way he connects meaning *nn* with audience recognition of the agent's intentions. He wants to

* One of Grice's main philosophical interests has actually been the exploration of cases where speakers would be held to have 'implicated' something by their words, as in the basketball case, without what they have implicated being in any strict sense part of the meaning of their words. It should be noted, though, that, as in the case of the conventional implicatures which are part of the meaning of what one says, Grice rejects any causal account of the functioning of non-conventional or conversational implicatures.

distinguish cases where acts of mine coincidentally produce beliefs and other attitudes in audiences from cases where the attitude production is dependent on audience recognition of my having the intention, and to say that only the latter are cases of meaning *nn*. Thus my carelessly leaving a photograph of Mr Y and Mrs X lying around so that Mr X found it might well have produced the same belief in him, without there being any question of my meaning *nn* anything by my careless behaviour. I mean *nn* only when my audience is intended to fulfil my intention that they should acquire an attitude or belief through recognition that I do have such an intention.

In 'Utterer's Meanings and Intentions', Grice works with the following definition of meaning *nn* for utterances, based on the more general characterizations of meaning *nn* arrived at in 'Meaning': utterer *U* meant *nn* something by uttering A if and only if for some audience, *H*, *U* uttered A intending

  (i) *H* to produce a particular response *r*

  (ii) *H* to think (or recognize) that *U* intends (i)

  (iii) *H* to fulfil (i) on the basis of his fulfilment of (ii).

What *U* means *nn* by A thus turns on the identification of the intended response. It should be clear that in talking in general terms of a *response* here, Grice can account for utterances (and other acts of meaning) which are intended to produce responses in audiences other than beliefs. In other words, in linguistic terms, he can account straightaway for non-indicative modes of utterances, such as orders, pleas, complaints, and the like, and this may at first sight seem to be an advantage his analysis of meaning has over those concentrating on the informative uses of language, which seem to overlook the myriad types of intention utterers can have in speaking. (Very rarely is language used *just* for conveying information.)

In the rest of the paper, Grice defends and refines his basic definition of utterer's meaning so as to accommodate subtle cases where people do not mean *nn* that which they are said to mean *nn* by his definition, and cases where people do mean *nn* what they are said by the definition not to mean *nn*. I shall assume that Grice is successful in dealing with these problems, and that in his definition of utterer's meaning he has said something important about the role recognition of intention has in communication, because I want to consider a more basic problem for him, which in the end undermines his whole attempt to explain (timeless) sentence meaning in terms of the intentions of the utterers have in uttering given sentences on specific occasions. Following Mark Platts[31] we can approach the problem like this. Utterer's meaning, as so far defined, applies to much more than sentences which are grammatically and semantically correct. In addition to including such things as the bus conductor's three rings as examples of meaning *nn*, it would also (surely quite rightly) allow coded utterances, bits of linguistic nonsense and the like to count, so long as we could imagine some audience correctly understanding the utterer's intentions in enunciating the nonsense. It is now natural to ask what there is in regular sentence meaning over and above the utterer's meaning that may be present in his coded or nonsense talk. One might say that the differences between the meaning *nn* involved in the utterance of a newly invented bit of code or nonsense and that involved in the utterance of a standard English sentence is that there is an established *regularity* between the intentions underlying the utterances of standard English sentences and those attaching to nonsense. After all, we could here and now decide to take utterances of 'bububu' to mean 'If it rains, I shall stay in', without cancelling any standard sense of the words, for 'bububu' has none. Now, for Grice the standard or timeless sense of a given English sentence, say 'Snow is white', consists in its regularly being used by English speakers intending to produce in audiences recognition of the fact that the speaker believes snow is white and intends through that recognition to produce a similar belief in the audience. The timeless sense of a word, say 'shaggy', derives from its regularly being used by English speakers in, among other things, assertions intended to produce in audiences beliefs that something or other (such as a particular dog) is shaggy or hairy-coated. How, though, does it get established that people are using 'shaggy' in that way? Grice suggests that this might be done by means of what he calls 'ostensive correlation': the speaker utters 'shaggy' in the presence of a number of hairy-coated objects, intending to point out just those objects, presumably hoping that his audience will latch on.

But, as Grice himself recognizes, many speakers engage in no such explicit acts of correlation-intention for many of their words. We will for such cases, he says, have to invoke the idea of a non-explicit correlation between, say, my use of the name 'Fido' and Jones's dog, and 'it is tempting to suggest that a non-explicit correlation of "Fido" and Jones's dog *consists* in the fact that [I] *would*, explicitly, correlate "Fido" and Jones's dog'.[32] Why this idea is tempting rather than fully satisfactory from Grice's point of view is because when a speaker undertakes the appropriate explicit correlation for some word of standard English, he will not regard himself as stipulating a sense or inventing a new one. It would not be like my stating that in future utterance of 'bububu' was to be understood in a certain way, or that two waves of my hand were in future to be taken as a signal for impending rain. In the case of words and sentences of an existing natural language, any correlations I make between words and things will be seen by me as constrained by existing procedures, as Grice puts it himself. It seems that in participating in established linguistic practices, one is actually bound by sets of rules determining meaning, which have been cut adrift from any original acts of explicit correlation, or the particular intentions of particular speakers, rules which determine precisely which future explicit correlations of words and things are correct and which intentions one might intelligibly be supposed to have in making utterances of specific sorts.

Taking the opposite position to Grice, and saying that timeless (or standard or literal) meaning is not explicable in terms of individual intentions on individual occasions of utterance, but that the direction of dependence is the reverse, shows why certain other features of language use may well be problematic for Grice. There is first the multifariousness of intentions with which actual words and sentences are uttered, which suggests that it is unlikely that there is any such thing as a standard intention regularly going with utterances of given words or sentences. Yet, it seems reasonable to suppose that words and sentences do have standard meanings through all their utterances, however odd the circumstances. Then, second, Grice's account does not explain how, without some prior grasp of word and sentence meaning one's audience is supposed to grasp one's intentions in utterance, except by speaking of the established sense of one's words and sentences. But, in invoking a notion of an established sense to explain what one's actual linguistic intentions might be, one is drawn naturally in the direction of regarding the elements of a natural language as something independent of and logically prior to the actual intentions actual speakers have in making their utterances. In this way, we would be able to see how language, as a pre-existing abstract structure, itself makes possible the intentions speakers have in using it, in much the same way that the existence of chess and its rules makes it possible for us to avoid an attack on our queen from our opponent's bishop.

Grice is, of course, right to see language as in some sense rooted in human life and intentions. An act would hardly be a linguistic act if it could not be conceived in intentional terms, exemplifying some intention of some speaker, and Grice has also shown how the effectiveness of communication through language presupposes a general trust on the part of speakers and hearers – that as a speaker I intend my hearer to recognize my intentions, and as a hearer that the speaker's intentions are what they seem to be. But, from these facts, it does not follow that meaning can be analysed directly in intentional terms, without some irreducible semantic component.

However, even if Grice could show that the meanings of sentences and their component words were ultimately analysable in terms of speakers' intentions, in giving a systematic account of a natural language he will have to show how the meanings of whole sentences – of which there are potentially infinitely many in a natural language – are dependent on the meanings of their parts, the individual words and constructions that make them up. It seems, moreover, that for reasons of economy, if for nothing else, even an intentional account of a natural language would deal separately with those elements of utterances which determine the subject matter of an utterance from those which determine the force with which it is uttered. (We can, for example, distinguish a common element of meaning in the different speech acts involved in the assertion 'Jones is buying a shaggy dog', the question 'Is Jones buying a shaggy dog?', the order 'Buy Jones a shaggy dog!', and so on.) So a Gricean account of a natural language might well mimic much of what is involved in an account of linguistic meaning which sees a natural language as a rule-governed structure floating free of considerations regarding speakers' intentions, and which regards the analysis of meaning as something separable from a treatment of the rules governing the types of force which actual utterances have. What would such an account of meaning look like?

Donald Davidson has made a proposal for such an account, which combines many of the elements which have emerged so far from our study of language: Fregean logic, the idea of a natural language involving a grasp by speakers of the rules underlying a finite vocabulary and stock of constructions, as well as explanations of sense and reference rather similar to the ones suggested earlier in this chapter, together with Tarski's theory of truth. Very briefly, and glossing over important technicalities and qualifications, what Davidson suggests is that we take truth for granted and regard a Tarskian definition of truth for a language as providing us with a theory of meaning for that language. The Tarskian truth definition will consist of axioms like

'Richard Nixon' stands for Richard Nixon

for proper names, and

'cat' is satisfied by an object x, if and only if x is a cat

for predicates, and

⌜A and B⌝ is true if and only if A is true and B is true

for logical connectives.

The axioms, which will of course have to cover all the elements of language, and not just those mentioned, will yield an account of truth which generates as theorems all and only equivalences of the form

(5) 'Snow is white' is true if and only if snow is white.

As already suggested, however, when discussing Fregean logic (above, p. 151), giving a truth definition for the whole of a natural language is going to involve us in extremely difficult problems when we come to deal with adverbs, modalities, verbs ascribing propositional attitudes, and the rest. We want to know what the right form for the clauses dealing with such parts of speech might be. Are adverbs, for example, to be dealt with by taking events as primitive entities, on a par with material objects, or do modalities require that we introduce possible worlds? The problems involved in constructing the axioms for these parts of speech, so that they do yield all and only equivalences like (5), (and indicate how we might draw the right logical consequences from our utterances), are not the merely technical ones of coming up with something formally correct; in the end, we are talking about the elements that turn out to be basic to our language and our picture of the world.

However, we cannot simply lay out the Tarskian definition, assuming we have one, and say that we have thereby given an account of meaning for English, or even for another language such as German if that is the language we are talking about. (The language for whose sentences truth is being defined is called the object-language.) For, as will be remembered, the crucial test which Tarskian definition has to satisfy is that in giving the truth conditions of any sentences of the object-language we have to use a sentence equivalent in meaning to the one we are giving the truth conditions of – either the original sentence itself or a translation of that sentence, where that is appropriate; in other words, Tarski assumes that we know what equivalence of meaning is in order to define truth. So it would be circular to use Tarski's procedure to define meaning.

What Davidson does is to invert Tarski's procedure and to assume that we know what truth is. We then, as in Quine's radical translation, establish by observation what the truth conditions are for some of the sentences of the language we are studying, identify the meanings of terms and progressively, through trial and error, build up a Tarskian-style definition with axioms for the terms and constructions which will produce theorems such as:

(5) 'Snow is white' is true if and only if snow is white

which are all true; our evidence for thinking that our theorems are true will be that the 'native' speaker assents to 'Snow is white' or whatever the sentence is, just where we as linguists would expect him to on the basis of our truth definition (that is, where snow is white), allowing presumably for occasional marginal error of judgement on his part. Now, Davidson is not saying that we can simply reduce 'means that' to 'true if and only if' for there are many instances in which a sentence is true if and only if some condition holds where that condition in no sense gives the meaning of the sentence; for example:

(6) 'Snow is white' is true if and only if some buses are red.

(It will be remembered that the 'if and only if' expression implies only that what is on the left-hand side has the same *truth-value* as what is on the right-hand side, not the same meaning.) Davidson is not claiming that *any* true sentence stating that some sentence in our object-language is true if and only if . . . gives the meaning of that sentence we are looking at. Nor can he be saying that if we construct a theory for the whole of a given language, which yields *only* true T-sentences, and no false ones, then those T-sentences can be regarded as giving meanings, because, as he realizes, we can take any contingently true sentence of English and add it to any of our axioms, and we will still get true T-sentences. For example, we can add 'and the earth moves' to our clause defining the relational term '— is a part of —', and we will get a T-sentence saying, for example,

(7) 'Putney is a part of London' is true if and only if Putney is a part of London and the earth moves.

(7) is clearly true, but equally clearly it does not give the meaning of 'Putney is part of London'. Further constraints on the construction of the T-sentences have to be added if they are to be regarded as giving meanings, or, indeed, before they will be the sort of T-sentences envisaged by Tarski where what we find on the right-hand side of the 'if and only if' is a translation of the object-language sentence on the left-hand side. We *may* be able to get genuinely Tarskian T-sentences without assuming that we have translations of the object-language sentences by imposing certain psychological constraints on our construction of the theory of meaning for the object language.

These constraints would have to do with the best possible guesses we could make as to the beliefs our 'natives' have in asserting their sentences and the evidence they appear to appeal to in establishing them. We would notice that, for example, in establishing that something was a part of something else they did not make observations of the surface of the earth, that in asserting the whiteness of snow they did not inspect the greenness of grass, and so on. In other words, we observe what it is plausible to think of them believing or thinking when they make specific utterances, on the basis of our knowledge of human psychology in general and their environment in particular, and we observe these psychological and environmental plausibilities in mind in constructing our truth definition.

Let us assume that it is possible to construct a Tarskian truth definition for our object-language without assuming that we have translations of its sentences and which is subject to the constraints. What is now being said is that the meaning of any sentence of that language is given by the appropriate *T*-sentence. This is often stated as the thesis that the meaning of a sentence is given by its truth conditions: it need not mislead, so long as we remember the way in which those truth conditions have been established, and the human and psychological constraints on their establishment. Now, it follows from what has been said that understanding the object-language is, in some sense yet to be analysed, equivalent to having implicit knowledge of its truth definition. Now, clearly this knowledge is not being thought of here as explicit propositional knowledge of the theorems. Such knowledge is not necessary, fortunately as it happens, as no one has succeeded in giving the logical form on which we could base axioms for many parts of our speech (cf. above, p. 151). But nor would explicit verbal or propositional knowledge be enough, as we already saw in the case of the Richard Nixon and cat axioms. The knowledge that understanding English consists in must be something other than the ability to *say* what the truth conditions of various sentences are. What we appear to need and what we have been pushing into the background for some time now is an account of what it is for a speaker to know these conditions.

If the knowledge in question cannot be the purely verbal knowledge that 'Snow is white' is true if and only if snow is white, saying that someone understands the meaning of 'Snow is white' must involve their ability to use the sentence or – what comes to the same thing – understand what is involved in the fulfilment of the truth conditions in some way.

Davidson sometimes appears to be suggesting that we can explain a speaker's understanding of 'Snow is white' or any other sentence in terms of his knowledge of its truth conditions. But, it might be urged, we have got to say something more about what understanding the fulfilment of the truth conditions consists in for there to be any genuine explanation here. Davidson is not, of course, suggesting that this understanding of truth conditions is some comparison of pure unconceptualized reality and our words, so that more is going to have to be in terms of the use a speaker makes of this knowledge. This does not contradict what we said earlier about the understanding of proper names and general terms; indeed, we stressed there that this knowledge would be manifested in an ability to use the terms in question in speech acts plausibly expressive of the speaker's psychological states. What we are now asking is, in effect, if anything more systematic and less general can be said about this.

Michael Dummett, who more than anyone else has criticized the idea that understanding the meaning of the sentences of one's language consists in knowing their truth conditions on grounds of lack of explanatory power, has suggested that what we need is an account of meaning in which our understanding of the sense of sentences is seen in terms of an ability to recognize the circumstances in which an utterance of a sentence would be justified. Knowledge of meaning (and hence of truth conditions, if truth conditions are taken as they appear to be by Davidson as equivalent to the sense of a sentence) amounts to an ability to recognize when those conditions obtain. Dummett writes 'We no longer explain the sense of a statement by stipulating its truth-value in terms of the truth-values of its constituents, but by stipulating when it may be asserted in terms of conditions under which its constituents may be asserted.'[33] Understanding for Dummett, then, consists in knowing assertibility conditions, and sense appears to be equivalent to such conditions. However, putting our understanding of sense in this way has the consequence that with many sentences not only will we never be able to manifest our understanding, because we are never in and can never envisage ourselves as being in a position conclusively to verify or falsify them, but also apparently, being ignorant of when they may be asserted, we do not fully understand their sense.

Examples of such statements might be statements about the remote past, statements about universal natural laws, statements in mathematics we can neither prove nor disprove, and for which an effective means of proof or disproof does not exist, certain open-ended statements about the future, such as 'A city will never be built here', and counterfactual statements. What would our understanding of such statements amount to? Does it amount to the possession and manifestation of whatever procedures we have which are weaker than conclusive proof, but which would count in favour of or against the assertion in question? This is something that non-realists about meaning such as Dummett need to clarify.

One can, of course, object to any account of linguistic meaning and understanding in terms of knowledge of assertibility conditions, whatever these conditions are taken to be, on the grounds that a clear distinction needs drawing between a statement's meaning and truth, on the one hand, and the grounds we might have for asserting it, on the other. One very obvious drawback is that such a doctrine would entail that the meaning of many statements would alter depending on when and by whom they were uttered, even though they appear to be about the same event. Consider, for example, a statement made by us in the twentieth century to the effect that Caesar crossed the Rubicon in 49 BC and a statement of one of Caesar's companions at the time to the same effect. The grounds on which the two statements are asserted must be entirely different, yet it seems implausible to suggest that what they mean is different. They appear to be about the same event, and made true or false by the existence or non-existence of the same event. Looked at like this, it seems most implausible to suppose that the sense of the two statements is different, or that the way we would set about justifying them has anything to do with their meaning. Indeed, to suggest that it does also implies that, when we discover better means of investigating what would normally be regarded as a given subject matter, our talk about that subject matter actually changes in meaning. The position we have now reached is something like this. Understanding a sentence is first analysed as knowing its truth conditions. But, it is said, this cannot be a merely verbal knowledge of what those truth conditions are, so it must be an ability to recognize the fulfilment (or at least the partial fulfilment) of those conditions. So into understanding what a sentence means enters our grasp of the ways we would set about verifying or falsifying it.

Mode of verification is thus seen as at least part of the meaning of a sentence. The idea we find in Dummett that understanding the meaning of a sentence consists in the ability to recognize when its justification conditions are fulfilled will naturally be located on the non-realist pragmatist–coherentist side of the dispute about truth which we examined in Chapter 2. For Dummett, learning a language involves first and foremost learning when it is correct to assert something, as we have seen, and he has difficulty in accounting for the meaning of sentences which outstrip our recognitional capacities. Dummett's view also has the consequence that new types of justification can, if they are central enough, change the meaning of terms involved, especially when these supersede older ones, rather in the same way as on the Kuhnian position on changes in scientific theory, and perhaps should be rejected for the same reasons. Even if we are unhappy with a naïve correspondence view of truth or meaning, we surely want the truth and meaning of our sentences to be unaffected by changes in procedures of justification, as well as in changes of the position of speakers relative to the state of affairs being described.

Is it possible to develop a non-realist theory of meaning which gives some role in our account of meaning to procedures of justification, but which is less susceptible than Dummett's to objections of the sort mentioned? These objections appear in part to depend on the way Dummett construes meaning in terms of actual procedures of justification, because at least some of the problems are to do with the use or introduction of different procedures: the different procedures we have to use in verifying Caesar's Rubicon crossing from those of his lieutenant, the change in verification procedures from one scientific paradigm to another. Putnam, who says that he has been persuaded by Dummett on many of the issues in these areas, suggests that we regard truth (and hence, presumably, meaning) in terms of idealized justification conditions, rather than in terms of justification on present evidence, as he is insistent that assertibility can be revised for the better as our empirical knowledge increases.[34] A suggestion of this sort, however, would not help us much with accounting for the assertibility conditions of many of the sentences Dummett saw as posing such a problem for the truth conditions theorist.

Dummett objects to the idea that we, or even some superhuman being, one day or in different circumstances might simply observe directly the truth of a counterfactual statement by direct insight into counterfactual reality, unless we were able to provide a picture of what this power might consist in.[35] We might, on similar grounds, say that talking of an idealized notion of warranted assertibility by itself tells us nothing of what the assertibility conditions – or the meaning – of, say, statements about inaccessible regions of space and time, or of many counterfactuals, might be. Certainly, it is hard to see how even the most ideal experimental conditions or procedures of investigation could ever allow us to produce decisions on myriads of sentences such as 'Caesar had exactly two hairs more on his head on the day he crossed the Rubicon than when he entered Rome', or 'If Mussorgsky had not been alcoholic, he would have lived to a good old age.' We seem to understand these sentences perfectly well, but we cannot account for their truth or falsity, or their meaning, in terms of theories which would tie truth and meaning down to verification, even in the most ideal conditions. Arguing as we have that the meaning (and hence truth) of sentences depends on their place in systems of sentences is not the same as saying that those systems must give us ways of deciding on the truth of all the sentences they generate.

Against the analysis of meaning in terms of assertibility conditions, while it is true our picture of the world is initially based in our practices, including those of verification, elements of that picture outstrip our procedures of verification. Our probing gives us the possibility of referring to things that are beyond our powers to know, and our conceptualizing of reality itself leads us to the idea that there are things we can speak about without being able to verify, or even have any idea how to verify or falsify, sentences about them. In this fairly strong sense, there are mind-independent realities, and the intuition behind a correspondence theory of truth is, up to a point, vindicated. We need a verification-independent theory of truth and meaning to account for the workings of our language, which appears to enable us to talk and speculate about things which we regard as being true or false quite beyond our powers of justification, though how far this realism should be taken with the more theoretical claims of science is, as we have said (p. 136), problematic. In contrast to the views of Dummett and Putnam, such a theory is just what is provided by the analysis of meaning suggested by Davidson, in terms of the truth conditions of sentences and modest axioms governing the senses of terms. Davidson's theory is itself seen as part of an attempt to ascribe intelligible speech acts to particular speakers on the basis of their utterances, but, to repeat once more, the empirical constraints on the construction of such a theory of meaning for a given language will not be whether the assertions thus ascribed to speakers of that language are verifiable by them, nor should we regard the theory itself as being constrained to give an account of how we get ourselves in a position to recognize of some object x that that object is, say, a cat. What counts is rather whether, from our own point of view, it is intelligible that these speakers should be having the beliefs we ascribe to them. We know, at least from our own case, that such beliefs go along with our conception of ourselves as living in a world that exists and manifests regularities to some extent independent of our perceptions of it, even if we cannot get any purchase on that world except through our own concepts and categorizations.

It might be felt, however, that even if we do not need to fill out our account of meaning with a fuller account of the sense of terms than the modest clauses such as '"Richard Nixon" stands for Richard Nixon' and '"cat" refers to an object x if and only if x is a cat', this leaves the very notion of referring to objects which is assumed in these clauses up in the air, and, especially if we are materialists, we need some general account of our ability to refer to things in the world which would root that ability firmly in physical facts about objects and about ourselves. In other words, we will only really understand language if we understand the causal (physical) connections that exist between us and the things we refer to. Hartry Field[36] has argued that the notions of reference and truth (which are based on the axioms where reference is apparently presupposed) which emerge from Tarskian truth definitions are woefully inadequate, that all we are told by them about reference, say, is in effect that, for all x and all y, x refers to y if and only if x is (the name) 'Richard Nixon' and y is Richard Nixon, or x is 'Hubert Humphrey' and y is Hubert Humphrey ... and so on until we have listed all the names and all their bearers. Similar lists will be given for the reference of general terms, and the definition of truth, too, simply consists in pairings of sentences with their truth conditions. But in chemistry, we would not be satisfied if a request for a definition of valence was answered by a similar list pairing all the chemical substances and their numbers. Moreover, Field argues that unless we can give a fuller (physical) account of what reference is our conceptual scheme breaks down from the inside, concluding that, on our theory of the world, it would be 'extremely surprising' if there were some non-physical connection between words and things. What Field seems to be implying is that the notion of reference, or, perhaps more accurately, each occasion on which a speaker uses a word to refer to an object, involves a physical link-up between the word and the object, via the speaker, which explains how it is that the word and the speaker may be said to refer to the object. He is claiming that in the absence of something like this, language, with its ability to link words with things, and so to say true or false things about them, will remain an anomaly, something not part of the natural-causal order at all, and so, presumably, will we, the speakers of languages. Such a thought would clearly be anathema to materialists (or physicalists, as they are sometimes called). Like McDowell,[37] we can respond to Field in the following way. What Field is looking for is a cueing in of our theory of meaning to the world at the point of the primitive axioms (for 'Richard Nixon', 'cat' etc.). But this is to mislocate the point at which our theory connects with the world. Our theory of meaning is primarily a theory of understanding other people. Its empirical content and contact, if any, are to be looked for there, as to whether it allows us to link up people's utterances and their behaviour (both physical things), so as to throw light on their behaviour, including of course their utterances. The theory will be adequate to the extent that it provides satisfactory interpretations of their utterances, in the light of their behaviour, in such a way that, whenever the theory says that an utterance of theirs, say A, says that p, their behaviour would make a saying that p reasonable. We do not require that empirical contact be made *within* the apparatus that allows us to read an utterance of A as a saying that p, and the axioms governing single terms are devices within that apparatus. They are not themselves the point at which our theory is rooted in the observable realm, so there is no requirement even for a physicalist that anything physical should directly underlie what they say, so long as the theory itself is based in hard physical facts.

McDowell goes on to argue that a physicalist need not expect that even at the level of the interpretation of whole utterances as speech acts revelatory of speakers' behaviour anything interesting or systematic would turn up relating the utterance to what we are reading it as being about. It is true that an utterance is a physical event, describable in terms of sound waves, etc. So there is no utterance, and, indeed, no piece of behaviour, that is not a physical event, and if we are physicalists and believe that all physical events are governed by physical law, then there is no utterance or piece of behaviour that is not so governed. But, in interpreting people's utterances as speech acts and their behaviour as action, we are treating the utterances and behaviour as intended by them; indeed, it is as intended by them that our interpretation makes sense of it.

Now, as we shall see in the next chapter, it may be that there is no systematic linking of any sort between bits of behaviour considered as physical events, and the same bits of behaviour considered as intentional actions. All that physicalism requires is that every piece of behaviour should, *qua* physical event, be describable in terms of physical law. It does not require that any description of it as intentional be translatable directly into physical-law terms. The intentional and the physical, as levels of description, may just fail to link together in any systematic way. Applying this to linguistic behaviour, take my utterance of the words

'Richard Nixon was not so stupid!'

Somone interpreting these words as they fall from my mouth will only be able to interpret them as being about the former President of the US if it is at all plausible that I might be in a position to utter an opinion about that person. Indeed, as we saw earlier, this sort of constraint operates at the very construction of a truth-definition of my language. We can then agree that, in regarding the utterance-event as being about Richard Nixon, there will be *some* physical–causal relation between my utterance and Nixon. But it does not follow from this – what Field wants and what, in a different way, Kripke wanted – that there will be just one physically describable relation between any occurrence of any name and its denotation, as McDowell puts it. Even if it so happened that there was such a relation this discovery would not amount to a reduction of the semantic notion of reference to the physical.

The case would be quite unlike the discovery in biology that genes were DNA molecules, because, as we shall see in Chapter 4, relations which obtain in the intentional sphere are governed by quite different types of consideration from these governing physical events and relationships, and meaning relationships are, as we have said, an example of the intentional. We say that someone's words refer to some object or person not *because* of some causal or physical relation that exists between his words and this object, but because looking at his words in this way helps us towards forming a conception of his words and actions as a rational, coherently related whole, in which his words serve as a plausible expression of his attitudes, his actions seem reasonable given his desires, and his desires, to complete the circle, fit with his words. In regarding language and the understanding of language as a part of a task of interpreting what people do and think, so as to yield a picture of an agent as (in the main) a being who exhibits rational coherence between thoughts, words and deeds, we are introducing elements and constraints that play no part in our descriptions of physical events in terms of physical law. Whatever physical facts underlie our claims that peoples' words refer to particular objects, claiming that they do is true in so far as seeing them as referring to those objects helps to make their words and behaviour rationally coherent.

Rules and Conventions

Throughout this chapter on language, we have encountered the idea that speaking a language is a rule-governed activity, and that we can describe its systematic nature by giving sets of rules which explain the meanings of the terms and lay bare the logical structure of the language. Logic, itself, that which governs correctness in argument and inference, comes to be seen as a formal system, moving smoothly and necessarily from statable axioms and rules of inference to valid conclusions or theorems. Encouraged by the prospect of analyses of logic and language as governed by statable rules, we might then hope to throw light on two of the deepest problems in philosophy. We may hope to explain our speaking of language in a rule-governed way and the nature of logical (and mathematical) necessity in terms of the initial adoption of rules or conventions, which then guide our future practice in such a way that the correctness of a new application of a term we have learned or the necessity of the truth of a logical (or mathematical) conclusion are determined by our initial choice of the relevant convention. On the nature of logical and mathematical truth, Ayer put it in *Language, Truth and Logic* that propositions of logic and arithmetic, 'simply record our determination to use words in a certain fashion. We cannot deny them without infringing the conventions which are presupposed by our very denial, and so falling into self-contradiction. And this is the sole ground of their necessity.'[38] What I want to show in this section is that neither our speaking of a language in a rule-governed way nor logical necessity can be explained in terms of the adoption of conventions.

To take the question of logical (and mathematical) necessity first, the attraction of a conventionalistic explanation is that, as we saw in the quotation from Ayer, it appears to reduce the problematic notion of necessity to something quite open and familiar. Instead of looking for logical facts which bind our thought in a non-empirical way, we simply appeal to our decision to adopt certain rules, as in a game like chess or football. In chess it might be said what makes a move, such as a pawn going three squares at once, a false move is simply the fact that we have agreed that pawns should not move in such a way. What we have here is an arbitrary choice, but one by which we agree to be bound so long as we play chess. Perhaps some international chess authority could change the rule, but, until they do, we have to stick with it. This, I think, is what people mean when they talk about a rule or decision being conventional, and there is nothing more mystical about it than there is about any other talk about human decisions and agreement, though, to be sure, that is problematic enough.

The model of the conventions governing logic and mathematics is probably going to be rather more complicated than the game case. The conventions adopted will be adopted 'because they serve the ends of inquiry' or something of the sort (though presumably rules of games, and modification of them, will be responsive to the overall aim of the game): moreover, whatever else international logic conferences do, they don't stipulate new rules of logic. We will be told that the conventions governing logical inference which we adopt for the purposes of speech and argument are adopted first in our behaviour and only later put into words and formalized. When we formalize them, we are effecting a rational reconstruction of our practice, showing where its necessities derive from in reality. However, as Quine has shown in 'Truth by Convention'[39] a model of logical necessity as based in conventions adopted (even without explicit formulation) arbitrarily and prior to the validity or necessity of any logical inference is incoherent. The first reason for this is roughly the same as that given by Lewis Carroll in 'What the Tortoise Said to Achilles' and is that, if we treat a general rule by which we draw a conclusion from various particular premises as itself a further explicit and particular premise in our argument, we will then need another general rule permitting us to derive our conclusion from our now enlarged set of premises. We can, of course, add the new rule as a further specific premise, but we will then need yet another rule to deal with the yet larger set of premises, and an infinite regress is under way. The relevance of this infinite regress argument to the idea that the truths of logic can be regarded as deriving from conventions is that logic (in the form of the unexpressed rule) is needed at every point in order to derive our specific logical conclusions from the conventions, if we are treating those conventions as part of the set of specific premises in an argument. Quine's second point is simply that, in expressing the conventions which are, on the conventionalist account of logic, supposed to govern the meanings and implications of the logical terms 'if', 'not', 'all', and so on, we will not be able to avoid making free use of those very idioms which we are attempting to circumscribe;[40] in other words, we will succeed in expressing the relevant conventions only if we are already conversant with the idioms. So both in understanding and in applying the conventions to derive logical inferences, we will be presupposing some logical truths. Logic thus lies too deep in our thought and language for it to be secondary to any set of conventional stipulations, even as a rational reconstruction of our procedures. The rules determining our logical practices cannot be explained or justified by appeal to anything like the adoption of conventions, because at least some of the conventions themselves will, as Quine puts it, 'be incapable of being communicated until after [their] adoption'.[41]

Are we then to conclude that what we do at the deepest logical level we do naturally as opposed to conventionally? Something of this sort would appear to follow from the analysis of rule-following given by Wittgenstein in his *Philosophical Investigations* and related writings. One way of interpreting Wittgenstein's point, which is a deeply sceptical one, is to say that we cannot invoke the notion of following a rule as an explanation of why we use a word in a certain way on future occasions of its use or of why we declare a certain conclusion to follow logically or necessarily from certain premises, because nothing that can be stated as a rule contains within itself all its future applications. On the contrary, in Wittgenstein's view, neither language nor logic (or mathematics) can be regarded as having foundations in this sense. Rules, whether stated in language or regarded as thoughts or mental images, do not and cannot guide our behaviour in speaking and drawing conclusions, because more than one outcome can be regarded as conforming to any rule or image. In fact, any bit of behaviour can be regarded as being in conformity with any rule. What we do is to speak and act, fortunately, as it happens, by and large in concert. We simply agree in the main on the future applications of linguistic terms and on what follows from what in logic and mathematics.

We can retrodict from our communal behaviour and say that we are following such and such rules, but this cannot be regarded as anything more than an *ex post facto* summary of our behaviour, perhaps like the case where we see people throwing a ball around aimlessly as it seems, and someone says that the whole time they are playing a game with definite rules at every throw. But rules that are retrodicted in this way do not determine future behaviour in the way that a gramophone record determines the sounds that emerge from the speakers, nor would they justify what we do at any very deep level.

How does Wittgenstein reach these radical conclusions? His basic insight in this area can be presented as very similar to Goodman's new riddle of induction, only applied to the inductions we might make about the linguistic and logical behaviour of our fellows, rather as if Goodman's grue-bleen speakers did not use the words 'grue' and 'bleen' at all, but used 'green' and 'blue', only (we would say) to say what ought to be said by 'grue' and 'bleen'. What Wittgenstein is out to smash is the hold on us of the idea that we can have in our minds or in verbal form an image or a set of instructions (such as a convention) which will tell us how to apply some term or some logical or mathematical operation in the future. So, we have an image, let us say, of something green (or a physical sample – it does not matter) and we want to use it to determine our future use of 'green'. Can it do this? What if we are grue thinkers and call a blue object observed after 2000 'green'? Have we made a mistake? It is Wittgenstein's contention that there are circumstances in which it would be wrong to say that we have made a mistake, rather than that we are just different from those who use 'green' in the 'normal' way.

The most famous instance of this form of argument in Wittgenstein occurs at section 185 of the *Philosophical Investigations*.[42] We are asked to consider a pupil who is being taught the principles of addition, how to add plus one plus two, etc., to a series of numbers. All our examples and tests are with numbers of less than 1,000, and he goes on as we do up to 1,000. But when we tell him to continue a series (say plus two) beyond 1,000, he writes down 1,004, 1,008, 1,012. We try and point out his mistake, telling him that he is not going on in the same way as he had done before, but he simply insists that he is:

In such a case, we might say, perhaps: It comes natural to this person to understand our order with our explanations as *we* should understand the order:

'Add 2 up to 1,000, 4 up to 2,000, 6 up to 3,000 and so on'. Such a case would present similarities with one in which a person naturally reacted to the gesture of pointing with the hand by looking in the direction of the line from finger-tip to wrist, not from wrist to finger-tip.

Wittgenstein's point appears to be that the notion of going on in the same way, even when preceded by explicit instructions as to how one is meant to go on, is crucially and necessarily under-determined.

There are all sorts of unspoken presuppositions and expectations about how someone will go on when presented with an instruction. We can, of course, guard against and correct some misunderstandings, but never all potential misunderstandings, because in our very process of correction we will be assuming communality of understanding at other points. Explanation and correction must come to an end at some point, at which we expect the pupil to 'see' how he is meant to go on, just as justification of our practices does:

> If I have exhausted the justifications I have reached bedrock, and my spade is turned. Then I am inclined to say 'This is simply what I do.'[43]

Fortunately, at these points, as with pointing a finger in a certain direction, we generally all act in the same way. So, communication generally, and language in particular, becomes possible. Within the framework of shared action and reaction, it is possible to give explanations and rules that go far enough to initiate others into our linguistic and calculating practices. But what makes the rules we give in doing this guides to action is the fact that we do share a form of life, and do, naturally, tend to agree on the future application of these rules. It is not something inherent in the rules themselves or indeed expressible by means of them; without us all following pointing gestures in one way rather than in another, and countless other unspoken agreements in practice, rules would be quite useless in determining how we were to speak or reason.

Indeed, Wittgenstein goes so far as to say that without a community of people speaking and reasoning similarly, the very notion of following a rule would lose its sense because on some interpretation any bit of behaviour can be made out to accord with a rule. What makes some bits accord and other bits fail to accord is not a relationship between a rule and a single piece of my behaviour but the fact that other people in my community act similarly. (In his paper 'Wittgenstein on Rules and Private Language' Kripke has very pertinently pointed out the parallels between Wittgenstein's analysis of rule-following in terms of the behaviour of many people and Hume's account of causality in terms of the constant conjunction of many events.)

We should not underestimate the implications of Wittgenstein's claims. According to G. P. Baker and P. M. Hacker, in their monumental commentary on the *Philosophical Investigations*, they completely undermine any hope of accounting for linguistic understanding in Fregean terms, in terms that is of some calculus of rules for using words so as to yield sentences whose sense is determined by the truth conditions that result from particular combinations of the words used to form the sentences.[44] Why language is in order and possible depends rather on the fact that there is agreement in our judgements and in our actual ways of explaining expressions. In Wittgenstein's view, they say, there are multiple criteria for understanding expressions and explaining their use with different standards of explicitness and exactness, depending on need; further, there is no assumption that assertion is primary, or that truth conditions are central to understanding. In this, as in so much else, philosophical concentration on explaining sense in terms of the truth conditions of assertions deviates from and distorts our actual practices. In our actual practice, so much tacit understanding is presupposed, that the attempt to capture anything significant by means of a calculus of rules determining the sense of whole sentences in terms of the senses of their parts is doomed from the start. The sort of phenomenon one might point to here, is the way an expression can contribute differently to the sense of one sentence from the way it contributes to the sense of another. An example would be 'on' in 'They established a base camp on Mount Everest.' and 'The calendar is on the table.' In the one case 'on' can be replaced by 'on top of' but not in the other. How could this sort of fact, which occurs countless times in ordinary language, be dealt with systematically? Would we have to give different rules for 'on' to deal with the different cases? The point seems to be that the sense of words is highly sensitive to the context of their utterance, so much so as to destroy the hope of any general theory of meaning which took the words out of the context in which they actually have sense. Indeed, one could go further and point to the incredible and ultimately unspecific amount that is taken for granted and is part of our actual understanding in any actual use of something as ordinary as the words of the second sentence quoted to yield an assertion to the effect that a particular calendar is on a particular table. Frege, in the view of Baker and Hacker, was, in his conception of the way language works, the great myth-maker of contemporary philosophy, and Wittgenstein has exploded the myth, whether people have understood him or not.

Kripke regards Wittgenstein's analysis of rule-following as even more destructive than Baker and Hacker. He appears to have shown '*all* language, *all* concept formation, to be impossible, indeed unintelligible'.[45]

And Wittgenstein's 'solution' – that we can be said to mean things by our words only if our practice in the application of expressions coincides with that of others – seems hardly to solve the mystery. What he is really saying is that there is no fact of the matter about me or my words or my understanding of them which determines that I shall be correct in calling the creature at my feet a dog, or in saying that 1,000 plus 2 is really 1,002 and not 1,004. What makes these things correct is simply that I belong to a community that will corroborate my saying these things. Of course, I *feel* bound to say these things, I *feel* that in saying them I am being faithful to my original understandings of 'dog' and 'plus 2' but that is all I can say, so long as I consider myself in isolation. What I feel does not constitute correctness, and, as in this case, so long as I simply concentrate on myself, there is no more than what I feel, and hence no sense in asking whether what I feel is really right or wrong. So Wittgenstein concludes 'To *think* one is obeying a rule, is not to obey a rule. Hence it is not possible to obey a rule "privately"; otherwise thinking one was obeying a rule would be the same thing as obeying it.'[46]

So, as Kripke points out, Wittgenstein's scepticism about meaning and necessity makes it impossible for us to say that we all say that 1,000 plus 2 = 1,002 *because* we all grasp the concept of addition in the same way, any more than for Hume we can say that heat follows fire because of a heat-producing power in the fire. All we can say about fire and heat is that the two are regularly observed going together, and all we can say about addition is that, as a brute, 'natural' fact, people in our community sharing our form of life tend to say that 1,000 plus 2 makes 1,002 not 1,004. But there is no reason why either of these regularities might not break down: the next instance of fire might feel cold to me, people might start giving all sorts of different answers even to simple sums. If they did, not only would mathematics collapse, but we could not say that everybody had started making mathematical mistakes, because of the loss of the very background of agreement in judgement on which talk of some calculations as being correct and others as being mistaken depends.

Wittgenstein's view on rule-following is incredible at the very point at which it goes beyond Humean and Goodmanian scepticism about induction. For although, as I suggested earlier, it is possible to see his position in terms of a 'green–grue' dilemma as applied to the linguistic usage of others, in the most fundamental case, in the denial that I can obey a rule privately, what is at issue is a scepticism regarding knowledge of my *own* intentions concerning my linguistic usage and my calculating practices. Even if I cannot be sure simply by observing their behaviour what anyone else will do when confronted by the first emerald after A D 2000, assuming that it is the colour we would now call 'green', I can at least know whether *I* would call it 'green' or 'blue' in A D 2000 and this suffices to fix my own understanding of 'green' and 'blue' (i.e. my use of 'green' is not equivalent to Goodman's 'grue', nor my use of 'blue' equivalent to 'bleen'). I can thus envisage some future behaviour of mine as being in conformity with my present linguistic intentions and other behaviour, say, if other people called it 'blue', which would be in contrast to my present intentions and understanding of terms. But if I can ask myself what I would call something in the future and get a definite answer, I can also ask other people what they would do, and so discover whether or not they are really meaning 'grue' when they say 'green'. So the prospect of a wholesale inductive doubt concerning the future linguistic practice of myself and others can be avoided, once we realize that questions about future linguistic practice are, in part, questions about people's present intentions and what would or would not be consistent with those intentions. Wittgenstein's views about rule-following are incredible because they suggest that we cannot know what would be or would not be consistent with our own or with others' present (linguistic) intentions until we or they *decide* how to treat the next case. And, in his picture, these decisions cannot be made right or wrong by anything that is the case now, for to say that would be to admit the very point he is at pains to deny.

The last point comes out particularly clearly in his writings on mathematics. He says that far from a proof being justified because in it we are faithful to the sense we have already given to the expressions involved, accepting a new theorem is a decision, an invention, like adopting a new rule of language. Laws of calculating and inference, in his view, compel us not like a railway locomotive stuck on parallel tracks, but more like other laws of human society: we get punished or inconvenienced if we do not do the same as others, people generally expect others to conform, such practices are general. If they were not then there would be no such thing as calculating or inferring, but the foundations of these practices are the brute facts of psychology and anthropology, namely, that we just happen to act in concert on these matters.

Without denigrating the fascination of much of what Wittgenstein says, it is hard to take his central contention about proof seriously. Is the example of the deviant calculator adding 2 to 1,000 even coherent? It seems coherent, but only so long as we do not probe deeper. We are being told in effect that it might have been open to some calculator of such a sum to come up with 1,004 as an answer, on the grounds that 'it comes naturally to this person' to understand the order as we would understand the order 'add 2 up to 1,000, 4 up to 2,000, 6 up to 3,000 and so on'. But adding 2 to 1,000 would surely be equivalent to adding 4 to 998 or 502 to 500 or to multiplying 2 by 501? There is no clear way the 'adding 4 up to 2,000' rule could be applied directly to these other cases, so, unless yet more deviant rules are introduced, it looks as if we are going to get 1,002 in these cases. But if we had 1,002 physical objects, we could surely demonstrate that exactly the same quantity could be represented as 1,000 plus 2, 998 plus 4, 500 plus 502 or 2×501. If Wittgenstein took the course of having yet more deviant rules to cover these other cases, then it will become increasingly doubtful, as the deviations increase, that the deviant reasoner ever had the same concept of number as ours in the first place, in which case it is not shown that, given the same initial understanding of the rules, deviant applications are possible.

What remains defensible in the Wittgensteinian account of rules, whether these are rules for calculating and inferring, or rules for the use of language, is that many of the rules in question are either our constructions, adopted no doubt for various purposes of ours, or, at a deeper level (as Quine showed), pre-conventional tendencies we have to draw inferences of various sorts. But what Wittgenstein fails to convince most philosophers of is that there is no sense in which we can objectively succeed or fail in being consistent in our applications of these rules and tendencies. And, if this is right, this is a deep and significant conclusion, for it shows that the notions of consistency and of rationality (in so far as consistency is part of rationality), which are central to our use of language and of calculation, are not themselves revisable or malleable by decision. Indeed, to represent these just as pre-conventional tendencies of our mind is overly naturalistic, if it suggests that that is all they are and that they could have been different had our make-up been different. In fact, given that they are presupposed in any discussion of rules or anything at all, it is hard to see any reason for not saying that they are *a priori*. What, though, of Baker and Hacker's scepticism regarding a Fregean account of language? I do not see that the reasons they adduce concerning the tacit presuppositions of utterance and the sensitivity of the sense of words to context would necessarily rule out as impossible the comparatively limited, though hardly simple, programme for philosophy of language suggested here, for that programme does not purport to do more than show in a systematic way how the parts of sentences yield the truth conditions of whole sentences. It is hard to believe, despite the effect of context on utterance, and the prevalence of non-literal usage, that the meaning of whole sentences does not depend in a systematic way on sentence parts, as the Davidsonian account suggests. In so doing, it leads us into all sorts of difficult questions about analysis of proper names, general terms, adverbial constructions, modality and much else besides, including of course the relations between assertive and other uses of languages.

It does not, however, say anything about how the statements of truth conditions are themselves to be understood, or how we, as speakers of the language in which they are expressed, relate our words to the circumstances in which we find ourselves. To say something on the first point might well involve us quickly in the circularity of attempting to say what language means by means of language, while it may well be true that nothing can be said about the second point which is not, in effect, a full description of human activity and intelligence. (Perhaps this is what Baker and Hacker are really after.) Putnam, commenting on the failure of attempts to programme a 'translating machine' (in contrast to the ability of linguists to learn new languages in a matter of hours), says that to simulate translation in general, one would have to have a simulation of full human intelligence, interests and so on, because what one is doing in translation is to project one's own ideas and interests on to the words of the alien.[47]

We have seen the philosophy of language very much in terms of effecting systematic translations of the utterances of others into plausible ascriptions to them of belief and other attitudes, or, if we are working on our own language, to show how the parts of our utterances contribute systematically to the sense of the wholes. The rules and regularities underlying these utterances, which we hope to uncover in this way, will be those that allow us as interpreters to move systematically and explicitly to an interpretation of the utterance. But they will not and cannot also give us an interpretation of the interpretation; that would be to attempt to say the unsayable.

Chapter Four

Human Beings

In this chapter, we will consider the nature of human beings. What type of thing are we? Are we physical objects, or is there something irreducibly non-physical about us? Is there such a thing as the mind, apart from the brain? What is meant by speaking of a person acting, apart from saying that certain bodily movements occurred? Is human action free, or are we to regard ourselves as in some way outside the causal chains that compose physical nature? Then, what is the essential *me*? What is it that makes me the same person as the person that grew up in Lincolnshire so many years ago? Is this essential me constituted by sameness of body, or is it something more mental, a psychological continuity in some sense? If the latter, could I, the essential me, survive the death of my physical body?

These questions are, as we shall see, distinct. Nevertheless, running through them all is a tension between two distinct ways of looking at human beings, which has been aptly characterized by Thomas Nagel as that between a subjective perspective and an objective one.[1] In the objective perspective, we look at things, as far as possible, from no one's point of view. This is the perspective of natural science. Its descriptions and explanations are not couched in terms which make reference to an observer, to his position or point of view; ideally, too, they make no reference to his particular type of experience or to features specific to it. The ideal that science approximates to is an account of the world that would be intelligible to creatures with senses and experiences quite different from our own. The subjective point of view is one which is from the perspective of a single being experiencing the world. It assumes the centrality of my position and the type of experience of creatures like me.

However much we may wish to ascend to an objective viewpoint, we cannot, of course, completely prescind from our here and now, as we saw in our discussion of time, nor can we dispense entirely with our human experience of the world, for that would be to cut our science adrift from the experiential grounds which give us reason to accept it as true, as we have also seen already. Nevertheless, it is in considering ourselves that the tension between the subjective and the objective points of view becomes most pronounced, for if we are, at least in part, part of the physical world, the world of nature, we are also creatures with a subjective experience and consciousness of that world. The problem in discussing human beings and their behaviour – or ourselves and *our* behaviour – is to keep the truth of both perspectives in view, and not to emphasize one at the expense of the other.

The temptation to over-emphasize the objective account may seem to be the more dangerous at this time, both because of the prestige of science and because of the feeling that an impersonal account of the world, purged of subjective elements, gets closer to the essential nature of things than a viewpoint centred on one individual and based on experiences shared by members of only one species, but the subjective point of view is not without its problems, too, if it leads people to consider themselves as being in effect outside the world of nature and simply looking in on or floating free of its operations, and occasionally interfering with them from outside as it were. This latter tendency is exemplified most directly in dualist accounts of the mind, to which we shall now turn.

The Mind

When we look at ourselves in comparison with the rest of nature, it becomes apparent that we have certain characteristics and abilities that are not shared by inanimate things. We feel, we suffer, we react to our environment in the light of our consciousness of it. We have, in other words, a point of view on things, something which could not be said of my table or of Mount Everest. Of course, consciousness and the potentiality for felt pleasure and pain are also characteristics of other living things, animals, birds, insects, fish, among others. But human beings have specific intellectual and moral capacities that set them apart from other animals. Examples of these capacities include our abilities to calculate and to reason abstractly, to construct and develop social institutions and cultural and artistic traditions, and to appeal in our activities to values such as justice, courage, generosity and the like. Not implausibly, many have seen our possession of language as a common factor in all these other capacities. More debatably, some have gone on to suggest that it is actually the ability to speak language that differentiates us from other creatures.

This is debatable, because it is not clear that human beings are the only creatures with a language, and so long as the question is posed in such general terms it remains too vague for serious discussion. More importantly, however, for present purposes, is the question as to whether language itself might not be simply a symptom of something else about us that gives us these capacities, as well as the ability to speak language, rather than being an explanation of these other abilities. Since Plato, indeed, it has been common to explain specifically human intellectual abilities, including our possession of a developed language, in terms of something non-material in us, a spiritual soul or mind. This view is usually regarded as a form of dualism, because on it human beings are regarded as consisting of two distinct substances, a physical body, in which we are like the rest of nature, and an immaterial mind, which sets us apart.

The view of the mind which purports to explain our mental abilities, our creativity and our sense of freedom and moral responsibility by reference to a non-material substance in us, which, as Descartes puts it in his *Sixth Meditation*, is intermingled with our body, and which is responsible both for our intellectual abilities and our consciousness generally, is not the only form of dualism; there are other forms of dualism in which the mind is regarded as separate from and different from the body, but in which the mind is not regarded as initiating bodily activity. Thus, there are parallelisms, in which the mind and body follow parallel courses but do not mutually interact, and epiphenomenalisms, in which the mind is acted on by the body and is conscious of bodily inputs in the form of thoughts and sensations, without itself initiating anything in the other direction. Parallelism has the obvious difficulty of explaining how the remarkable way in which mental and physical events appear to reflect each other ever got set up, how a blow on the leg is followed by a sensation of pain, how a thought that I will do something precedes my actually doing it. How is it the mental sequence and the physical sequence go together so well, without any mutual interaction? Epiphenomenalism admits one-way interaction only, from body to mind, but not vice versa. The idea that thoughts and other mental acts cause physical acts is an illusion. Nietzsche, arguing like an epiphenomenalist, questioned whether the thought actually preceded the deed, or whether this might not just be a distorted perception, as when a man dreams he hears certain things that actually happened in the waking world, but in the reverse order. I shall have more to say about the implications of epiphenomenalism at the end of this section, but it clearly does not use the mind to answer the question about the source of our creative, moral and intellectual activities, which Platonic dualists have usually been interested in. For this we need to envisage the mind as acting positively on the body; our dualism will be interactionist in both directions.

Interactionist dualism is probably the most widespread form of dualism, and perhaps the most widespread view of human beings altogether among ordinary people. Apart from its connections with many religious and quasi-religious views of survival, according to which it is the immaterial soul or spirit which continues after death, and its links with the phenomena investigated in psychical research, it does appear to explain the fact of consciousness and to answer how it is that we are able to do many of the things that we are able to do, which appear to require a non-material explanation. Thus, it is because of our mind that we are able to calculate and deal with abstract ideas, and to perceive moral truths and necessary truths; no mere observation of particular phenomena could lead us to abstract ideas, nor could it assure us that, say, the law of non-contradiction obtained in all possible worlds, or that murder was wrong.

Now, while we might agree, as we saw in connection with nominalism, that these are problems in accounting for the abstraction of ideas in terms of the mere observation of particular phenomena, and that necessary and moral truths are not simply derived from observation, it has yet to be shown either that these things cannot be done by purely material beings, or, more crucially, that invoking an immaterial mind or soul would be of any help in explaining them. To put the latter point bluntly, if a material substance cannot be envisaged as forming general ideas or necessary truths or moral propositions, how is an immaterial substance supposed to do it? What is it about the immaterial substance that enables it to have these insights into generality, necessity and goodness? Here we are likely to be told Platonic stories about its contact with, or participation in, a superhuman world, but however transcendent this world is it is still a particular, not itself endowed with or capable of conferring insight into generality and necessity, hard to see as good in itself apart from some evaluation some being makes of it.

Actually, the problems with dualist interactionism are rather worse than just suggested. For it is not simply unclear how the immaterial mind is supposed to solve the specific problems it is invoked to deal with. Very little else about it is either clear or unproblematic. Significantly, most of what we are told about it is what it is not, rather than what it is. We are told that it is immaterial, not what it is made of, that it is not connected to the body as a pilot in a ship, but not how it is connected, that it does not decay even apart from the body, but not how it lives or survives. We are not told why or how it gets into contact with a new-born human person, nor how it is motivated to make its choices, except that it is not determined by physical law. We are, in short, told virtually nothing about the operations of this substance, about its relationship to the physical world, or about how it gets into the physical world at all. Moreover, the problematic aspects of human activity – consciousness, rationality, choice, and so on – are all dispatched to the mind, without any further explanation of how the mind does these things. The mind is like an immaterial little man, or homunculus, behind the physical man; it is hard to see how this is not simply a matter of deferring rather than of solving the difficulties. The dualist neurophysiologist Sir John Eccles claims to have found evidence for sudden and physically inexplicable brain activity when people will to make certain bodily movements.[2] This is clearly the sort of consequence dualist interactionism would be expected to have, and anyone espousing this view must be prepared to look for this sort of ghostly intervention in the physical world.

To many philosophers, both a belief in naturalism and the particular difficulties of dualist interactionism have suggested that materialist accounts of human activity should at least be shown to be inadequate in some rather strong sense before one settles for the ultimately mysterious postulation of a non-material mind. Some have felt, in addition, that the dualist thesis, that the immaterial mind is the source of our creative, intellectual and moral activity, rests on a misunderstanding of the nature of the concepts involved. This is very much the line taken by Gilbert Ryle in *The Concept of Mind*.[3] Ryle's position, very baldly, is that when we speak of an action done intelligently, or voluntarily, or with concern and so on, the point of the qualifications is not to suggest that the actions are preceded or initiated or accompanied by some mental act of intelligence, or will, or concern, but rather that the actions involved meet certain standards of intelligence or concern, or that they were not forced on the agent by anyone else. Similarly, speaking of someone as intelligent, or charitable, or a free spirit, is not to say anything about his mind or its qualities. It is rather to speak of the way he usually acts, or is disposed to act (with intelligence, with concern, in defiance of convention). The mind is not a thing; 'mentalistic' predicates do not refer to acts going on in the mind in parallel to bodily activity. They refer instead to a person's behavioural dispositions and to the type of descriptions we are inclined to give to his behaviour.

It must be said that there is a great deal right about a Rylean analysis of mentalistic talk from a phenomenological point of view. Generally speaking, I am not aware of mental acts, such as thoughts or acts of decision, preceding actions of mine which other people might describe as intelligent, creative, free, and the rest. I might drive a car intelligently, or treat others with openness, but to say this is not to say anything about my internal mental states. Even where I might actually think before I act, the cleverness of what I go on to say or do is not constituted by my having thought. It refers rather to what I achieve in acting or talking, and how others judge my behaviour. On Ryle's view, when we talk about someone's mental qualities or states, in very many cases we are not talking about the state of something (the mind) which is behind what he does and pulls the physical strings – the ghost in the machine – we are really referring to various qualities (or lack of them) in his behaviour.

Ryle's position has close links with the more scientific form of behaviourism, associated with psychologists such as J. B. Watson and B. F. Skinner. The characteristic claim here is that a scientific explanation of human behaviour should eschew reference to the mental which is regarded as private, subjective, unobservable and above all non-explanatory. In science, causes must be both intersubjectively accessible and independently checkable, but neither is the case with people's mental states and impressions. All the data we have on people are their actions and their probabilities for actions of various sorts. Talk of people believing, hoping, fearing, and so on does not do more than say that in given circumstances certain actions are probable. In no sense is it to explain why they do what they do, or to identify any underlying cause of their actions. It is simply to repeat that they do or have tendencies to do actions of certain sorts in certain conditions. With both Ryle and the scientific behaviourists, then, there is a strong sense that talk of peoples's states of mind or mental attitudes is not really explanatory. Such talk must be reduced to or cashed out in terms of talk about behaviour. Even talking of a man's seeing green on a given occasion ought to be regarded as an oblique way of referring to his disposition to say 'green' at that time, or to move his car from the lights, or to do any one of a number of actions associated with the recognition of something green in his environment. Indeed, analysing talk of sensations in terms of the perceiver's dispositions to behave in various ways appears to offer a neat solution to one of the most intractable and vexatious problems in this area. The problem is that of other minds, and amounts to questioning how we know that other people have the same types of sensation as we do, or indeed actually have any sensations at all. Dualism, with its hidden mind behind the bodily shell, makes the problem insoluble. We just have no way of knowing what someone else might be experiencing in their private self, if indeed they have such a thing at all, or feel anything in it. The most we can say is that as their bodily reactions are similar to ours when we undergo feelings of various sorts, we can assume that they are having similar feelings, but this argument from analogy is weak in a number of respects, not least in that the sample class, in which we have direct perception of both the feeling and the associated behaviour, consists of only one member (myself). For behaviourism, on the other hand, there is no intractable problem of other minds. If what we mean when we refer to someone's perceptions and sensations is that they behave or are disposed to behave in certain ways, then given that they do manifest the behaviour and the dispositions, they necessarily have the perceptions and sensations, for that is all that is meant by speaking of such things and that is all there is to it.

But, it will be said, that is not all there is to it. When I speak of myself being in pain, I do not just mean that I am disposed to behave in certain ways. I refer to something I feel, and I also intend to refer to the feelings of others when I speak of their pains and pleasures. Behaviourism must be wrong if it denies this obvious and primitive fact; I would not care in the way I do about my pains, or indeed those of others, unless they were horrible, that is unless they felt horrible. If behaviourism cannot account for the felt quality of our feelings, then it is wrong or, at best, quite inadequate as an account of the mind.

We shall see shortly that failing to account fully for the facts of consciousness and feeling is a criticism that can be made of accounts of the mind other than behaviourism. But a weakness more specific to behaviourism arises from its general tendency to equate talk of mental states and attitudes with talk of behaviour and dispositions to behave. In the first place, common-sense psychology tells us that when we speak of someone being jealous, say, we are not simply referring, however obliquely, to his behaviour, actual or potential. While it is true that we would have no grounds for speaking of his jealousy unless he behaved or appeared likely to behave in particular ways – and stressing this link between the mind and behaviour is the truth at the basis of behaviourism – we believe that in saying that he is jealous we are saying something about what causes the behaviour. A person's jealousy is what causes his jealous actions. Similarly with beliefs, desires, sensations and other mental states and attitudes; these are what cause the linked behaviour – they are not the behaviour itself under another name, which is what behaviourists would have us believe.

While it is true that we cannot simply accept the common-sense view of human behaviour without some reason in its favour, it is clear enough that it does have some strong empirical support in that our beliefs about what other people will do, based on assumptions about their beliefs, desires, perceptual states and characters generally, are very often confirmed in practice. Compared with the predictive attainments of behaviouristic psychology, in which reference to mental states is eliminated as far as possible in favour of measurable stimulus inputs, common-sense psychology does pretty well, particularly when we are dealing with behaviour which is a response to some complicated human situation, as opposed to the typical laboratory test in which the subject is tested in a very artificial way regarding some precise perceptual discrimination or short-term memory capacity. It would be fantastic if our ordinary predictions and explanation of people's behaviour did not, at least obliquely, rest on insights into the causal determinants of that behaviour.

Then, secondly, behaviourism purports to account for our ordinary talk of beliefs, desires, perceptual states, and so on, in terms of our actual and potential behaviour. It is certainly true that there is something suspect in speaking of someone being angry or jealous or afraid if he or she never did anything appropriate to being in those states. But the problem for behaviourism is that what counts as behaviour appropriate to the states in question will be appropriate only given other beliefs and desires of the agent. It is sometimes claimed that the mental is marked by the fact that we can take up mental attitudes, such as belief or fear or anger, to things that do not actually exist, and that this constitutes a problem for any attempt to account for the mental in material or physical terms. Thus, I can be afraid of a Trotskyite conspiracy to disrupt industry; even though there is no such thing, my actions could be very much affected by this false belief. This phenomenon, whereby verbs describing mental attitudes can have as their objects non-existent things, is often referred to as the intentionality of the mental. In itself, however, the so-called intentional inexistence of the objects of mental attitudes does not preclude analysis of those attitudes into behavioural terms. The man fearing Trotskyite infiltration will no doubt tend to behave in certain predictable ways, depending on his own circumstances and influence. The problem with a behavioural analysis of this fear, however, is that the behaviour which, on the analysis, is taken to be what that fear amounts to will have the necessary connections with the fear only given that the man has other beliefs and desires. Thus, we can take his subscribing to the Economic League as being an aspect of his fear (or even more simply as a manifestation of it), only if we assume that our subject believes that the League might actually help to root out the moles. He could, of course, subscribe to the League for quite other reasons, in which case the behaviour would have nothing to do with that particular fear; equally, he could have the fear, but have nothing to do with the League because he thought it ineffective, disapproved of its methods, had fallen out with its organizers over golf, or for any one of a host of other reasons.

In general, the point is that actions are the actions they are – means to ends the agent has – only in the context of the whole complex of the other beliefs and desires the agent has. It is not coincidental that behaviouristic analyses of mental states are characteristically open-ended and in-defeasible, saying that, if a man wants *p*, then he will tend to do *s* or *t* or *u* or *v* or ..., and so on; short of knowing all the rest of what our man wanted and believed and what weights he gave to each of those wants and beliefs, we could not say in advance that some specific belief or desire of his would issue in any specific piece of behaviour, or that any piece of behaviour, however bizarre, might not be consistent with his having some specific belief or desire, given that other beliefs and desires of his were strange enough.

Behaviourism, then, fails both because we rightly regard our mental states and attitudes as being causally efficacious, and because behavioural analyses of specific mental status and attitudes depend for their validity on the presumed existence of other behaviouristically unanalysed mental states and attitudes. But behaviourism is not the only form scepticism about a spiritual mind need take. It is true to say that most modern materialistic analyses of the mind begin by accepting that mental states and attitudes are causally efficacious, and do not attempt to reduce them or translate them out into something else. One notable attempt both to accept the causal efficiency and reality of the mind and to bring it within contemporary scientific theory is known as central-state materialism, or sometimes, for reasons that will become clear, as the mind–brain identity theory. On this view, the mind is a thing, and talk of it is not just an oblique way of referring to behaviour. The thing which the mind is and the events and states which make it up have the unusual property of having two aspects, one subjective and conscious, and the other objective and material. The mind, in fact, is the brain, and mental events (such as thoughts and sensations) and states (such as beliefs and desires) are brain events and brain states. Saying that the mind and the brain are identical, on this view, is not to say that a mental term, such as 'pain', means the same as a neurophysiological one, like 'c-fibre stimulation', any more than 'lightning' means 'electric discharge', or 'water' means 'H_2O', even though lightning is electric discharge and water is H_2O. All these identities are the subject of empirical discovery and confirmation, and according to the proponents of the mind–brain identity hypothesis merely contingent. Water might have been some other substance, electric discharge in the air might not have produced the appearance of lightning, likewise pain might have been some other type of brain activity (or none at all). Kripke, who does not regard the identities of water and H_2O or of lightning and electric discharge as contingent (or indeed any identity between rigid designators as contingent), regards this aspect of the mind – brain identity theory as utterly confused. 'Pain' and 'c-fibre stimulation' are both rigid designators, so the identity between pain and c-fibre stimulation (if any) must be necessary. But pain, in its essence, is what is felt, and it is surely possible for some sentient beings to have c-fibre stimulation without feelings of pain and vice versa. Hence there can be no necessary identity here, hence no identity at all. However we have found reason to reject Kripke's views on the necessity of identity (pp. 178–9 above), so we should perhaps allow the identity theorist his contingent identity between mental and brain states, at least for the sake of argument.

In us, then, as human beings, mental states happen to be identical to brain states. But how, it will be said, can this be? Mental states and events such as pain or my thoughts about the Acropolis have quite different properties from brain states. Pains can be severe and cutting while brain states cannot; thoughts can be intelligent or funny or original, while these are not appropriate ways to characterize brain states. On the other hand, brain states, but not pains or thoughts, can be located precisely in space, measured electrochemically and subsumed under neurophysiological laws. What we have here are entities of such difference in type that they could not possibly be identical. Here the identity theorist will probably answer that what is being identified with brain process XYZ is not my thought that the Acropolis should not be open to tourists (clever, radical, presumptious, élitist or whatever), but the event which is my thinking of that thought. Why should this event not have two (or more) aspects, depending on the frames of reference in which it is perceived, just as the event which was yesterday's performance of Beethoven's 'Eroica' was quite indubitably also a particular configuration of sound waves in a certain auditorium? Of course, someone looking into my brain would not know what I was thinking or feeling, unless he knew the relevant correlations between subjective states of mine and my brain processes, but neither would a physicist of sound necessarily know what he was analysing was perceived by us as the 'Eroica'.

The mind–brain identity theory was originally advanced in the belief that it would have a degree of empirical testability. The hope was that correlations might eventually be discovered between types of experience and mental attitude, on the one hand, and types of brain event or state, on the other. The pain–c-fibre stimulation correlation would be the ideal here. Once correlations of this sort were discovered, laws could be framed and tested, so that we can see if it is true that whenever there are feelings of pain, there are c-fibre stimulations, and vice versa. However, even if type–type correlations of this sort could be discovered and confirmed, it would not show that mental events were identical with brain events. The evidence would be equally consistent with the two types of events being entirely different in type, but invariably correlated. Even a Cartesian dualist could accept that, because part of his thesis is precisely that there is constant and consistent interaction between the body and the inter-mingled soul. On the other hand, if the descriptions of the events in neurophysiological terms were part of a more general system of theories and laws, in which they turned out to be predictable in those terms, without any reference to mentalistic descriptions, the tendency to think of a separate mind (as opposed to the brain) as being causally efficacious in human behaviour would be correspondingly weakened, and this is perhaps the most critical problem in this whole area: whether the mental is at most an inefficacious by-product or epiphenomenon of events which are fully describable and predictable in physical (neurophysiological) terms.

However, returning to the identity theory, there is in fact no reason to suppose that for most of those mental events and states which involve cognition in any way type–type correlations of the pain–c-fibre stimu-lation sort will ever be found. Even if *my* belief that the Acropolis should be closed forthwith were a brain state of mine under another description, it is hardly likely that my brain state would be remotely similar to that of a Greek who had the same thought. Even an English speaker with the same thought would probably have quite different neural representations of the Acropolis, depending on his experiences of that place. Then, another slippery aspect of the mental is that there are considerable difficulties in knowing how to establish identity of mental attitude. We just do not know how to establish that two people are having the same thought or hope or fear, and hence we do not know how to pick out the candidates for the mental side of the mental–physical correlation.* The reason for this is that although you and I might both be consciously intending to catch the 3:00 p.m. train, the train I am intending to catch is that from Edinburgh, whereas you want the one to Edinburgh. But we have the same conscious

* I am following Kathleen Wilkes's *Physicalism* (London, 1978, p. 26), in the remainder of this paragraph.

thought, as far as its verbal formulation goes. Should we expect to find the same neuro-physiological state in both of us, or not? Equally, I believe Cicero denounced Cataline, you believe the Consul for 68 BC did. Do we have the same belief or not? Again, if I am remembering Athens, and how the Acropolis is always visible from odd places, and how you might cross Syntagma in the rush-hour, and the smell of the trolleybus tyres, and the place where Nikos Gatsos sits in Floca's, how many thoughts am I having? Am I to include states called memories, prejudices and moods among them? On all these points Wilkes comments that

there is no such thing as an objective answer to these difficulties, for the mental flux does not come ready-sliced. We can carve it up as we like: one sort of carving will give us very many mental states, another much fewer.[4]

Furthermore we know from neurophysiology that the firing patterns of neurons depend on the firings immediately preceding and the patterns established in the brain. So it is hardly likely that even two occurrences of the same (or similar) thought in different people or even in the same person at different times will be correlated with the same brain state. The prospect, espoused by the mind–brain identity theorist, of finding law-like correlations between types of mental state and types of brain state is now looking extremely unlikely.

One reaction to the problems raised by dualism on the one hand and the identity theory on the other is to say that both these theories create quite unnecessary problems for themselves by an over-fixation on the stuff of the mind, to the detriment of more interesting and more relevant questions concerning the things the mind can do. After all, what interests us about people is not what they are made of or what is inside their skulls, but what they can do, how they react, and how generally they get themselves about the world. If we found other creatures who behaved like us and responded to us, would it matter if we found that their brains were made of some quite different sort of stuff, or even if inside their heads there was no physical matter at all? Surely if their behaviour could be regarded as a reasonable way to attain the ends they appear to have, given the beliefs and desires and feelings our observation of their behaviour also leads us to attribute to them, we would still speak of them believing, hoping, fearing, experiencing, feeling pain, and so on, in the same way we apply these concepts to ourselves and other human beings. The suggestion is that these mentalistic terms, both those involving cognition of some sort and those referring to feelings, are primarily used to describe and explain the functioning of organisms, and do not in themselves have any implications regarding the make-up of physical structures which manifest the behaviour. In this context, analogies are sometimes drawn between accounts of human behaviour in our common-sense psychological vocabulary, and between the abstract programmes different types of calculators carry out. For we can say all we want to say about a programme like adding or subtracting without any reference to the physical make-up of the calculators (or people) who are going to carry out the programmes. The behaviour of anything or anyone who adds or subtracts, say, can be seen as exemplifying a certain programme, whatever their physical realization, and even whether or not they explicitly go through all the steps of the programme. The relevance of this analogy to the claims of both dualism and the identity theory is that, on the one hand, no one would dream of saying that a given programme can only be fulfilled by something immaterial, while on the other hand, it would be just crazy to say that the ability to add is identical with having such and such a physical constitution, when it is quite clear that calculators with many different types of physical make-up can all add correctly. If mentalistic terminology is a way of referring to behaviour, then it is quite clear that theories like dualism and the identity theory are wrong because they miss the main point of using mentalistic terminology in the first place, which is to engage in a fundamentally abstract characterization of behaviour, so as to enable us to explain and predict the behaviour of those beings we regard as being in the states in question. We see their behaviour and conclude that they are in certain states (or programmes); we then confirm (or falsify) these conclusions by using them to predict future behaviour, given specific circumstances (or inputs).

This view of mental language is sometimes known as functionalism, and has been advanced by Putnam in his paper 'Philosophy and Our Mental Life',[5] in which he argues that the (psychological) questions we are interested in when we discuss human behaviour have no bearing on whether our basic stuff is copper, cheese or soul, or vice versa, any more than explaining why a square peg will not go into a round hole calls for a description of the atomic structure of the peg and hole in question. Apart from being incredibly complex in practice, the atomic description would not explain why a square peg would not go through a round hole, because it would not be generalizable to other square pegs and round holes. What we are after here is a geometric explanation; geometry is in this sense autonomous of physics, and similarly, Putnam wants to say, talk of human behaviour will be autonomous of physicochemical descriptions of our brains. Physicochemical descriptions of our brain are not likely to explain our mental states, because, as in the case of the peg and the hole, so much that would enter the physicochemical description would be quite accidental and irrelevant to the form of the psychological description, and not generalizable to other similar psychological states of other people. Putnam is, in effect, agreeing with some of the criticisms we made earlier of the search for neurophysiological correlates for types of mental state, but suggesting that the search for such correlates would in any case be quite misplaced, because it is to mistake the point of mentalistic talk, which is to describe behaviour at a level which purposely abstracts from consideration of the physical realizations of mental states.

Putnam's functionalism has some affinity with behaviourism in its intentional disregard of questions of the stuff of the mental, although it would have no truck with behaviouristic reductions or translations of talk of mental causes. It has a boldness and freedom which is undeniably attractive, but one wonders whether the autonomy it secures for the mental may not be somewhat precarious, and whether his functionalist premises actually imply any very substantial autonomy beyond the truism that we can, within certain limits, talk of human beings doing things like believing, hoping, fearing, feeling and so on without referring to their brains. It does not show in any way that, given they are in physical state x, they could not but be believing so-and-so, any more than the autonomy of the geometrical shows that, given our peg was a lattice of atoms of such and such a sort and our hole a region of such and such a sort, no trajectory of the lattice could pass through our region. The autonomy accorded to geometry and ordinary mentalistic talk by Putnam's argument may be no more than an absence of any interesting translatability between various levels of discourse, combined, in the geometrical case at any rate, with a lack of interest in performing any breakdown of one level of discourse into another. But it is far from clear that with mental talk there is no interest in investigating the physical stuff that actually (though, to be sure, contingently) realizes the functional descriptions of ourselves in mentalistic terms.

Indeed, as Wilkes has argued, following D. M. Armstrong, a functional account of human behaviour may not only be compatible with what she calls physicalism (the claim that the physical sciences with their non-purposive explanations are adequate to describe, predict and explain the purposive behaviour of humans and animals[6]); it may be a prerequisite to physicalism. In her view, a functional analysis will be applicable to anything that can be regarded as consisting of systematically organized parts which work together to produce effects, such as stability in a society or the behavioural repertoire of human beings. The functions to be analysed will be the effects we are interested in. These effects can, of course, in many cases be seen as the result of the operations of sub-functions. Thus, if we regard the overall function of an automatic washing machine as being the washing of clothes, a function it shares with other systems incidentally, the washing machine may work through fulfilling the sub-functions of soaking, soaping, agitating, rinsing and spinning (which may or may not be present in other clothes-washing systems). In breaking down the functions of a system into sub-functions and sub-sub-functions and sub-sub-sub-functions (if necessary), we shall eventually hit upon structural items (or bits of matter) which are actually responsible for the execution of specific functions.* The idea is that in the system the structural items, by working together, produce the big effects we might be interested in explaining, without themselves doing the big thing. Thus, in the washing machine, the soap dispenser, the pump, the thermostat, the drum and so on all have their small functions; none of them individually washes clothes, but together they all do.

Now the structural-functional account of the mind will as a first step take certain mental functions, such as remembering or perceiving or problem-solving, and attempt to break them down into sub-functions and sub-sub-functions, perhaps by using computer models or analogies of these activities, checking, of course, to see how likely it is that the functional models that are constructed might be similar to the ways in which human beings do these things. Evidence from neurophysiology and from brain-damaged patients can sometimes show whether or not it is likely that a specific sub-function is part of a human ability, although there are problems in knowing the 'steps' a human being might go through in remembering, when these 'steps' are not themselves part of our conscious experience. Ultimately, of course, the hope is that certain structural items in the human brain will be identified as performing certain specific lowest-level functions, which, our models show us, could combine with other structural items performing other low-level functions to produce memory or perception or problem-solving or whatever cognitive ability we are interested in. The reason why a functional account of the human mind is a prerequisite to physicalistically inspired brain research is because, although most of our ordinary-language psychological notions (such as

---

* How far we go down in the material level is very much a matter of decision depending on our specific interests. In the washing machine example, the pump might be regarded as a basic structural item or as itself a sub-system consisting of sub-functions, themselves needing structural realization right down to the particles of elementary physics.

belief or motive or memory) are so imprecise and wide-ranging as to be of little help in any research, without some ideas of the sorts of high-level things brains do and how they might do them – which is where the functional analysis is supposed to start from – we will have no idea what to look for at the immensely complex neurophysiological level. So ordinary-language psychology is an indispensable starting point for physicalism. On the other hand, in practice, it is more likely that actual scientific work will begin only at the point at which the science of psychology hands us clearly defined functions such as retrieval of information bits, or pattern recognition, which are not recognized in ordinary-language psychology but which might plausibly be seen as part of what we do when we remember something or see something. The point is that with these psychological terms of art, laws have been forthcoming, something which could never be the case with the gross ordinary-language 'remember' or 'see' or 'think', precisely because of their vagueness, something that dogged us when we tried to discover when two thoughts were the same, whether a thought was really a memory, and so on. Arguably, part of the richness and versatility of ordinary-language psychology is due to this vagueness. Whether this is so or not, it is the clearly defined mental functions recognized by scientific psychology that are most likely to be susceptible to neurophysiological analysis. At the same time, however, it will be a vindication of the psychological terms of art if some distinct type of neurophysiological process does turn out to be correlated with it. On the structural-functional view, then, central-state materialism was far too simplistic in its search for specific correlations between the mental and the physical, but not wrong in looking for correlations of some sort between types of psychological function and types of brain process.

The structural-functional version of physicalism hopes to avoid one of the classic problems in the philosophy of mind. In breaking big tasks (such as perceiving) into little ones, carried out presumably by the firing of neurons, it appears to dispense with the homunculus in the brain, the little man who would be required to see the images, decode the representations, and do all the other mentalistic tasks that are often left to do by supposed explanations of mental activity. The homunculus crops up whenever one mental act (such as seeing) is analysed in terms of a type of thing (such as an image in the brain) which itself requires mental activity in order to be dealt with. On the structural-functionalist view, just as water-heating is not itself a type of washing, but is part of it, so is neuron-firing not itself a type of seeing, but part of it. But the question which worries many people at this point is the question as to how events like the firing of neurons could ever produce something like seeing, and here it is unclear that functionalism can give the answers. What is being asked here is how the unconscious (neuron-firing) could ever produce the conscious (seeing). Maybe, it is said, there are all these sub-systems in me, which are not conscious, but surely in me there is still the one that knows and oversees the rest and which is in that sense conscious, a sort of king-homunculus if you like.

Daniel Dennett has attempted to deal with this question by comparing the mind first to a chess computer in which we can think of there being overall intelligent functioning (chess-playing) on the top level, then at lower levels other examples of intelligent functioning (move generation, move criticism, time-keeping and so on). The move criticism function, say, looks pretty intelligent, but it can be broken down into smaller, less intelligent functions, down and down until we get structures that simply react automatically and non-intelligently to the inputs they are given:

> but put these together in large armies, mustered like Chinese boxes, a whole system of these stupid elements can exhibit behaviour which looks distinctly intelligent, distinctly human.[7]

Fine, we might well say, but a chess-playing computer, however intelligent, does not have to be conscious or to feel. It can react intelligently to what it is presented with (or 'intelligently', if you like, but the functionalist will say does it really matter?) but is it conscious of sensory quality? Is it conscious of what it is presented with in the way we are conscious of the stimuli we react to? Does it exhibit sentience as well as sapience? Dennett tries to defuse this question by turning to a different analogy, that of a large organization, in which individual specialists all perform their pretty unintelligent functions, like the stupid elements of the chess computer, but in which there is also a 'press secretary' that represents (pretty inaccurately, as it happens) what is going on in the system to the outside world. But, as Dennett himself recognizes, this analogy, although in some ways suggestive, does not really help with the problem of consciousness.

In the first place, large organizations are not conscious or self-conscious, even if they issue statements or print-outs about their activity. So, in the second place, even if we include in our organization a system-observing functionary, like the press secretary, and build in the suggestion that the system is to react to and report on its own goings-on, we still do not get the system *feeling* what is going on inside it or knowing what it is reacting to. Nothing is easier than to envisage a complicated machine reacting to, say, a green light by printing out 'green', setting itself in motion and doing all sorts of other things; but nothing is harder than to imagine this machine having an experience of green, or being aware that when it prints out 'green', what it prints out refers to a certain colour. On this last point, John Searle has argued forcefully that machine analogies are quite inappropriate to explaining the mental, because, however complicated the machine and its programme, all it will ever do will be to transform inputs of some sort into outputs of some other sort. It would no more know what those inputs were about than I would if I was locked in a room and given messages in a language I did not understand, such as Chinese, and which I then transformed into other Chinese messages I also did not understand, according to sets of transformation instructions for such messages that I had been given. We could, of course, infiltrate a press secretary into the proceedings, who was not simply reacting to stimuli and 'representing' the goings-on in the system for the benefit of outsiders, but who was actually aware of what things meant and how they felt, or a king-homunculus who had feelings and awarenesses derived from the machine-like inputs and transformations going on in the system (computer or brain). But I need hardly say that any such manoeuvres would be admissions of defeat, if our aim is to explain awareness in purely functional terms, because we would still be left with the problem of accounting for the awareness of the press secretary and the homunculus.

The problem with structural-functionalism, in short, is that we can envisage all sorts of machines or organizations in a certain sense replicating human responses and human behaviour (our *functions*), without there being the least hint that these machines or organizations might have feelings or awareness generally. Furthermore, as Nagel has insisted, there are plenty of other types of creature lacking fundamental human abilities, such as language, whom we intuitively and immediately accept as sentient. The lives of these creatures, and of us, is not to be analysed in terms solely of reacting and behaving, however rationally and intelligently; it is also a matter of experiencing, which is not at all the same as the self-monitoring of a thermostat or a computer, even if it is possible to regard some aspects of experience as having a self-monitoring function.

In his article 'What Is It like To Be A Bat?'[8] and elsewhere, Nagel has emphasized the essentially subjective nature of experience, that the feel of my experience can be conveyed only to creatures of a type similar to me. There is a very strong sense in which I, as a human being, cannot know what it is like for a bat to be a bat, yet it seems quite in order to think of it being like something to be a bat. As we have just seen, systems exemplifying functional and even intentional behaviour can be envisaged which have no subjective feelings or awareness at all. That is, it is not like anything to be a computer. At the same time, an objective description of the neurophysiology of a bat or of a human being and a functional account of their beliefs, intentions, reactions and so on which would be intelligible to creatures with different types of perceptual faculties will not convey to the alien creature what it is like to be a bat or a human being. We seem to be left in the predicament that, while matter organized in certain ways clearly does produce sentience, we have no idea how this might come about or even what form an explanation of the problem should take. Indeed the more 'functional' and 'structural' our accounts become the further they take us from sentience, and the more they are compatible with a quite different type of sentience or with the absence of sentience altogether. This should not be thought to favour dualism; if we can make sense of the soul at all, the soul is as objective a thing as the body, and we have no idea how to explain how this thing can also be a centre of consciousness and of feeling.

There is a great divide here between those philosophers, like Wilkes, Dennett and Rorty, who are prepared to think of sentience largely in terms of the self-monitoring of neurophysiological systems, in terms, in other words, of its capacity to enable these systems to react flexibly to the environment, and those philosophers, like Nagel, Kripke and Searle, who feel that this leaves out of the picture the most important, indeed the essential aspect of sentience, in which, as Kripke puts it, 'its immediate phenomenological quality'[9] is what pain is, whatever its function or underlying physical cause might be.

Wilkes, it will be recalled, expected that a physicalistic account of human behaviour would be able to describe, predict and explain the purposive behaviour of humans and animals without recourse to purposive idioms. The firing neurons physicalism puts at the bottom of its analysis are not themselves regarded as having intentions or beliefs or any mental states or attitudes at all.

In answer to the question as to how non-purposive activity can become purposive we are given the machine analogies, in which any behaviour can be regarded as intelligent, purposive, based on beliefs, and so on, provided that such talk enables us to give an adequate description and explanation of the machine's behaviour in playing chess, or whatever. At one level the analogies are certainly persuasive. Part of the role of our talk of beliefs, motives, intelligence and so on is to enable us to discern a projectible pattern in the behaviour of the organism or machine we are studying. But at another level, one wonders if this is all there is to it and if the inverted commas the critic of functionalism insists on putting round talk of a machine's intelligence or beliefs or intentions (see above, p. 226) might not be justified. Is there in fact a link between sentience and beliefs, intentions and intelligence, a link the functionalist wants to deny, but which might justify caution in speaking of something non-sentient as having beliefs and the rest?

Ascribing sentience to an organism suggests that it is not simply a system of discrete parts which function as if to produce a whole system; it suggests, rather, that, in some way we do not fully understand, the organism forms itself into a single unified consciousness, in which what is happening at various parts of the system are perceived and felt at a single point; *I* see, hear, feel pain, and so on, and not my eyes, my ears or my hands. A single subject with a single point of view is the subject of the 'immediate phenomenological quality'; without this unity of perception it is doubtful whether we would be able to speak of sentience proper in an organism, as opposed to different parts of the organism simply reacting to different stimuli without the organism as a whole feeling them. So sentience presupposes a unity of consciousness, but so, I shall now argue, does the predication of beliefs, intentions and other psychological attitudes.

The concepts of belief and intention, and other concepts which we use to describe people's cognitive and affective attitudes to things, presuppose the idea of a subject in some degree in control of his thoughts and his actions. It is just this idea which is lost in the structural-functional analysis of intentional talk into 'stupid' elements doing non-intentional, non-intelligent things, and which, arguably, is never really present in the activity of a machine, however complex its programme and however 'intelligent' its execution of its programmes. Bound up with the notion of belief are the ideas of respect for truth and evidence. A man who said that he did not care whether what he believed was true or not could hardly be said to know what it was to believe, because to believe just is to hold something true. Equally, if a man is confronted with clear counter-evidence to some cherished belief of his, and recognizes it as such, then he can hardly go on holding the belief, however much he might regret the impossibility. So speaking of people believing things implies that they are, at least in the main, rational beings, controlling what they believe in the light of argument and evidence. (This is not a matter of charity: it is rather a matter of understanding what they say when they say they believe something.) Inherent in the concept of belief is the idea of a rational subject not simply 'believing' as a result of non-rational factors, such as the firing of neurons, but exercising, no doubt imperfectly, but exercising never-theless some sort of central, global control over his beliefs and standards of belief. In the case of intentional activity, we also have the idea of a person in some sort of global control. We contrast actions that are really intended, and desires and motives that are really those of the person, with things that he or she could not help doing because of some physical reflex beyond his or her control. Once again in intentional activity we have the idea of the agent as a centre of consciousness in some sort of global control of activity. Neurons firing, in whatever complexity, look like physical reflexes. Where, in this picture, does the intentional agent fit in? If, on the other hand, we envisage the possibility of a subject of consciousness as a centre of experience, there is no great distance to be travelled to see this centre of experience as also in control of some of its thoughts, and, perhaps, of some of its actions too.

It cannot be pretended that we have reached a satisfactory point in our discussion of the mind. Physicalism is attractive in many ways especially if we wish to see ourselves as part of nature, and wish for a unified account of natural processes, but it leaves too much out. Putting back in what has been left out simply leaves us with the problem, intractable in physicalistic terms, of an organism which is a centre of consciousness and an initiator of action rather than just a passive reactor whose reactions are simply the sum of hordes of mindless microscopic reflexes. This problem is intractable because there is no room in the concepts we use to describe the physical for such things. But, it might be said, this appearance of intractability arises only because we are tacitly assuming that physicalistic explanation of human behaviour must in some sense explain how the psychological attributions we make to ourselves – of our attitudes of hope, belief, fear and so on, and of our feelings of pleasure, pain and so on – are derivable from a purely physicalistic description of our bodies and brains in physio-logical and neurophysiological terms. If it could be shown that no such derivation were possible, and that what we had here were two distinct and non-interlocking ways of talking about the same behaviour of the same organism, would it not in a stronger sense than that suggested by Putnam show that the mental is autonomous of the physical without necessarily leading to the abandonment of that adherence to physicalism which our belief in naturalism demands?

It is just this position that Davidson has attempted to occupy with his thesis of anomalous monism. Davidson's position regarding the mental is monistic, because he holds a weakened identity theory. Mental events are, in his view, physical events. Indeed for him they have to be, because they are causally effective. My desire to hear Bruckner's Eighth is what will get me to the Festival Hall on Wednesday. But, according to Davidson, talk of desires and of other mental attitudes is not the sort of talk that can feature in closed universal theories of the type required for talk of causation. So the events or states that constitute my desires and mental attitudes must be describable in a way in which they can feature in and be deductible from universal causal theories. So they must be physical (neuro-physiological) states and events.

What Davidson is appealing to at this point is the principle, already considered at the end of the section on causation, that an event which is the cause of another event can, like any other event, be described in various ways. While the event, if it is a cause, can truly be said to be the cause of whatever it causes, however it is described, it does not follow that all descriptions of the same event will be subsumable under a genuinely universal causal law, and, as we have seen, the possibility of being brought under such a law is central to the truth of the claim that we have a genuine instance of such a claim. Davidson's point is that, while descriptions of mental events in neurophysiological terms may readily be conceived of as falling under a closed system of causal laws, this is not the case with descriptions of the same events in mentalistic or psychological terms. The language we use to describe our psychological attitudes, our beliefs, our choices and so on precludes their being part of a closed causal theory, like that of physics in which every event is describable in such a way as to be amenable to causal laws, or even of being put into any systematic relation-ship with the terms of such a theory. This is partly because there is clearly much that affects the mental that is not itself part of the mental, but a deeper and more significant reason for the autonomy of the mental is that ascriptions of mental attitude are constrained by and must be sensitive to considerations of rationality, something which is not the case in the closed systems of the physical sciences. What we have to do in ascribing beliefs, intentions, desires and choices to others is exactly analogous to what we do in interpreting their language. Indeed, given that their mental attitudes will often be expressed in language, the two tasks have a high degree of overlap. We have to ascribe mental attitudes to them in such a way as to make their behaviour intelligible in the light both of the other attitudes we are ascribing to them and of their behaviour and circumstances. The point is actually similar to one we encountered in considering behaviourism. An action can be seen as the instantiation of a given intention only on the assumption of a whole set of other beliefs and desires on the part of the agent. My handing flowers to a girl can be seen as an attempt on my part to woo her, only given that I also believe that she likes flowers, does not suffer from hay fever, will recognize that I am giving them to her with the intention of pleasing her, and so on, and so on. My beliefs, equally, will be attributable in the light of my behaviour, but only given the assumption of various intentions and desires, with which they and the behaviour rationally cohere. As Davidson himself puts it:

> when we use the concepts of belief, desire, and the rest, we must stand prepared, as the evidence accumulates, to adjust our theory in the light of considerations of overall cogency; the constitutive ideal of rationality partly controls each phase in the evolution of what must be an evolving theory.[10]

Our attribution of physical properties is not sensitive in this way to the overall cogency and rationality of what is attributed. This is what constitutes the openness and autonomy of the mental, and why mental events and attitudes, though identical with physical ones, are unlikely precisely to parallel them.

Davidson is undoubtedly right in thinking that our attributions of mental attitudes to others have to produce a degree of rationality and consistency in our picture of the mental life of others, on pain of their behaviour and the ascriptions themselves beginning to be unintelligible. But he combines this degree of autonomy of the mental with a belief that the behaviour of human beings is, on a physical neurophysiological level, determined and predictable. But, it will be felt, most of my actions are physical movements. If these movements are predictable and determined, what does the autonomy of the mental amount to? If what we have are simply two alternative ways of describing the same physically determined events (that is, my bodily movements), is not the alternative mode of description which does not refer to the physical determination of those events the secondary one and, in the final analysis, redundant? Relative to the physical, doesn't the mental here take on a purely epiphenomenal role?

To put the same point in another light, Davidson writes as though what we are doing in ascribing mental attitudes is to impose a form of description on some behaviour which is fully predetermined in other terms. But this is to neglect the subjective aspect of mentalistic talk. When I speak of myself believing, intending, and so on, I do not conceive of myself describing something that in a sense already exists; I conceive of myself rather as formulating and sometimes choosing those attitudes in the light of what appears true and desirable, and, in attributing such attitudes to others, I will be speaking of their own formulations and choices, and not simply attempting a retrodictive account of their behaviour. The defender of physicalisms and identity theories of various sorts may well say at this point that this conception of mental attitudes as constructed by ourselves in our own reflections and deliberations is fundamentally misguided, that we know from our own experience of ourselves and of others, that agents are not the best authorities on what they believe and intend, and that in many cases outsiders are in a better position to judge what someone really believes or intends than they are themselves, for all their reflecting and deliberating. Without denying a substantial element of truth in this in many cases, it is still open to us to question whether this is always the case, and whether sometimes, and in ideal circumstances no doubt, I do not have the sort of control over my beliefs and intentions which would be denied by the suggestion that they are just there, inside me, as they are, whether I acknowledge the fact or not. Moreover, we might want to add, in my constructing my beliefs and choosing my intentions I may well be led to initiate physical movements in the form of bodily actions, in a way that would appear to be denied by the claim that my bodily movements are totally determined according to physiological and neurophysiological laws.

To hold such a conception of human mental activity and its effects on the physical world, one is not compelled to retreat to a Cartesian dualist conception of the self, for one does not have to regard the human person as consisting in part of a spiritual substance, separable from the body. The main objection to this conception is that it explained nothing, and in any case, as Nagel has insisted, there are just as many problems in explaining how a spiritual object could be the possessor of subjective experiences as there are in explaining how a physical object could be. But I am a physical object *and* I am conscious etc. This is something that may defy explanation, and something which physicalist and functionalist accounts of human beings omit, for we can perfectly well imagine machines making decisions, responding 'intelligently' to problems, reacting with aversion to certain stimuli, and the rest, without for one moment imputing subjective consciousness to them. Of course, the remarks just made in criticism of Davidson attribute to human beings more than consciousness. They also attribute to them the ability to reflect on their beliefs and intentions, and to change them – and the world – in the light of these reflections. Human beings are being envisaged in these remarks as the initiators of some of their actions, and not as totally subject to the laws of nature and pre-existing states of affairs. But is this actually an intelligible supposition, and is it part of what is meant by speaking of human beings as free rational agents? To these problems we will now turn.

Freedom of Action

At the end of the previous section, I suggested that we are aware of a conception of human beings which entails that they can judge and act with some measure of independence of natural law, and that this conception is closely linked to our ideas of ourselves as free and rational in judgement and action. We can add to this that such a conception is also entailed by those notions of moral responsibility, of praise and blame, of gratitude and resentment, of love and hate, and the like, which envisage ourselves and those with whom we enter into moral and affective relationships as being on occasion able to do otherwise than they in fact do, not simply in the excuse that they could have done otherwise had they so willed, but in the stronger sense that they could actually have willed to do other than they did, and, of course, have done so. The strongly libertarian conception of human life which I am here describing holds, in short, that human beings are, potentially at least, in control of their desires and actions in such a way as to escape complete determination of their actions by factors over which they have no ultimate control, such as their heredity and environment, their neurophysiology and the rest. This conception, however, turns out on examination to be profoundly problematic, so much so in fact that many profess to find it unintelligible, claiming indeed that the notions of rational choice and responsibility which the libertarian view is concerned to make room for actually require for their intelligible application the very determinism in our behaviour which the libertarian would seek to free us from.

Physical determinists hold that everything that happens does so in accordance with physical law. Applied to human beings, such determinism would entail that all our behaviour is caused by a variety of factors inside and outside us, which in one way or another are ultimately simply given to us, and on the basis of which we react to stimuli. The deterministic picture of human behaviour becomes rather complicated, however; in the first place, some of the factors which contribute to bringing about what I do are deeply embedded within me, in my personality and character. I was either born with them, or, through upbringing and other environmental influences operating on me long ago, they have long since become part of the comparatively stable centre of the person I have become. Their effect on what I do can be distinguished from the effect on me of transient and external factors, such as the behaviour of other people and things, which impinge on me briefly and from outside. As we shall see, the determinist makes considerable play of the distinction between factors which influence what I do from the inside, as it were, and those impinging on me from the outside. Then, a second complication in any deterministic account of human behaviour is to decide on the terms in which the account is to be given. Is it to be given in terms of ordinary psychological and sociological concepts, in terms, in other words, of a person's perceptions, beliefs and desires and the factors such as environment, teaching, class position and the rest that operate on a person from without and the actions that result from the combinations of these factors, or is it to be given in terms of the person's neurophysiological states, the electro-chemical stimuli impinging on these states, and the bodily movements that result? Current theory would make the latter possibility the only likely candidate for a fully deterministic account of human behaviour. We have already remarked several times on the vagueness and open-endedness of ordinary psychological concepts which would seem to preclude their ever being worked up into anything more than a statement of tendencies of people of various types and in various states to react in particular ways to other probably equally vaguely delineated types of situation. Statements of tendencies within populations are quite consistent with individuals within those populations having a high degree of individual randomness and unpredictability, so, if that is the best that even a scientific tightening-up of psychological concepts could produce, determinism would be quite unproven at the level of the psychological. Determinism with any claim to scientific rigour or backing would appear to rest on the hope that we would one day have a complete and closed set of laws enabling us to predict the bodily movements that would follow brain states of various sorts, and the brain states that would follow other brain states and external stimuli of various states.

Determinism at the neurophysiological and physiological level would be determinism enough, at least to show that the behaviour of the human organism was fully subject to laws of nature. It is not, of course, what armchair determinists are usually thinking of when they 'explain' the behaviour of (say) a convicted criminal as due to his deprived childhood and low intelligence. And the armchair determinist may well have grasped the germ of an important point. The explanations of human behaviour we are actually interested in are explanations which represent that behaviour as actions endowed with human meaning through their being consequent on an agent's motives and inclinations and his or her perception of his or her circumstances. In other words, we want to know what someone *does* when he makes physical movements of various sorts, what I say when my larynx and tongue moves, what I am signalling when my arm moves, whether I am striking or greeting or congratulating someone when my hand strikes them, and so on. An account of human behaviour which is restricted to physiological and neurophysiological terms will leave entirely out of account the significance of the physical movements which it predicts. So we have, in theory at least, two parallel ways of describing and referring to human behaviour, one of which speaks, to put it broadly, of human actions and their associated beliefs, desires and motives, the other of which speaks simply of bodily movement and the preceding brain activity. It is this duality of description and interest that Putnam was exploiting when he disclaimed interest in the stuff of the mind in favour of functional (or psychological) accounts of human behaviour. Now, some may feel that so long as we have these two parallel schemes of description and explanation, each usable and useful in its own terms, neither need impinge on or presume to discredit the other. In particular, a deterministic neurophysiology need have no tendency to invalidate any of the things we say at the psychological level in attributing motives of responsibility, guilt and the like, and in ascribing praise and blame. The types of interest that the two schemes subserve and the circumstances in which they would be used are just so different as to rule out any conflict or overlap in practice. After all, to apply or use neurophysiological theory we would have to get people into laboratories, whereas we are far more interested in dealing with them outside laboratories. Further, even if neurophysiological determinism were true, it would not show that our ordinary psychological talk would be any less efficacious and central than it actually is in everyday life.

While admitting the differences of interest and application that undoubtedly exist between neurophysiological talk and ordinary psychological accounts of human activity, it may be doubted that the two are as independent as just suggested. After all, if we had good reason to suppose that neurophysiological theory was deterministic and complete, allowing us in principle to predict in its terms every movement I make now and in the future, would this not have a profound effect on the way I conceive myself and my behaviour? I see myself as free up to a point in some of my choices and actions: my responsibility and the praise and blame I am accorded make sense only on the supposition that some of my actions are free. Yet, neurophysiological determinism will be telling me that the movements that constitute my actions and the brain states which are (or cause) my beliefs and desires are themselves determined. However separate in practical application the two modes of discourse might be, theoretical knowledge that my actions and my beliefs and desires are determined, even at a neurophysiological level, cannot but have a profound effect on the way I conceive myself and others. In reply to this very natural response to the possibility of determinism prevailing in human behaviour, many philosophers, of whom Hume may be taken as an outstanding example, have argued that there is in fact no incompatibility between our thinking and speaking of ourselves as free on the one hand and the presumption that our psychological states and actions are (on whatever level) determined by physical law.

Hume's statement of the thesis that free will and determinism are compatible (or compatibilism) appears in Section 8 of his *Enquiry Concerning Human Understanding*. What his compatibilism rests on is, first, a denial that talk of causality (or of determinism) involves any presumption of an effect being forced or necessitated. Many defenders of libertarian positions on freedom (which I shall now take to involve the denial that all human actions are caused or determined according to physical law) use in defence of their position the absence of any feelings of constraint or compulsion when they take themselves to be acting freely. But, argues Hume, for this to be taken as evidence in favour of libertarianism, we would have to be thinking of causality in terms of force or necessitation. As we have already seen, Hume is sceptical of any such force: once it is realized that 'we know nothing farther of causation of any kind than merely the *constant conjunction* of objects', we will see that failure to feel forced to act when I think of myself as acting freely has no bearing on whether the act was caused or determined in accordance with physical law. In fact, if we reflect further, we will see that it is evident that what we call free actions 'have a regular conjunction with motives and circumstances and characters' so as to enable us to draw inferences from one to another. They are, in fact, determined by these factors, and the determining factors themselves are the effects of other determining factors. But this in no way undermines the everyday distinction between free and unfree actions. A free action is not an uncaused or undetermined action; it is, rather, an action which is determined by our own choice, as opposed to an unfree action, one imposed on us by the choice of another or by circumstances we have no control over, and 'this hypothetical liberty is universally allowed to belong to everyone who is not a prisoner and in chains'.

Hume's compatibilist position amounts to saying that all actions are determined, but that some (the free ones) are determined from within, while others (the unfree ones) are determined from without. He also makes some play of the claim that the libertarian is in effect thinking of free actions as uncaused ones, but, as he says in speaking of voluntary actions, the ones for which we are to be held responsible and for which we are praised and blamed are ones which are caused by us:

> We cannot surely mean that actions have so little connexion with motives, inclinations and circumstances, that one does not follow with a certain degree of uniformity from the other.

An action which is uncaused would be a chance action. Hume denies the existence of chance effects, saying that talk of chance is tantamount to an admission of ignorance regarding a cause, but even if we disagree with Hume on that, and accept a degree of randomness in nature, an action for which we hold the agent responsible can hardly be one that happens for no reason at all, unconnected to the agent's steady motives or inclinations. A purely random piece of behaviour would hardly be an action at all; an action is something envisaged as intended by the agent, in the light of his desires and his beliefs about means of furthering them.

It is true that Hume concentrates in his account of free action on the causation of actions, but he would obviously extend his deterministic arguments to the motives and inclinations that he sees as the causes of actions. A present motive or inclination of mine is one that follows naturally and deterministically from my past motives or inclinations, while a free choice is one that I make in the light of my own motives and inclinations and not one that is forced on me. The contrast Hume would insist on in every case is not what he regards as the illusory contrast between an undetermined act or state and a determined one, but the contrast between an act or state determined from within, as it were, as opposed to one determined from without. And certainly, looking at other people's free actions, and looking back over my own free choices, it is often possible to discern a pattern and an inevitability about a life that may have been far from obvious from the subjective point of view.

After our reflections on psychological concepts we may be less sure than Hume that actions and motives, inclinations and circumstances, can actually be worked up into anything genuinely law-like. But this hardly affects the substance of his claim, which is that the difference between a free act and an unfree one is not that between something determined and something undetermined, but rather between ways in which the act is determined. One that can be regarded as following from my own desires will be free, the rest unfree. This distinction remains unaffected by the neurophysiological type of determinism, for we can still identify our desires and what follows from them even if we believe that the states that constitute (or cause) our desires are determined. So a version of compatibilism based on that defended by Hume can survive the claim that it is brain states and physical movements rather than desires and action that will feature in any plausible deterministic account of human behaviour. It survives because a deterministic neurophysiology would reinforce a general determinism regarding human behaviour, without in any way undermining the grounds on which (according to Hume) we distinguish between free and unfree action.

But are Hume and other compatibilists right in thinking that the distinction between voluntary and involuntary action simply amounts to a distinction between types of origin of my actions, given that the origins are in both cases seen as part of a deterministic history of the interactions between the organism that is me and the world? The compatibilist picture would, it is true, lead one to expect that one would feel differently about the choices that appeared to follow naturally from the complex of beliefs and desires which have gone to make me up, from those that were forced on me by pressure from outside and against what I wanted. We can speak from this point of view of an individual being responsible to the extent that his actions follow from those beliefs and desires of his that we could envisage being changed or reinforced by pressure from outside; praise and blame would be seen as fundamentally forward-looking, ways of extinguishing or reinforcing aspects of an agent's character. But we clearly could not speak of an agent being responsible for his actions in the sense that he could, all things being the same, have made a choice other than the one he did make. Equally, his character in the long term must, from a deterministic point of view, be regarded as the result of what he was born with and what happened to him. In a way, on the deterministic view the agent becomes the passive recipient of his beliefs and desires, and his choices and actions the predictable outcome of his beliefs and desires. It is just this basic passivity with respect to what I am, what I believe, and what I choose which the libertarian will want to reject, and, in rejecting it, he will claim that the compatibilist gives a false account of what a free action or choice consists in.

The libertarian believes what I think we all believe about ourselves, namely, that when we make a decision or actually do something or form a judgement about something we are not simply performing in a way already determined, in either psychological or neurophysiological terms. This last point is important to emphasize because whatever autonomy the psychological has from the neurophysiological, if my psychological states and attitudes are still regarded as identical to or in causal relations to my neurophysiological states and these latter states are neurophysiologically determined, then it follows that the corresponding psychological states will be neurophysiologically brought about, and the control I think I have over them will be an illusion. As Nagel puts it, however, to be my own, actions are not happenings or events at all, and certainly not happenings or events supervenient on neurophysiological events. They are things I do, and I regard the actions of others as things they do.[11] When I praise or blame them, for example, I do not regard myself as indulging purely in forward-looking control of their future behaviour. But it is just the thought that I do things in a way that I am free of physically determining causes and effects that the determinist finds unintelligible and why he will be inclined to offer accounts of notions like freedom and responsibility which preserve at least some of their conventional senses, while being compatible with determinism.

Compatibilism fails, I have argued, to do justice to the sense of personal agency and choice we have. But it does not follow from this that this sense is itself intelligible or defensible. How, it will be urged, could we make decisions and have thoughts which themselves bring about effects in our brains and which interrupt or change whatever neurophysiological processes were already in train? At the very least the libertarian position entails that there could not be a complete and closed deterministic science of the brain. This may not in fact be so implausible. Brain science could, like contemporary microphysics, be indeterministic, thus allowing room for neurophysiologically unpredictable brain events, as Eccles claims it actually does. Of course, determinism in the brain on its own would provide only a necessary condition for what the libertarian wants. Freedom in human activity is not, as we have already seen, mere randomness, though it may look like that from the point of view of the brain. What the libertarian wants is some sense that I do and decide things in a way which is intelligible and according to my reasons and desires, but which is not determined by physical law. Here the autonomy of psychological explanations and their inability to enter into deterministic frameworks may well be crucial. Hume could conceive of 'motives and inclinations' as being intelligible only if they were part of a closed causal system. But we have seen that the very language in which we speak of such things is too indeterminate and too shifting in application ever to fit into such a framework. We cannot universally form definite predictions which are confirmed about how people will behave on the basis of even a very good knowledge of their psychology, although on the basis of such knowledge we can have some idea of what they are likely to do and understand why they do the things they do, even when what they do is unexpected. In other words, in our ordinary-language psychology we already have a non-deterministic way of accounting for, explaining and, within limits, predicting human behaviour. Hume could envisage no way in which an action or a choice could fail to be determined unless it was a purely chance happening. An effective reply to Hume at this point would be to point out that we already know and use a scheme of explanation in our everyday accounts of people's behaviour and the reasons for it which assumes that actions can be intelligible, without being either random or totally determined.

The determinist, however, will continue to find all this totally mysterious. What does the choosing and deciding, on this picture, and on what basis? Doesn't the libertarian picture in fact lead ineluctably to metaphysical dualism, with a non-physical self pulling the strings of the brain according to its wishes? And how, in any case, would its wishes escape being random if they were not determined to go one way or the other, by a preponderance of evidence or motive pushing it in that way? Can a genuinely libertarian freedom be more than liberty of indifference, where we are not being strongly pushed in any particular way (by reasons or evidence or anything else), and so we choose something more or less randomly? The problem for the libertarian here is to explain how a reason for an action can seem good to him, without his being thereby determined to choose it, and if this is conceded, he will then be asked to explain how some reason can seem good to him except as an effect of past conditioning. In other words, the Humean view of motives and inclinations reasserts itself regarding an agent's choice of reasons for his actions. Practical reasoning – the relations between an agent's actions, on the one hand, and his beliefs and desires, on the other – may evade capture by deterministic theory, but it is hard to see how individual decisions can avoid all taint of randomness if they are not determined to seem the best by the standards and criteria the agent has already accepted, and these acceptances themselves will in their turn be either random or determined by earlier choices, and so on, and so on.

Wiggins, in a sophisticated and subtle defence of libertarianism,[12] has spoken of biographies unfolding non-deterministically but intelligibly,

non-deterministically in that personality and character are never something complete, and need not be the deterministic origin of action; intelligibly in that each new action or episode constitutes a comprehensible phase in the unfolding of character, a further specification of what the man has by now *become*.[13]

He goes on to quote the Sartre of 1969 as saying that freedom consists of that which makes a totally conditioned social being someone who does not render back completely what his conditioning has given him. This is perhaps better from the libertarian point of view than Wiggins's own statement, which is consistent with a character which develops in fact in a random way, later having some pattern read into it. The essence of libertarianism is that I make something of myself, that I take responsibility for my actions, that I choose my course, not that these things are rendered unto me. As I have said, these notions are deeply embedded in our conceptions of ourselves and our lives, but I fear that we are no nearer making sense of them. Libertarianism has, as one critic of it says, a blank where an essential element ought to appear.[14] It does not explain who the 'I' is, or how the 'I' can be motivated to make choices, even motivated by reasons, without thereby being determined. In what does our spontaneous but non-random control over our deeds and decisions consist? As Honderich insists,

the blank occurs at that point where one should have an account of the non-causal agency that is ordinarily supposed to enter into responsible action. No one has ever offered more, by way of explanation, than a certain amount of dubious machinery, notably the 'Creative Self'. It is pretty hard to maintain the required suspension of disbelief in such items, or rather, it is hard to see what it is that one is trying not to disbelieve.[15]

The onus is on the libertarian to explain his concept of acting on reasons I choose and which I assess and in a sense control, without my being deterministically motivated by them or by the factors that led me to find my reasons convincing. The indeterminacy of quantum physics, which he alleges characterizes the operation of the brain, provides him only with the space he needs to work. But, as Honderich says, the space is currently filled largely by a blank.

Of course the problem of freedom of action is central to our conception of ourselves and our world. The libertarian maintains that we as human beings have the ability to step outside the possibilities of either determinism or randomness afforded by natural law, and that we can assess and control our actions and our beliefs by assessments and choices we are not determined to make, and that judging something to be true or good or rational is quite unlike being caused to do something. He may well cite here the difference between believing something on good evidence and being caused to have a belief by some chemical interference with my brain. The determinist will admit the distinction, but say that the distinction operates only between types of cause – that one belief is caused in me in one way (perhaps because I am determined to be the sort of person who mulls over evidence), the other in some other way. The libertarian will point out that much of our moral, penal and social lives depends on the idea that we are capable non-deterministically of forming our own judgements and of making our own decisions, and that this is what justifies our praising someone who does these things in the light of what is true and good and blaming someone whose standards are lower. Our discussion in this section has tended to underline the revisionary nature of a determinist interpretation of responsibility and other moral and quasi-moral notions, and the way in which we do not subjectively conceive of ourselves as determined, but much needs to be done to show convincingly that these notions and conceptions are coherent, let alone rationally acceptable.

Personal Identity

The distinction between the subjective and objective points of view that has been a running theme through our considerations of the mind and action becomes a central concern in a philosophical consideration of personal identity. For we appear to have two distinct ways of looking at questions of personal identity, of deciding, that is, whether a person at one time is the same person as a person at another time. On the one hand we can appeal to the person's own memory and experience and ask him whether he was the person who did such and such in the past. In the limiting case of one's own life, this is almost inevitably the way in which one will first attempt to deal with such questions. It was I that did the deed in question because I can remember doing it. And whatever problems memory has as a test of personal identity, it appears that from the subjective point of view, what matters to me about myself, about my past and my future, is precisely the psychological continuity that exists between my present state and my past, and which I envisage as being projected into the future. One of the psychologically implausible aspects of Eastern doctrines of reincarnation is that most people have no memories of their past existences, and if, when I am in my future states, I cannot remember the state I am in now, there seems no more reason for me to care about those future states than there is for me to care about other people quite distinct from me, whose lives I can influence in various ways.

On the other hand, it is easy to show that appealing to psychological states, such as one's sense that one has done or experienced something in the past, cannot in many cases settle questions of personal identity. In the first place, there are many things I have done, particularly in my early years, which I have no memory of, and secondly, my memory has on many occasions proved inaccurate and unreliable. I often 'remember' having seen or heard something, and it is later proved to me that I could not have done any such thing, either because such a thing never happened or because other people had observed me elsewhere or had failed to observe me at the event I 'remembered'. My memory of my past, then, seems open to correction by others, based on what they have seen and heard. That this should be possible is part of our conception of ourselves making our way through a world which exists independently of us; our own mental states taken individually are not the final arbiters on how things are in the world, or, indeed, on how we make our own way in that world. The objective side of personal identity was memorably summed up by Bishop Butler in 1736 in his *Analogy of Religion* in the words

One should really think it self-evident, that consciousness of personal identity presupposes, and therefore cannot constitute, personal identity, any more than knowledge, in any other case, can constitute truth, which it presupposes.

If we take 'consciousness of personal identity' to include one's memory of having done or experienced certain things in the past, then Butler's point would be that talk of actual memory, as opposed to purported or supposed memory, presupposes that one actually is the same person as the person that did or experienced those things. In other words, saying that one is the same person as the one in the past is not equivalent to saying that one has certain memory-like experiences of a certain existence or experience in the past, for one's memory can be wrong as it would undoubtedly be if I claimed to remember putting gunpowder under the House of Commons in 1605. One's memory that one did something must be checkable by other non-psychological means, and this entails that the doer of the things 'remembered' be identifiable as the same person as the one who remembers by non-psychological means. Saying that felt continuity of experience with some other existence in the past is not the same thing as being the same as the person who had those experiences or did those things does not, however, tell us what it is to be the same person as someone in the past, or whether we have the necessary non-psychological means for deciding such questions. In law and in ordinary life, however, it seems clear enough that we do have a firm idea both of what constitutes personal identity and of how, in theory at least, such questions are to be decided. Bodily continuity is what constitutes personal identity, and proof of bodily continuity is enough to establish personal identity. Moreover, we have pretty foolproof means of establishing bodily continuity; despite several changes of bodily material throughout a full human life, the configurations recorded in fingerprinting and dentistry apparently remain constant throughout. Finally, the phenomena of consciousness, memory impressions, character traits and the like, tend to remain stable through life, altering only over long periods and often in concert with bodily change and development. The general coincidence of subjective and objective factors in establishing personal identity reinforces our tendency to allow the greater objectivity and reliability of tests of bodily continuity to override and correct the comparatively occasional instances where subjective feelings are doubtful or disagree with objective tests, while at the same time allowing us to rely on memory alone for unimportant cases or cases where no non-psychological tests are possible. But the assumption remains that my body is continuous with the body that has the experiences I remember, and this is why, whatever 'memory' experiences I have and whatever light on Stuart police methods is thrown by them, I could never actually be Guy Fawkes, because my body is not continuous with his.

The view just described would see human persons as physically embodied beings, and their lives and identities as being coextensive with the life of the physical beings that they are, but it will be questioned by some whether the account is really as adequate as it seems. In the first place it may be said that it trades on an important ambiguity in talk of the person being coextensive with the living human being. For we cannot say that a human person is coextensive with his body. My corpse is not the person that I am. In what then does my life consist, as it does not seem to be the same in temporal duration as the existence of my body? The thought that there is a distinction to be made between my personal existence and that of my body takes us back once more to the role of experience and other psychological factors in measuring the extent of my life (or when I was a *living* body), and raises the possibility that the life that I lead may be connected for a time with the particular body I now have, but that this connection may be contingent, and that what really counts as my life is the lived continuity that exists between various experiences of mine. This view can be formulated to avoid the objection we have considered to any criterion of personal identity based on subjective memory feelings alone by stipulating in the first instance that the experiences remembered be experiences of an embodied being (and hence that the experiences be checkable by others), while denying that the being be embodied always in the same body. What is being suggested in effect is that a person can shift from one body to another. The point of the suggestion is not, initially anyway, to convince us that such things might happen, but rather to cast doubt on the commonsensical stress on the centrality of bodily continuity to personal identity. After all, it will be said, to answer the Butler point, while it is required that a person's memory experiences be checkable through the observation that they were part of a continuous history of some body, it is not required that the person in question was always associated with the same body.

Locke was an early exponent of the view that persons could change bodies. An *Essay Concerning Human Understanding* (Bk II, Chap. XXVII, Section XV) entertained the possibility that a prince and a cobbler might go to sleep one night, one in his palace, the other in his hovel. Adapting Locke's example slightly, the man in the hovel wakes up with his head full of thoughts and memories that would fit the prince, and the man in the castle appears to be continuing the mental life of the cobbler. Does this radical personality change amount to a body-swap between prince and cobbler? It is tempting to say so in the context of the example, given the background story and symmetrical exchange of memories, personalities and so on. Although Locke was a supporter of the memory account of personal identity (and Butler was attacking Locke in his attack on that view), the prince–cobbler example does not make memory the sole criterion for the past history or identity of the prince (now in the hovel), for the memories of the prince are linked systematically to the observed behaviour of the prince in what we will now call his former body. What Locke's story does is to suggest rather strongly that bodily continuity may not be sufficient or necessary to establish personal identity.

The actuality of organ transplantation has given something of more than science-fiction relevance to recent updatings of the prince–cobbler case in terms of imagined brain transplantation. Again the point of the examples is to bring out what is at issue in our talk of personal identity, and to see just what is important to it. Let us follow Sydney Shoemaker in his exposition of a brain-transplant case.[16] Mr Brown and Mr Robinson are being operated on for brain tumours, the operation involving extraction and replacement of the brain. However, the brains are inadvertently replaced in the wrong skulls. One of the patients dies, but the other – the one with Robinson's body and Brown's brain – regains consciousness, and exhibits great shock at the appearance of his body. Pointing to himself, he says 'This isn't my body, the one over there is!' He automatically answers to the name 'Brown', has all Brown's memories, prejudices and character traits, and none of Robinson's. As Shoemaker says, we would surely be strongly inclined to say this man is Brown. If we do, 'we must be using psychological criteria of personal identity and allowing these to override the fact of bodily nonidentity'.

Natural as the inclination may be, in the Shoemaker example, to say that the man who survives is Brown, Bernard Williams has shown that it is possible to describe cases whose outcome is qualitatively just the same – a body with total transformation of psychological attributes – which we would be far less inclined to think of as cases of Brown in Robinson's body.[17] Let us, for example, imagine Robinson undergoing some very unpleasant process, entering a torture machine or the like, in which he successively undergoes total amnesia, changes in character and implantation of fictitious 'memory' beliefs appropriate to someone else entirely. Is there a new person here in Robinson's body? The temptation to say there is so far is not strong, though it might be strengthened somewhat if the newly implanted memory beliefs turned out to be those of a real person, Brown, and would be increased even more if Brown underwent a similar procedure in the reverse direction, ending up with Robinson's psychological traits. But not only is it far less clear that we would speak of body-exchanges even in the final stage of this example than in the Shoemaker case, but the *only* reason for doing so appears to be the purely external addition to the example of the information that the newly implanted 'memories' happened to be those (or like those) of some really existing person. If this were not so, we would simply say that Robinson had undergone a peculiarly unpleasant experience. Two questions remain crucially difficult to answer in all this. First, why should the purely external fact of the new memories being in some sense non-illusory make any difference to whom we are now speaking of? Secondly does this example not show, contrary to what the Shoemaker example seemed to show, that personal identity can survive total psychological discontinuity?

In answer to the second question it is, as Williams emphasizes at the end of his paper, no use saying that what we have here are cases which stretch our existing conceptual apparatus in such a way as to be undecidable, and that all we can do in such cases is to make a stipulation (to the effect that what we have is Robinson, or Brown, or some new person altogether, Brownson, or the like). For, at least from Robinson's point of view, what is at issue is not the application of a concept. Suppose that Robinson were told that he was going to undergo the experiment. Might he not, very properly, fear all this as something that was going to happen to *him*, as something about *his* future? And how, in addition, could he be deflected from such a concern about himself, even if it turned out that someone else (Brown) was undergoing the same thing in reverse? Williams is not absolutely sure that Robinson would be right to have such fears for himself, but he finds it totally unacceptable that someone should be told that a future situation (such as the experiment on Robinson) was such that it is conceptually undecidable or a matter for decision whether it would be happening to *him* or not, for this would be to leave him without any emotional attitude appropriate to that situation.

The disposition, despite Shoemaker's case, to think that personal identity must be rooted in bodily continuity, whether psychological changes take place in one, can be reinforced by pointing out, as Williams does in the conclusion of his article, that the experimenter could have changed Robinson in the way indicated in the example, and then in the final stage gone on to produce two people with Robinson-like character and memories (by splitting the original Robinson brain, say, and putting one half into each body) and perhaps introduced Brown-like character and memories into other bodies than Robinson's, as well. Such cases make it even more difficult to know what to say; they would make it particularly difficult to speak of Robinson continuing in Brown's body; he also continues in the other body (say Smith's), into which his character and memories have been inserted, and so we have the same (one) person in two bodies. Not only that, but once the operation is over, the two new bearers of Robinson's character and memories will diverge and pursue different histories, so on the body-swap view Robinson will be identical with two different people, 'Robinson-Brown' and 'Robinson-Smith', which is absurd; for if Robinson were the same person as 'Robinson-Brown', and the same person as 'Robinson-Smith', then 'Robinson-Brown' and 'Robinson-Smith' would be the same person, which they clearly are not. But it is equally rational to say that Robinson is 'Robinson-Brown' as to say he is 'Robinson-Smith', and worse, since the reason for our original intuition that in the Shoemaker case Robinson survives in Brown's body is exactly the same as our reason for saying that Robinson survives in each of 'Robinson-Smith' and 'Robinson-Brown'. Williams concludes by appearing to reject the whole notion of a body-swap, suggesting that the example Shoemaker has presented us with is the one out of a range of equally possible situations (and in many relevant ways precisely parallel situations) which we should be most inclined to call a change of bodies. 'As against this,' he concludes, 'the principle that one's fears can extend to future pain whatever psychological changes precede it seems positively straightforward',[18] and hence that I should continue to think of myself in terms of what happens to my present body, whatever happens to my memory or character.

However, we may want to question whether Williams is correct in his emphasis on bodily continuity, to the exclusion of psychological continuity. As I remarked at the start of this section, psychological continuity seems peculiarly important to us in our thinking and concern about ourselves; even if we admit that failure in occasional cases of amnesia does not destroy the identity of the amnesiac, it seems doubtful that our concept of a person could survive frequent dissociations of psychological and bodily continuities. The examples introduced by Williams are just such dissociations, but implicit in the discussion so far has been the assumption that what really matters to us is our personal identity through time, and that psychological continuity is important in so far as it is a criterion for personal identity. Because, as Williams has shown, two persons can be psychologically continuous with an original psychological source, whereas identity is always a one-to-one relation, we had to conclude that psychological continuity could not constitute personal identity. But Derek Parfit has argued in 'Personal Identity' that this is exactly to reverse the correct order of importance. [19] According to Parfit, we are interested in personal identity precisely because it normally entails psychological continuity or survival, which is what really matters to us. If psychological continuity took a branching form, as in the Williams examples, then what we ought to do is leave questions of identity aside and examine instead how our notions might survive cases of psychological branching where one psychologically continuous tract of experience is split into two or more, by something like Robinson's brain being split and one half placed in Brown's body and the other in Smith's, with each resulting person having all Robinson's memory and character traits up to the time of the operation. Parfit, in other words, seeks to disentangle questions of survival (which matter to us) from questions of personal identity (which don't, according to him).

Suppose I were Robinson? Which (if any) of 'Robinson-Brown' or 'Robinson-Smith' would be me? According to Parfit, there is no further answer to this question over and above as full a description as we can give of the relevant continuities and discontinuities, psychological and bodily, no further fact which my identity could consist in. What we should, in any case, be concentrating on is the extent to which 'Robinson-Brown' and 'Robinson-Smith' are psychologically continuous with the original Robinson, and this is something that admits of degrees. Both new people can speak of the original Robinson as 'my past self', as the original Robinson would, in anticipation, speak of both the future people as future selves of his. Soon after the operation, both the new selves would be psychologically very close to the past self, but, later on, it is possible that 'Robinson-Brown', say, would have virtually no memory of Robinson, in which case he would speak of Robinson as 'not in any way one of *my* past selves, just an ancestral self'.

Parfit in fact suggests that this sense of being nearer or closer to past or future selves is one all of us actually have in our own lives, and that our lives are in fact actually made up of bundles of such selves, in greater or lesser continuity with each other. There is, on the way of thinking Parfit proposes, no essential or underlying person, an 'I' which binds the successive selves. What matters in the continued existence of any of us are just the relations of degree of psychological connectedness and continuity that exist between the phases of our life. A consequence of this view of human life, which Parfits admits, is that it would weaken the hold on us of the idea that we ought to care especially about the interests of our distantly future selves, more, say, than we care about the interests of other people or as much as we care about the satisfaction of our present self. It is clear enough that Parfit's picture of human beings as consisting of successions of not necessarily closely related selves would indeed have radical consequences for our notions of rationality and consistency, as applied to a person's life, as well as for our attempts to undertake long-term personal commitments and our expectations that others should, in justice, feel themselves bound by promises and contracts.

Parfit's view of what matters in human life, and of psychological continuity being a relationship of degree as well as potentially a one–many relationship, may provide an answer to some problems raised by the notion of survival of death. He does not, to be sure, provide any support for the idea of disembodied survival of death, and there are great difficulties in even imagining a disembodied human life. For our lives and experience are centrally oriented through our existence as embodied perceivers and agents. But a disembodied perceiver, a perceiver from no point of view, is of doubtful intelligibility, and even more difficult to accept is a disembodied agent, one who acted without a body. Would such a being simply will things to happen? But what would that be like, and how would we distinguish cases where what happened did so of its own accord from cases where it did so because we had willed it? And how would disembodied beings communicate with each other? What would there be in the stream of contents which occupied the consciousness of a disembodied being to enable it to distinguish between a content which was merely fantasized and one that was really a message from some other being? Without perception, action or communication, a disembodied life would consist in little more than a succession of memories and images passing before the mind which we could in no clear sense control or assess, except on the basis of past embodied experience, a shadowy and ever-diminishing type of life for beings used to embodied life, assuming disembodied consciousness is possible at all. But the survival through some sort of bodily resurrection, which Christians look forward to, is not survival in a disembodied state. Some have objected that my survival in a resurrected body would be indistinguishable from the existence of a replica of myself and consistent with several replicas existing in different places, but on Parfit's view this would not matter. I might be able to think of one of my future selves as being in a different future body from the one currently living and acting here and now, and of others in other bodies, and, in this future state, the various selves might feel themselves to be in some sort of psychological continuity and connectedness with the self I currently am. The replica objection holds only against the view that survival entails personal identity, and would not be effective against a view like Parfit's which allows for several selves continuous with the one I now am continuing in different bodies.

Still, it cannot be said that Parfit's idea of succession of selves in more or less psychological contact with each other would be likely to appeal to any orthodox religious believers in bodily resurrection, for orthodox Christianity puts considerable stress on the one essential me that persists through all my physical changes in life and death itself. (Indeed, much of the motivation in favour of dualism comes from orthodox religion.) And certainly the inadequacy of Parfit's conception of human selves to account for our moral intuitions provides one telling line of objection to it. But, following Wiggins,[20] we can perhaps put the objection in a context which explains and grounds the idea that bodily continuity is indeed a central and indispensable part of our concept of a human self or person.

In considering Parfit's argument, we have been assuming that we understand what it is to be a human self. But it seems clear enough that what he initially means by a self is some tract of a person's history, bound together by a strong degree of psychological continuity and connectedness. (Indeed, it is surely significant that in a postscript in later reprintings of his original article, including the one referred to here, he says that talk about successive selves is only a *façon de parler*, liable to mislead if taken any more literally.) Parfit's notion of a self is, then, parasitic on the notion of a human person, and at least part of our interest in human persons, from both the subjective and objective points of view, is in constructing 'internally consistent, mutually consistent, indefinitely amplifiable, individual biographies'.[21] It is the construction of a determinate individual biography that is of course precluded by branching or overlapping selves, for in such a conception there is no clear answer to questions concerning which self did such and such a deed or whether indeed several selves after a fission might not equally claim to have done some deed performed before the fission. There is not even any clear criterion for deciding when one self begins and another ends.

Against Parfit's plurality of selves occupying the life of one human being, Wiggins insists that our concept of a person is in fact akin to a natural-kind concept, a natural kind, it will be remembered, being something with a scientifically discoverable nature, which explains its behaviour and constitution. According to Wiggins, it is no accident that we all feel such an intuitive certainty that 'man' (*homo sapiens*), 'human being' and 'person' are coextensive, and that the identities of persons (and even of selves, we might add) are precisely equivalent to the identities of the animals that we are. Indeed, we might add further that the speculations we engaged in about the possibility of the same consciousness existing or continuing indifferently in more than one physical body grotesquely distorts the extent to which one's self-consciousness and sense of who one is is determined by one's body, that one is conscious of oneself as a person with such and such physical characteristics, and that one is conscious of one's making one's way through the world with a particular physique and sex, and a particular history in which that body is central. It is quite unclear to what extent one could recognize one's continuing consciousness as surviving anything like a body-swap, or whether, in the event of such a thing, the consciousness that awoke from the operation would be like a total amnesiac learning what it was like to be a human person all over again, though puzzled from time to time by some strange and troubling images of another and oddly disconnected life, altogether distinct from that which one is now leading.

Accepting that human personhood and self-consciousness are intimately tied to both one's existence as an animal with definite limits in space and time and one's consciousness of that existence would not only explain the pervasive idea that, despite the speculations of Locke and Parfit, bodily continuity is central to identity and selfhood, but would also provide some backing for the views on the interpretation of the language of others canvassed several times in the previous chapter, as well as for the idea, to be considered in the next chapter, that human beings have certain naturally given limits on their needs and desires that cannot be changed by free choice, either individually or collectively. For if human beings are animals, with a given biological constitution, then the presumption that they will agree on much, in both factual and evaluative matters, need not be defended on purely methodological grounds. We can, as Wiggins suggests, base our assumptions about what people are likely to think or want or need in a shared human nature, 'supervenient on contingencies of human *biological* constitution'.[22]

Whether or not one finally accepts that human selves and human self-consciousness are intimately bound up with existence as a specific human animal, with a definite birth, death and physical embodiment, it can be said in conclusion that the defenders of the bodily continuity view of personal identity have gone some way to suggesting the connections between what one says on this issue and the way in which one is likely to approach ethical and social questions. For if selves are free-floating in the way Locke and Parfit imply, then there seem to be no naturally imposed limits on the desires that might be foisted on them or the functions that might be assigned to them. The free-floating view of the essential me is, whether its defenders initially realize this or not, a close ally of those managerial political and economic systems that treat individuals as bundles of transiently and temporally connected desires, manipulable and malleable as occasion or opportunity offer. A sense that I am a living organism, and that my history is history as that organism, with certain limits and possibilities given to me thereby, not only roots my existence firmly in the physical world and biology, hence providing the essential link between the subjective and the objective conceptions of my existence, but it also suggests a natural background against which ethical choices and political decisions might be measured.

Chapter Five

Ethics and Politics

In this chapter, we will consider the basis of moral judgements and the nature of the ties that bind men together in societies. We will ask whether political ties and moral obligations are founded in individual choice and consensus, or whether there is something about them that transcends individual choice. As we shall see, the liberal individualist will stress the aspects of individual commitment and decision involved in accepting that one has an obligation or a duty of a certain sort, whether personal or social; his opponents will stress in various ways how individuals arise out of a context, social, political and moral, over which they have no control, and against the background of which their own identities and personalities are formed. In considering various theories of the nature of moral and political obligations, we will see how the theorists involved tend characteristically to stress one aspect of the matter, while leaving out other aspects. We have various intuitions as to what the right and the good consist in, and about how we are to assess moral and political judgements, and it is often easy to show that theories about the right and the good stressing one set of intuitions conflict with other equally plausible intuitions. But are our intuitions on these matters in fact compatible, and, if not, how can we justify the choice of one set rather than another?

The Nature of Morality

At one time (or so we are often told, though without always being told exactly at which time) people simply accepted that the moral thing to do was determined by some objective standard, such as a divine command or some natural law. If someone wanted to know what he or she ought to do, then he or she had simply to consult the standard. This might involve asking a teacher or, slightly more sophisticatedly, be a matter of reflecting rationally on one's problem in the light of the nature and purpose of human life. In either case, however, the answer was already determined by the facts, even though there might be difficulty on occasion in determining what the relevant facts were. The underlying assumption was that human life has a purpose, either given directly by God or in some way written into human nature. Human flourishing will be achieved if we regulate our lives according to that purpose, but not otherwise. Morality consists broadly in submitting to that purpose, where the purpose is conceived as something laid down in advance by an authority – God or nature – which we have no say on.

One problem with seeing morality as arising directly from divine or natural law is that there are competing versions of what the law is. While this in itself is not a compelling objection to this conception of morality, it does mean that human judgement has to be exercised in deciding which of the competing versions of morality is the correct one; this admission opens the door to Kant's famous objection to any attempt to found morality on divine commands or law-like facts about human nature. Kant says that even if the Holy One of the gospel were to stand before me, I would still have to decide within myself, on the basis of my own idea of moral perfection, that this was indeed the Holy One of God.[1] In other words, before accepting any message as being the truth about morality, I would still have to exercise my moral judgement in deciding that the message and the messenger were good. My moral judgement, then, cannot be subordinated to any positive fact about a divine message or how human nature is. I have still to judge that the content of the message or what promotes the flourishing of human nature are what I ought to do, and this may be problematic, as can be seen when we reflect that the Holy One of the Gospel invites us to accept that the wicked will be condemned by Him to eternal damnation, and that it would be by no means implausible from an evolutionary point of view to think of human flourishing being promoted by preventing the handicapped from reproducing.

Kant's demonstration of the role that human judgement has to play in the formation of moral decisions is often taken to be an illustration of the way a genuine morality is in a sense autonomous; a heteronomous morality – one in which people simply submitted to the moral codes imposed on them by authorities, natural or divine – would really be no morality at all, for it is an evasion of the fundamental responsibility of each of us to evaluate moral matters for ourselves. We still have to show that any supposed moral authority and its pronouncements are such that we should be guided by them, and that remains an open question, until we explain why we should. But if this is what the autonomy of morality amounts to, it does not amount to very much, because an exactly parallel argument could be mounted against a man who accepts certain things as true just because the Pope, or Einstein, or anyone else says so. His attitude is irrational to the extent that he is unable or unwilling to show why the pronouncements of his chosen authority are likely to be true. What the Kantian argument shows is the irrationality of uncritically basing one's beliefs in any field on the mere say-so of an authority. It does not show anything peculiar to morality, and it certainly does not show what it is often taken to show, that morality is not a factual matter or that moral judgements are in some sense independent of any facts there may be relevant to human flourishing or human destiny.

That moral judgements are unlike ordinary factual judgements in various ways has, however, been a familiar theme in moral philosophy since the time of Hume. Hume himself pointed most forcefully to one aspect of this, that in judging that some course of action is right or wrong we are speaking about what ought or ought not to be done, and that in doing so we are going beyond a mere statement of what is or is not the case. Logically, Hume is quite right. Even if one accepts that because one *has* made a promise to visit some relation, it follows logically that one *ought* to visit the relation, this can only be because lurking in the background is the institution of promise-keeping, with its built-in understanding that one ought to keep one's promises. In engaging in the institution on a particular occasion I may be said to be taking on the obligations that this entails, so my admitting that I have promised to do something is tantamount to my admitting that I am recognizing that I ought to do it. This in no way threatens the point Hume wishes to make, which is that where we are not implicitly relying on the mutual acceptance of institutions or forms of description (such as speaking of some course of action as 'mean' or 'disgusting'), which have some built-in moral content, judgements that one ought to do something cannot be derived logically from judgements that such and such is the case.

But Hume draws a conclusion from the 'is–ought' distinction that might be regarded as more questionable than the distinction itself. He argues that the new affirmation 'ought', as when we say murder ought not to be committed, serves to express nothing more than that reflection on murder produces in us a sentiment of disapprobation. The viciousness of murder does not consist in any empirical property observable in a murderous act:

in whichever way you take it, you find only certain passions, motives, volitions and thoughts. There is no other matter of fact in the case. The vice entirely escapes you, as long as you consider the object.[2]

If moral wrongness is not, in Hume's view, an empirical property, it is not a matter of reason either. Reason, for Hume, is a method of discovering truth and falsehood, which in turn depend on either logical relations or on matters of fact. Given what has just been said, morality is not a matter of fact, nor is it a purely logical matter. Against this background Hume's claim that ''tis not contrary to reason to prefer the destruction of the whole world to the scratching of my finger'[3] makes perfect sense. Only given a certain desire could I prefer one to the other. But the presence or absence of the desire, like the feelings of approbation or disapprobation in me that moral talk properly refers to, is something that escapes rational control or justification.

Most people would accept Hume's claim that the rightness or wrongness of an action is not an empirically observable feature of it; clearly it is not something that scientific research would be expected to turn up. But it would not follow from that that the moral quality of an action did not consist in its having some observable feature which was what made it moral or immoral. If we see some children gratuitously tormenting an animal, we might naturally conclude that the wrongness of what they were doing consisted in the fact that it caused unnecessary pain to a sentient creature. Conversely, the goodness of a famine relief worker in the Sahel, saving the lives of starving babies, would seem to be due to the tendency of his or her actions to alleviate suffering. From this, one might conclude that good and evil, though themselves unobservable, are simply tendencies of actions to produce pleasure and reduce pain, and vice versa. Something like this indeed is what utilitarians claim, and I shall have more to say about this in due course. However, there is an argument, due to G. E. Moore, which purports to show that it is impossible that moral goodness should consist in the possession by an action or an agent of some property other than goodness itself.[4] Moore's reason for saying this is that if goodness did consist in, say, the possession by an action or state of affairs of the property of relieving pain or of promoting pleasure, then it would be analytic, or true by definition, that a pain-relieving action or state of affairs was good. However, according to Moore, it cannot be analytic that goodness is equivalent to pain-relieving (or any other property whatever), because it is not self-contradictory to deny that a pain-relieving action or state of affairs is good (or that an object of any other specified sort is good).

This argument has an air of speciousness about it, resting as it does on the questionable analytic–synthetic distinction, and on intuitions about what it would be self-contradictory to say. Moore may indeed be right about the indefinability of 'good', if it should turn out that there can be no single definition of the morally good in terms of some finite list of properties, but this needs to be shown; his argument, though, gains plausibility from the fact that there are a number of competing accounts of moral goodness, and even if we hold one to be correct, we still understand what is intended by the others. It is clearly a substantive question as to what moral goodness consists in, and it would be quite trivial to rule out competing accounts on grounds of definition. Surely the utilitarian is not or should not be saying that moral good is by definition what relieves pain and promotes pleasure, even if Bentham did, on occasion, do this. He might, on the contrary, claim that, starting from the rough-and-ready idea of moral goodness he was brought up with, as consisting in certain types of action one ought to do, he has refined and revised what he was taught and discovered, or invented a more adequate and systematic account of moral goodness, in the light of which, perhaps, he is led to revise some of his earlier beliefs. But the fact that it is not linguistically deviant to say that moral goodness is not the same as (say) relieving pain and promoting pleasure does not mean that an account which claimed it was might not be preferable to any other, just as water is H₂O, though it is not self-contradictory to deny it.

Moore, however, concluded that goodness could consist in no natural property or set of natural properties at all. (Thinking that it did is what he called the 'Naturalistic Fallacy'.) However, he did not accept Hume's subjectivism. He did not think that moral judgements were simply descriptions of the feelings various acts and people arouse in us. On the contrary, Moore was certain that moral goodness is as objective a property as any natural quality, such as redness or the propensity to relieve pain. It is not a natural quality, so it must be a non-natural quality; it is not detected by the means appropriate to discerning natural qualities, so it must be detected by some sort of ethical intuition. Though Moore does admit that talk of ethical intuition is really no explanation of our grasp of moral qualities, it does not seem unfair to follow normal practice in characterizing his position as intuitionism, for what he says amounts to claiming that the unanalysable property of goodness is simply apparent to the morally sensitive eye.

It is easy to see what is wrong with naked intuitionism once we consider what happens when two conflicting ethical intuitions, for example, on the morality of abortion, confront each other. Unless the whole subject is to degenerate into simple assertion and counter-assertion, the two protagonists will presumably advance reasons of various sorts for their views; that abortion is always wrong, because it involves a destruction of life, or sometimes permissible, because unwanted pregnancies lead to multiple unhappiness. If this is the way the discussion proceeds, it is hard to see how each disputant is not in fact using some quasi-naturalistic account of morality to justify his intuitions. Of course, it may be in the end that each ends up with a simple statement of some basic value judgement he can give no further justification for. He simply knows, like Tolstoy, that life must never be destroyed, say, or that there is a divine command against abortion. But this latter view, if it is to be a moral position, involves accepting the goodness of the divine command, as Kant's argument showed; and, in all probability, intuition will be appealed to here, both in identifying a particular edict as a divine command, and in accepting its goodness. His opponent, meanwhile, simply knows something else, perhaps that what counts morally is quality rather than quantity of life. But, even assuming goodwill and rationality on the part of both protagonists, it looks as if there is no neutral way of deciding whose intuition is the properly discriminating one. Intuitionism, intended as an ethical objectivism which is at the same time non-naturalistic, is an inherently unstable position. It either relies on having naturalistic reasons for one's intuitions (certain courses of action *are* right or wrong because of natural properties they have) or it becomes little more than a matter of standing on one's unjustified and unjustifiable intuitions. And it is hard to distinguish that from Hume's subjectivism, that moral discourse is ultimately a matter of people appealing to their feelings. Unlike the yellowness of an object, which can be seen as the cause of our perceiving it as yellow, supposedly objective moral properties play no obvious causal role in bringing about our feelings that one thing is right, another wrong.

Moore was right to emphasize the role intuitive judgements play in moral life and discourse. It is quite likely that a society of human beings could function satisfactorily only if most of the members of that society in ordinary life accepted certain courses of action as just right and others as just wrong, without further argument, as if such facts were obvious to any person of goodwill.

Maybe many people will never get beyond this stage of moral reasoning, and be none the worse for that as friends, lovers and colleagues. But a philosophical inquiry into morality might be expected to try to get further, and the widespread existence of moral disagreement shows the importance of making such an attempt. Some people, however, would regard any such attempt as ultimately doomed; at least, doomed at the point at which we are simply confronted with different ultimate values. Moral argument, it would be said, can go a certain distance. Often enough, there will be enough shared background between disputants to enable one to show that some proposal of the other contravenes some shared value in a way the other had not realized. Thus, if both protagonists are committed to both the protection of old people against street crime *and* to the upholding of civil liberties, a move in a discussion on the desirability of heavy policing of the young unemployed might be to show that such tactics infringed the liberties of the young in an unacceptable way. There might also, within the same framework, be an empirical investigation into the likely effects of various police methods, whether they actually reduce crime levels, seem unreasonable to those so policed, lead to increases in police brutality and unaccountability, and so on. But the discussion may begin to take on an intractable air when it comes to ranking the values involved. Can personal liberty be overridden in order to prevent street crime? And why has personal liberty such a high value anyway? Basic intuitions are likely to re-emerge at these points, and it has seemed plausible to many to follow Hume in thinking that what we have here are just differences in feeling. Thus, A. J. Ayer argued in *Language, Truth and Logic* that precisely because it is impossible to specify any test to distinguish correct from incorrect ethical intuitions, in expressing a moral judgement one is actually making no statement at all. If I tell someone he was wrong to steal some money,

it is as if I had said, 'You stole that money', in a peculiar tone of horror, or written it with the addition of some special exclamation marks. The tone, or the exclamation marks, adds nothing to the literal meaning of the sentence. It merely serves to show that the expression of it is attended by certain feelings in the speaker.[5]

It can be objected that this so-called emotivist view of ethical statements would make moral disagreement really impossible, because if I say that thrift is a virtue and you say it is not, we will each really be doing no more than expressing our respective feelings regarding thrift, and in so far as neither of us states a proposition there can be no disagreement between us. Ayer simply concedes the point, adding that people really never argue about basic questions of value (because all that can be done is to express one's attitudes, for or against, and discover whether or not others share them).

Whatever one might think about this last claim, Ayer's emotivist theory does have one great advantage over accounts of ethical language which would see ethical statements as descriptions of states of affairs of some sort. For if it were the case that saying that stealing is wrong was a matter of describing a certain property stealing had, then people could agree that stealing was wrong, without concluding that they were under any obligation not to steal. Descriptivist views of ethical statements sever the crucial link between moral judgements and a person's affections and conduct, but this link is at the heart of the emotivist theory.

On the other hand, saying, as Ayer does, that moral judgements are used to express feelings, and in addition to arouse feeling and stimulate action, is surely too broad a characterization. 'Up the Spurs!' does all that, but it is hardly a moral judgement or even an expression of moral feeling. We need some more precise characterization of what makes a feeling or a judgement moral. R. M. Hare has attempted to provide such a characterization, while still remaining faithful to the basic emotivist theme of the non-cognitive nature of moral discourse. What he does is to emphasize something inherent in emotivism, but to develop it in an original way.[6] In Hare's view, moral discourse is a form of action-guiding or prescriptive discourse. It tells people what to do; when I say 'Stealing is wrong', this is to be understood in terms of my telling people not to steal. But unlike a prescription or order proposed for one specific occasion, such as my telling a particular garage attendant to park my car on a particular occasion, a moral judgement I make is to be regarded as universal, a command issued to all people (including myself) to behave in such and such a way on all relevant occasions. So if I say 'Stealing is wrong', I am to be understood as commanding everyone, irrespective of who they are, not to steal. Similarly my saying that Jones did wrong to take the money means that I should order anyone in similar circumstances to Jones not to take the money. Thinking of moral judgements as universal, impartial and applicable to the maker of them as much as to anyone else puts Hare in a long tradition of moral thinkers, from Kant and the utilitarian Bentham to the present, as Hare himself points out, quoting Bentham as saying 'Everybody to count for one, nobody for more than one' and Kant's injunction 'Act only on that maxim through which you can at the same time will that it should become a universal law.'[7]

Hare thinks that the universalizability of moral judgements makes moral argument possible at the level of basic values and principles. For I will in effect have to take the preferences of others into account in enunciating my basic principles. If I say that other people ought not to steal or cheat, I must be prepared to say that I shouldn't. If I say that it is morally permissible for me to exploit the poor of the world, then I must be prepared to allow them to exploit me, unless I can specify any relevant difference between me and them. Hare thinks that it is likely that I would not generally be prepared to allow others to act in a way that trampled on my perceived interests; hence I cannot consistently adopt a moral system that allowed me to trample on theirs. And in this he is undoubtedly correct, as far as most people go. So, his prescriptivism has this advantage over emotivism, that it provides a way of ruling out some proposed ethical judgement as morally wrong, those, namely, that are not universalizable. Indeed, if we were to extend our universalizing method by saying that we should adopt those moral principles which produce the greatest satisfaction of everybody's preferences, it seems as if we might have a way of ranking and deciding between competing moral and political proposals, and this indeed is just what Hare has proposed in his more recent work, in which he claims that the requirement of universalizability actually generates a form of utilitarianism, whereby we should each judge moral and political principles and proposals by putting ourselves in the position of all those affected by them, and reckoning how the preferences of all these people would be helped or hindered by them, and to what extent. Thus, we might accept a general principle to the effect that stealing is wrong because everyone's preferences will be satisfied by such a proposal in various ways, while only those few who are able to get away with stealing, or can profit from the stealing of others, will have any preferences satisfied by stealing being morally acceptable. However, before considering utilitarianism and its special problems, we have to ask whether the universalizability of moral judgements on its own does lead directly to our having to take the preferences of other people as equal to our own in our choice of values. What, after all, is there in logic to stop a fanatical racist from holding that the interests of members of the 'master race' should be allowed to override the interests and preferences of other, lesser breeds? It is true that, in consistency, he would have to allow that he himself would have to be done down, and even done away with, if it turned out that he was not of the right racial origin, but what is to stop someone, against a background of collective psychosis, with Hitler and Himmler striding high, from doing just that? Hare obviously hopes to make those making grossly unjust and inhumane proposals admit to their logical inconsistency when they put themselves in the shoes of their victims, but it is not clear that some fanatics might not accept the consequences of their proposals, even to the extent of acquiescing in their own destruction. Even if the 'principled' Nazi, turning his detestable view on himself, may seem unlikely to us (though there are stories of such people), Western democracies are full of people who regularly vote in a way that is quite inconsistent with their own perceived preferences and interests, let alone their real interests, because they feel some moral or political obligation to do so.* The problem prescriptivism has to solve is to show how the mere fact that one engages in moral talk commits one to anything like an impartial respecting of the interests and preferences of others, when many would be prepared to see their own interests and preferences overridden by moral imperatives.

At one time, Hare admitted that the pure fanatic – the one who was prepared to be done to as he would do to others – did restrict the effectiveness of the universalization of moral judgements as a tool in moral argument, but claimed that this problem was more theoretical than real, because most actual fanatics were inconsistent reasoners: they would change their minds if they realized what was entailed by moral judgements, and accordingly put themselves in their victims' position.[8] Subsequently, however, he has attempted to deny the very possibility of the type of pure fanatic who could not be budged from his project of trampling on others by being asked to put himself in their shoes, and which would present a genuine difficulty for his derivation of utilitarianism from the nature of moral judgements.[9] The reason for this is that if I, a fanatical racist, put myself in my victim's situation, I will have to represent myself not as being as I now am, with my present preferences, but as *he* now is, with his actual present preferences. And, in actual fact, according to Hare, my actual victims very strongly prefer not to be done down by my racial prejudice; so my putting myself in their position will at once present me with preferences counter to my own. (As we shall see, though, Hare's position is that *if* my victims did not have preferences against what I was doing, there might be no objection to my doing them down.)

Hare underestimates the power of the 'Klemperer effect' – the power of persuasion, crisis and propaganda to get victims to assent to victimization, but even apart from that, it is not clear that accepting that moral judgements should be universally applied means that in making them one would have, logically, to test the rule on which they were based by considering how the various people affected by them would feel about it.

* Nor was this unknown in Germany in the 1930s. The great conductor Otto Klemperer was by no means the only Jew in Germany in 1933 to welcome (for a time, a time of madness, he later called it) the rise of pro-Aryan German nationalism, and what he called the *'rinascimento'* of Germany and 'victory over the devilish powers of Communism, which prescribes atheism and the denial of God', arguing that even if he was one of those adversely affected, the country could not continue to be run as it had been. The *Verband Deutschnationaler Juden* actually endorsed the *Deutschnationale Volkspartei* in the 1933 election, and this was the largest element in Hitler's coalition of that year. (On all these points, cf. Peter Heyworth's *Otto Klemperer: His Life and Times*, Cambridge, 1983, Vol. I, pp. 413–17.) The point is that people can easily be manipulated into preferring what is clean contrary to their own interests. This is something Hare fails to account for.

The sort of utilitarianism Hare proposes in his later work will accept as correct moral rules those principles whose outcome maximizes the preferences of all the people involved, so we would quite naturally get rules against murder, lying, stealing, and so on, given that most people would accept that having rules like these would best help them to satisfy their preferences in various ways. But, one might ask, how have we got from universalization to calculating preferences in this way? Kant, it will be remembered, interprets universalizability in terms of what we can rationally will should universally obtain. This allows for the possibility of a moralist arguing that people might be generally misguided about what is in their true interest, and attempting to work out a moral code accordingly. Equally, for Bentham, we are supposed in morality to aim to maximize happiness, and to take everyone's interest into account, but it is not clear that this means we have to give much weight to people's conscious preferences, even if they are strong, if we believe these preferences are likely to lead to their own unhappiness (as those of the *Verband Deutschnationaler Juden* certainly did).

Both emotivism and prescriptivism have been frequently accused of operating in a sort of moral vacuum, in which everything about morality depends on the criterionless choices of the subject. From this perspective, they are not very different in spirit from the vulgar existentialist view that each individual should simply choose what to do as each situation confronts him or her. Hare's prescriptivism, of course, imposes a structure of consistency and logic on ethical judgement which is quite lacking from existentialist ethics, but it is like at least some version of existentialism in providing no content to morality. That is to be provided by the preferences of the society or the age, by a process of adopting as moral rules those principles which are seen by critical ethical thinkers as best furthering the preferences of all. This leads to a strange conclusion; that, if we can actually do the calculations on the preferences of each person and their relative strengths (and this is a big if), we will all be able to agree on what the right principles are, so there is a rationality and objectivity about ethical judgement, but if preferences of people change, then the right moral principles will change too. The facts on the basis of which moral principles are to be justified are, as he puts it, 'shifting facts about people's prescriptions'.[10] But, to many, this will appear intolerable, an intolerability accentuated by the fact that the preferences and prescriptions of sadists, Nazis and other moral deviants are to be put into the calculations, and by the suspicion that, if these preferences were very strongly held by the vast majority, then their victims' preferences could in effect be morally overruled. Hare admits that if the preference of a fanatic was strong enough on some point, it might outweigh the preferences of all the others who would suffer through its realization,[11] but a more difficult case for him to treat is one in which the majority wish to treat the minority in a way most of us would regard as inhumane, immoral and unacceptable.

What I have just said suggests in turn that moral judgements are not to be seen as dependent on possibly transient and changing feelings and preferences as emotivism, existentialism and prescriptivism in their different ways seem to suggest. Perhaps it would be nearer the truth and better to think of the true object of morality as something existing outside us, a good drawing us on, and not something arising from inside our will, either individually or collectively. Such, at least, is the suggestion of Iris Murdoch (in *The Sovereignty of the Good*[12]), who regards the moral elevation of the will implied by some of the doctrines we have recently been considering as something Satanic, given the proneness of human beings to wickedness and self-deception. Murdoch herself sees a need for morality to be rooted in a looking outside ourselves, at a transcendent Good, but, as she admits, this is an idea hard to make sense of outside a religious context. Nevertheless, her belief that individual preference and choice cannot and do not form the basis of morality might be thought to derive support from the fact that the language in which we naturally describe people and their actions is deeply moralistic. By this, I mean that in describing someone or what he does as 'mean', 'loyal', 'cowardly', 'patriotic', 'generous' and so on, we do not (as a rule anyway) first realize that what we are describing has such and such properties, and then take up an attitude for or against it. The description and the evaluation go hand in hand, once we realize that the description fits, which might suggest that the evaluation is something evoked by the person or the action, rather than arising from within us as Hume suggested. Without denying the pervasiveness of evaluatively loaded descriptions in our daily lives, or the difficulty of separating a so-called evaluative element from a descriptive element in the descriptions, the use of such terms need provide no very great difficulty for Hume. The fact that we naturally characterize people and actions of certain types in certain ways which imply our approval or disapproval does not show that any evaluations implicit in the descriptions are not ultimately due to human feelings, reactions and social patterns; they do not in themselves demonstrate the existence of a quality of goodness or an objective good apart from us. Indeed, we can, either as individuals or groups, dissociate ourselves from the attitudes we originally learn in learning how to apply morally loaded descriptions. It would not be inconsistent for someone to disapprove of patriotic behaviour, nor even especially implausible that someone should do so if he were to adopt a form of internationalism, much in the same way that we, unlike their contemporaries, may have a far from approving attitude towards the cunning of Odysseus or the great-souledness of Agamemnon. Moral reformers, indeed, characteristically attempt a re-valuation of existing values, and this may also involve linguistic reform, making, say, 'humble' a term of approval, rather than of contempt.

Moral judgements, then, are not frozen in language. It may nevertheless be felt that the individual will is not the ultimate arbiter of moral judge-ments; that moral judgements and the preferences on which we might base them have to be constrained by considerations that relate to the prevention of harm to human beings and the promotion of their well-being. Our intuitions and feelings as to what is morally good count as moral intuitions and feelings because they can be shown, or at least argued, to be relevant to the promotion of happiness and the relief of unhappiness. So, as Philippa Foot has argued against Hare's attempts to explain what a moral judgement is simply in terms of a man's willingness to act on it and to universalize it, we can regard a proposal as a moral one only if it connects in some way with our current conceptions of human good and harm. If someone said that it was morally good to clasp his hands three times every hour, or morally evil to have the hairs on his head reduced to an even number, we would fail to understand what he said. She claims that 'it is surely clear that moral virtues must be connected with human good and harm, and that it is quite impossible to call anything you like good or harm'.[13] We see here one of the ways in which morality is connected with prudence, for we all have an idea of our own personal good and harm, and an interest in these things, as well as ways of making comparative evaluations between our various preferences, short term and long term. Morality can be seen as building on this sense, as an attempt to formulate principles that would further good and prevent harm to people in general, and moral discussion will, in so far as it is rational, be aimed at demonstrating that the principles arrived at and the consequent actions do indeed do this.

It might be questioned at this point why people should be interested in the moral evaluation of actions and principles at all, as it means regarding the interests of others as something to be taken into account when we decide what to do. One can, of course, argue that a society of doves, where moral principles, such as respect for life, property and freedom, are generally valued will be helpful to everyone, because no one wants his life, property or freedom interfered with by others. But this would not necessarily give *me* a reason for being moral, rather than prudential in all my own actions, especially if I knew that the law and social disapproval were strong enough to keep most people in line. I might gain more for myself by a form of hawkish free-loading on the dove-like moral behaviour of others. It is, in fact, impossible to provide a conclusive argument against a hardened and determined free-loading amoralist, though to say that is little more than to admit a logical difference between prudence and morality. At the same time, one can point out that as we all have an interest in keeping morality going, we also have an interest in maintaining sanctions in favour of morality, making it uncomfortable or worse for people who offend too dramatically, so morality becomes naturally reinforced by prudential considerations. Further, as Hare has argued, the best way to bring children up to be moral – which, presumably, we all have an interest in doing as we all want morality to obtain in general – is to inculcate moral feelings in them, and it is easy to underestimate the pain of the 'cognitive dissonance' involved in acting against strongly entrenched attitudes.[14] So there is a further prudential support for morality in practice, a support no doubt based in our genetically inherited feelings of sympathy for those fellow-sufferers at least that we can see as part of our own group or tribe. So, as Mrs Foot points out, while it is true that

if people in general did not take an interest in the good of other people, and the establishment of rules of justice in their society, the moral use of 'ought' would not exist[15]

we can suggest reasons, social, personal and genetic, why they should take an interest in the good of others. Indeed, people who take no interest in the good of others will presumably find satisfactory relationships of any sort impossible.

Given, then, that we all have an interest in the good of others, as well as of ourselves, we need some basis on which to assess the morality of various courses of action, which takes us beyond the merely formal requirements, implicit in the words of Kant and Bentham quoted earlier, to take into account the interests of others. The simplest and most straightforward proposal in this area may well be the slogan adopted by the early utilitarians: always act so as to achieve 'the greatest happiness of the greatest number'. Unfortunately the simplicity and objectivity are entirely deceptive. We are not told how happiness is to be measured or happiness compared. If we are to include more than the promotion of physical pleasure and the removal of physical pain, as we surely should, how can we compare the happiness arising from reading a book of philosophy with that of bringing up a family, or either with the pain of suffering cold for a number of years. Is it more in a man's true interest (or happiness) to live as a fool satisfied, or as Socrates dissatisfied, or even to be a pig satisfied rather than a man satisfied, to raise J. S. Mill's famous dilemma.[16] Mill says that the only competent judges, those who have experienced both 'lower' and 'higher' pleasures, judge in favour of the higher, but this is by no means clear. In any case, even if they did, what would it show? If we are talking here about the values of higher culture and education, Rousseau and Tolstoy might say that it showed only the power of vanity and metropolitan silliness to corrupt the minds of light-headed men, who would be far happier living a more mediocre and simple existence as peasant farmers. Are such disputes decidable simply in terms of quantities of happiness? In the absence of some standard or concept of what a human life ought to be like, they are not, and this in the end is the most weighty objection to attempting to base morality on utilitarian considerations, at least if these are regarded as objective summings of data on happiness. It is easy to see why Hare and many writers since Mill interpret utilitarianism much more subjectively, in terms of the satisfaction of preferences; not that doing the sums between competing preferences and strength of preference is going to be easy, for how should my very strong preference against racism, say, be weighted against twenty *Daily Mail* readers' ill-informed and ill-focused hostility to further immigration? Nevertheless, in dealing with subjective preferences, we do not have to ask what is in people's true interests or what will really promote their happiness.

There is, however, an objection to utilitarianism which is commonly made, but not clearly unanswerable from a utilitarian standpoint. Roughly, the objector contends that utilitarianism leads inevitably to the condoning or even the prescribing of actions which are clearly, by any standards, immoral. Suppose for example I have promised to take my daughter to the zoo next Saturday, and I discover that Horowitz is giving a recital on television that day. My pleasure in staying in and watching television will far outweigh my daughter's pleasure in going to the zoo, so, it is said, on utilitarian grounds I ought to break my promise. But, in fact, utilitarian grounds would sanction no such thing, if we take into account the damage such behaviour would do to the institution of promise-keeping in general and my daughter's attitude to me and to promise-keeping in the future.

Utilitarianism tells us, in effect, that we should examine carefully the consequences of actions in assessing their morality; this, indeed, is one of its best features, and the reason why it is a far healthier approach to moral and political questions than dogmatic authoritarianism or empty-headed intuitionism. But it does not and, indeed, should not be taken to say that we should examine only the immediate consequences of actions considered in isolation from the place the action has in the general framework of our personal relationships and social institutions. The effect of actions in supporting or undermining trust in relationships and institutions must also be taken into account. The building up and maintaining of trust in promise-keeping in my daughter and others is a good, leading in the end to far greater general happiness than the small surplus of happiness my watching Horowitz brings me, to say nothing of the generally deleterious effects if promise-keeping is undermined as an institution. The utilitarian can, quite consistently, give a very large weight in deciding on general rules to the general quality of life made possible by having or not having the rules in question. Thus, it would be quite possible for a utilitarian to adopt a rule saying that individual life and freedom were always to be respected, for in a society without such a rule everyone would be much worse off, particularly in that they would be unable to envisage their lives as depending on their own choices and plans.

So utilitarian considerations can actually support the keeping of promises and the abiding by other general moral principles, such as truth-telling and respect for individual life and property, even in cases where one act of breaking one of these rules would appear to bring greater happiness to those immediately involved. But this appearance is due in most cases only to our taking too narrow a view of the action and its consequences. Indeed, one can go further here, and suggest that utilitarians should not in general recommend the weighing-up of consequences of each individual action before deciding what to do. The consequences of particular actions are highly uncertain; weighing them up will take far too much time and effort; people, in assessing consequences of actions, are only too easily inclined to overlook the uncomfortable and disadvantageous ones. So, there are good utilitarian reasons for the general adoption and upholding of moral rules which will tell us what to do in particular circumstances. Furthermore, once such rules are generally recognized, we will be able to calculate our own behaviour on well-grounded expectations regarding the likely response of others, something that would not be easy if everyone was forever engaging in calculations of consequences all the time. On this more sophisticated view of utilitarianism, then, the assessment of consequences comes in not at the stage of deciding on individual actions, but in deciding on or justifying general principles. Indeed, a *rapprochement* between utilitarianism and intuitionism can be made at this point. In bringing children up, we should try to inculcate moral intuitions in accordance with our general principles, so that generally they act instinctively on those intuitions. At the same time, we justify the principles (and hence the intuitions) in the light of utilitarian considerations.

But still, it will be objected, this can lead to a dilemma for the utilitarian where a moral intuition, say, to keep one's promises, that can in general receive a utilitarian justification conflicts on a specific instance with clear utility. In such a situation, the utilitarian must either reject the intuition in the specific case or modify his utilitarianism. Furthermore, there can be cases where rejecting the intuition can seem clearly immoral. Hence utilitarianism cannot be an adequate account of morality. The sort of case the objector has in mind would be one where, unknown to anyone except those involved, the organs of some solitary down-and-out are removed from him, thereby causing his death, to save the lives of people with great potential for good in the community; or where an innocent sympathizer with some guerillas is tortured to reveal data that might prevent a terrorist outrage; or, even more fantastically, where someone is told by a mad soldier in some remote jungle to shoot one innocent prisoner in order that the soldier should agree not to blow up nineteen others. What we are supposed to conclude from these examples is that overwhelming moral intuitions – such as the right of innocent individuals to life and liberty – ought, in certain circumstances, to be put aside if we are consistent utilitarians, even though the intuitions are in general supported on utilitarian grounds. Crucial to each case must be some proviso to the effect that word would not get around about what had happened, or the utilitarian could quite justifiably reply that the potential damage to the rule in question would outweigh the gains from breaking it. But it is quite open to the utilitarian to stress that this proviso is unlikely in practice actually to be fulfilled – doctors and nurses talk, and so do torturers and prisoners – and that his system of moral judgement is one geared to the actual world, and not to some imaginary one where secrecy and confidence can be guaranteed.* In the fantastic jungle case, the soldier is obviously deranged; so why should we take him at his word

* Cf. Hare, *Moral Thinking* (see notes), p. 134. I have been following Hare in my defence of utilitarianism against the stock objections.

when he says that he will release others if I kill one? Moreover, in the other examples, the effect on the doctors and the torturers involved could well be extremely harmful regarding future potential victims, if they thought they were allowed to decide on such things, rather than submitting to a blanket condemnation of them.

I have been suggesting that there is a certain inconclusiveness in the handling of these typical counter-examples to utilitarianism, in part due, no doubt, to uncertainty on both sides about the actual outcomes were such cases really to occur. If the utilitarian wants to show that his position does not necessarily lead to his making what most people would regard as the wrong decision, he can stress the uncertainties and difficulties of the example. Of course, it remains possible to construct examples where some grossly evil consequence follows from sticking to a moral rule, where the utilitarian answer would be to break the rule. Suppose I promised someone in good faith, as they were dying, to carry out the provisions of some secret will known only to me, and the provisions involved disinheriting their needy dependants in favour of an enormous bequest to some organization to promote the cult of garden gnomes; would I be wrong on any account of morality to break the promise? It is not clear that the obvious utilitarian answer would be the wrong one here. There certainly can be cases where the consequences of sticking blindly to moral rules is simply irrational, and if the utilitarian stress on examining the consequences of actions in terms of their propensities for good and harm leads us to recognize this, then it may well be the advance in moral thinking its original proponents believed it to be.

Nevertheless, even if it is possible to defend utilitarianism against certain characteristic objections to it, the deeper significance of the objections is perhaps to emphasize the emptiness there is at the heart of utilitarianism. It looks at first as if it is a hard-headed empirical doctrine, and that all we have to do is to work out the best ways of maximizing happiness, but it actually tells us nothing about what this happiness is. In fact it is only against some more substantive conception of human good and harm that we could regard it as a strong objection to a policy that it gave doctors more power over life and death, or allowed torturers to exist at all. A simple summing of happiness can give us no guidance here, because we simply do not know how much weight to give the various elements that would go into the sums – physical contentment, sense of self-respect, security, political freedom, integrity and so on. Although, as I suggested earlier, a utilitarian can, quite consistently, give a lot of weight to the overall quality of life deriving from full respect for individual rights, it is not clear that he has to. It is not then coincidental that some modern utilitarians stress the satisfaction of felt preferences rather than the maximizing of happiness because it seems that what is meant by the latter is very far from clear or objective, whereas the former is in a sense objective and might even be measurable. On the other hand, it is natural to suppose that letting moral values arise from some equalizing machinery whose input is human preferences is exactly to reverse the true order of dependence, and that what we need is some guidance on the morality of various preferences, and some means of distinguishing moral aims and desires from immoral ones. To see morality in terms of the maximization of acceptance-utility – what people would accept – is not only immoral; it may be felt it also gives *carte blanche* from the moral point of view to those who would manipulate the preference of others for their own ends.

A more substantive conception of human nature than one in which the persons or selves at the basis of moral decisions are simply bundles of whatever preferences they happen to have seems to be what is needed here. It is, of course, a more substantial conception of a human person, as a natural kind, with consequent objective needs and interests that Wiggins was looking for in his criticisms of Parfit, and the basis of his claim that a Parfittian view of the self combined well with a managerial attitude to human beings and their preferences. For a more substantial view of human nature, it is natural to look back to Aristotle, for whom human good and harm were to be seen in terms of naturally predetermined aims and goals, which, whether we realize it or not, are what bring about happiness. Aristotle himself put his moral views in the context of a teleological account of biology; individual members of a given species have a certain end or *telos*, to which they strive, and to which their physical make-up – their limbs and organs – is directed. Morality was for Aristotle its own reward, because to be virtuous was to fulfil one's human nature, including one's reason. Aristotle would have had no truck with the anti-intellectualism of romantics like Rousseau or the modern advocates of 'education for work', though more important in general is the implicit anti-consequentialism of Aristotle's position, for this suggests and implies a major difference between his position, which will stress the way a man's acts and decisions contribute to his own integrity irrespective of consequences, and that of a utilitarian's, for whom consequences are all-important. Moreover, and most important for Aristotle, the human condition is essentially a social or political condition. A man outside a city is no man, but a beast or a god. One's identity, while based on one's biological nature, is actually formed through the various and multifarious ties that bind one to other men, which is part of the explanation for Socrates' preference for death over exile from Athens. From our social and political relationships we derive not only many of our obligations, but also sets of shared values and common purposes, which will be a substantial component of any viable concept of a good life, and in terms of which we can measure our progress through life.

When we look at the types of behaviour Aristotle thought to be virtuous, however, we cannot help being struck by the way that central and universal virtues like truthfulness, justice and courage are supplemented by such traits as pride in one's own position and an aristocratic magnificence or 'great-souledness', which might appear to us to be appropriate only to certain strata of certain types of society. Indeed, Aristotle's belief that his moral system applies only to free men and not to slaves (or 'living tools'), together with his view that some men are slaves by nature, emphasize the historical relativity of much of what he says. How much of what he says can survive the transition to a completely different type of society, with a plurality of values and a democratic form of organization?

Against the individualism implicit in the emotivisms and utilitarianisms we have been examining, in which the individual is seen as the source and arbiter of moral values, it can certainly be urged with F. H. Bradley that the individual, 'the man into whose essence his community with others does not enter, who does not include relation to others in his very being, is a fiction'.[17] Neither the individual, nor his ethical world, can be conceived of as starting from scratch, any more than our system of knowledge is born anew in each one of us. In the matter of empirical knowledge, this dependence of individuals on already existing and socially transmitted bodies of knowledge is reflected in the way in which, in learning a language, we also acquire large bodies of knowledge and theory about the world. But we do not simply learn theories; we also learn who we are, what we should do, who we are related to, what our obligations and rights are, and so on. We also learn in learning language, as we have already seen, all sorts of attitudes to particular types of conduct and people, and something about what it is to be a person of integrity, wisdom, and so on.

It is unlikely that anyone, even an extreme individualist, would attempt to deny any of these obvious facts, but the question is the significance that should be put on them. The autonomous moral will of Kant is represented to us as judging the pronouncements of Christ himself, but, one might ask, from what point of view. He must be using some criteria by which to judge, these criteria must be supplied from somewhere, but whatever they are and wherever they come from, we can always ask the Kantian question again: are *these* good? We now know too much, it seems, just to accept the moral ideas we inherit. And so, it seems, all we are left with at the end are our basic feelings (intuitionism, emotivism) or a machinery for maximizing the preferences that exist (prescriptive utilitarianism). In this latter view, moral argument looks like a sort of contractual system whereby disconnected and isolated individuals work out a method of each individual satisfying as many of the preferences they have with the least impediment to all the rest satisfying their preferences, severally and individually. Indeed in one of the most influential works of recent moral and political philosophy, John Rawls's *A Theory of Justice*,[18] it is claimed that in determining principles of justice we have to regard ourselves as being in the so-called original position, behind a 'veil of ignorance', and seeing what we would unanimously accept from there. This veil of ignorance hides from us all knowledge of who we are, what abilities or status we have, how old we are, what sort of society we are in, and, above all, what our conception of good is. In other words, the individual moral agent is reduced to a bare arbiter, whose only function, it seems, is to decide on the morality or justice of certain proposals (which will, of course, affect him). The Rawlsian perspective on justice is one in which rational individuals come together in a state of mutual ignorance to create the form of social organization for mutual protection and cooperation in which each can best further his or her own interests, without detriment to the interests of the others; Rawls takes it to follow from the original position of ignorance that no one will agree to any inequalities of distribution which do not in themselves directly benefit those worst off and most incapable of fending for themselves, because, for all each of us knows, it might be us that are the weaklings. Rawls's conclusions are, therefore, opposed to utilitarianism, at least in any simple form, because the total sum of happiness could be increased by schemes of distribution which would be unjust in his terms, and unacceptable to those in the original position, who might find themselves at the bottom of the utilitarian heap, increasing the total sum of happiness, to be sure, but not their own.

Rawls, however, has had many non-utilitarian critics, not simply because his proposals imply egalitarian redistributions of the goods of society, but also because he appears to leave no room for the notion of entitlement. A man is entitled, it is said by Robert Nozick, to those goods which he has acquired by just means, and no one, above all not a redistributing state, is entitled to take them from him. It would be intolerable to our sense of natural justice to think otherwise, and any state that attempts to do this by force, presumably, 'violates people's rights';[19] propriety of means of acquisition is what determines justice, rather than the comparative amounts owned by different people. Now, while it is true that Nozick's view conforms to the moral intuitions of many people, it cannot be said that Nozick offers much argument in favour of his premise about the inalienable right to keep and pass on what one acquires by morally unobjectionable means. He simply follows Locke in asserting that, in a state of nature, people have a natural right to life, health, liberty and possessions which have been gained by the work of their own labour, which no one may transgress, even in order to provide someone else with life, health, liberty or possessions. Individuals and their inalienable right to forge their own way through life are taken by Nozick to be the essential givens from which the rest of morality stems. From the distinctness of individuals, he claims, follow those rights they need to lead and plan their own lives.[20] But recognizing the moral significance of the distinctness of individuals (something implicit in the requirement that moral judgement be fully universalizable) does not in itself show us what the consequent rights accorded to individuals should be, nor, more crucially, how we should settle conflicts between conflicting claims about what is necessary for different people to lead their lives. A Rawlsian would surely say that a Nozickian should be made to waive his 'inalienable' property rights and rights of transfer of property, which, after all, are sustained and made viable by the institutions of the state, and would not otherwise exist, in order that other distinct individuals be allowed to live in reasonable circumstances, without there being anything unjust about such compulsion.

The essentially negative Locke–Nozick interpretation of human rights is not the only or even the most influential current interpretation of natural human rights. People outside strictly legal contexts who talk about a right to work do not usually mean that no one should stop them from finding work. They mean that the state has a duty to provide them with work. In similar vein, someone who reflects seriously on Rawls's original position might conclude that each individual has a right to his or her Rawlsian share of the national product, and that the state has a duty to see to it that they get it. Who is right about rights? Where do rights come from and how can claims to rights be justified? There is very little to be gained in following Locke, and saying that they pertain to individuals in a state of nature; this looks like a particularly unconvincing attempt to derive an ought from an is, as nature is clearly no respecter of rights. Ronald Dworkin, in his book *Taking Rights Seriously*,[21] talks of individual rights in cases where collective goals are not sufficient justification for denying an individual his or her wishes, but claims that he needs no metaphysical foundation for this talk, other than a sense that each individual should be treated with equal concern and respect. In other words, for Dworkin rights are founded on a principle of equality, but one wonders just how such a principle can consistently generate anything that may never be overridden by collective goals, a suspicion that may be increased by some of Dworkin's own claims, that, for example, reverse discrimination is permissible in certain circumstances, or that liberty may often be compromised in the advancement of equality, by bussing school children, for example. The man who is not being allowed to enter college despite his qualifications, in order to let some other person in for purely racial or egalitarian reasons, may not find it very convincing when Dworkin tells him that he is in fact being treated with equal concern and respect. Nozick would certainly not agree. The suspicion is that people talk about rights when they want to claim particular importance for some moral intuition or political preference. I would be very far from wanting to pour philosophical scorn on those who claim a positive right to work or to be fed, but it seems to me that any talk of rights must be based in some shared general conception of how we are and how we should live. Even the general injunction to treat others as ends rather than means, which some have claimed to derive from the very logic of moral discourse, needs some determinate conception of what it is to treat someone as an end rather than as a means before it can yield any specific rights or sense of when one 'right' can be overridden by another 'right', or even by a very large utility. Does treating everyone as an end or as worthy of equal respect lead to a Nozickian individualism or an egalitarianism of the sort favoured by Rawls and Dworkin? In the absence of any such shared conception, talk of rights looks like mere intuition, mere emotion.

I shall have more to say on the details of the positions of Rawls and Nozick (and of Dworkin) in the next section, but, as Alasdair MacIntyre has suggested, the most striking thing about Rawls and Nozick is not their disagreement on practical policies, but their fundamental agreement on the nature of social life

... as – at least ideally – the voluntary act of at least potentially rational individuals with prior interests who have to ask the question 'What kind of social contract with others is it reasonable for me to enter into?' Not surprisingly it is a consequence of this that their views exclude any account of human community in which the notion of desert in relation to the contributions to the common tasks of that community in pursuing shared goods could provide the basis for judgments about virtue and injustice.[22]

The crucial question, of course, is whether in present circumstances we can regard identities and aims through life as being given to us through our (changing) position in a moral and social community and our pursuing shared goods, or whether this perspective is forever lost with the passing of the city state and other cohesive social organizations. In the city state it made sense to think of a person's identity and consequent rights and obligations as flowing from membership of the city. But if in the modern pluralist state all we have are competing interest groups, with no shared sense of community, the state apparatus itself can be at best a sort of arbiter between these groups (each of whom will claim their own sets of rights to set against the others), or at worst (and as, I shall argue in the next section, is actually the case) an instrument of control of the dominant sections of society; while the individual's social role and position, which did determine his ends, are now replaced by the goals and meanings which he chooses for himself (and from the ability to form which Nozick, for one, appears to derive the whole of morality). To these conceptions of society and the individual, the starting points of Rawls and Nozick are appropriate, but at the same time they show us the distance we have travelled from the perspective in which the rootless ego castigated by Bradley is really a fiction.

However, even in a pluralist, individualist society, in which the social whole is largely a matter of the adjustment of conflicting interests, it is not clear that the whole of morality has to be conceived in terms of utilitarian trade-offs between individuals' basically arbitrary preferences and interests, nor our only goals the ones we actually choose. Even if there is no overall city state for us to owe allegiance to, we are all plunged by birth into networks of smaller communities, and as we make our way through life, we enter other such groups, families, clubs, intellectual disciplines, sports, professions and social institutions of various sorts. Now participation in such groups is characterized by the recognition on the part of all of reciprocal duties, rights, loyalties and deserts, which are not a matter of individual choice or preference. The family itself is perhaps the most striking example of the way a person can have rights and allegiances simply because of who he or she is, and quite independent of individual choice or decision. In saying this, I am not endorsing any particular concept of the family, or attempting to defend the nuclear family against, say, the Soviet system of child-rearing; but I am pointing out the way human beings are inevitably born into contexts of personal rights and allegiances which have nothing to do with choice on their part. Then, as an individual grows up, he or she will also participate in all manner of relationships, activities and organizations in which one's status, obligations, rights and deserts will be due at least in part to the activity or discipline concerned, and not to the private preferences of those involved or to utilities other than the furthering of the relationship, activity or organization itself.

So, even given the absence of universally shared schemes of values in contemporary pluralist societies, there will be important areas of life within those societies in which strategies of calculating the preferences of individuals seen and seeing themselves in isolation from interpersonal contexts will be unable to account for the facts of moral obligation, our recognition of others as morally significant possessors of inalienable claims on us and our allegiance to them as they present themselves in those areas. As Nagel points out, in looking after one's children, say, one may be acting on what would be good from the utilitarian, impersonal point of view, but this is not why one does it (or feels obliged to do it).[23] One does it because of one's own relation to these children, and one's own relations to parents, children, colleagues and so on are part of what makes one who one is. Indeed, one could go further and follow Nagel in distinguishing the essentially agent-centred evaluations implicit in these cases, where what is at issue is myself and my relationships, and their and my integrity, from the generally outcome-centred and utilitarianly based evaluations that would be relevant to deciding on which general rights and principles should obtain in a society, although, as we have already seen, decisions on general principles cannot be taken in total abstraction from ideas about what we think people are and how they should be.

Caring for one's children may be a case where agent-centred and utilitarian evaluations coincide in general, but it cannot be denied that there may be conflicts even here – between, say, one's responsibility to do one's best for one's own children and the utilitarian insistence that a greater increase of happiness is to be preferred to a lesser one. Lavishing my resources on my children will not increase their happiness as much as giving the same quantity of resources to people much worse off will do for them. Should I then give the money I was going to spend on my daughter's Christmas presents to War on Want in order that other children might have their sight saved? Ought I to feel remorse at not doing this? Actually, if I put it to her in the right way, my daughter would tell me not to give her any presents, and so perhaps there is no genuine moral dilemma in this case, only my own conformism and lack of moral conviction; but should I make her live her life on or just above the British poverty line so that numbers of Sahelian children can survive at all? The point I am making here is that the obligations and allegiances that derive from who we are and who we are in relationship with can come into conflict with impersonal demands for justice or equality, as represented by the universalizing tendencies of Kantian and utilitarian moral systems. Both types of demand are aspects of our moral thinking. Universalization, and taking the interests of all affected by a course of action into account, are part of what distinguishes a moral system from a prudential system, and, unlike Aristotle, we see no relevant moral differences between Hellenes and barbarians or slaves. Indeed, a further important aspect of universalization is precisely the way it forces us to extend the boundaries marking out the kinds of being who should be treated with moral concern. If, for example, what generates part of our moral concern for other humans is their ability to feel pleasure and pain, should not that same degree of moral concern be shown to other creatures, such as higher animals, not relevantly different from us in respect of feeling pleasure and pain? On the other hand, much of the content of our moral evaluations, of how in depth we think people ought to be as well as our original understandings of what it means to treat others as ends and not as means, derives as much from our experience of relationships and communities and engaging in shared projects with others, as from impartial reflection on which outcomes would be fairest or most generally acceptable. In cases of conflict between the universalizing and the agent-centred evaluations of a course of action, we have no superior position from which to make *the* moral decisions. If in some situation I have to choose a course of action which will involve me in choosing to enact one moral value rather than another – and, as I have suggested, such cases are not rare – is all that is left me a personal preference or feeling for one decision rather than another?

Perhaps there is, and perhaps it is at this point that emotivism is correct. Against emotivism, though, it is not the case that just anything could be a moral choice. There are far too many constraints on the content of morality for that. A moral choice is one relevant to the furthering of the good and harm of human and other sentient beings, and, as with knowledge in any other area, we inherit a whole range of ideas about what that consists in, and about what a good life or a good person is, and central to these ideas are undoubtedly the respect for the individual we find in Locke. There can be no total revaluation of values, at least none that can be expressed in the language of moral evaluation. But we are not heirs to a single, determinate conception of the common good, or even of the individual good, nor are we always clear about what should happen where the common good and individual goods conflict. To that extent, those who emphasize the role of choice and preference in moral discussion are correct, and, as just suggested, there may be points at which one cannot exactly justify one's choice of values: one simply prefers to emphasize one source of moral evaluation at the expense of another. One might hope to bring the features of one's moral landscape into some sort of reflective equilibrium, as Rawls has suggested,[24] by taking our various intuitions about moral matters, examining their implications and mutual inconsistencies, comparing them with competing conceptions, and then moving on to some more all-embracing and better-argued conception. But even if we were able to do this with regard, say, to our concept of justice, as Rawls tries to do, it would not follow that the conception we arrived at was the only way a state of reflective equilibrium could be arrived at for that concept, or, as the subsequent discussions of Rawls's own proposals has shown, that the features stressed in the revised conception were those universally regarded as being most important. Then, a final and to many most irritating limitation on moral philosophy is that it cannot actually forge the link between thought and action which seems so important in this area. There is a sense in which someone might agree that such and such a course of action was morally required of him, yet fail to find that course of action compelling on him. He might even be adept at the deployment of moral arguments, particularly of an *ad hominem* sort. I have tried to suggest in the course of this section that such a man would, if consistently amoral in this way, find it very hard to enter into human relationships and communities at all. But his position would be pathological, rather than formally inconsistent or open to cure by philosophical argument; and this shows once again a certain element of truth in emotivist accounts of morality, in that morality (and hence philosophical reflection on morality) must ultimately be based in shared feelings and ways of life. The forms of moral discourse, universalization, appeal to the individual rights of others, and so on, can get to work only where people have some sense that others should be treated as ends, not as means. To be without this sense is not in any straightforward way irrational, as Hume indicated. But – and this is where there is an element of truth in more naturalistic accounts of ethics – these shared feelings and ways of life will naturally tend to manifest themselves in the language we use to describe human behaviour as well as in our institutions and ways of living together. Moreover, these institutions and ways of living together will reflect our biological conditions and needs, and the idea that we are embodied beings making a historical progress through life, a history framed and partly determined by the human world through which we are travelling, and partly made by our own choices. The analysis of moral discourse should reflect the complexity of this situation, the ways in which our lives are both social and individual and in which what is good is both given to us and chosen by us.

Society and State

A natural and sympathetic reaction to the horrible excesses of modern dictatorships in the name of collectivism has been to insist that only individual human persons truly exist and that corporate entities, such as states, races and nations, are simply collections of individuals, no more than the sum of their parts. Against Bradley, who said that the individual outside his community was a fiction, the individualist will say that any community itself becomes a logical fiction as soon as it is personified and regarded as having special rights and duties of its own. The politician* who said that a nation's only duty is to preserve itself in existence is, on the individualist view, talking utter nonsense, albeit dangerous and influential nonsense, for nations as such cannot have duties, only individuals can. Hence, individual rights to life or property should not be trampled on in the name of a nation, race, class or any other collectivity, and to claim the right to do so is bogus mystification; although it does not follow from this that groups of individuals might not often and quite legitimately claim rights of redress against other individuals, the individualist thesis would require that their case be made out as a case of individual interests against other individuals, which is precisely the task shirked behind collectivist rhetoric.

Individualism, then, has both a metaphysical dimension and an ethical one. The metaphysical aspect – the denial of the reality of social wholes which cannot be reduced to the individuals composing them – can,

---

* Mr J. Enoch Powell.

however, be separated from the ethical thesis, that individuals should not have their rights overridden by appeal to the needs of collectivities. It is as well for liberals that this should be so, because individualism in an extreme metaphysical form cannot be sustained. Extreme individualists would hold, as Karl Popper did at one time[25] and as Tolstoy may have done in *War and Peace*, that notions essentially involving groups of people, such as 'war' and 'army', are abstract constructions, whose role is to explain the behaviour of individuals. On this view, the task of social theory is to show how talk about collectivities can be analysed in 'nominalist terms, that is to say, *in terms of individuals*, of their attitudes, expectations, relations, etc.'. Popper calls this view of social science 'methodological individualism'.

Now, while it may be true that some concepts used in social science are reducible in this way, it is not true that all human behaviour can be explained in terms of the behaviour of and desires of individuals, taken in isolation from their social groupings. The reason for this is that many of my desires have an essentially social dimension. It is precisely because I see myself as a member of groups of various sorts that I am in a position to want to impress my commanding officer, or to serve my country. These aims of individuals are possible only because of the existence of social objects, such as armies and countries. Tolstoy may have wished that men were not so constituted, and that soldiers recognized what they do as individuals when they kill each other. But he would be overstating his case if he refused to distinguish between what a soldier does in a battle and what he does in a drunken brawl, even though the physical consequences are the same (the death of some other men). Tolstoy points out that the army moves only because of millions of individual actions and decisions, but he overlooks the fact that many of the individual decisions are intelligible only given the existence of the social object which the army is. Indeed, if it is true that armies operate only because individual soldiers act, it is also true that men are *soldiers* (as opposed to individuals fighting) only because of the existence of social organizations like armies.

Individualism can seem an attractive thesis when one wants to bring home to members of corporate bodies that they are still responsible for the things they do on behalf of those bodies. But if it means that social actions and decisions are to be regarded as the outcome of individual desires in which there is no reference to social institutions, then it would make it very hard to account for what people do in engaging in activities such as marrying, playing in a team, working in a university, voting, and so on.

These activities make sense only because the agents see themselves as members of larger social wholes, and this self-perception is not, as Popper suggests, simply introduced by us to explain what we would do anyway. The point is that someone who did not see himself as a member of some nation would not be able to act patriotically – or unpatriotically – because the necessary background of meaning would be absent.

Does this, then, mean that a social whole, such as a nation or a team, is somehow greater than the sum of its parts? As this is a highly emotive issue, we must be careful to distinguish just what might be meant by accepting or denying such a claim. The individualist is certainly right in claiming that social wholes are composed of individuals. If every member of a tribe dies, then the tribe ceases to exist. On the other hand, it is not the case that all statements about social wholes or indeed about human action are analysable into statements about individual behaviour and motivation which make no mention of social concepts or institutions. This is what we have already argued. But the individualist might assert that despite this irreducibility of social talk to individual talk, only individuals are truly real. Here he would be wrong. States and armies are as real in their own way as the individuals that compose them, and survive as complex organizations, despite the passing of those individuals that compose them at any one time. Indeed, as I suggested in the previous section, it is a fundamental trait of human beings to participate in groups, from which they derive much, if not most, of the value and meaning they find in their lives, starting, of course, with language and basic social and family relationships, to say nothing of the more articulated traditions and activities they will enter into in later years. On the other hand, it does not follow from the way that individuals derive so much of meaning and value from various social groupings that individuals exist for the sake of any such groups. One can quite consistently admit the importance of community to one's life while still insisting on individual rights, which corporate ends may not override. Moreover, the communities one does recognize as constitutive of one's personality in many ways are not necessarily the same as those organizations claiming political and legal authority over one. The society or societies to which everyone owes so much from birth on cannot be identified without further argument as the state under which one lives, to which one may feel one owes little or nothing. It is important to recognize that a theory of political authority cannot be straightforwardly derived from reflections on the essentially social nature of man, and to realize that Thomas More, in writing that 'when I consider and weigh in my mind all these commonwealths, which nowadays anywhere do flourish ... I can perceive nothing but a certain conspiracy of rich men procuring their own commodities under the name and title of the commonwealth', is not necessarily denying the essentially social nature of human existence.

It is, in fact, very difficult to write neutrally about the state. One can easily be brought to agree with the classic liberal view of the state as a necessary agency of mutual protection, the guarantor of individual rights within and general security without. At least, one can easily be brought to agree that such a thing would be desirable. But the actual practice of most states, West and East, is very far from this ideal: in them we find, as More did, that the rich and powerful 'invent and devise all means and crafts, first how to keep safely, without fear of losing, that they have unjustly gathered together, and next how to hire and abuse the work and labour of the poor for as little money as may be', and they then attempt to legitimize these unjust gains by means of laws and appeals to the common good. People who talk about the actual state in Britain, or the USA, say, as if it were a mutual protection agency which we had all in some sense contracted into are actually upholding the myth of the legitimacy of the powerful, if they do not combine their 'contractarian' view with a vivid sense of those aspects of state activity which are concerned more with exploitation than general protection. (This is why it is hard to be politically neutral when writing about the state.)

When we ask what political obligation derives from, we find three main types of answer, apart from the claim that the state is simply an organ of oppression, backed up by police forces and armies. We should perhaps be reluctant to accept this latter view as the whole truth, because it is reasonable to suppose that no state can exist in normal circumstances over a long period without some degree of consent on the part of the governed. That is to say, most people feel some allegiance to their rulers and to their authority, even though they may dislike much of what they do. Moreover, most revolutionaries and freedom fighters do not want to do away with the state altogether; they want to set up better ones. Now, the simplest view of state authority, somewhat akin indeed to ethical intuitionism, is that it is simply there to be obeyed, and that disrespect for the rulers on the part of the ruled is obviously wrong. This view, which is perhaps a throwback to belief in the divine right of kings, has the disadvantages of intuitionism in any sphere of discourse in making argument about competing claims impossible, and one competing claim in this area is that political authority is conditional and rests on the discharge of certain obligations on the part of the rulers. One way in which political authority can be seen as conditional is the requirement that the ruler's actions be expressive of the general will of the ruled. Something like this, indeed, was the view of Rousseau. Although he was scathing in his criticisms of all the states that existed (in terms that strikingly foreshadowed Marx), he believed that in an ideal state, set up by a free social contract, the decisions that were taken would be representative of the higher moral feelings of each citizen, who would put aside his own selfish and subjective concerns to seek the good of all. For Rousseau, the individual, in giving up his original liberty through the social contract which sets up the state, actually achieves true freedom, because in the state he will act on the dictates of universal reason rather than being moved by his individualistic passions. Whether or not Rousseau would have been a totalitarian himself, the dictatorial potential of his doctrine that subservience to the general will amounts to true freedom is only too obvious if recent practice is any guide, and sufficient reason to look for a more modest account of political obligation.

The more modest account is, in contrast to Rousseau's insistence that the individual only becomes himself in conforming to the decisions of the state, strictly utilitarian and consequentialist in claiming that political obligation is justified to the extent that membership of the polity confers important benefits not otherwise attainable. This is the line of thought we find in Hobbes and Locke. For Hobbes, the only refuge from the brutish and brutal state of nature was in the mutual security a state and a sovereign could provide. We each owe allegiance to the sovereign to the extent that he does protect us from enemies within and without the state, though not if he fails in his duty to us. Locke took a more sanguine view of the state of nature, although in nature each individual had to provide his own protection against loss of property and attacks from outside. So men contract to put themselves under a power with the 'right of making laws ... for the regulating and preserving of property' and to employ 'the force of the community' in executing such laws and in defence of the commonwealth from foreign injury.[26] As with Hobbes, if the rulers break their trust with the ruled, the ruled have the right to replace them with other rulers.

Hobbes, Locke and Rousseau all appear to place considerable stress on the notion of a social contract, but this should not perhaps be taken too seriously except as a heuristic device. For none of us ever entered into such a contract, nor, even if we had, would its existence be necessary to our continued obedience to the rulers, provided that the reasons for general obedience to the state continued to convince us. In seeking the source of political obligation, we should look to what the state can do for us now, rather than into its murky past. The implications of Hobbes's and Locke's social contract are clearly that the rationale for the state is primarily as a protection agency, and its activities should be confined to this as far as possible. In this narrow conception of the ends of the state, they were followed by the classical utilitarians, Bentham and Mill, while writers closer to Rousseau, notably Hegel and Marx and, in his own way, the conservative Edmund Burke, have of course suggested far more intimate and organic connections between the state and the lives of its citizens. Each of this latter group, in his own way, suggests that it is only in and through the state that the individual becomes fully human, although Marx, of course, sees this coming about only in the classless society. Our original question about the status of political obligation has thus led quite naturally into a consideration of the ends of the state, for it is there, if anywhere, that political obligation can find a rational basis. But what should the ends of the state be? How are we to decide on competing claims in this area?

It is the great virtue of the works of John Rawls and Robert Nozick that they have pushed these questions back into their rightful place in the centre of political philosophy. Rawls's starting point in his theory of justice is, as we have already indicated, to determine those principles 'that free and rational persons concerned to further their own interests would accept in an initial position of equality as defining the fundamental terms of their association'.[27] In order to do this, he wants us all to imagine ourselves behind a veil of ignorance about our particular position and identities, though knowing all that needs to be known about human nature in general. What we decide from such a perspective will, in his view, constitute fair and justifiable aims for governments in the real world, for societies are best regarded as cooperative ventures for mutual advantage, and 'a society satisfying the principles of justice as fairness comes as close as a society can to being a voluntary scheme', allowing for the obvious point that societies will naturally have to moderate between conflicting interests, imposing whatever degree of compulsion is necessary to do this.

In Rawls's scheme, provided there is only moderate scarcity of basic material essentials, those in the original position will opt for two principles. The first (and overriding one) is a principle of liberty: 'each person is to have an equal right to the most extensive total system of basic liberties compatible with a similar system of liberty for all'. Then, secondly, there is a principle of distribution such that 'social and economic inequalities are to be arranged' so that they are 'to the greatest benefit of the least advantaged' and any inequalities of opportunity for office or position are to benefit those with the lesser opportunity.[28] The conception underlying Rawls's system of justice as fairness is that all social primary goods (rights, liberties, opportunities, powers, income and wealth) are to be distributed equally unless an unequal distribution can be shown to be to the advantage of those least favoured by nature or by initial starting point in life or any subsequent working of the system.

If we are to regard the state as having a function beyond the night-watchmanly one of providing an ambience of social stability and security, then Rawls's idea that it should aim at a fair sharing-out of material and social goods can seem attractive; certainly any state that subscribed to Rawls's conception of justice would be immune to objections such as those of Thomas More, and this would not, I think, be any mean accomplishment. Objections to Rawls's view, however, can be raised from several different points of view. First there is the utilitarian objection, that people should not be restrained from seeking great amounts of good even for themselves simply because their doing this would increase the gap between the better-off and the worse-off without any consequent improvements for the worse-off, and that the roots of that egalitarianism which would condemn the mere existence of such a gap may well be an unworthy envy on the part of the worse-off. This was Nietzsche's view, and Nietzsche combined it with an insistence on the need for outstanding individuals to strive for excellence (by definition, something beyond the mean), though whether this should be regarded as a licence for élitism in all fields is naturally debatable. Nevertheless, even though few, if any, actual states are just on Rawlsian principles, it is not clear that the mere existence of inequalities between people is something the state should strive to eliminate.

That it is not, and that even to attempt it is to offend against both justice and liberty, has been strongly argued by Nozick, who sees the proper role of the state as the restricted one of providing the minimal protection needed to allow people to exercise their rights. His fundamental objection to egalitarianism such as that of Rawls is that an analysis of justice as fairness leaves the most important aspect of justice out of the picture. This is what Nozick calls entitlement. A man is entitled to any goods he has acquired legitimately, and it is just this thought which Rawls's veil of ignorance hides from us. We are asked by Rawls to assume that all the goods that exist in a society are, as it were, just there, like manna from heaven, and not worked for or cultivated by the efforts of specific individuals, planning and directing their lives in accordance with their projects of saving and acquisition. Nozick will argue that this idea of a man's property as an integral part of his life-project is central to our idea of being a person. Rawls's original position is precisely engineered to deprive people of the idea of entitlement; Rawls says this is based on justice, not envy, but this argument will be undercut if 'the very considerations which underlie the original position [yielding Rawls's two principles of justice] themselves embody or are based upon envy'[29] – the wish of the dispossessed to deprive those who are possessed of their legitimate entitlements.

Nozick's political philosophy is, by contrast, based on a very simple and Lockean notion of justice as entitlement. A man is entitled to any previously unowned thing which he acquires by a process (such as work or discovery) 'if the position of others no longer at liberty to use the thing' is not 'thereby worsened'.[30] The position of others is held by Nozick not to be thereby worsened if I merely deprive them of the liberty to acquire the thing, or if my acquisition means that I am now in competition in some market with other owners, though it would be unjustifiably worsened if by some process of acquisition I acquired a monopoly on an essential commodity such as all the drinkable water in the world. What I have legitimately acquired, I can legitimately transfer to others; equally I can legitimately acquire what others have acquired, if they allow me to. Nozick holds that it is a fundamental and unjustifiable infringement of my liberty if anyone else takes from me what I am entitled to, and that the worst offender in this respect is the state, which through taxation forcibly deprives me of what I am entitled to in order to give it to others. Making people participate in something like a state health service, say, is tantamount to forced labour; it is making them work hours they would not otherwise have worked, not for their own benefit, but for the benefit of others. Above all, it is forcing them to do something against their basic right to freedom. Any attempt by the state to redistribute wealth within the community in accordance with Rawlsian principles will not only distort the history of production within a community and the efficient and overall beneficent operation of its mechanisms (the view of free marketeers, like F. A. von Hayek), but it will also infringe the rights of those from whom their entitlements are removed, and their liberty in so far as the removal is done under threat of force. Nozick argues that the Marxist slogan 'From each according to his ability, to each according to his needs' implies a fundamental violation of individual rights as well as encouraging the fantasy that objects appear in the world out of nothing, not already earned and worked for. He would replace it by the words

'From each as they choose, to each as they are chosen' (by the free market, presumably).[31]

It is clear that Nozick sets great store by history. Indeed, much of his criticism of Rawls's and other redistributive accounts of justice is that they neglect the way goods arise, and the intimate connections between men's efforts and their entitlements (or feeling of entitlement). But Nozick's view of history turns out, on examination, to be so one-sided as to be hardly less illusory than the fantasy that goods are just there, independent of the work and effort of individual men. For it is simply not the case that the majority of present ownerships of goods can be traced back to legitimate acts of original acquisition; Nozick does suggest that otherwise illegitimate acts of acquisition can be legitimized by compensation of the victims of *force majeure*, although his discussion of compensation and rectification is as obscure as the proviso about the conditions under which a previously unowned thing would be illegitimately possessed. Still, this need not worry us, as conquerers are not in the habit of compensating their victims in any respect. It is really extraordinary that the words 'war', 'empire', 'imperialism', 'conquest' and 'serf' do not appear in the index of Nozick's book, given the centrality in his system of original acts of acquisition, while the notion of slavery is introduced only to imply that paying taxes to help the needy through state systems of health, insurance and education is actually a form of slavery. Only a man with a totally impoverished historical sensitivity could have supposed that a theory of justice based on the concept of a legitimate act of original acquisition could have any significant application in the twentieth-century world, where the not implausible claim of the dispossessed (the vast majority of the human race, after all) is that they have been cheated and robbed over and over again, and that their position is now so far behind the rich that they are never likely to break out of the cycle of their deprivation without some major redistribution of goods, both within countries and throughout the world. To show that what I have just said is not prejudice on my part alone, I will quote MacIntyre:

The property-owners of the modern world are not the legitimate heirs of Lockean individuals who performed quasi-Lockean ... acts of original acquisition; they are the inheritors of those who, for example, stole, and used violence to steal the common lands of England from the com: aon people, vast tracts of North America from the American Indian, much of Ireland from the Irish, and Prussia from the original non-German Prussians. This is the historical reality ideologically concealed behind any Lockean thesis. The lack of any principle of rectification is thus not a small side issue for a thesis such as Nozick's ...[32]

Rawls's system, of course, does embody a principle of rectification, but by neglecting any historical perspective at all, and much of what Nozick says about this is pertinent; significantly, though, Rawls does see the type of social contract and redistributions which could be predicated on the basis of his original position as being viable only on the assumption that all the individuals in the original position are conceived of as co-existing in a definite geographical territory under conditions of moderate (that is, not extreme) scarcity.[33] Does this mean that Rawls's theory of justice can have nothing to say about the justice or injustice of the world economic order? But how can justice be so circumscribed within geographical frontiers, when the wealth of some nations is so tied to the poverty of others that nationalistic attempts to curb the operation of 'free' markets within those countries is regarded as subversive and threatening by the richer nations, an excuse to reimpose, overtly or covertly, their own versions of 'freedom', 'democracy' and 'peace'?

Ted Honderich has written that 'there is no question in political philosophy more fundamental and encompassing than the question of how the goods of the world and the goods of society ought to be distributed among us'.[34] Although he would not have been able to command general agreement on this among political philosophers prior to the works of Rawls and Nozick, it cannot be said that either provides more than partial answers to the fundamental question. Rawls emphasizes the state of the actual distribution of goods, but at the expense of people's personal claims of entitlement, as Nozick shows, while Nozick emphasizes entitlements and legitimacy. But even if all present holdings of wealth could be traced back to the sort of non-violent exploitation of untapped resources that the Lockean picture conjures up, should we be satisfied with the resulting distribution? If entitlement made a wretchedly unequal job of distribution so that millions starved while others wasted the fruits of the earth, should it be regarded as sacrosanct? If the very rich have to be forced to give up some of their goods (as they no doubt would have to be), and protest at the resulting infringement of their liberty, do we have to regard this liberty as inalienable? It is the disadvantage of Nozick's intuitionistic approach to 'inalienable rights' that he forecloses discussion of such questions; presumably, once discussion is allowed, we admit that entitlements and individual liberties are not necessarily pre-eminent values in deciding questions of justice. But this, in turn, simply emphasizes the way in which people seek different and not necessarily compatible ends in politics. Liberty does not always square with justice, nor justice with utility, nor security with liberty. In practice, there are few who are not prepared to compromise their favoured end in each of these areas. Few would find a purely Rawlsian or a purely Nozickian approach to questions of distribution satisfactory. This in turn raises the question as to whether political philosophy can be realistically expected to provide some theoretical hierarchy of ends enabling all such conflicts to be settled in advance, or whether its role should be seen as the more restricted one of bringing out what is implied by adherence to the various conflicting principles. Perhaps, too, consideration of Rawls and Nozick might suggest that the choice of guiding principles in the political sphere cannot be made on *a priori* grounds, in blithe abstraction from how the world actually is. Thus, Nozick's entitlement approach seems far more applicable to a world of largely disconnected societies, with plenty of empty space. Its model of pioneers seizing tracts of the world for the first time is singularly inappropriate when the rapacious exploitation of those underdeveloped forest areas that do remain threaten the very future of the planet, and when it is very hard to see how the poor are not in a thousand ways continually exploited by the rich. Rawls's model, on the other hand, at least in the eyes of its critics, presupposes something like a philosophical year zero, in which people without memories or deserts frame a new order from scratch. Of course, one can regard a Rawlsian perspective as expressing the type of distribution a state concerned with justice should be aiming at in its legislation, but the legislation looks like an attempt continually to undermine the sense that many people have that their own efforts and work must in themselves be worth something for them, and worth something that can be passed on to their descendants, and not rewarded merely because a central state committee decides that doing so is going in some way to improve the lot of the worst off. But this is not to say that it might not be a very good thing if this sense were undermined and corrected by political education. Nozick claims that without a sense of inheritable and disposable property, all individual rights will disappear, while von Hayek appears to believe that material inequality is the very condition of material progress. Those who wish to argue for redistribution of social goods according to a principle of equality need to question these assumptions, and they might well begin by considering Rousseau's words at the start of Part Two of the *Discourse on the Origins of Inequality*: 'You are undone if you once forget that the fruits of the earth belong to us all, and the earth itself to no one', and go on to reflect that our present institutions of private property, particularly those regarding the passing on of goods, are viable only because of a massive framework of law and policing. They protect, and even encourage, the amassing by a few of vast amounts of wealth, far more than could be needed by an individual to provide for himself enough security to lead an independent life, free from coercion by others, while others are, by comparison, utterly deprived. Nozick appears to move from the plausible, though not self-evident, idea that a man needs some property rights of some sort as a bulwark against unjust coercion by others, to the utterly implausible conclusion that a man's basic liberty from such coercion would be totally undermined by any public curb on greed or acquisitiveness.

Rawls and Nozick, as already noted, both regard the state as something justified in terms of agreements between independent individuals; the role of the state is one of protection and arbitration between those individuals in matters of security and property rights. Both regard morality as something at once more general and in certain respects more private; and private areas of morality are outside the proper province of the state and legislation. In this they follow J. S. Mill, with his celebrated distinction between acts which are prejudicial to others and those which affect the agent alone (cf. *On Liberty*, Ch. IV). In the latter case 'there should be perfect freedom, legal and social, to do the action and stand the consequences'; in other words, law should not interfere in activities which harm no one but those freely engaged in them. A conception of the law which attempts to make a clear distinction between public and private areas of life is one that is fitted to societies in which there is a plurality of values and moral ideals. People should be allowed to regulate their own lives, so long as their self-regulation does not infringe the rights and liberties of others. But this conception of law is harder to work out or to accept in practice than it seems at first sight. Does it mean that there should be no legislation against dangerously addictive drugs or suicidal sports, or in favour of compulsory health and unemployment insurance? Then, how are we to determine the boundaries between a public and a private act? Does a man who pays large sums of money to secure a privileged education for his children do something merely private? Or is he doing something eminently public, in reinforcing social inequalities and gaining (intentionally or not) unfair advantages for his children? And, the most vexed type of question in this whole area: do not private indulgences in pornographic displays or prostitution, say, have public and social repercussions in their effect on the moral climate of society as a whole? Are there any acts I do which affect me alone?

These last questions strongly suggest that it is very hard to draw the sort of clear distinction between public and private activity which Mill is looking for, even if one were to agree with him that the state has a duty not to legislate on such matters as crash-helmets for motor-cyclists, voluntary euthanasia or private agreements between workers and employers to operate closed shops. However, it is not clear that denying a clear distinction between private and public activity entails the conclusion that a prominent judge, Patrick Devlin, notoroiously drew, that it is the role of the state to enforce morality by means of law. Devlin claimed that moral matters were not purely private, that a recognized morality is necessary to society and that the state has a *prima facie* right to legislate against immorality as such.[35] He argued that an established morality is essential to the welfare of a society, and that it follows from this that 'the suppression of vice is as much the law's business as the suppression of subversive activities'.[36]

There is indeed a point of substance in Devlin's premise, and one that can be overlooked in purely contractarian and instrumentalist views of the state. It is very hard to see how one might speak of a social organism, such as a state or a nation, unless there was a degree of moral consensus within the organism. A state or a nation is not a prison, and could not be operated like one without gross inefficiency and unhappiness. No police force could impose standards of conduct on a whole society for long, and this implies that in a viable society people will generally agree that they have a moral duty to respect such things as the sanctity of life, truth and the property of others, at least in certain cases and in certain respects, without being forced to do so. In this sense, viable law will have to be based on moral consensus; laws, such as the prohibition of alcohol, that go against the underlying moral climate of a society in too drastic a way are likely to provoke resistance, resentment, corruption and a damaging hostility to political authority and to law itself. So laws should not be judged and evaluated purely in terms of formal correctness of enactment (by correct procedure, and so on); it does seem sensible on the part of legislators to allow for sensitive interpretation and application of the law on the part of the judiciary, taking into account the moral attitudes prevailing in the society. But saying that a society rests on a broad moral consensus, and that law should within certain limits reflect that consensus, is not at all the same thing as saying that the law should intervene in every moral matter.

What Devlin entirely overlooks is the possibility that a society might have toleration of moral and other significant differences in all sorts of areas as part of its broad moral consensus. Is society going to fall apart because people have different religious beliefs or sexual practices or cultural traditions? It is not clear that this is a purely empirical question:

a society that attempted to enforce uniformity on such matters might very well break up if there were large groups of dissenters within it, as has happened not infrequently. H. L. A. Hart, in answering Devlin from a broadly liberal point of view in 'Immorality and Treason', suggested that the law should not forbid acts which do no harm to the agent or others, but which the majority of the community simply found immoral.[37] This is a significant weakening of Mill's principle, because it would allow legislation on such things as the wearing of motor-cycle crash-helmets and drug abuse, but it hardly provides an answer to someone following in Devlin's footsteps who argued that homosexual practices are not *merely* immoral, but so abominable that their mere presence is an offence, and in themselves deeply injurious to a society that tolerated them by making them legal. Devlin's own position here is not clear. But he is emphatic that if homosexuality were deeply abhorrent to the majority, they could not be 'denied the right to eradicate it'. Could those who object to this position, though, define an area of basic rights and liberties, which we would wish to keep the law out of? We could, but in doing this we will inevitably be deciding on all sorts of controversial matters, like the liberty of a man to work in a given industry without having to join a union, or to indulge his taste for cocaine, or for Danish pornography or for anti-Semitic propaganda. Utilitarian thinkers, like R. M. Hare, would argue that questions of this sort should be decided in terms of the overall acceptance-utility of adopting legislation of one sort or another, but many would argue that, whatever the utilities involved, the law has no right to, say, interfere with my freedom of association or my sexuality, or that the law should move towards producing a better life for the worst-off, even if this was not agreed by the majority of a society.

Utilitarianism does have the advantage, however, over inalienable-rights theories that it forces one to monitor the actual consequences of a particular piece of legislation (or its absence), and to make adjustments accordingly, but, as we saw earlier, it leaves uncertain how we should evaluate the consequences or how we should weigh up different types of preference regarding the consequences. At some point each person has to take a moral stand on just what he or she thinks should be the limits of legislation, in terms of striking a balance between such factors as individual dignity and rights, general welfare, and so on, and in doing so they will not regard themselves as simply waiting on or contributing to the total acceptance-utility of what they decide. In a pluralist society, with competing values and conflicting interests, the law cannot simply take a shared morality for granted and proceed to enforce it. It may indeed be the existence of pluralism in a society that forces us to regard certain areas of life as outside the scope of formalized social disapproval in the shape of law. (In closed societies, both a man's thought and his 'private' life are seen as well within the proper ambit of legislation.) From a pluralist perspective, it is natural to look at the law as something like an umpire, holding the balance between conflicting interests and allowing individuals the room to work out their own projects and life-styles, where doing so does not impinge too intimately on the room of others to do the same. But while there is some truth in this picture regarding the day-to-day work of the courts, it would be deeply misleading if it led us to think that it was possible for the law to be neutral as between conflicting interests in a class-divided society, and simply judge impartially between them. This is because, as became abundantly clear in considering the work of Rawls and Nozick, there is no concept of justice which is neutral in the necessary way. Nozick's analysis of justice clearly favours the haves, while Rawls sets up his original position precisely so that everyone thinks of him or herself as a potential have-not. How could the law be neutral as between someone who finds the present state of distribution of goods grossly unfair and someone who regards the *status quo* as basically just? In practice, of course, the law tends to uphold the *status quo*; this underlying reality is often masked behind the formal impartiality the legal system may affect, in its insistence on due process and the observance of correct procedure.

What I have just been saying about the law assumes by and large the truth of legal positivism, that is, that the law is to be seen in terms of the laws enacted by the authority of a society and that individuals have legal rights and duties only in so far as these are recognized by written law or explicit social practice. According to legal positivism, lawyers and judges speak and act correctly when they say and judge in accordance with what is entailed by these institutions. But this view has a problem with hard or disputed legal cases, where it is unclear just what existing statute or precedent do entail. In such cases, according to legal positivism, judges will use their discretion in making decisions, one way or another, and their decisions will actually be creating new law. In advance of the decision, there is nothing to be right or wrong about; and neither party in such a case strictly has a right to win before the decision. When a judge speaks of the right a successful litigant *had* in his case, he is in fact invoking a bit of legal fiction, because before the judgement there was neither right nor wrong in the case.

Now, this view of the law and legal rights and duties has been strongly criticized by Ronald Dworkin, who claims that it rests on an unacceptable anti-realism about meaning: that just because the truth-value of a proposition is unclear (such as the one about my legal position in a hard case in which judicial discretion is invoked), it does not mean that it does not have a truth-value.[38] Dworkin claims that anti-realism is as unacceptable in law as he thinks it is in science or in history, and he proposes an alternative theory about propositions in law that are not clearly covered by legislation or explicit precedent. Judges, he thinks, can be right or wrong about how they exercise their discretion, and they are not to come to their decisions by putting themselves in the shoes of the legislators or of the majority of society or, indeed, by giving force to their own moral opinions. Their decisions are to be judged as right if a general political theory which supplies the best justification for non-controversial propositions of law also provides for the rights or duties which their controversial judgement allows. Thus, for example, we might claim (as Dworkin does) that a general theory which takes equality (or right to be treated as an equal) to be the right from which other constitutional liberties are derivative is the one that provides the most coherent synthesis of the various rights and liberties admitted by British and US law. Arguments for specific rights and liberties have to be made out in terms of that background right, and thus, again to illustrate by example, Dworkin will conclude that cases of reverse discrimination (which may be legally controversial, in that both employer and the would-be employee who is not employed because he comes from a privileged group may claim conflicting rights in the matter) can be justified, where they can be shown to be serving a general policy of respecting the right of all members of the community to be treated as equals, and the needs of some sections of the community are greater than those of others.

Dworkin's position takes issue with legal positivism, because it holds that there are legal truths and rights which are not explicitly enshrined in positive law. It could undermine my suggestion that the law tends naturally to uphold the interests of the powerful, because the law might – almost despite the intentions of its framers – invoke certain general rights and principles, which would themselves entail some sort of egalitarianism, against which some particular laws could be judged as bad laws (if, for example, they deprived workers of the right to withdraw their labour). But is there any reason to think that Dworkin's claims about there being one best theory of the law are correct? And how would one judge between competing claims to have the most coherent and simple system of justification for the non-controversial propositions of law? It is, of course, true that judges, in deciding disputable cases, will often make appeal to various principles they derive from other parts of the law, and, indeed, to appeals to natural justice, but it is far from clear that there is or could be any overarching political theory to ground all the positive laws in a single system, or, even if there were, that appealing to that theory would always be the best way of exercising judicial discretion. In some cases, attention to the particularities and details of the case might be more to the point than seeking general principles on which to judge it.

As with Rawls's reflective equilibrium, I must confess once more to being sceptical about there being any single theory or conception from which all that is in the law or in our more general moral attitudes can be shown to follow most smoothly, and in terms of which various competing claims to rights, either legal or moral, are to be assessed. In part this is because it is unclear that all our moral attitudes and all our laws are actually consistent with each other, as I suggested earlier in considering the tension that may exist between my duties to my family and a proper regard for equality. This suggests that we would have to choose which attitudes and laws are the more fundamental, in order to rule out others as inconsistent with the overall synthesis. Moreover, even if all our attitudes and laws were consistent, there may be many ways they could be synthesized equally smoothly: Dworkin appeals to the theories of science to support his general realist position on the law, but, as we saw in discussing these theories, there are many possible but inconsistent theories, any of which could systematize a given set of data with equal smoothness, simplicity and coherence. The comparison with science supports an anti-realistic pluralism in law and morality, rather than the realism of a single correct theory. If we are realists about scientific theory, this will be because of our belief that a true theory corresponds to the physical world; but in law and morality there is no external world, only a synthesizing of our intentions and practices.

It might also be felt that Dworkin's general appraoch to law is still broadly within the positivist tradition, in that the political theory on which he bases his talk of legal rights has to take positive law as its data base. But far from being an objectionable feature of Dworkin's theory, this dependence of argument on existing practice points to an important aspect of discussion in both law and morality, and highlighting it will enable us to consider from a new angle the general question of the justification of moral attitudes which we considered at the end of the last section. Some people – and Rawls and Nozick may be examples of this from one point of view, classical utilitarians from another – hope to found the whole of ethics or political theory on a firm and unquestionable basis, which they attempt to derive from some impeccable source, such as a rationalistic 'original position' or a pure intuition of basic rights or some very general principles about the impartial nature of argument as such. But each of the ensuing systems suffers from at least two kinds of defect. First, they characteristically fall foul of other moral judgements of ours (Rawls underplays desert, Nozick the notion of fairness, the utilitarians the way general well-being can trample on individual duties and commitments). Secondly, each system has to justify its own basic premise against those who would criticize it – and how could this be done except by attempting to show that other moral judgements, which everyone would accept, can be seen as applications of the basic premise? My point here is that in developing a system of morals or politics, we are going to be appealing, in a holistic way, to other judgements of morality and politics. As there is a web of belief in epistemology, so there is a web of evaluation in ethics.

Our moral and political evaluations depend in the first instance on all sorts of beliefs and principles we are given in our childhood and in our language, about what is fair, reasonable, kind, humane, compassionate, honest, and so on. A great deal can be done in showing how these initial and generally accepted judgements should, in logic and consistency, be applied to cases beyond those in which we originally learned them. If moral judgements are initially based on standards of behaviour we regard as appropriate to those we are related to and feel for, we may learn that in consistency the same standards should be extended to those beyond our immediate circle, when they are not significantly different from those in our circle. If, for example, we refrain from hurting someone we know on the grounds that it will cause him or her pain, in consistency we should refrain from doing things that will cause anyone pain, whether we know them or not. In such a way have the rights of slaves, of women, of the dispossessed, been argued for, and, at times, won. People may argue in a similar way about the morality of eating and experimenting on animals: as sentient beings, do they share enough of those aspects of human life which would lead us to say that it is wrong to use even mentally retarded humans or infants for ulterior purposes of our own?

In addition to seeing just what principles are implicit in our moral judgements, and how they might be extended, we should also look carefully at the actual or likely effects of certain rules of conduct or public policies. If, for example, we felt that it was inconsistent with what we believed about the dignity of the individual to attempt to prevent a person from committing suicide when they were old and infirm, we should still look to see whether legislating to allow for voluntary euthanasia meant in practice that old people unwanted by their relatives were put under pressure by those relatives to agree to a far from voluntary death. This kind of monitoring of the effects of principles and policies is an essential part of the rationality of both morality and politics, as our decisions will inevitably have unforeseen consequences.

So moral and political argument has both a logical and an empirical aspect; does this mean, though, that we are restricted in these areas to casuistry (the analysis of the logical structure of a moral system) and sociology? I think not, and for a reason already touched on. The principles we have may well be mutually conflicting, and are in any case largely tailored for a world that is undergoing extraordinary change. In examining our moral and political attitudes and their effects we may have to try to bring them into a consistent whole, by choosing in the light of current circumstances which to stress and which to play down. But we will also inevitably have to ask ourselves whether our principles and the image we start with of the good life are in all respects appropriate to our current predicament. In this way, ethics and politics can be both rational and open-ended. Something can be preserved of the Kantian ideal of an autonomous ethic, without, at the same time, pretending that we are the choosers of all our moral values and political assessments, or that we exist as individual moral beings apart from the ties and demands of the circumstances into which we are born.

Suggestions for Further Reading

In these suggestions for further reading, I will mention books that should be fairly easily available. I do not, for obvious reasons, mention here works I have discussed in any detail in the text.

On many topics in metaphysics and epistemology A. J. Ayer's *Central Questions of Philosophy* (London, 1976) is both stimulating and original, as well as very probably accessible to readers of this book. So should many of the articles in *Perception and Identity* (edited by G. F. MacDonald, London, 1979), a volume discussing Ayer's work with replies by him. More specifically, on phenomenalism and related issues to do with our basic conceptual scheme, mention should be made of J. L. Austin's *Sense and Sensibilia* (Oxford, 1964) and P. F. Stawson's *Individuals* (London, 1959). On nominalism and many topics in the philosophy of language and mathematics, Michael Dummett's *Truth and Other Enigmas* (Harvard, 1978) contains essays that are hard, but challenging and indispensable. A number of Quine's most important essays on metaphysical and linguistic topics are in *From a Logical Point of View* (New York, 1963). On causality, an important recent study is J. L. Mackie's *The Cement of the Universe* (Oxford, 1974).

On issues in the philosophy of religion, Brian Davies's *Introduction to the Philosophy of Religion* (Oxford, 1982) will be found useful: so will J. L. Mackie's *The Miracle of Theism* (Oxford, 1982) and, I hope, my own *Experience, Explanation and Faith* (London, 1984).

On epistemology generally, mention can be made of three recent books, all radical and challenging: Richard Rorty's *Philosophy and the Mirror of Nature* (Princeton, 1980), Hilary Putnam's *Reason, Truth and History* (Cambridge, 1981) and Nelson Goodman's *Ways of Worldmaking* (Hassocks, 1978). A useful historical survey of scepticism and discussion of sceptical issues is Nicholas Rescher's *Scepticism* (Oxford, 1980). Sir Karl Popper's *Conjectures and Refutations* (London, 1969) is the best introduction to his thought. The current scene in philosophy of science is surveyed by W. Newton-Smith in *The Rationality of Science* (London, 1981) and excitingly and critically discussed in Ian Hacking's *Representing and*

Intervening (Cambridge, 1983). Mention should also be made of Bas van Fraassen's *The Scientific Image* (Oxford, 1980), as a controversial and well-argued defence of anti-realism about scientific theories.

My discussion of logic has drawn heavily on Geoffrey Hunter's *Metalogic* (London, 1971). An excellent and very accessible account of the philosophical roots of modern logic is given by Anthony Kenny in his *Wittgenstein* (London, 1973). Kenny's book is also the best introduction to Wittgenstein's work. Useful introductions to the philosophy of language include Bernard Harrison's *Introduction to the Philosophy of Language* (London, 1979) and Mark Platts's *Ways of Meaning* (London, 1979). Davidson's work on the philosophy of language is now easily available in his collection *Enquiries into Truth and Interpretations* (Oxford, 1984).

A good little survey of the body–mind issue is Keith Campbell's *Mind and Body* (London, 1970). Daniel Dennett's *Brainstorms* (Hassocks, 1978) contains essays on the mind that are both accessible and highly thought of. *Essays on Freedom of Action*, edited by Ted Honderich (London, 1973), is a fine collection of original work on its subject. Derek Parfit's original work on personal identity, including its ethical ramifications, has recently been very much extended in his *Reasons and Persons* (Oxford, 1984); too late, unfortunately, for any consideration in this book.

On recent moral theory, Geoffrey Warnock's *Contemporary Moral Philosophy* (London, 1967) is brief and excellent. Two recent subjectivistic accounts of ethics, both interesting and worthwhile, are Gilbert Harman's *The Nature of Morality* (New York, 1977) and J. L. Mackie's *Ethics: Inventing Right and Wrong* (Harmondsworth, 1977). On utilitarianism, apart from the work of Hare, there is *Utilitarianism: For and Against* by Bernard Williams and J. J. C. Smart (Cambridge, 1973).

While Rawls and Nozick continue to dominate political philosophy, F. A. Hayek's works should not be neglected, especially *Law, Legislation and Liberty* (3 volumes, London, 1973–9) and *The Constitution of Liberty* (London, 1960). H. L. A. Hart's *The Concept of Law* (Oxford, 1961) has acquired something of the status of a classic.

On how philosophical discussion of contemporary moral issues can be done, Jonathan Glover's *What Sort of People Should There Be? Genetic Engineering, Brain Control and Their Impact on our Future World* (Harmondsworth, 1984) seems to me to be exemplary.

Much of the work of contemporary philosophy is carried out in articles in professional journals, such as *Mind, Philosophical Review* and *Journal of Philosophy*. However, the Oxford University Press does publish useful paperback collections of important recent articles on many topics in philosophy, which also include editorial introductions by a philosopher working in the relevant area. A one-volume collection containing some most important recent articles together with helpful introductions to each one is *Philosophy As It Is*, edited by Ted Honderich and Myles Burnyeat (Harmondsworth, 1979).

Notes

Chapter 1: Metaphysics

1. Carl Hempel, *Philosophy of Natural Science*, Englewood Cliffs, 1966, p. 102.
2. W. V. Quine, *Word and Object*, Cambridge, Mass., 1960, p. 1.
3. A. J. Ayer, *Hume*, Oxford, 1980, p. 41.
4. John Locke, *An Essay Concerning Human Understanding*, Bk IV, Ch. II, Section XV.
5. Ludwig Wittgenstein, *Philosophical Investigations*, Oxford, 1953, p. 94.
6. Nelson Goodman, *The Structure of Appearance*, Dordrecht, 1977, p. 98.
7. A. Eddington, *The Nature of the Physical World*, Cambridge, 1928, Introduction.
8. Michael Dummett, 'Common Sense and Physics', in *Perception and Identity* (ed. G. F. Macdonald), London, 1979, pp. 33–5.
9. Donald Davidson, 'Radical Interpretation', *Dialectica*, Vol. 27, 1973, pp. 313–27.
10. Rudolf Carnap, 'Empiricism, Semantics and Ontology', *Revue Internationale de Philosophie*, 1950, pp. 22–40.
11. Locke, op. cit., Bk II, Ch. II, Section IX.
12. Goodman, op. cit., pp. 104–5.
13. ibid., p. 262.
14. For a detailed survey of such cases, see David Wiggins, *Sameness and Substance*, Oxford, 1980, Ch. 1.
15. Quine, *From a Logical Point of View*, New York, 1963, p. 149.
16. Wiggins, op. cit., pp. 134–5.
17. ibid., p. 121.
18. Ayer, 'Replies', in *Perception and Identity* (see above), p. 312.
19. David Hume, *A Treatise of Human Nature*, Bk I, Pt III, Section XIV.
20. F. P. Ramsey, *The Foundations of Mathematics and Other Essays*, London, 1931, p. 252.
21. Hume, op. cit., pp. 65f.
22. Hempel, op. cit., p. 55.
23. C. Peacocke, 'Causal Modalities and Realism', in *Reference, Truth and Reality* (ed. M. Platts), London, 1980, p. 45.
24. Hempel, op. cit., pp. 57–8.
25. Ayer, *The Central Questions of Philosophy*, Harmondsworth, 1976, p. 183.
26. Pierre de Laplace, *A Philosophical Essay on Probabilities*, 1819, Ch. 2.
27. Davidson, 'Causal Relations', in *Essays on Actions and Events*, Oxford, 1980, Ch. 7.

28. Quine, *Word and Object* (see above), p. 172.
29. ibid., p. 170.
30. J. M. McTaggart, 'The Unreality of Time', *Mind*, Vol. XVII, pp. 457–74.
31. Dummett, 'A Defence of McTaggart's Proof of the Unreality of Time', in *Truth and Other Enigmas*, Cambridge, Mass., 1978, pp. 351–7.
32. ibid., p. 355.
33. Richard Swinburne, *The Existence of God*, Oxford, 1979, Ch. VII.
34. J. L. Mackie, *The Miracle of Theism*, Oxford, 1982, p. 100.

Chapter 2: Epistemology

1. C. S. Peirce, *Collected Papers*, Cambridge, Mass., 1931–5, Vol. V, p. 407.
2. Hilary Putnam, *Meaning and the Moral Sciences*, London, 1978, p. 125.
3. ibid., p. 126.
4. Ayer, *Language, Truth and Logic*, Harmondsworth, 1971, p. 118.
5. Ramsey, 'Facts and Propositions', in *The Foundations of Mathematics and Other Essays* (see above), Ch. VI.
6. Marshall Swain, 'Knowledge, Causality and Justification', *Journal of Philosophy*, Vol. LXIX, 1972, pp. 291–300.
7. Alvin Goldman, 'A Causal Theory of Knowing', *Journal of Philosophy*, Vol. LXIV, 1967, pp. 357–72 (at p. 369).
8. Quine, 'Two Dogmas of Empiricism', in *From a Logical Point of View* (see above), Ch. II.
9. ibid., p. 41.
10. ibid., p. 43.
11. *Meditation I*, as in *The Philosophical Works of Descartes*, translated by E. S. Haldane and G. R. T. Ross, Cambridge, 1969, Vol. I, pp. 145–6.
12. Margaret Wilson, *Descartes*, London, 1978, pp. 17–31.
13. Descartes, *Meditation VI*, as in *The Philosophical Works of Descartes* (see above), p. 199.
14. Wittgenstein, 'Notes for Lectures on Private Experience and "Sense Data"', *Philosophical Review*, Vol. LXXVII. pp. 271–320 (at p. 306).
15. Goodman, 'The New Riddle of Induction', in *Problems and Projects*, Indianapolis, 1972, pp. 371–88.
16. Ayer, *The Central Questions of Philosophy* (see above), p. 178.
17. Goodman, 'The New Riddle of Induction' (see above), pp. 387–8.
18. Quine, 'Natural Kinds', in *Ontological Relativity and Other Essays*, New York, 1969, pp. 114–38.
19. ibid., p. 125.
20. ibid., p. 126.
21. Sir Karl Popper, *Conjectures and Refutations*, London, 1969, pp. 34–6.
22. T. S. Kuhn, *The Structure of Scientific Revolutions*, Chicago, 1962.
23. ibid., p. 121.
24. ibid., p. 149.
25. Davidson, 'On the Very Idea of a Conceptual Scheme', Presidential Address to the American Philosophical Association, 1973.
26. ibid., p. 19.

Chapter 3: Logic and Language

1. Davidson, 'Truth and Meaning', *Synthese*, Vol. XVII, 1967, pp. 304–23 (at p. 321).
2. Davidson, *Essays on Actions and Events* (see above).
3. Mark Platts, *Ways of Meaning*, London, 1979, pp. 195–6.
4. Gottlob Frege, 'On Sense and Reference', in *Philosophical Writings of Gottlob Frege*, translated by P. Geach and M. Black, Oxford, 1960, pp. 56–78.
5. Bertrand Russell, *The Philosophy of Logical Atomism*, Lecture II (available in *Logic and Knowledge* (ed. R. C. Marsh), London, 1956).
6. Dummett, *Frege: Philosophy of Logic and Language*, London, 1973, p. 97.
7. Saul Kripke, *Naming and Necessity*, Oxford, 1980.
8. Ayer, 'Identity and Reference', in *Language in Focus* (ed. A. Kasher), Dordrecht, 1976, pp. 3–24 (at p. 21).
9. Kripke, op. cit., p. 163.
10. Evans, 'The Causal Theory of Names', *Supplementary Proceedings of the Aristotelian Society*, Vol. XLVII, 1973, pp. 187–208.
11. Gareth Evans, *Varieties of Reference*, Oxford, 1982, p. 315.
12. John McDowell, 'On the Sense and Reference of a Proper Name', *Mind*, Vol. LXXXVI, 1977, pp. 159–85.
13. ibid., p. 170.
14. Colin McGinn, *The Character of Mind*, Oxford, 1982, p. 39.
15. Wittgenstein, *Philosophical Investigations* (see above), p. 217.
16. Wittgenstein, *Tractatus Logico-Philosophicus*, Section 4.002.
17. Evans, op. cit., p. 45.
18. Putnam, *Realism and Reason*, Cambridge, 1983, *passim*, esp. pp. xii and 19.
19. Putnam, *Realism and Reason* (see above), p. 71.
20. Putnam, 'The Meaning of "Meaning"', in his *Mind, Language and Reality*, Cambridge, 1975, pp. 215–71.
21. Ayer, *Philosophy in the Twentieth Century*, London, 1982, p. 270.
22. Quine, *Word and Object* (see above), Ch. 2.
23. ibid., pp. 51–2.
24. ibid., p. 73.
25. Examples of real-life indeterminacies in translating Japanese into English are given in Quine, *Ontological Relativity and Other Essays* (see above), pp. 35–9.
26. Quine, *Word and Object* (see above), p. 79.
27. Putnam, *Reason, Truth and History*, Cambridge, 1981, pp. 32–5.
28. H. P. Grice, 'Meaning', *Philosophical Review*, Vol. LXVI, 1957, pp. 377–88.
29. Grice, 'Utterer's Meanings and Intentions', *Philosophical Review*, Vol. LXXVIII, 1969, pp. 147–77.
30. Grice, 'Utterer's Meaning, Sentence-Meaning, and Word-Meaning', in *The Philosophy of Language* (ed. J. R. Searle), Oxford, 1971, pp. 54–70.
31. Platts, op. cit., pp. 88–92.
32. Grice, 'Utterer's Meaning, Sentence-Meaning, and Word-Meaning' (see above), p. 68.
33. Dummett, 'Truth', in *Truth and Other Enigmas* (see above), pp. 17–18.
34. Putnam, *Realism and Reason* (see above), pp. xvi–xviii, 85–6.

35. Dummett, 'What is a Theory of Meaning? (11)', in *Truth and Meaning* (eds. G. Evans and J. McDowell), Oxford, 1976, pp. 67–137 (at p. 100).

36. Harry Field, 'Tarski's Theory of Truth', *Journal of Philosophy*, Vol. LXIX, 1972, pp. 347–75.

37. J. McDowell, 'Physicalism and Primitive Denotation: Field on Tarski', *Erkenntnis*, Vol. XIII, 1978, pp. 131–52.

38. Ayer, *Language, Truth and Logic* (see above), p. 112.

39. Quine, 'Truth by Convention', in his *The Ways of Paradox*, New York, 1966, pp. 70–99.

40. ibid., p. 97.

41. ibid., p. 99.

42. Wittgenstein, *Philosophical Investigations* (see above), Section 185, p. 75.

43. ibid., p. 85.

44. G. P. Baker and P. M. Hacker, *Wittgenstein: Understanding and Meaning*, Oxford, 1980, p. 381.

45. Kripke, 'Wittgenstein on Rules and Private Language', in *Perspectives on the Philosophy of Wittgenstein* (ed. I. Block), Oxford, 1981, pp. 238–312 (at p. 268).

46. Wittgenstein, *Philosophical Investigations* (see above), p. 81.

47. Putnam, *Meaning and the Moral Sciences* (see above), pp. 56–7.

Chapter 4: Human Beings

1. Thomas Nagel, *Mortal Questions*, Cambridge, 1979, Ch. 14.

2. Sir John Eccles (and Sir Karl Popper), *The Self and Its Brain*, Berlin, 1977, pp. 293–4.

3. Gilbert Ryle, *The Concept of Mind*, London, 1949.

4. Kathleen Wilkes, *Physicalism*, London, 1978, p. 27.

5. Putnam, 'Philosophy and Our Mental Life', in his *Mind, Language and Reality* (see above), pp. 291–303.

6. Wilkes, op. cit., p. 10.

7. Daniel Dennett, 'Artificial Intelligence and the Strategies of Psychological Investigation', in *States of Mind* (ed. J. Miller), London, 1983, pp. 67–81 (at p. 78). See also *Brainstorms*, Hassocks, 1978, Ch. 9.

8. Nagel, op. cit., Ch. 12.

9. Kripke, *Naming and Necessity* (see above), p. 152.

10. Davidson, *Essays on Actions and Events* (see above), p. 223.

11. Nagel, op. cit., p. 199.

12. Wiggins, 'Towards a Reasonable Libertarianism', in *Essays on the Freedom of Action* (ed. T. Honderich), London, 1973, pp. 31–62.

13. ibid., p. 52.

14. Ted Honderich, 'One Determinism', in *Essays on the Freedom of Action* (see above), pp. 185–215.

15. ibid., p. 210.

16. Sydney Shoemaker, *Self-Knowledge and Self-Identity*, Ithaca, 1963, pp. 23–5.

17. Bernard Williams, 'The Self and the Future', in his *Problems of the Self*, Cambridge, 1973, pp. 46–63.

18. ibid., p. 63.

19. Derek Parfit, 'Personal Identity', in *The Philosophy of Mind* (ed. J. Glover), Oxford, 1976, pp. 142–62.

20. Wiggins, *Sameness and Substance* (see above), Ch. 6.

21. ibid., p. 167.

22. ibid., p. 185.

Chapter 5: Ethics and Politics

1. Immanuel Kant, *Groundwork of the Metaphysics of Morals*, 2nd German edition, Riga, 1786, p. 29.

2. Hume, op. cit., Bk III, Pt I, Section I.

3. ibid., Bk II, Pt III, Section III.

4. G. E. Moore, *Principia Ethica*, Cambridge, 1903, Ch. I.

5. Ayer, *Language, Truth and Logic* (see above), p. 142.

6. R. M. Hare: (i) *The Language of Morals*, Oxford, 1952; (ii) *Freedom and Reason*, Oxford, 1963.

7. Hare, *Moral Thinking*, Oxford, 1981, pp. 4–5.

8. Hare, *Freedom and Reason* (see above), pp. 180–85.

9. Hare, *Moral Thinking* (see above), Ch. 5 *passim* and p. 171.

10. ibid., p. 228.

11. ibid., p. 226.

12. Iris Murdoch, *The Sovereignty of the Good*, London, 1970.

13. Philippa Foot, 'Moral Beliefs', in *Theories of Ethics* (ed. P. Foot), Oxford, 1967, pp. 83–100 (at p. 92).

14. Hare, *Moral Thinking* (see above), pp. 197–8.

15. Foot, *Theories of Ethics* (see above), Introduction, p. 9.

16. J. S. Mill, *Utilitarianism*, Ch. 2.

17. F. H. Bradley, *Ethical Studies*, Oxford, 1927, p. 168.

18. John Rawls, *A Theory of Justice*, Oxford, 1972.

19. Robert Nozick, *Anarchy, State and Utopia*, Oxford, 1974, p. 149.

20. ibid., p. 33.

21. Ronald Dworkin, *Taking Rights Seriously*, London, 1977.

22. Alasdair MacIntyre, *After Virtue*, London, 1981, p. 233.

23. Nagel, op. cit., p. 132.

24. Rawls, op. cit., pp. 48–50.

25. Popper, *The Poverty of Historicism*, London, 1961, pp. 135–6.

26. Locke, *Two Treatises of Government*, II.i.3.

27. Rawls, op. cit., p. 11.

28. ibid., p. 302.

29. Nozick, op. cit., p. 215.

30. ibid., p. 178.

31. ibid., pp. 159–60.

32. MacIntyre, op. cit., p. 234.

33. Rawls, op. cit., pp. 126–7.

34. Honderich, *Philosophy As It Is*, Harmondsworth, 1979, p. 57.

35. Patrick Devlin, 'Morals and the Criminal Law', in *The Philosophy of Law* (ed. R. M. Dworkin), Oxford, 1977, pp. 66–82.

36. ibid., p. 77.

37. H. L. A. Hart, 'Immorality and Treason', in *The Philosophy of Law* (see above), pp. 83–8.

38. Dworkin, *Taking Rights Seriously* (see above), esp. Ch. 4; *The Philosophy of Law* (see above), pp. 7–9.

Index

FOR THE BEST IN PAPERBACKS, LOOK FOR THE

In every corner of the world, on every subject under the sun, Penguin represents quality and variety – the very best in publishing today.

For complete information about books available from Penguin – including Pelicans, Puffins, Peregrines and Penguin Classics – and how to order them, write to us at the appropriate address below. Please note that for copyright reasons the selection of books varies from country to country.

In the United Kingdom: Please write to *Dept E.P., Penguin Books Ltd, Harmondsworth, Middlesex, UB7 0DA*

If you have any difficulty in obtaining a title, please send your order with the correct money, plus ten per cent for postage and packaging, to *PO Box No 11, West Drayton, Middlesex*

In the United States: Please write to *Dept BA, Penguin, 299 Murray Hill Parkway, East Rutherford, New Jersey 07073*

In Canada: Please write to *Penguin Books Canada Ltd, 2801 John Street, Markham, Ontario L3R 1B4*

In Australia: Please write to the *Marketing Department, Penguin Books Australia Ltd, P.O. Box 257, Ringwood, Victoria 3134*

In New Zealand: Please write to the *Marketing Department, Penguin Books (NZ) Ltd, Private Bag, Takapuna, Auckland 9*

In India: Please write to *Penguin Overseas Ltd, 706 Eros Apartments, 56 Nehru Place, New Delhi, 110019*

In Holland: Please write to *Penguin Books Nederland B.V., Postbus 195, NL–1380AD Weesp, Netherlands*

In Germany: Please write to *Penguin Books Ltd, Friedrichstrasse 10–12, D–6000 Frankfurt Main 1, Federal Republic of Germany*

In Spain: Please write to *Longman Penguin España, Calle San Nicolas 15, E–28013 Madrid, Spain*

In France: Please write to *Penguin Books Ltd, 39 Rue de Montmorency, F-75003, Paris, France*

In Japan: Please write to *Longman Penguin Japan Co Ltd, Yamaguchi Building, 2–12–9 Kanda Jimbocho, Chiyoda-Ku, Tokyo 101, Japan*

A CHOICE OF PENGUINS AND PELICANS

Asimov's New Guide to Science   Isaac Asimov

A fully updated edition of a classic work – far and away the best one-volume survey of all the physical and biological sciences.

Relativity for the Layman   James A. Coleman

Of this book Albert Einstein said: 'Gives a really clear idea of the problem, especially the development of our knowledge concerning the propagation of light and the difficulties which arose from the apparently inevitable introduction of the ether.

The Double Helix   James D. Watson

Watson's vivid and outspoken account of how he and Crick discovered the structure of DNA (and won themselves a Nobel Prize) – one of the greatest scientific achievements of the century.

Ever Since Darwin   Stephen Jay Gould

'Stephen Gould's writing is elegant, erudite, witty, coherent and forceful' – Richard Dawkins, *Nature*

Mathematical Magic Show   Martin Gardner

A further mind-bending collection of puzzles, games and diversions by the undisputed master of recreational mathematics.

Silent Spring   Rachel Carson

The brilliant book which provided the impetus for the ecological movement – and has retained its supreme power to this day.

FOR THE BEST IN PAPERBACKS, LOOK FOR THE

A CHOICE OF PENGUINS AND PELICANS

The Apartheid Handbook   Roger Omond

This book provides the essential hard information about how apartheid actually works from day to day and fills in the details behind the headlines.

The World Turned Upside Down   Christopher Hill

This classic study of radical ideas during the English Revolution 'will stand as a notable monument to . . . one of the finest historians of the present age' – *The Times Literary Supplement*

Islam in the World   Malise Ruthven

'His exposition of "the Qurenic world view" is the most convincing, and the most appealing, that I have read' – Edward Mortimer in *The Times*

The Knight, the Lady and the Priest   Georges Duby

'A very fine book' (Philippe Aries) that traces back to its medieval origin one of our most important institutions, marriage.

A Social History of England   New Edition   Asa Briggs

'A treasure house of scholarly knowledge . . . beautifully written and full of the author's love of his country, its people and its landscape' – John Keegan in the *Sunday Times*, Books of the Year

The Second World War   A J P Tavlor

A brilliant and detailed illustrated history, enlivened by all Professor Taylor's customary iconoclasm and wit.